Good-bye, Machiavelli

Good-bye, Machiavelli

GOVERNMENT AND AMERICAN LIFE

Bernard Wishy

Louisiana State University Press
BATON ROUGE
AND LONDON

04 03 02 01 00 99 98 97 96 95   5 4 3 2 1

Designer: Amanda McDonald Key
Typeface: Sabon
Typesetter: Moran Printing, Inc.
Printer and binder: Thomson-Shore, Inc.

Library of Congress Cataloging-in-Publication Data
Wishy, Bernard W., 1925–
   Good-bye, Machiavelli : government and American life / Bernard
W. Wishy
       p. cm.
   Includes bibliographical references (p. –) and index.
   ISBN 0-8071-1923-7
   1. Political science—United States. 2. State, The. 3. United
States—Politics and government. 4. Reason of state. I. Title.
JA84.U5W53 1995
320.5'1'0973—dc20   94-45182
                                            CIP

For John Howie

Fellow citizens, we cannot escape history.
—Abraham Lincoln

Can't repeat the past? . . . Why of course you can.
—Jay Gatsby

Contents

Preface

Americans have dreamt many dreams in their history, but no political fantasy has stirred them more than the idea of escape from powerful government. Starting in the seventeenth century with specific irritations about English rules for religion or their local governments' land policies, Americans gradually developed the idea that government was intrinsically hostile to liberty and opportunity. Whether they reached high for salvation from sin or low for the vulgarest success, Americans developed the hope that in their new world the state and statecraft, the whole sorry and sordid scene of Machiavellian politics, would be left in Europe. Government here would play a far smaller role than the trustworthy individual and his private associations in taking care of citizens' needs. In a virgin land "commensurate with man's capacity to wonder," not only a new Adam, but an almost stateless society would be created. In time, Americans were so led to deprecate government that European observers like Hegel and Tocqueville held that, rightly speaking, in America there had been little or no state in the fulsome sense that Europeans knew all too well.

This book attempts to lay out the main controversies in the history of whatever state America has had. It is also about the workings of our principal government institutions and the larger patterns of our politics concerning the state. Any bias in telling this tale is not for or against state intervention, but that we understand, as we have not, how Americans have actually dealt with government and thought about it across almost four centuries. Such understanding requires that we put aside contemporary liberal ideas that government action is usually preferable to private initiative, as well as today's conservative notions to the contrary. If support for "free enterprise" is our mission in exploring the past or if we look solely to validate what Jefferson decried as energetic government, we can find both. We shall miss, however, the actual pattern of how state power, while waxing and waning about particular policies across our history, has steadily increased over the long pull. But even questions about the wisdom of that growth seem secondary, since effectiveness, not size, is, in fact, the principal but neglected American issue. That neglect, as well as the complex dynamic of state growth, is analyzed in what follows.

No analysis of how we have been governed should imply that if we had the right ideas about the state better government would follow. A history of our uses of the state and of our quarrels about them cannot deliver us from current quandaries even if, *pace* Santayana's warning, we get that history straight and remember it. But history can make clear what our dilemmas have been and how we created them. The past may thus reveal the limits for our choices today, and its perspective may be a practical use for this study. The subject is so large, however, that, understandably, a view scanning four centuries is perilous and has remained untended. I have no illusion that my effort can be more than initiatory, an outline suggesting paths for fuller inquiry and trying to present main themes rather than giving detailed attention to this or that state government's banking policies or to federal legislation about farming or education. Were it not for many such special studies, however, the overview here would have been impossible, and I want to acknowledge how much the more particular scholarship that has preceded me has made my ambitious but, one hopes, not pretentious venture possible.

Good-bye, Machiavelli

I

THE FOUNDING

The Shadow of Machiavelli

In the beginning, said John Locke, all the world was America, a paradise. But America itself began long after the loss of paradise. "All the world" of America's founders was one, not of Lockean innocence, but of the disorder and power-mongering that marked the advance of centralized state power in Europe. Even as Jamestown was settled, in 1607, it was amid bitter English quarrels with overreaching government and complaints that "the prerogatives of princes may and do daily grow."[1]

As the struggle in England between throne and Parliament mounted, the royal policies about taxation and true religion suggested to their opponents the arrogantly immoral politics that was spreading across Europe, inspired by the "wicked Machiavelli."[2] About a century earlier, Machiavelli's handbook on government, *The Prince* (1513), had heralded an extraordinary change in political consciousness. With Machiavelli, not God's but man's will, not securing justice but manipulating power, had emerged from Christian shame as admissible premises for politics. If beyond *The Prince* there was another Machiavelli, the advocate of a virtuous republicanism,[3] that influence remained far more limited than his portrait as the evil one, teaching that lies, fear, and cruelty were to be judged only for their effectiveness in keeping power and enhancing control by the ruler of the state.

In 1600, of course, the idea of "the state" had a lineage far older than the teaching of Machiavelli, and its meaning had changed over the centuries. By that time under the Stuart monarchs, "state" implied a clearly

1. "Form of Apology and Satisfaction," in *Constitutional Documents of the Reign of James I. A.D. 1603–1625*, ed. Joseph R. Tanner (Cambridge, Eng., 1930), 217–31.

2. Felix Raab, *The English Face of Machiavelli: A Changing Interpretation, 1500–1700* (Toronto, 1964).

3. J. G. A. Pocock, *The Machiavellian Moment* (Princeton, 1975).

defined and supreme government within national borders that claimed a monopoly on the use of force; increasingly centralized legal, fiscal, military institutions and exclusive powers over war, peace, and diplomacy; control by a dynastic ruler or ruling elite using a corps of at least semi-professional officials to conduct government business; and control over the faith that taught obedience to God and demanded supreme loyalty for all subjects to the ruler. After Machiavelli, these powers and claims of the state began to acquire an open justification, called *"raison d'état,"*[4] declaring that the prince could invoke whatever standard was convenient in pursuing his needs. Machiavelli's teaching went deeper, however, for *raison d'état* also meant that by the very nature of politics, with its limited choices and the unpredictable play of "fortuna," officials of any government might have to act against God, reason, common morality, or even their own consciences in order to protect the state. Both meanings were quickly regarded as the essence of the teaching of the unspeakable Machiavelli. They became moral and religious anathema while also winning converts in the conduct of professedly Christian princes and governments of Europe.

If America began under the European shadows of these ideas, its English founders also had a heritage of liberty that dated back at least to Magna Charta (1215). In 1600, however, any fabled English liberty was much narrower than it was to become in the next century. Under the early Stuarts, political liberty did not imply our broad, sacrosanct rights of man, but largely meant only the recognized right of the leading commoners of England, acting on behalf of "the people," to be consulted in Parliament when the sovereign wanted to move on large issues such as taxation and religion. Beyond politics, liberty also supposed the right of any freeman of England to be protected in property and person from arbitrary action by government. Law was the unseverable companion of that liberty, and with the growing claims of the throne it was becoming all the more important for the Stuart opponents that state power be checked by the rule of law. That concept already included opposition to punishment without just and demonstrated cause as well as to imposition of taxes without consent.

Of course, what most Englishmen of 1600 experienced day by day was more likely to be authority and obedience rather than political liberty or the niceties of the law. For common folk, any liberty was mostly catch-as-catch-can. They knew an informal freedom that derived from skill in evading commands to conform to the law or to the wishes of their betters. Many Englishmen who had no quarrel with established religion

4. Friedrich Meinecke, *Machiavellism: The Doctrine of Raison d'Etat and Its Place in Modern History* (New York, 1965).

might, nevertheless, try to avoid the rules about labor or markets in a society as drenched as England then was in the belief in the importance of hierarchy and stability and of avoiding social disorder. Some Englishmen despaired of the authorities precisely because they failed to provide order against starvation, misery, and unemployment. Probably most colonists who came to the New World from England and the Continent fled because of the deficiencies of order rather than its excesses.[5] They left because of what the Old World was doing to their bodies rather than to their consciences.

Most English leaders who did protest the Stuart religious impositions and invoked the old ideals of law and liberty did not leave for America but stayed behind to resist James I and to approve the trial and execution of Charles I, in 1649. In the 1620s, John Winthrop of Boston and William Brewster of Plymouth, like their devout followers, yearned more for order than for modern liberty—but their kind of Christian order, free of the royal arbitrariness that, in their view, had violated "trew faith" or proper Christian standards of government. They also wanted strong and righteous authority to counter human sin and error, but one strictly bound by law that they or their representatives had made or to which they had assented. Other leaders at Providence, Baltimore, and Philadelphia were to emigrate for quite different religious ideals than had the divines of Massachusetts Bay. All may have rejected the official Anglican order of priests and rich liturgy, but far from minimizing the state or deprecating order, they looked to governments of their own that would uphold a true reformed faith and create a proper social discipline. Only the few anabaptists or a "seeker" like Roger Williams thought that true Christianity precluded any state intervention in faith and worship, provided that all sects kept the peace. Because the new politics of Machiavelli seemed to make the will of the prince superior to all law and set no limits on what the sovereign might do to impose his corrupt order, the Stuart monarchs, James and Charles, became insufferable to their opponents.[6] For some of those opponents, abusively called "puritans," the Antichrist ruled England. Perhaps truth and order could be found only at a distance, in America, safely beyond royal corruption.

America the Exception?

Looking back from the mid-nineteenth century, European historians such as Tocqueville and Burckhardt were to sense something fated

5. Peter Clark and Paul Slack, eds., *Crisis and Order in English Towns, 1500–1700* (Toronto, 1972).

6. John P. Kenyon, *Stuart England* (New York, 1978).

and dreadful in the seemingly relentless increase in the power of the state already obvious in Stuart England and on the Continent.[7] In the long, painful growth of central authority in Europe in contest with a still-fragile liberty, the American colonies may seem the happy exception. Our mythology holds that as state power after 1600 was evermore felt in Europe, the oppressed fled from noxious order to American freedom. In America, government diminished and, some think, virtually disappeared. For 169 years after Jamestown, however, in law and loyalties the Americans were subjects of the same would-be aggrandizing governments as were Europeans—almost as long as they have lived as a republic. Considering the later and deplored fractiousness of Americans about order, discipline, and the powers that be, it is ironic that their purported adventures in individual freedom and social experiment often began more as a search for better order and more attentive government than could be found in Europe. For most of their history, colonial Americans expected government to help provide the plot of land, the tiny shop, the access to a craft or markets denied them in overpopulated, underfed, and blood-drenched Europe. Even in 1776, alongside the denunciations of the king in the name of liberty, we still sense the complaints that he had failed grievously to provide his subjects with the proper order.

The better order for a would-be colonist included relief from numbing poverty, unemployment, and lawlessness in the English towns and countryside with their thieves or roving gangs of desperadoes. America as "the best poor man's country" caught the imagination of prospective immigrants, who also envisioned relief from state-enforced social stations and duties that closed ranks and doors to social inferiors, to those deemed "dependent" because they lacked property or, even if owning land, were still too lowly to have "connection" with the great and near-great. There were countless numbers also willing to risk the crossing to find an order that would lessen the threat of debtors' prisons.[8] There were English and Europeans who were better off and had little or no religious complaint but felt held back from fruitful enterprise. For them, there were to be trading companies and proprietorships to open Virginia, New Amsterdam, New Sweden, the Carolinas, and New England.[9]

Unlike the direct role of the state in underwriting the colonization

7. Alexis de Tocqueville, *The Old Regime and the French Revolution* (Garden City, N.Y., 1955); Tocqueville, *Recollections* (New York, 1949); Jakob Burckhardt, *Force and Freedom* (New York, 1943).

8. Carl Bridenbaugh, *Vexed and Troubled Englishmen, 1590–1642* (New York, 1968); David B. Quinn, *England and the Discovery of America* (New York, 1973).

9. Charles M. Andrews, *The Colonial Period of American History* (4 Vols.; New Haven, 1934), I, 28–31.

of New France and New Spain, private enterprise had immediate responsibility for opening much of British North America.[10] But it was not our "free enterprise." From Walter Raleigh in the 1580s to James Oglethorpe's associates in Georgia in the 1730s, although men interested in the new world for investment did put up the money, they had no right to send colonists across the Atlantic without a state charter and without promising the state that English law and religion, London-set boundaries for their "plantations," and royal decisions in foreign policy would be observed. Free enterprise usually is taken to mean freedom to ignore the state in starting and conducting whatever business one wants. But using the state to approve or underwrite enterprise was with Americans from the beginning. Indeed, that role never ceased, although it was to become a hidden, powerful motif in a self-flattering history depicting the individual American meeting all his needs by himself.

By about 1580, the English state might not yet have had the money nor wanted to provide it for colonies, but its strategic interests and those of adventurous merchants began to coincide. With the Spanish Armada defeated in 1588, the throne wanted enhanced prestige and secure power against its perpetual enemies across the Channel in France and Spain. About then, the first colonization efforts began in Ireland and, in much frustration with those ventures,[11] across the ocean to North America. As the colonies grew and brought profits as well as power and prestige, England was more prepared to underwrite private investment by committing troops and ships to colonial defense. By 1650 it had passed the first Navigation Acts to protect imperial trade, and by 1664 it had chased the Dutch from New Amsterdam. Eventually, the state paid off the descendants of the proprietors who had founded colonies such as Maryland and the Carolinas and put most colonies directly under resident royal governors. This thickening involvement indicates how important the state was to the rich as well as the poor in the founding of British North America, however strong the later myths that, from our earliest times, Americans were blessedly free of the state and power politics. Broadly, amid all the groups and motives that helped populate America over the century and a half of English rule, we can discern the state as a gathering image of authority trying sporadically to extend its grasp over religion, trade, or taxes, failing its Christian duty to nur-

10. For a comparative history of imperial policies in the Americas, see James Lang, *Conquest and Commerce: Spain and England in the Americas* (New York, 1975). For other comparisons of states and empires, consult the works on Spain by J. H. Parry, Woodrow Borah, Charles Gipson, and Bailey W. Diffies; G. M. Wrong on French America; Richard Beeman on Portuguese Brazil and Virginia.

11. Quinn, *England and the Discovery of America*.

ture its subjects. In other directions, it encouraged, underwrote, and defended those who were willing to take the risk of investing or coming across the ocean.

It was the later American struggle against the British empire that nurtured the idea that American political life had been state-free and innocent of English, Machiavellian corruption until George III acted otherwise. From the hostile perspectives during the imperial travail after 1763, the eight generations under kings were not only foreshortened but put into the service of liberty and against the state from the first landings. Jamestown in 1607 was a prelude to 1776. The rights of man and demand for the rule of the law that inspired the strictures of Jefferson against George III were American ideals from the beginning. All that remained in 1776 was to cut a few remaining weakened strands and to let the colonial "states" become what they largely already were: fully competent societies with governments or states of their own.[12]

All this was a gloss by Jefferson, John Adams, and the late colonial historians on what was later called the Whig theory of English history. They traced English liberty and the consent of the governed from before Magna Charta through the parliamentary lawyers Coke and Selden, who opposed James I and Charles I. From the 1620s onward, liberty quickened in English republican writers such as John Milton, James Harrington, and Algernon Sydney and came down to our revolutionary generation. English history was thus construed as a ceaseless struggle for liberty not in tandem *with* the state but *against* it, with the parties and basic issues remaining much the same: Saxons versus Normans after 1066, King John versus the barons in 1215, Charles Stuart versus Cromwell, and George III opposed by Whig friends of liberty in Parliament and the colonies. Americans of 1776, still largely British in origins, not only widely assented to this tale but added their most recent grievances in a long list in their exasperated Declaration of Independence.

The famous American version of Whig history is the "legend of the Founding Fathers," in which every generation of Americans after 1607 had to repeat the fight for liberty to be taxed only with consent, to trade where they wished, to have an adequate currency, to manufacture for one's needs, to ship where one willed, to practice a chosen faith, and to be able successfully to call on the law against overreaching and corrupt government. The climax of that struggle, the vindication of liberty by the virtuous Americans separating from sinful England, was the task of 1776. The painful but providential purpose of the 169 years un-

---

12. There is an old debate about the distinction between *state* and *government*. For simplicity here I use the terms almost interchangeably with the admitted danger of distorting some historical issues, especially about law and sovereignty.

der kings was thus to prepare Englishmen to become Americans and to rescue English liberty from a near-fatal loss to George III. English liberty was redeemed when it became American freedom.[13]

Strains on the State

Fascinating and still popular as this tale is, it obscures and distorts much, like all myths of birth and redemption. The role of government in colonial times was not limited to approving casually the founding of the colonies and then looking the other way. The colonists did not use their new-found freedom in the wilderness to build a society that forswore the state. On the contrary, most of the colonial period was not an age of free politics, free religion, and free speech. Nor was it an epoch of free markets or free labor. The product, price, and labor controls of the mercantilist world in England also were standard in each colony and locality. The era also created the American race system with laws to maintain whites over blacks and to subdue those called Indians. The colonial years also brought, even more widespread than slavery, bound or "indentured" labor for whites and imprisonment for debt followed by legal and political disabilities. Some of these limits on white liberty lasted well beyond the revolution of 1776 for the rights of man.[14]

A less-known tale than the legend of the Founding Fathers suggests that, springing from England as so many did, most colonists in their ideals and institutions long thought of themselves as Englishmen or Britons. They willingly played the imperial game, toasted the king, and rejoiced in his triumphs over the French and Spanish. A notion of life in America being different, better-off, and morally purer than the home country also began to develop early, with, for example, the Massachusetts Puritans' idea that in fleeing England they had escaped to holy living from defilement. But this drift toward a moralistic self-enhancement among the colonists was long inseparable from dependence on imperial trade and defense and on government, local and imperial, for land grants, bounties, market rules, and English law and soldiers. And when they had the chance to choose a stylish life, well-to-do colonists did not repair their log cabins but copied England in their fine houses, portraits, furniture, carriages, gardens, dress, and colleges.[15]

13. Contrast Herbert Butterfield, *The Englishman and His History* (Cambridge, Eng., 1944), with his *The Whig Interpretation of History* (London, 1931); Wesley F. Craven, *The Legend of the Founding Fathers* (New York, 1956); Jefferson's gloss is in Otto Vossler, *Jefferson and the American Revolutionary Ideal* (Washington, D.C., 1981).

14. David W. Galenson, *White Servitude in Colonial America* (New York, 1981).

15. Louis B. Wright, *Cultural Life of the American Colonies, 1607–1763* (New York, 1957).

The facts of English power and trading advantages, English law, language, and anti-Catholicism, the commands of English colonial charters as well as feelings of a common tradition and familial connections helped support a transported impulse to English fullness of government in North America. Yet, whatever weight we give to this momentum, colonial life was bound to create important variants on the European state, forcing it to adjust the play between liberty and order and ultimately to create prejudices against intrusive government per se. Under American conditions change had to occur, but not because every generation of colonials was waiting for the Declaration of Independence or thought the king and his ministers corrupt. Love England and cheer the king's forces as one might, America was not England. Nature's setting for farming and trading were different. Distances from London and within the colonies were far beyond the mere four hundred miles that separated Cornwall from the northern edge of Scotland, and the English in America had to accommodate themselves to a growing potpourri of settlers from all over western Europe.[16]

At first, the tiny settlements in alien and frightening places had to huddle together for protection and to observe the old laws and new rules needed for survival. The first American gold rush in Virginia soon after 1607 showed what chaos would follow if order was ignored and authority flaunted.[17] In Massachusetts Bay the Puritan ideal of strong Christian government, not a search for boodle as in Virginia, was the purpose of the leaders in emigrating. At first, the communal ideal was reinforced by the common perils of life such as the shortage of food and the Indians. In most of New England, the "saints" who controlled church and state confronted a majority of "strangers" who had emigrated for more mundane purposes than God's word or to be herded and harangued by haughty leaders.[18] Very soon, irritations accumulated about the direction of the new Zion, over which most settlers had little say. As the magistrates and divines of the first generation in Massachusetts and Connecticut developed their highly articulated, state-enforced Christian order, disaffection arose about voting rights, religious status, and landholding.[19] Alienation and anger in all social ranks bred thoughts of moving on, but the hope that greater and more profitable liberty would be found

16. Daniel Boorstin, *The Americans: The Colonial Experience* (New York, 1958).

17. Edmund S. Morgan, "The First American Boom," *William and Mary Quarterly,* XVIII (1971).

18. Darrett Rutman, *Winthrop's Boston* (Chapel Hill, 1965).

19. Edmund S. Morgan, *The Puritan Dilemma: The Story of John Winthrop* (Boston, 1958); Alan Simpson, *Puritanism in Old and New England* (Chicago, 1955); Michael McGiffert, "American Puritan Studies in the 1960s," *William and Mary Quarterly,* XXVII (1970).

elsewhere was qualified by fears of the unsettled interior and of losing the protection and the favors in land distribution and legal tenure that the charter authorized only the colony government to dispense. "Out there" were death and disease, Indian capture and torture, the devil unchecked by Christian order and free to roam and tempt, uncleared lands and an unprecedented isolation of souls without society, church, and law. The settlement of colonial New England by towns, rather than direct grants to individuals by Boston or New Haven, thus responded to demands for both liberty and order.[20] A new town tapped initiative and appealed to the discontented. But the colony laws and courts, needs for defense, new churches, albeit of the established Congregational faith, and a host of communal needs ensured that even those living on their own farms outside a town would be kept close to the eyes and arms of local government.[21]

In other colonies, elaborate initial plans to constitute European communities based on manorial estates and obligations, noble titles, lordly privileges, and dependent subjects went awry. Dutch New York, Maryland, and Carolina quickly moved away from attempted recastings of English manorialism or of a feudalism already long gone. Revival of a fixed hierarchical social order made no sense for an America intent on attracting settlers. The expansiveness and mobility that stemmed from natural wealth, geographic size and distances, and diverse nationalities and religions frustrated making America into a Europe.[22] Manorialism was to wither on American soil and leave behind only scattered, thin remains. By 1776, despite his great complaints, no tenant farmer in New York or any colonial payer of quitrents approached being the serf or cowed peasant of a European lord and master. In Europe, the low horizons of life, with space filled and land staked for generations, frustrated the aspirations of most commoners. But America's immense space provided a tonic as the close-knit communal and patriarchal life of Europe began to unravel.[23] That tale, in effect, of how Eu-

20. Philip J. Greven, Jr., "Historical Demography and Colonial America," *William and Mary Quarterly,* XXIV (1967); Daniel S. Smith, "The Demographic History of Colonial New England," *Journal of Economic History,* XXXII (1972); Kenneth A. Lockridge, "The Population of Dedham, Massachusetts, 1636–1736," *Economic History Review,* XIX (1966).

21. George L. Haskins, *Law and Authority in Early Massachusetts* (New Haven, 1960); Timothy H. Breen, *The Character of the Good Ruler* (New Haven, 1970).

22. Wesley F. Craven, *The Southern Colonies in the Seventeenth Century, 1606–1689* (Baton Rouge, 1949); Rowland Berthoff and J. M. Murrin, "Feudalism, Communism, and the Yeoman Freeholder," in *Essays on the Amercian Revolution,* ed. Stephen G. Kurtz and James H. Hutson (Chapel Hill, 1973).

23. Gordon J. Schochet, *Patriarchalism in Political Thought* (New York, 1975).

ropean villagers became American individualists has been deeply documented, but the general effects of American expansiveness on the development of government created patterns that we still need to understand, especially since so many of them are enduring.

As every textbook tells us, the American wilderness suggested freedom and opportunity. Less emphasized is that besting the wilderness required collective and public, as well as individual and private, effort.[24] In clearing new land the need for labor and companions might be met by family, but once settled on his terrain and producing a surplus, the colonist sensed the wider world of markets and money. Mere subsistence did not satisfy for very long and profits beckoned. But getting to markets was very difficult. In the wider context of our ongoing debate about "economic development," colonial life on the incipient huge American scale helped create new interests that soon outstripped the individual's power to serve them. "Boundless horizons," as they develop in America or elsewhere when resources as well as ambitions are large, require the state, whatever the prejudices against government intervention.[25] Whatever laissez-faire or socialist ideology tempts people to believe about the state, the historical record everywhere reveals the so-called modern economy, *i.e.*, expansive and rationalizing, developing in tandem with state power and functions. Through thick and thin, in calm and crisis, the state grows in response to awakened needs. But it also waxes because of politics. For their own reasons of extending or stabilizing their power, from colonial times to today, government leaders had a stake in stimulating economic growth, sponsoring with public aid where capital was thin or timid, and soothing those whose wounds in market or social strife it could not afford to ignore. These are the impressive characteristics of the long swell of the history of American government, whatever the surface waves of American debate about the state. Much of this study will bear on this claim as well as trace the tensions within and about government that ceaseless ambition, "growth," and its mystique have generated.

Already early in colonial life, once his blood was stirred and opportunity seemed graspable, the American found his solitary powers insufficient for his appetites. Stuart Bruchey has emphasized, however, that the vastness, riches, and novelty of the new continent, although nurturing aspirations, also imposed natural and human limits on the scale of enterprise. These did not really begin to give way until after the revolu-

24. Michael Zuckerman, *Peaceable Kingdoms* (New York, 1970); Mody C. Boatright, "The Myth of Frontier Individualism," *Southwest Social Science Quarterly,* XXII (1941).
25. On boundlessness generally, see David B. Davis, *Ante-bellum American Culture* (Lexington, Mass., 1979), xx; Rowland Berthoff, *An Unsettled People* (New York, 1971).

tion, but as Americans struggled against the colonial limitations, they found the state indispensable, even if a nuisance or worse, in breaching the barriers of nature and simple technology.[26] Within all the dreams of a new beginning, for fresh immigrants and for farmers moving on, lurked "needs." All human beings have needs, but they are not always conscious and directed toward government as they were by the colonists: for law and order against the predator and sharpster; for defense against the Indians, French, and Spanish; for communication with family and authorities "back there"; for provisioning with powder, muskets, and nails; for access to navigable streams and shipping lanes; for labor, usually scarce, whether free, bound, or slave, to help work the land; for capital, ample currency, credit, and fair interest; for codified legal entry onto new land and for secure titles to it to avoid eviction; for allies against natural barriers or competitors whom one could not take on alone. An old ideal endured with the new land hunger. Patrimony had to be preserved and estates passed without contest to designated heirs. This hope alone implied a large world of law.[27] Probate especially brought forth a maze of colonial law of inheritance that was added to the English rules.[28] No common folk in the Western world at the time held more land and were more astir about their property and thus more often in court than the colonial Americans. Their frenzy for their interests and for the litigation to protect them also implied constant recourse to the state. In forsaking a closed-in village life, with authority close at hand, the pioneer on the frontier or the freeman farmer behind him may have increasingly nurtured a conceit that he could succeed without government. But the colonial records, not only of probate, but of government regulations, bounties, petitions for relief and favors, and public and private trials, show abundantly that pioneers under pressure scurried toward the state when life turned too grim or "opportunity" seemed too risky.

Colonists sought the state—for bounties on naval stores, for prohibiting the growing of tobacco in England, for maximum access to Caribbean trade—but they also started to shame it for interference or neglect. Such seeking while shaming is perhaps the most enduring pattern of American ambiguities about government. As colonists moved away from imperial government in the coastal areas and into the backcountry, the colonial authority, as well as London, gradually gath-

26. Stuart Bruchey, *The Roots of American Economic Growth, 1607–1861* (New York, 1968), 71–72.

27. Richard B. Morris, *Studies in the History of American Law* (New York, 1930).

28. Jackson T. Main pointed out to me the significance of the world of probate. I also draw on his *Social Structure of Revolutionary America* (Princeton, 1965).

ered an aura of being distant, haughty, unreliable, ineffective, insensitive to needs, and resistant to backcountry demands for representation, defense, or tax relief.[29] As colonial life expanded westward, "London" as a presence faded more than did colonial government, although appeal for a London role could suddenly come to mind in frontier areas if Williamsburg or Boston seemed insensitive about defense against the French or Indians or about access to western lands. For most of the colonial period London was too distant for daily needs, so when colonists called on the state or the state took an initiative, principally the colony or local government was involved. American government, and an American governing class sprung from commoners, grew in response to a wide variety of burgeoning needs, including finding better paths to satisfying those needs than London or the royal governors' retinues might provide. Over a century, the colonists grew accustomed to providing for themselves, and this increased self-reliance set the stage for the great imperial struggle after 1763. When London under George III did assert itself forcefully against colonial practice and sentiment, it confronted aggressive and educated colonial leaders who had been schooled for generations in their own lively politics of local sufficiency. They were also prepared to resist London to the utmost; they had already successfully trimmed the royal governors' claws on colonial taxation and patronage.[30]

Reach and Grasp

Colonial expansion and the imperial ambitions of London moved together, but for different reasons. On the books, the total variegated apparatus of the laws and officials from London, the colonial capitals, the counties, towns, parishes, and localities marked a spread of the state. The increase in the functions *formally* assigned to government would never lessen throughout American history. The later growth, however, would be pragmatic, not based heavily on the Christian principles that sinful or fractious men must be governed or on the mercantilist theory that the interests of the community, regime, and empire should be protected. During the colonial period, however, one must especially watch, not merely the state's reach "on the books," but its grasp or effectiveness. "On the books," in the helter-skelter adding of task to task, law to law, office to office, appointee to appointee, regulated product to other products, or as a *considered* matter of general policy, government

29. Jack M. Sosin, *The Revolutionary Frontier, 1763–1783* (New York, 1967).

30. Bernard Bailyn, *Origins of American Politics* (New York, 1968); Jack P. Greene, *The Quest For Power* (Chapel Hill, 1963).

piled up.[31] In the periodic redoing of imperial administration from the 1660s to the 1760s, government *tried,* erratically and clumsily, to make its weight felt. Overall, the colonist of 1760 was far more heavily involved in a web of government than he may have liked or than he was portrayed in later myths of his freedom from the state.

If there is a word to describe any rationale for the accumulating aspirations of colonial government, *i.e.,* for its pretenses or reach, it is *mercantilism.* As a theory, the word belongs more to scholars after Adam Smith coined it than to the vocabulary of Stuart or Hanoverian statesmen.[32] Neither needed the theory, for the facts seemed patent. Mercantilism was a policy for survival. In a world of nations often at war and dominated by a sense of scarce resources (especially of gold and silver), the state felt impelled to regulate economic activity just to endure, let alone to become rich and prosperous. Colonies came to be prized as sources of wealth, as bases for ships and troops, and as sites for royal flags far from the homeland but testifying to its power. With wealth from colonies as one of the sinews of statecraft, the lands and waters of America, with their tobacco, iron ore, grains, fibers, furs, fish, lumber, and naval stores, became irresistible temptations for settlers and their governments to try to pass beyond an economy of mere European "make-do" or subsistence to American amplitude and profits. Everywhere in the colonies one finds, against those sizeable natural and institutional limits, the push to productivity and restlessness about markets, profits, currency, investment, and fevers for speculation. This economy was not run in our free-swinging way for the individual entrepreneur. "Individualism" in farming, fishing, and trade helped a person accumulate private treasure, but it had to work in conjunction with government. Under the charters the colonist owed loyalty to the throne, and his economic links with London tied him to imperial interests.[33] But his own governments within the colonies regulated not only religion and morals but wages, prices, markets and market days, and conditions of labor.[34] They granted him favors, paid him the bounties for indigo or naval stores, provided incentives for exploration and further settlement, and ordained the rules for ocean commerce and trading. All this put the colonist far from the limited state of later laissez-faire theory. Over eight generations, by every sign of government activity—by tasks undertaken, agen-

31. Herbert L. Osgood, *The American Colonies in the Seventeenth Century* (3 vols.; New York, 1904); Osgood, *The American Colonies in the Eighteenth Century* (3 vols.; New York, 1924).

32. Eli Hecksher, *Mercantilism* (London, 1935).

33. Michael Kammen, *Empire and Interest* (New York, 1971).

34. Richard B. Morris, *Government and Labor in Early America* (New York, 1946).

cies created and offices filled, bills introduced and acts passed, government costs, official buildings constructed—colonial government grew in its reach and even in penetration to some of its mercantilist goals.

The growth, however, was inchoate and sporadic, proceeding in fits and starts. This suited a world with a politics and economics that were less widely debated than ours and without governments legislating programs under ideologies for making ever-better societies. This was the time before Bentham and before modern statistics and analytic studies of policy aiming at more rational government or at "growth" as good in itself. It was also an age before "legislation" became the major business of government. Much of governing day-by-day involved courts and judges rather than the other branches of government. What initiative government had came less from below or from legislative leaders than at the behest of a royal governor who could summon, dismiss, or veto a House of Burgesses or the General Court. The ideal at the grass roots and the tree tops was to maintain the going system sufficient unto the day rather than to "introduce novelty into the state," as Burke was later to moan about the new revolutionary age of "sophisters, economists and calculators." Indeed, it was the *mess* of this mercantilist politics that later inspired both Adam Smith and Bentham to ask that government be cleansed, simplified, rationalized, made "modern."

"Mess" as the normal and expected limit on the state's grasp helps account a great deal for the compatability of the expanding reach of the colonial state with personal liberty. The government in London might at different times act with a law from Parliament, a Privy Council ruling, or a regulation from the Treasury, the Board of Trade, or the "Southern Department."[35] But there was poor "follow-up." Illegal squatting on land, or cutting trees in reserved forests, or refining iron, or not paying the duty on molasses did not quickly bring down "revenooers" on one's head, if at all. And the vast accumulation of rules about prices, wages, credit, apprenticeship, forestalling, quotas of crops, as well as about law and order, morals, and religion, could be enforced only sporadically and with difficulty over the ever-vaster and thinly settled terrain. The pretension of mercantilist government was thus ambitious, but the reach in the colonies increasingly exceeded its grasp, as well as the will of its growing corps of officials, open as they were to smuggling, bribes, and favors.

Profit from the offices of state brought great corruption, but that was then endemic to government. The laws laid out, not salaries, but fees for each service performed by sheriffs, tax assessors, and other petty offi-

---

35. Thomas C. Barrow, *Trade and Empire* (Cambridge, Mass, 1967).

cials.[36] This made office in a cash-starved land attractive. But these fees were only the legal proceeds. The favor-granting of the mercantile state so berated by Bentham and Smith did, by our lights, pervert government. And there were signs even before 1763 that the colonists were feeling fed up and cynical, however much they played the game and celebrated English liberty. But corruption, like mess, could also mean that the state seldom pounced. Pressed enough or given the opportunity to crack down, it could act and did, but only in spurts of activity coinciding, for example, with a new energetic governor such as Andros in Massachusetts (1684 to 1689) or in yet another round of imperial reform as, fatally, after 1763. The squabbles over favors and "places," not so much "policy," were the notable reasons why colonial politics bubbled, and it is another myth of the revolutionary generation that all before 1763 was tranquil between the energetic colonists and languid government. If anything, American colonial politics was more continuously and more bitterly contentious and reached deeper into the grass roots than politics did in England.[37] By 1763 Americans had been busily wheeling and dealing in seeking government favors for generations, however much, again, they were to depict themselves as orphans and innocents called reluctantly to battle the king.

Waxing and Waning

Along with exhibiting reach without grasp, as well as mess and slack, and despite the widening scope of laws and offices on the books, colonial governments waxed and waned about the concerns they would press or forego.[38] The level of government that pressed or relaxed similarly varied. Government in London or Charleston could lessen its reach in one respect, only to increase it in others. This pattern, like seeking and shaming, was to endure down to today and has become an important mark of our federal system. Activity at Williamsburg or London might retreat for a while from concern about the Indians, but localities nearer the Indians would have to maintain their concern or enlarge

36. See, for example, *Acts and Laws of the State of Connecticut in America* (Hartford, 1786). Assistant judges were given twenty-four shillings per action tried. Sheriffs and constables were to have four pence per summons served. The list of fees for other services is extensive. Other colonial records have similar lists.

37. See James Henretta, *The Evolution of American Society, 1700–1815* (Lexington, Mass., 1973), for general characteristics. To sample deeper detail in one colony, see Patricia U. Bonomi, *A Factious People* (New York, 1971).

38. The theme of waxing and waning is derived from J. B. Brebner, "Laissez Faire and State Intervention in Nineteenth Century Britain," *Journal of Economic History, Supplement VIII* (1948).

it with, for example, new rules for a more effective militia. By not sensing such patterns in colonial as well as later American history we can be misled about the total reach and grasp of government. A notable case of this waxing and waning on one large concern of colonial times is apparent in the regulation of religion, a many-sided tussle among London, the colony seats, localities, and religious groups.[39]

Generalization is difficult because of the multiplicity of American sects and churches, the diversity of colony governments and their policies, and the cross-purposes, reversals, and fits and starts in London. Most of the colonies (New Amsterdam, Rhode Island, and Pennsylvania were exceptions) began with a high emphasis that orthodoxy be guarded. At first, the governments accepted the age-old task of the state to promote, in the words of E. B. Greene, "not merely religion in general or Christianity in general, but a particular form of Christian faith and polity."[40]

Diversity of creed and observance, however, was present from the beginning, even within the most zealous colony, Massachusetts Bay, with religious "strangers," such as Quakers and Presbyterians, eventually suppressed.[41] Among all colonies the early religious diversity, like the mixture of nationalities, could not be eliminated. Instead, it was accepted in the attempt to attract settlers. Inevitably, this policy led to a gradual decrease in the number of colonists who accepted the established faith or zealously pursued it. Because of the passing of ardent leaders, as in Massachusetts, or a general drift of the populace toward indifference, slackening in the official faith also made religious policy less oppressive.

Beyond Massachusetts and Connecticut, from the outset, the variety of creeds among would-be settlers often confounded the initial incentive for an effective orthodoxy. In New Amsterdam, that pillar of the Dutch Reformed Church, Governor Peter Stuyvesant, was told by his superiors in Holland to relent in his moves against Lutherans, Quakers, and Jews and to "shut your eyes."[42] When the deeply Catholic Duke of York (afterward, James II) obtained New York in 1664 from the Crown just after it was secured from Holland, the English had already promised the Dutch government that the Dutch church there would have liberty, as would all Protestant congregations with properly ordained ministers. How "American" in cross-purposes it already was that an ardently Catholic proprietor had to establish the Anglican Church by state com-

39. The leading general history is Sidney E. Ahlstrom, *Religious History of the American People* (New Haven, 1972).

40. Evarts B. Greene, *Religion and the State* (Ithaca, N.Y., 1959), 46.

41. Perry Miller, *Orthodoxy in Massachusetts* (Cambridge, Mass., 1934).

42. Greene, *Religion and the State,* 30.

mand while also promising toleration to dissenters. Soon too, as in the officially Anglican Jersies and in Carolina, the dissenting colonists outnumbered the Anglicans. The charters for the Jersies required Anglicanism, but that stipulation had to be ignored to encourage settlement. In Carolina the original provision for toleration was reinforced by the influx of non-Anglicans, to the discomfort of the more assiduous Anglican settlers. They had to bear with the situation or see immigration drop.[43]

Of all the colonies, Maryland best illustrates how official religious policy could wax and wane repeatedly and rapidly in response to internal and external pressures.[44] In order to gain an American haven for fellow Catholics, the original proprietor, Lord Baltimore, had to foster toleration for all Christians. Maryland's celebrated Toleration Act of 1649 provided for peace between Catholics and Protestants on the basis of common belief in specified Christian tenets. Maryland thus waned from orthodoxy. Simultaneously, however, it tried to wax toward the past with another law in 1649 that imposed the death penalty for those denying the Trinity (although that law seems never to have been enforced). Soon, the tumult in Cromwell's England in the 1650s over religious policies drove Maryland to and fro about both orthodoxy and toleration. After cancellation in 1654, the Toleration Act was revived in 1657, and a religiously diverse immigration to Maryland resumed. But after 1689 there were, again, new harsh laws against Catholics, as there were in originally tolerant Pennsylvania after 1701.[45]

Everywhere in America, waxing and waning in official religious policies were affected by the travail of the children of God's Word against the temptations of the rich and vast American world. Then as now, the lures of the world posed hard choices for pious Americans who wished populace and state to follow a stringent, world-denying word of God. The expansive world in America also took other tolls on official orthodoxy through intermarriage, the dearth of churches and ministers, and conflict among diverse faiths and sects.

For those who could not remain true to the Word while pursuing the ways of the world, the state not only conveniently waned in enforcing established faith but eventually waxed, ironically, in supporting toleration. The colonial state was thus not inevitably the enemy of religious freedom. Roger Williams used the state in Rhode Island to secure the broadest toleration in early colonial America. In earliest Maryland

43. Ahlstrom, *Religious History of the American People,* 196–99.
44. Greene, *Religion and the State,* 53–56.
45. Isaac Sharpless, *A Quaker Experiment in Government* (2 vols.; Philadelphia, 1902), I.

and freshly founded Pennsylvania it was the state that declared religious liberty for all trinitarians or Christians, although this might not bring political rights for Catholics or Jews. Governor Andros, who came to New England after the suspension of the Massachusetts charter in 1684, was an Anglican deeply hostile to the Puritan establishment. To obtain the rights of the Anglican minority to worship in the officially Congregational colony, Andros forced toleration onto Massachusetts.[46]

Overall, it is difficult to escape the impression that the state would not have waned from orthodoxy and waxed toward toleration without the competing fires of many sectarian faiths, with none able to dominate. Even more, all creeds in time asked less of followers than had John Cotton and Thomas Hooker in the 1630s. Only as skepticism, worldliness, and merely moral issues replaced theological truth could government's powers over religion have waned significantly. Still, by 1776 official orthodoxies had been deeply confounded rather than thoroughly routed. In Virginia after the revolution, Patrick Henry was loathe to allow the recent disestablishment of Anglicanism to extend to the state's withdrawing, as Madison wished, all support for religion. Indeed, had the Anglican faith in Virginia and elsewhere not been the king's religion, requiring loyalty to him from its priests and communicants, it is debatable whether its full disestablishment would have come.[47] During and after the war, established Congregationalism in Massachusetts, New Hampshire, and Connecticut—not, significantly, the obligatory royal religion in those colonies—remained. These establishments coexisted unsteadily with dissent, skepticism, and anti-Catholicism.[48] All of these, in turn, were affected by movement to toleration (the state policy) and tolerance (the public attitude). By 1800, only some stones of a "wall of separation" between church and state were actually in place in America, and Jefferson's phrase scarcely described the high informal status and influence of protestant Christianity in his time.

An important novelty for the colonial state as it waned toward tolerating religious diversity was how to deal with zealous subjects who shook state and society with demands for a renewed and enforced faith. In the eighteenth century particularly, private sloth or official ease about doctrine or diversity could suddenly be challenged by "awakenings."[49]

46. Greene, *Religion and the State*, 63–64.

47. Hamilton J. Eckenrode, *The Separation of State and Church in Virginia* (Richmond, Va., 1910); Rhys Isaac, *The Transformation of Virginia, 1740–1790* (Chapel Hill, 1982), 278, 283–85.

48. William G. McLaughlin, *New England Dissent* (2 vols.; Cambridge, Mass., 1971); John Tracy Ellis, *Catholics in Colonial America* (Baltimore, 1965).

49. J. M. Bumsted and J. E. Van de Wetering, *What Must I Do To Be Saved?* (Hinsdale, Ill., 1976).

Reeking of truth as those aroused by these revivals often were, they could demand that the state command orthodoxy. But by the 1740s, the religious slack that angered the revivalists had advantages for worldly governments and their subjects who were more interested in peace and getting and spending than in truth. The enthusiasm of the awakenings was also threatening to good order because it suggested a wild individualism or heterodoxy not only about faith but about other accepted ideas of civic obedience and social conduct. In other words, evangelical intensity might spill over from "mere" religion to the general order and stability still so prized by government.[50]

Waning in the state's will for orthodoxy introduced a recurrent American problem: could government that had moved to support toleration wax again toward orthodoxy to support citizens who were dogmatic and demanded that state and society reembrace "truth"? In the late colonial period a notable example of this tension was Congregational New England's immense upset when London mandated security for Catholic worship in newly acquired Canada.[51] But such problems were to endure long after 1776 as American religiosity recurrently clashed with the official policy of separation of church and state. Intense religious conscience reappeared cyclically in America with controversial demands that state power wax to confront "evil" that ranged from general impiety to disregard for the sabbath, chastity, or sobriety, the decline of Bible reading, and absence of prayer in public schools.[52]

In the colonial economy and in social and moral concerns the patterns of waxing and waning were equally intricate. If the state withdrew gradually from its early extensive "blue law" activity about sexual and drinking habits, it waxed toward regulating race relations[53] or improving public health and hygiene, particularly in growing towns with concentrated populations so open to pest and plague and contamination of food, water, and air.[54] As settlement and the scope of markets expanded, government had to increase activity and resources to ease communication and transport by clearing streams or improving ports. When, despite mercantilist government support, colonial ventures in wine and silk failed, the state waned from encouraging them, only to wax in concern about rice, indigo, and dairying, both to stimulate production of and in regulating markets for those products. As an imperial economy

50. Ronald Knox, *Enthusiasm* (New York, 1950).

51. Victor Coffin, *The Province of Quebec and the Early American Revolution* (Madison, Wis., 1896).

52. Martin Marty, *Righteous Empire: The Protestant Experience in America* (New York, 1970).

53. Winthrop Jordan, *White over Black* (Chapel Hill, 1963).

54. Richard H. Shryock, *Medicine in America* (Baltimore, 1966).

developed after 1660, wool, iron, hats, sugar and molasses, tall trees, naval stores, and the currency supply became familiar items in the story of the contest about regulation within the waxing empire, but these were only some of the items on the lengthening list for state reach.[55] Had the grasp of colonial government, both from London and the colony seats, matched its reach about what it professed to regulate, American colonial history might have been quite different.

Government waxing and waning, as its objects of concern shifted, also came with stretching or withdrawing geographically. Roads and navigation hazards, defense needs, and marketing rules might start as small, local concerns but reach proportions making a county seat (for militia marshaling) or a colonial capital or London (for rules about tobacco growing, pricing, storing, and shipping) more active, or at least a growing partner, in such responsibilities.

Currency supply and the value of coins and paper issue became especially vexatious problems as trade became intercolonial and international with the West Indies, Africa, or southern Europe. It was beyond the practical or legal power of both the colony and its localities to create one metal currency that would be reliable and usable from the Caribbean to Canada. Sporadically, adequate currency was the concern of London. The chronic problem within the colonies was largely dearth. Generally, the currency supply was affected by the waxing and waning of inexpert and haphazard government.[56] If the state waned in strictness about the amount or hardness of currency, floods of paper or wooden issue could lead to inflation that would then require governments to try to repair damage by once again waxing in currency controls. These extensive colonial contests about the money supply, with various levels of government waxing, waning, and then again returning to repair currency and credit deficiencies, prefigured similar contests over the money supply and interest rates during the Revolution and after, down to today's savings and loan epic and struggles about the role of the Federal Reserve Board.[57]

Generally, therefore, the waxing and waning between the federal and other levels of government that we still experience on matters like education, welfare, exploration for off-shore oil, "revenue sharing," and so

55. Edward C. Kirkland, *A History of American Economic Life* (New York, 1954), 98–129.

56. Joseph A. Ernst, *Money and Politics in America, 1755–1775* (Chapel Hill, 1973); Curtis P. Nettels, *The Money Supply of the American Colonies Before 1720* (Madison, Wis., 1934).

57. Fritz Redlich, *The Molding of American Banking* (New York, 1951); Milton Friedman and Anna J. Schwartz, *A Monetary History of the United States, 1867–1960* (Princeton, 1963).

on, was thus implicit in the colonial maze of allocated powers and responsibilities between London and the colonial seats of government as well as between the colonial capital and its counties or towns.[58] The overall complexity already apparent in colonial waxing and waning warns us of the difficulties of reading the general history of the reach and the grasp of the state too simply. Assessing the weight and import of government activity at any time in American history requires analyzing what subject or aspect of a problem is coming under scrutiny, what type of regulation or intervention is increasing or declining, the difference between the reach of legal power and grasp in actual enforcement, and at what tier of America's governments intervention appears or disappears, perhaps only to appear elsewhere then or at another time.

Problems of Liberty

Toleration created many dilemmas, but another recurrent American difficulty about liberty as an aim of government began to emerge during the founding generations. The colonial world had counted heavily on personal initiative and profit as incentive to produce wealth but had used state subsidies and regulation to reconcile energetic enterprises with official views of social and political well-being. But as the economy grew and diversified, it became more difficult for the state to cope with the varied activities that its wish for growth had helped stimulate. Notable examples include rum and raw iron production, the hunger for more land, and the search for adequate masts and naval stores for the navy. Although the argument for less-fettered enterprise was forming before Adam Smith,[59] it was also apparent before the Revolution that if the state honored what Smith was to call the "natural and beneficent tendencies" of individual effort, freedom from the state could lead to disruptive social or economic results. In the colonial-imperial economy many investment "bubbles" had burst, land claims involved fraud, booms and busts occurred in tobacco, and attempts were made to corner markets in many products and services.[60] Such problems left many colonists feeling cheated and also threatened the stability, resources, and income of government. The colonists demanded government action to counter fraudulent land claims or engrossing of grain or excessive charges

58. Ian K. Steele, *The Politics of Colonial Policy: The Board of Trade in Colonial Administration, 1696–1720* (Oxford, Eng., 1968).

59. Joseph Dorfman, "Political Economy of the Eighteenth Century," in Dorfman, *The Economic Mind in American Civilization* (3 vols.; New York, 1946), I.

60. Morris, *Government and Labor in Early America*, 20–21.

for interest or shipping. Since colonial times, Americans have thus known cycles of unregulated or deregulated enterprises leading to hues and cries about the "social costs" of injustice, "bigness," favoritism, or "ruinous competition." Perennially, preserving free or fair competition has implied as intervening a state as the mercantilist government that, from the outset, bestowed favors and set market conditions in fear of excessive competition.

Additionally, after all due allowance for how little anyone then knew about economic policy, colonial regulation made no clear case that the state, merely because it is powerful or can claim to speak for the public good, has superior talent for policing the economy. Keeping colonial enterprise controlled for the good of the empire involved fallible and power-conscious government in judgments about alternative and competing policies with many variables: what the good of the empire meant, what was fairness for London and for the colonies, whom to favor and what group to punish, and, ultimately, what the rights of Englishmen were under a seriously enforced imperial policy. Repeatedly, when the colonists moved into a freer or more competitive mode in producing tobacco[61] or in issuing their "pine-tree shillings" or other currency, they so deranged "market forces," as then dimly understood, that imperial government was called upon again to regulate the abuses. Ever since colonial times, therefore, when government regulates or withdraws, waxes or wanes, complaint and struggle about any state path seem unavoidable.

Officialdom and Liberty

In the long pull, we find a double momentum in each colony, toward an impressive practical freedom within ever-growing government either as sponsor or regulator of enterprise. In politics in the colonies as in England, ambitious government gradually had to adjust to the demand for and practice of greater liberty.[62] But most often that involved shifting its concerns rather than abandoning all intervention. Considering all geographic levels and types of intervention, it is dubious that the degree of state intervention on the books as well as in actual grasp has ever justified later American assertions about a golden age of individual freedom or of laissez-faire. State power and liberty in America have grown inextricably entwined with each other, with each available to check the other.

---

61. Jacob M. Price, "Economic Growth of the Chesapeake and the European Market, 1697–1775," *Journal of Economic History,* XXIV (1964).

62. Greene, *The Quest for Power.*

Because liberty as a theme in American history was to gain greater prestige than the suspect idea of the state, histories and stump speeches have praised the advances of freedom rather than the growth of government in ceaseless conjunction with freedom. Indeed, the state has been indispensable to American freedom—to develop the West, to end slavery, to challenge the Kaiser or Hitler, to grant women the vote or equal pay, to secure rights for blacks.

Long before the final imperial crisis, colonists had been establishing this pattern, empowering their assemblies, for example, to help expand the economy and to send agents to London to serve their interests or liberties. However, much of the early history of state-seeking among the colonists is still overshadowed by the patriots' claim that the revolutionary crisis succeeded years of London's "salutary neglect" of America under a placid and free colonial life marked by a mere handful of officials and generally passive government.[63]

Whether London or a colonial government grasped or only reached on imperial policy, both reach and grasp implied increases in numbers and types of officials. In later colonial language borrowed from England, this meant more "placemen," "connections," and "influence."[64] In each colony, the expanding maze of officialdom is impressive for a supposedly increasingly state-free world. Few posts such as sheriff or assessor at local and county levels were created for imperial administration and few, if any, disappeared with the Revolution. By the end of the colonial period, a village of a few hundred inhabitants, such as Sturbridge, Massachusetts, had created about two dozen distinctive offices to do its work.[65] Listing them makes the scope of local government vivid: assessors; auctioneers; constables; engine (fire) men; fence-viewers; field-drivers (for stray animals); fire-wards; hog reevers; health committee; measurers of wood and bark; moderator (of town meetings); overseers of the poor; overseers of work and pauper houses; pound-keeper; school committee; sealers of leather; sealers of weights and measures; surveyors of lumber; surveyors of highways; tax collectors; the sheriff; bailiffs; and justices of peace. The "selectmen," who also belong on the list, were the principal administrators of the town. The scope of their responsibilities also underscores the breadth local government had attained. Besides passing laws and hearing the townsmen, the selectmen

63. James A. Henretta, *Salutary Neglect: Colonial Administration Under the Duke of Newcastle* (Princeton, 1972). Contrast with Murray N. Rothbard, *Salutary Neglect: The American Colonies in the First Half of the 18th Century* (New Rochelle, N.Y., 1975).

64. Alison G. Olson and Richard Maxwell Brown, eds., *Anglo-American Political Relations, 1675–1775* (New Brunswick, N.J., 1970).

65. Isaac Goodwin, *Town Officer: Or Laws of Massachusetts* (N.d.; rpr., Worcester, Mass., 1825).

could license hospitals, innkeepers, liquor sellers and entertainments, slaughterhouses, and distilleries; maintain the jury lists; appoint guardians for the insane; and so on.

Sumner Powell's study of another colonial town, Sudbury, Massachusetts, reveals, similarly, not only "a staggering number" of 650 ordinances for governing the community but how far beyond English borough "legislation" this number was at the time.[66] Admittedly, these offices and powers were in New England towns, where government reached and could grasp more than in other, more sparsely settled colonies, especially in the South with its lack of towns. But an examination of the lists of offices in colonies with county rather than township systems, and at the colonywide and local levels, reveals the similar growth of officialdom.[67]

The Prosaic State

Colonial government spread in order to reach large, often contradictory, goals of security, opportunity, and liberty. The spread suggests that control of government mattered and that the colonists' own struggles for power within their localities or at Boston or Williamsburg was intense. Because nods and favors from government could count so much in colonial life, would-be leaders fought hard to control it. But by 1776 colonial politics also involved more of the populace and familiarized more of them with public affairs then was probably the case in any larger society of the Atlantic world at that time.[68]

Political life in western Europe after the founding of the colonies was increasingly as secular as it was in the New World, but it took the French Revolution to strip away from the European state and church their ancient aura of miracle, mystery, and authority. Although the sanctity and uncontested sovereignty of the English monarch had shrunk in the train

66. Sumner C. Powell, *Puritan Village* (Middletown, Conn., 1963).

67. *The Colonial Records of the State of Georgia*, ed. Allen D. Candler (Atlanta, 1904–16); Maryland Historical Society, *Archives of Maryland* (Annapolis, Md., 1883–1919); Historical Commission of South Carolina, *The Colonial Records of the State of South Carolina* (Columbia, 1951–); *Laws of the State of Delaware* (2 vols.; New Castle, Del., 1797).

68. For politics in individual colonies, see Robert Zemsky, *Merchants, Farmers, and River Gods* (Boston, 1971), on Connecticut; Bonomi, *A Factious People,* on New York; Theodore G. Thayer, *Pennsylvania Politics and the Growth of Democracy, 1740–1776* (Harrisburg, Pa., 1953), on Pennsylvania; Bernard Bailyn, "Politics and Social Structure in Virginia," in *Seventeenth Century America*, ed. James C. Smith (Chapel Hill, 1959), 90–115, on Virginia; and Marion E. Sirmans, *Colonial South Carolina: A Political History, 1663–1763* (Chapel Hill, 1966), on South Carolina.

of the seventeenth-century revolutions, coronation rites and court rituals, elaborate etiquette and rules of precedence, "bowing and scraping," all continued to suggest that something more than unaided human will was at work in the origins and fortunes of the English state. In America a contrasting "embourgeoisement" of government had preceded the American Revolution. Just a few months before the break with England, Tom Paine, in *Common Sense,* had to harangue the patriots to give up fantasies about King George, kingship, and government generally. His argument was not only against a king thought to be God-given but against a lingering illusion that he had ever cared for the colonies and would eventually respect the liberties of his children.[69]

Paine could appeal to the workaday tone and extensive experience with politics that the patriot leaders had long been accumulating. Unlike the commoners in France who came to the fore only in 1789, the revolutionaries of 1776 had been involved in politics for generations. In towns and at county seats or courthouses, at Hartford and Charleston, from sending agents, appeals, and petitions to London, they knew "affairs." The leaders' wide experience and their reading in history and law tempered tendencies to become what Edmund Burke was to deprecate in the novice French reformers of 1789, as "men of mind," *i.e.,* mere theorists in politics. The Americans knew politics daily as "interests" as well as historic "English liberty," the rights of Englishmen, and, to strike another note, of order against "the mob." From the grass roots around Charlottesville, Braintree, or Philadelphia, where Jefferson, Adams, and Franklin lived, up to dealing in London with the House of Lords and Privy Council, American politics produced a wide range of talents that sought power and service. Seats in government continued to carry honor, but they did not bring titles of nobility, codified social privilege, or special treatment before the law like the French aristocracy's exemption from taxes. From England descended an idea that was to come into larger flower in America, the notion of a small freeholder being sufficiently propertied to be independent of another man's will and thus trustable to vote for a legislative representative to advise the king or royal governor. In America, starting with town meetings and selectmen or in the local militia, voice and seats were open to thousands of men of very modest means. Like more prestigious seats in the colonial assemblies and royal councils, the petty offices were also entry into the increasing swag of colonial mercantilism. A seat or an office gave a freeman not only his due but a say in religious and defense policies and in parceling out the mundane benefits and costs of government in

69. Eric Foner, *Tom Paine and Revolutionary America* (New York, 1976).

land policy, subsidies, tax rates and assessments, patronage, cuts from fees for serving summonses, or shares from fines. The local militia gave the commonest man with a musket a voice, as well as participation, in public affairs. The militia was one of America's first political clubs and a springboard to other offices in a town, county, or colonial capital.[70]

Colonial politics from the militia to the royal council was thus prosaic, bread-and-butter politics. As politicking became familiar stuff on the village green or at the county courthouse, it also became less remote and less secret than the politics of the monarchical court of flattering aristocrats. The workaday tone in America led to the desanctification and demythologizing of the traditional "majesty" of the state long before London's denunciations of American "irreverence and impudence" in the 1770s.

Christian and classical thought had put the source of the state in God (or a god), in mythic heros like Theseus or Romulus and Remus, or in a vaunted lawgiver or legislator like Lycurgus. Because politics in the colonies became so mundane and so participatory, quite another strain in the great tradition of Western political commentary on the state was to appeal to Americans, the origins of government in "convention."

By itself, that idea, especially as in an agreement or a contract between government and a people, came to colonists in various guises: through their charters and founding documents; through the more famous English writers about contract like Hobbes and Locke; and, most notably, from among that array of seventeenth- and eighteenth-century pamphleteers and theorists now known to scholars as the "countrymen" republicans or "commonwealthmen."[71] Harrington, Milton, Sydney, and their successors took up republicanism in the mid-seventeenth century as an alternative to the truncated Stuart monarchy. For them, power resided in "the people," but a propertied people deferential to the advice of their chosen wise leaders. Both populace and leaders had to remain diligent about the eternal corrupting power of government. The highest task was thus cultivating public-spiritedness or virtue. The busy and mundane political atmosphere of colonial life especially nourished the implicit notion of republican thought that government was a human arrangement among an alert populace, not a superhuman, patriarchal institution with unquestionable authority. In the latter respect, Machiavelli had urged the prince to keep apart from the multitude and put subjects in awe and fear of him if they could not love him. But awe and def-

70. Lawrence D. Cress, *Citizens in Arms* (Chapel Hill, 1982); John Shy, *A People Numerous and Armed* (New York, 1976).

71. Caroline Robbins, *The Eighteenth-Century Commonwealthman* (Cambridge, Mass., 1959).

erence were difficult to maintain in the moving colonial society with its rapid fluctuations in class and status, ceaseless migration, periodic rebellions, tenant riots, Regulator Wars, and rebel marches on the capitals, as well as with the known common origins of every leader in the public eye.[72]

In royal America, solemn and pious ceremony did surround the assuming of power by a royal governor, the convening of the assemblies, the opening of courts and of the royal councils or upper-houses.[73] All of these usually involved a minister invoking the holy to remind men of God's role in the workings of the state under a blessed monarch. Despite these invocations of august origins, the royal governor's position and powers, like those of the royal councils and the courts of justice, were inevitably known to be of this world, from recent time, transient and strongly limited by the colonial assemblies. In challenging London, the colonists had a special incentive to develop their own account of the origins and purposes of these offices. Political life in America had begun in liberty and self-sufficiency.[74] The colonies had started under specific charters still in hand a century later, negotiated by identifiable human ancestors who lived not too long ago. Changes in the charters, such as shifts from proprietors and single-house legislatures to governors and bicameral systems, involved relatively recent, recorded, earthly squabbles, not ethereal events or distant, fantasy scenes like the wolf suckling Romulus and Remus. By 1776, the forms of liberty such as those in the English Bill of Rights of 1689 were also man-fashioned and still con-

72. It is difficult not to qualify seriously the idea that colonial politics combined a broad suffrage with an elite leadership to which the folk "deferred." The concept is derived from Walter Bagehot's *The English Constitution* (1867). He used the idea of deference to describe mid-nineteenth-century politics in England, a quite different world than busy and on-the-move colonial America. There, difficulties in communication and travel, lack of newspapers and political parties, isolated and intense involvement of the populace with daily work, gave "insiders" willing to pursue politics great advantages. The rich and well-born had the time and leisure for politics, and politics thus fell into their hands without significant "deference," in Bagehot's sense, from the plebs. The American political elite faced major challenges in almost every generation, including violent opposition from at least the days of Bacon's Rebellion (1676) through the Regulator Wars a century later. Such turmoil does not imply deference. The elite, furthermore, complained chronically of *lack* of deference from the "multitude" and "mob." *Geographic,* not strong social, distance and the need to tend to daily tasks seem more likely explanations if social elites were left largely to govern as they willed and to be reelected.

73. Philip A. Bruce, *Institutional History of Virginia in the Seventeenth Century* (2 vols.; New York, 1910), II, pt. 5, describes offices, dignities, and ceremonies; Charles J. Sydnor, *Gentlemen Freeholders* (Chapel Hill, 1952), describes, in contrast with Bruce, the election hurly-burly.

74. Two famous accounts near the end of the colonial period are John Adams' *Novanglus* letters and Jefferson's *Summary View of the Rights of British North America.*

tested by flesh-and-blood human beings. The illustrious names in the American chronicles of liberty were known as wise men, not as mythic mighty servants of kings, as were Roland or El Cid. The great deeds were also in tangible documents that were "on file." The colonial assemblies had records of past proceedings and lists of yesterday's members, many of whom were remembered by or related to those still living. The powers of the assemblies, like colonial government generally, came from only a century or so earlier and had emerged from well-recorded struggles against the proprietors or Governor Andros, or against the Duke's laws in New York after the fall of New Netherlands in 1664. None of the pieces of state machinery in America had emerged, as even the Commons seemed in England, from a medieval swirl, a bewildering plethora of "bodies," *i.e.*, towns, shires, parishes, bishoprics, noble families, schools, monasteries, guilds. The assemblies and every other colonial governing body were created in rationally deliberated and recorded acts on specifiable months, days, and years: the House of Burgesses in 1619, the Massachusetts Common Court in 1634, the New York legislature on October 17, 1683. Similarly, each town, parish, or county had recorded dates of origin.

From the outset, also, the geographic lines of government were clear and consciously contrived. Constituencies, districts, parishes, towns, and counties had not congealed, as they so often had in England, as tracings of distant fiefs or of great family holdings with hazy outlines. The original colonial legislative districts were created by their governments and were empowered to send a certain number of representatives depending, in part, on the size and location of the area, not on the boundaries of its lords or mighty ones. There also evolved rationalistic, "modern" formulas for creating new districts and for calculating the number of representatives to be sent from them.[75] There was precious little in America of 1776 like the "ownership" of many Commons seats by aristocratic families in England.

Just as there was little religious or mythic mystery about the assemblies, there was little about the more honorific second or upper house, generally called the Council.[76] Convenience, connivance, and caution, all human and even humdrum considerations, had added this tier to the legislature. Unlike the House of Lords in England, the council members could claim no awesome lineage, no dignity of family equal, in origins

75. Jack R. Pole, *Political Representation in England and the Origins of the American Republic* (New York, 1966).
76. Leonard W. Labaree, *Conservatism in Early American History* (New York, 1948); Jackson T. Main, *The Upper House in Revolutionary America, 1763–1788* (Madison, Wis., 1967).

at least, to the dignity of dukes or earls or marquises as symbolized by the English nobility's titles, robes, coronets, and their inheritance of seats in the upper house in Parliament. Seats in the councils did tend increasingly to be given to the upper-crust and to be passed to sons, but only through specific appointment of each generation by the governor and throne, not automatically by right of blood for all time.[77] Nor, importantly, were the council members like the European aristocratic leaders of "estates," a legalized and enduring, special and privileged "order" of the ennobled. The councilors, however prestigious, could not invoke an inherent superiority given by God to the lords of the earth. Nor did they possess the English lords' inherited privileges of administering local justice or appointing the local curate, with powers undergirded by the lands entailed for centuries and constituting family realms within the greater royal realm in London. American councilors might be deemed "esquire," and most were wealthy, powerful, educated, and experienced in politics. But the Carter or Laurens families had moved into honorific positions from simple beginnings that anyone could discern. Their money, achievements, "connections," and loyal services to the governor and throne earned recognition but no ennoblement and only rarely knighthood. In theory, at least, the council, chosen for life, represented wisdom, experience, and continuity, compared with the assemblies whose comings and goings through popular elections made them seem less steady, more fractious, and thus less reliable for the purposes of the governor or London.[78] And men sought the council, not only for the honor and prestige, but, like membership in the assembly, for better access to government favors and to be in the front ranks in the doling out of the "places" in the ever-increasing patronage of colonial life.

So too with the colonial executive.[79] By 1763, nine colonies were under royal governors, whatever their charters had originally provided. Individual governors, however, came and went, usually with short stays in America. Family connections with Americans had nothing to do with naming and succession. Appointment by London, arrival in America, removal and departure were known to reflect the distant political and patronage situation in England with, in most instances, little consultation about colonial wishes or needs. As choice of the monarch and as symbol of the august majesty of the English state, the governor might be surrounded by a small "court" with pomp, prestige, etiquette, and ritual. He could summon the assembly, dismiss it, and veto its actions.

77. Labaree, *Conservatism in Early American History.*
78. Greene, *The Quest for Power.*
79. Leonard W. Labaree, *Royal Government in America* (New Haven, 1930).

But for the colonists, he was always a man. And the bitter controversy and criticism so many governors provoked from the seventeenth century on, not just after 1763, brought an ever-growing skepticism about their wisdom and a further secularization of politics. The entire apparatus of the state was thus a human contrivance, a "convention," for quite specific English rights and liberties. These liberties had existed even before Jamestown and government was to be held responsible for protecting them. The state and its helmsmen were not the divine idea on earth.

Much to this effect had already been thought through by many English leaders by 1689. The colonists thought that 1776 was to complete the job. A guarded version of the familiar Tocqueville line still holds: America was born in 1776 familiar with a liberty and an "equality of conditions" unmatchable at the time in the Atlantic world. The revolutionaries did not overthrow an *ancien régime,* install new institutions like the Civil Constitution of the Clergy, redraw the administrative map of the nation, or bring in a class of commoners as tyro political leaders. An American old regime of liberty was at stake in 1776, not a new order. So, too, the Jeffersonian leaders of 1800 thought they had *saved* the American Revolution by defeating the Federalist-aristocrats and an Anglophile world view alien to American aspirations. Nevertheless, they were of the same social stamp as the Federalist opponents. In class origins, the Democratic-Republican Jefferson, so intent on simplicity and spare government, and the Federalist John Adams, so often fussy about pomp and prestige, came from the same universe of advantage and intellectual training as did the earlier opponents of the throne within the Stamp Act Congress, the "Association," the First and Second Continental Congresses, and the Confederation. All of the Founding Fathers had come out of the quicksilver life of the colonies with its constant cycles of rise and fall, even ruin. History, again, known or knowable by every man, made apparent the modest origins, recent ascent, and valued experience, formal and informal, of the governing corps.[80] Even before Jefferson, Paine, and others gave us the democratic idea that in America any man of talent should be able to rise to the limit of his abilities, many an "everyman" in the colony had come from nowhere by midlife into chambers of the state. The "first gentlemen of Virginia" had risen from the first men in Virginia.[81] Who, then, might not succeed? Or lose out, or be removed?

Because their politics was about power and patronage, involved mere mortals, and enlisted men of common origins, the Americans felt increasingly free to use government as they willed, as a "convention."

80. Bailyn, *Origins of American Politics;* Sydnor, *Gentlemen Freeholders.*
81. Louis B. Wright, *The First Gentlemen of Virginia* (San Marino, Calif., 1940).

When the throne seemed to place insuperable obstacles to their wish that London government continue to respect established American liberty, the desanctification of the state, so long under way, proceeded further, ultimately treating George III as the mere human who happened to be a king and as "cashierable" as his predecessors Charles I and James II.

II

RECASTING THE STATE

Limits from the Past

Understanding both the ideas and the institutions of government in the 169 years Americans lived under kings makes it simpler to comprehend the forty-year struggle after 1763 to find an appropriate form of government for Americans.[1] The fight that began with concern about an empire turning against liberty evolved into a struggle to expunge the monarchial state and to guarantee what Jefferson would call the "empire for liberty" of a democratic republic.

By 1763 the long struggles to control colonial government and to shape the state to London or the colony government's wishes had produced frustrating stand-offs. The colonial legislatures had gained larger powers over the purse, including salaries, than the Parliament in London enjoyed, but the governors had the power to summon and dismiss the assemblies and to veto their actions.[2] Overall, patronage and favors had increased as by-products of the waxing of government tasks. Theoretically, more offices should have increased the effectiveness of the state as growing bureaucracy did in Europe. The governors with much power over the patronage and legislation should have been able to make good on the state's reach in colonial affairs. Instead, increasingly, the spoils in appointments had been split, with the assemblies obtaining their own array of "placemen" to augment their powers of purse and to counter the governors' wishes.[3] Meanwhile, London's apparatus for reviewing colonial activities had piled up by 1760 to include, just among the obvious offices, the Board of Trade, the Southern Department, the Admiralty, and the Privy Council.[4] The increasingly detailed royal instructions

1. For a recent survey, see Robert Middlekauff, *The Glorious Cause: The American Revolution, 1763–1789* (New York, 1982).
2. Labaree, *Royal Government in America.*
3. Greene, *The Quest for Power.*
4. F. B. Wickwire, *British Subministers and Colonial America, 1763–1783* (Princeton, 1966).

to the governors brought additional complication and delay and thus dampened the initiative of the governors and their retinue.[5] With turnover in the London and imperial bureaus so frequent and so corrupted, it was rare that anyone in higher officialdom had the mind, will, or time for serious work during a stay in America. The growing "mess in London," so to speak, was well known to the colonial politicians, reported as it was by the colonial agents or lobbyists in England, of whom Benjamin Franklin was the most famous. For long, the mess, like the division of spoils between the governors and the assemblies, was accepted as part of a game that was willingly played by the colonists, their agents in London, and their informal "connections" with the great and near-great who influenced policy.[6] Eventually, however, the London mire was to dramatize the distance between government on American soil that, being nearby and simple and staffed by fellow colonists, might be approachable and trusted and London's corrupt, distant great state. Even before 1763 London power was watched for signs of vice and veniality. Irritating and unpredictable reversals of colonial policy by London were often due to the vagaries of the games of English domestic politics, with little serious consideration of imperial policy.[7] Such banal intrigue, however, was to be transformed by the colonists into part of a deliberate plot by George III and the "king's friends" to subvert American liberty.[8]

By the time of the French and Indian Wars (1757 to 1763), a vexed London wanted officials in distant New York or Charleston who could be trusted to do as London wished.[9] It took to itself appointments from the governors' lists, positions like tax receivers, auditors, attorneys general, and naval officerships. Many colonists construed this increase in royal appointees as an attempt to bypass and snub them rather than as an expression of an accelerating appetite for more places for favorites in the London game. Whatever the motives, the increased appointments from London at the expense of the governors at the colonial capitals lessened the governor's patronage, one of his key weapons in keeping his colonial charges in line and fulfilling the royal instructions. This diminution occurred while his powers had also been clipped from within the

5. Leonard W. Labaree, ed., *Royal Instructions to British Colonial Governors, 1670–1776* (2 vols.; New York, 1935).

6. Michael Kammen, *A Rope of Sand: The Colonial Agents, British Politics, and the American Revolution* (Ithaca, N.Y., 1968).

7. Louis B. Namier, *England in the Age of the American Revolution* (Rev. ed.; London, 1961).

8. Bernard Bailyn, *Ideological Origins of the American Revolution* (Cambridge, Mass., 1967).

9. Bernhard Knollenberg, *Origins of the American Revolution, 1759–1766* (New York, 1960).

colony. By 1760 the assemblies had successfully fought to control the purse and to appoint officials like sheriffs, militia officers, and treasurers.[10] By the accession of George III in 1760, the double pressure from London on high and from the assemblies below, had already left the governor in the dangerous position of sporting an expensive prestige and irritating pretensions to power with decreasing ability to do what his mission required. To place into such weakened and contested hands after 1763 the responsibilities for enforcing imperial reforms like direct taxes or for disciplining recalcitrant assemblies while also seeking to invigorate unenforced or latent powers of imperial regulation was foolhardy.

In the previous twenty years the colonists' anger had been especially thickened by the governors' attempts to limit the damage to his control. Unlike the throne and the powerful brokers of English politics, however, the governor and his men in America owned no seats, had no rotten boroughs to provide loyal assemblymen, and could not nominate candidates for constituency balloting. The English practice of absentee grandees selecting candidates for legislature seats constrasted with colonial representatives clearly identified by their residence in and responsibility to their districts.[11] Harassed as he was by these colonial novelties in the legislatures (auguring the American system of numeric and geographic representation), the governor fought back, sometimes successfully, sometimes not, to limit the growth of new political districts. But his fight deepened animosity toward him and toward the royal state.

The effective powers of the governors, like the reach generally of colonial government, were further vitiated by the increasingly long distances and difficult terrain over which power and influence were to be exerted. Difficult distances helped increase colonial habits of self-reliance, local control, and voluntary group effort. The mere subjects of the European state gradually became participating American citizens with their own independent and experienced leaders. Their sensitivity about their achievements should have merited great caution in governing them.

By 1750 sovereignty over every aspect of colonial life remained, nominally, in "king in parliament." Montesquieu's famous description of the English separation of powers was ignorant about the royal prerogative and initiative as well as the ultimate judicial powers of the House of Lords. His idea was sensitive, however, to the tensions within the system. The separation of powers diluted the concentrated force of the state and was thus at least friendly to liberty. In colonial administration this tension encouraging liberty was reflected in laws and officials and loy-

10. Greene, *The Quest for Power.*
11. Pole, *Political Representation in England and the Origins of the American Republic.*

alties linked alternately to London, to the colony capital and localities, and to the separated powers at each level. Conflicts among the geographic levels of governments and among the branches of government made the colonists of 1763 already familiar with checks and balances and federalism, even if they did not use the now-famous phrases. A generation later, Madison's famous thoughts on faction, power, and liberty in *Federalist* 10 reflected not only his reading of English and classical history but also more than a century of colonial political experience. Several more lessons about faction and power remained to be written after 1763 before Madison's ideas about the threats of faction would have painful pertinence for Americans on their own in recasting the state.

The Crisis of Liberty

The imperial crisis that brought the American Revolution began primarily as a crisis of liberty under the English constitution. But it can also be viewed as a crisis of the state, for the conflict came to involve opposing views of the role of government and different views of how government in America had developed. The dramatic decade of imperial debate and its conclusion in revolution left indelible marks on American institutions and, even more, potent ideas about the nature of government.

After all weight is given to the economic argument about the incompatability of American colonial enterprise with British mercantilism[12] or to the abundant evidence of a distinctive American life consciously and honorifically set off from England,[13] the crisis after 1763 remains political. The manifest issue was liberty. The latent problem was the nature and scope of the state. New taxes or excises on stamps or tea, oppressive charges for interest and business services by Scottish merchants for shipping tobacco and other products through England, and restrictions on currency and western settlement all created deep economic grievances; but these ultimately produced revolution only because after the Boston Tea Party, in 1773, there was unprecedented will in Parliament, throne, and ministry to enforce London's wishes, and with soldiers and new political and judicial weapons in the customs service and vice-admiralty courts. These novelties sharpened the long-maturing political will of the patriots to resist any would-be effective grasp of the state and brought them from English remonstrance to American rebellion. Not only did London and the governors after 1763 present

12. Louis B. Hacker, *The Triumph of American Capitalism* (New York, 1940).
13. Max Savelle, *Seeds of Liberty* (New York, 1948).

new taxes and new imperial rules for trade, lands, currency, and so on, as well as press old trade regulations, but all of these were now to be pursued politically and earnestly by an enlarged enforcement bureaucracy with independently funded salaries that bypassed assembly controls, by special courts in distant places like Halifax that were not affected by local juries prejudiced for accused colonists, by dismissing the recalcitrant legislatures, and, eventually, by muskets and Hessian troops. Even those aspects of the London proposals that were reasonable and overdue, like an improved western lands policy and schemes for pacifying the Indians and reassuring the French-Canadian Catholics,[14] came up against potent colonial "irrationalities" like racial and religious hatred against Indians and Canadian Catholics and the ravenous appetite for land among settlers and speculators.

The new policies after 1763 for imperial revenue and defense seemed bad enough as such, but to obtain its ends, the state stretched its reach as never before to make the colonists feel its grasp. Despite the waxing and waning of controls during the dozen years of struggle, the new imperial policy after 1763 was too reminiscent of many past irritations. The cycles of waning between the Stamp Act (1765), the Townshend Duties (1767), the Tea Act (1773), and the restrictions on Massachusetts (1774) were too short to restore calm and allay suspicions, especially given the novelty of popular leaders and established elites organizing alerts and illegal opposition groups, like the "association," up and down the seaboard.[15] This time the royal state was serious: George III would do his will. The seemingly perfunctory Declaratory Act of 1765 that came with the repeal of the Stamp Act made no idle threat in reaffirming London's general right to legislate for the colonies.[16] Such new imperial determination went against colonial experience and expectations. Of course, the state from London or New York periodically had "reached," but the colonists had learned to expect that its reach would exceed its grasp and that the will to persevere would slacken or could be bought off or negotiated to ease. The Townshend Duties showed that the Stamp Act and the Sugar and Currency Acts (1764) were no transient enthusiasms of London. Even if the colonists could have been represented in Parliament with their own seats when those taxes were proposed, the acts would have been passed. So Americans would still have had to help pay the costs of empire.

14. Lawrence H. Gipson, *The Coming of the Revolution, 1763–1775* (New York, 1954).

15. Pauline Maier, *From Resistance to Revolution: Colonial Radicals and the Development of American Opposition to Great Britain, 1765–1777* (New York, 1972).

16. Edmund S. Morgan and Helen M. Morgan, *The Stamp Act Crisis* (Chapel Hill, 1953).

The longtime colonial ambivalence in seeking while shaming English government began, momentously, to change. The state as source of favors, "places," and protection for the colonists now became the intruder, eventually the "unnatural" enemy of law and those rights of Englishmen that Blackstone (1765) and others were now calling "natural rights." From the toasts to good King George, who had wisely rescinded the Stamp Act, to the Suffolk Resolves and Declaration of Rights and Grievances of 1774 was a decade in which, as Bernard Bailyn has shown, the rationalist principles of government and "rights" invoked in petitions and pamphlets were modulated by strong paranoiac themes of conspiracy, contamination, and corruption allegedly underlying London's attack on liberty. Not merely English liberty but simple American virtue was imperiled.[17] Distant vice-admiralty courts to try colonial offenders,[18] independent funding for the governor's minions, new and increased customs officials, a department of state for American affairs in London, a special American Board of Customs, and troops in unprecedented numbers to be quartered in leading towns—all these showed the *evil* behind the political will to bring Americans to heel.

Our reconstruction of the colonial argument must be cautious, insofar as "the state," government per se, was examined and criticized during the turmoil before 1776. The grievances were predominantly specific and pungent: lands, sugar, currency, stamps, Indians, lead, tea, new courts, and increase of soldiers. But the regulations came in such rapid succession that they drove colonial leaders, especially the many lawyers among them, to fundamental ideas available to them from their reading and education. Words like *state, government, sovereign, rights, prerogative,* were replete in the histories and political theory they had read. At least as important as John Locke as influences on them were those English writers who, despite the collapse of the Cromwell commonwealth, had continued to explore republicanism as a better guarantee for English liberty than was monarchy.[19] But even the former, it must be noted, was an English alternative.

The definitive turn to the republican idea came very late in the game, in 1775 to 1776. But the search for justification in invoking ideas such as weak executives and separation of powers should not make the colo-

---

17. Bailyn, *Ideological Origins of the American Revolution.*

18. Carl Ubbelohde, *The Vice-Admiralty Courts and the American Revolution* (Chapel Hill, 1960); Bernard Donoughue, *British Politics and the American Revolution: The Path to War, 1773–1775* (New York, 1964).

19. Gordon S. Wood, *The Creation of the American Republic, 1776–1787* (Chapel Hill, 1969); Robert E. Shalhope, "Towards a Republican Synthesis: The Emergence of an Understanding of Republicanism in American Historiography," *William and Mary Quarterly,* XXIX (1972).

nial leaders into men of texts and the candle. We do not know whom, specifically, most of the signers of the Declaration of Independence had read, and we know even less about how they construed or invoked texts from the many English republican writers. We do know from the extraordinary pamphlet literature of the time, which Bernard Bailyn has been making available to us again, what republican ideas were on the bookshelves, and we can generalize about their distillate that was in the air. Still, the leaders of 1776 were not "men of mind" like the French leaders of the third estate of 1789, overwhelmingly inexperienced with power and administration. However much royal oppression drove the Americans to higher consciousness about purposes and ideas, every institution that they were to set in place for a republican America came out of the inventory of their experience.[20] Republican ideology provided a gloss, an intellectual apology, for what American leaders wanted. They reformulated and made articulate English republicanism to justify their own colonial institutions. They were reclaiming English liberty from royal defilement and, soon enough after 1776, from aristocratic abuse also. If republican ideas had long been available for those colonists who chose to read them, they became more pertinent as the colonists were driven from specific grievances to purse and pride to seek protection in principles against monarchy.

By the time the debate reached Tom Paine and Jefferson in America and Price and Priestley in England, a portentous change was occurring in consciousness and in scope of argument. On the opening page of *Common Sense,* Paine declaimed that government is "but a necessary evil" and like dress, "the badge of lost innocence." Until then a "conservative" constitutionalism had so dominated the colonists' defense that Burke could admire them as fellow Whigs. The colonists gave greater space and fervor to republican alternatives to royal government only in desperation and in the last stages of their protest. Revealing, too, that it remained for two *English* radicals, Price in London and the newly arrived Paine, rather than veterans of the decade of resistance, to urge the colonists to understand their predicament philosophically and not only practically. Not merely George III, not solely monarchy, but government as institution and idea came before Paine's bar of universal reason, "nature," and justice.[21] As Otto Vossler, the noted German scholar of these matters, has shown, it was really Europeans like the French *philosophes* and Englishmen like Paine and Price who constructed a "mirage in the West" and invented the American Revolution as an *idea,* providing it with the abstract, universalist

20. Clinton Rossiter, *Seedtime of the Republic* (New York, 1953).
21. Foner, *Tom Paine and Revolutionary America.*

justification for equal rights that was later to link 1776 to the "spirit" of 1789.[22]

When the revolutionary arguments did get to "the state" as *the* issue, they immeasurably influenced future American, as well as European, ideas. Those ideas were to become the later, now famous, worldwide meaning of the Revolution as a new order of human affairs and not merely in the forms of government. In abandoning, as at last they did, king and parliament, the Americans were really trying to slip far away from the time-honored European idea that only strong, intrusive, omnipresent government can prevent chaos, sin, and selfishness from inundating the world. In all of their intense, conflicting historical, rationalist, and millennialist strains of argument[23] against their London connections and English crime, Americans forgot the positive and solicited roles that government had long played in colonial life. Only the noxious imperial pretensions were permitted to come to mind. Now, London governing had always been best only when done least. In actuality, in their localities and at the colony capitals and through their agents and other connections in London, the colonists had sought government if they could; but that was now obscured by the corrupting shadow of the oppressive Machiavellian state. When Jefferson spoke admiringly of the "integrity and good faith" of his own time he contrasted it with the "mean, wicked and cowardly cunning of the cabinets of the age of Machiavelli." Even before the revolution, Madison viewed the historic admiration for despotisms of "superiors over inferiors" as a maxim of Machiavelli, "whom others take to be a great politician for no other reason but for having ever been wicked." Embellishing such farewells to the wicked one, John Adams denounced interest in establishing a state religion as Machiavellian, for being "hypocritical, Jesuitical, and Pharisaical." What Americans in 1776 generally scorned about England was the illegality or insensitivity or arrogance or slowness or silence of government about their needs. The bill of particulars against the king in the Declaration was an indictment of a noxious regulatory state in which, Jefferson implies, the colonists themselves had no stake. Who could imagine from Jefferson's list of grievances that, for example, Americans wanted, bought, used, abused, and profited from slaves? In his original, but ultimately rejected, clauses on slavery, Jefferson denounced the king for forcing slaves onto America while, in the next few lines, excoriating him

---

22. Vossler, *Jefferson and the American Revolutionary Ideal;* Durand Echeverria, *Mirage in the West: A History of the French Image of American Society to 1815* (Princeton, 1957).

23. Henry F. May, *The Enlightenment in America* (New York, 1976).

for stirring those immorally oppressed slaves to rebel against their American masters.[24]

All that the colonial state had grasped for, successfully or not, whether once applauded or not, was now depicted as part of that wicked London design against liberty.[25] The threat to liberty had extended, furthermore, over the eight generations since the founding but had become fully apparent, and thus intolerable, only after 1763. It was clear, therefore, that almost two hundred years under kings could at last be seen as a single, unremitting struggle for liberty against unceasing English oppression. In the heated travail of farewell, reached only just before 1776, revolution suddenly became a faith and an independent America its church. Both, it was believed, had been founded on the rock at Plymouth.[26]

Shadows over the State as Idea

Les américaines libres, as their French allies were to call them, thus began to concoct an elaborate fantasy about the virtues of their colonial governments and about the minimal role the state had played in their lives. They created the aforementioned legend of the Founding Fathers, a history to support not only a version of English republicanism[27] but, with it, local liberty and the rights of man: in founding their colonies they fled from the state; in developing the colonies they made little or no use of it; in freeing the colonies they were rebuffing the attempts of the wolfish English state to destroy their freedom and opportunity and to suck profits from the admirable and honest colonial entrepreneurs; in establishing the United States they would soon show the world how little free and virtuous republicans needed the state and how alien, how "European," how "Old World," how hostile, the great state could be to virtue and liberty. These paradisical strains were to come in final rushes of rapturous release after twelve years of frustrating protests and negotiations. Along most of the way to 1776, however, there was little idea

24. Thomas Jefferson to Col. William Duane, April 4, 1813, in *The Life and Selected Writings of Thomas Jefferson,* ed. Adrienne Koch and William Peden (New York, 1944), 626; James Madison, "Commonplace Book, 1759-1772," in *The Papers of James Madison,* ed. William T. Hutchinson *et al.* (16 vols.; Chicago, 1962–), I, 13; John Adams to Benjamin Rush, August 28, 1811, in *The Spur of Fame: Dialogues of John Adams and Benjamin Rush, 1805-1813,* ed. John A. Schutz and Douglas Adair (San Marino, Calif., 1966), 192; Garry Wills, *Inventing America: Jefferson's Declaration of Independence* (Garden City, N.Y., 1978); Jordan, *White over Black.*

25. Bailyn, *Ideological Origins of the American Revolution.*

26. Craven, *The Legend of the Founding Fathers.*

27. H. Trevor Colbourn, *The Lamp of Experience: Whig History and the Intellectual Origins of the American Revolution* (Chapel Hill, 1965).

that they would have to bid England farewell, let alone so ecstatically. For that rapturous adieu alone, the colonists had to forget how slow they had been to break—sixteen months after Lexington and Concord. In the main, even as they moved near the end of protest to independence, the patriot leaders had been reluctant rebels.[28] Still, we must recall that the republicanism with which the patriots now felt compatible was thought to be an English tradition. And it had justified a general popular resistance to tyranny only after, as the Declaration was to put it, "a long train of abuses patiently endured" and with repeated peaceful and respectful protests against their pains.

The leaders of the protest, however, had felt threats not only from the king's governors, troops, and vice-admiralty courts but from among the more volatile populace, whom a century of colonial tumult had branded rioters, levelers, upstarts, and "the mob."[29] Whatever the opponents were called, in the 1760s once again the colonists had been fighting other colonists in New Jersey and the Carolinas about issues like rents, taxes, or representation.[30] Despite fears of losing power to the backcountry, the mob, or town demagogues if the patriot elite set a bad example by overthrowing royal authority, Adams, Laurens, Washington, Hancock, and the other leaders never really lost control of affairs during the coming of the Revolution nor after 1776 in the dozen years of experiment with the forms of a republic.[31]

The patriot accession to power in 1776 came with the end of English control. The royal governors and their supporters fled or holed up in enclaves like New York. The thirteen colonies now came into their own as they and their charters, laws, and administration passed into the already experienced hands of the patriot leadership. Continuity in the laws, forms, and substance of indigenous colonial institutions was esteemed. The corrupting monarchial elements were to be excised so that the colonial heritage of liberty would be available again. Overwhelmingly, the first changes in the charters and basic laws were to purge the worst royal element, the powers of the executive. However drastic this often was, it also represented continuity, easily traced back to the "rise of the assemblies" and the gradual clipping of the governors' claws about the purse and patronage.

28. Lynn Montross, *The Reluctant Rebels* (New York, 1950).
29. Maier, *From Resistance to Revolution*; Arthur M. Schlesinger, Sr., *The Colonial Merchants and the American Revolution, 1763–1776* (New York, 1918).
30. Richard B. Morris, *The American Revolution Reconsidered* (New York, 1967), chap. 2.
31. Benjamin Wright, *Consensus and Continuity, 1776–1787* (Boston, 1958). Contrast with Morris, "The Two Revolutions," in *The American Revolution Reconsidered.*

Shrinking the State

Beyond the former colonies, now independent states in their own right, the great state, royal government, was cashiered in writing on July 4, 1776. With it went what vestiges of mystique the monarchial state still had after 169 years of American demythologizing. The imperial impositions that had angered Americans since 1763 dissolved, and London and Tory placemen and their loyal followers were chased away with the governors. Gone also were the agents of imperial rules about shipping, iron, hats, and sugar. Control over forests, lands, currencies, and churches fell into private hands or to the new states or local powers. In these respects, the old imperial state, both in its reach and its grasp, precipitously waned to vanishing. Americans were now more open to the captivating idea that large and distant government with power and energy was always the enemy of freedom. With important Americans like John Adams dissenting, Paine and Jefferson let loose the corrective notion that good government was simple, cheap, and minimal.

Before liberty was redefined as maximum freedom from government, we must reemphasize, Americans had largely reconciled themselves to the mercantile system. It was a given part of the nature of things. But once principles, found after 1763 in the charters or common law or the "law of nature" and accented by the broadening sweep of resistance to London, revealed that the old, inevitable, and God-given order was, in fact, unspeakable, ephemeral, or against reason, the path to a more moral, simpler, "natural" politics of republicanism seemed open.[32] The confluence, therefore, of the revolutionary appeal to principles of liberty and the actual dismantling of so much of the soiled imperial structure was powerful. Now it could be seen that the old English system had no basis in "reason" or "nature" or in the "rights of man." New ideas about the purposes of government were in order.

Independence had not come to a recognized nation but to colonies allied with each other. The formal banding together of thirteen localities of liberty was unlike the ventures with the First and Second Continental Congresses, which were makeshift and illegal "protest organizations." The drafting of the new Articles of Confederation, whose lines were laid out by 1777, was the first occasion Americans had to consider what form of government beyond each state they would choose when there was no longer any higher power to constrain them.[33] Considering the growing colonial suspicion of fulsome, despotic, distant government that was brought to a head by the late imperial policies, it is impressive that the

32. Wood, *The Creation of the American Republic.*
33. Merrill Jensen, *The Articles of Confederation* (Madison, Wis., 1940).

new states gave as much power to the novel Confederation government as they did.[34] The new government's chief purposes were war, diplomacy to seek allies, victory, and the vindication of American virtue. Experience had yet to show Americans the need for national powers to tax rather than to request funds, to regulate interstate commerce rather than leave that largely to the states themselves, and to make citizens, not merely states, responsible to federal law. In 1776, with the reaction against royal centralization and the tender regard for locality and liberty, larger objectives for a first national government would have been chimerical and deeply divisive. Still, the Articles did give the Congress powers over diplomatic relations, coinage and borrowing money, Indians, disputes between the states, war and peace, and requisitioning the states for funds and soldiers. They also forbade the states any powers over foreign relations, war and peace, or restricting the rights of citizens from other states in travel and trading.[35] That colonies thinking themselves so abused by authority beyond their borders should have, by 1777, given as much to the first government of the United States as they did reveals the fear that too little government would lose the war, and leave the new union too weak before invasions and too open to European intrigue and insult. Still, distant government in America in 1777 had to be decidedly less than London's had been. In that sense, and at least until the war and the 1780s taught other lessons, the new confederation frame of government was as pragmatic as had been the search for comfort and profit within the empire.[36]

With our eyes on the future of American government, it is important to note that the patriots' attack on the state concentrated on distant and *regulatory*, not sponsoring, government. Despite the implication of the broad abstraction that the best government governed least and that all government was under a cloud, there was no cavil about local government. It was assumed to be a bastion of liberty, being near to the people, with familiar leaders and easy to control. This gap in the general indictment of the state became part of American ideology that must be called the myth of locality. Although it would have been news to slaves in the South, tenant-farmers in New York, or Catholics in Congregational New England, the American republicans took the locality, as expressed in the town meeting or county courthouse gathering, as the secure setting of liberty and virtue. This was not as eccentric or arbitrary as it may seem, since so much of the agitation for liberty against the crown had been carried on at the grass roots with tea parties, the burn-

34. Jackson T. Main, *The Sovereign States, 1775–1783* (New York, 1973).
35. Jensen, *The Articles of Confederation.*
36. For more on the Confederation, see below.

ing of revenue cutters, and the marshaling of minutemen. Under the aura of these defenses of liberty, the American crossroads and whistle-stop hamlet became bastions of sanity and freedom that are still seen as exemplars against the mess in Washington or the nefariousness of the League of Nations or United Nations. Similarly, by not abjuring sponsoring government that widened economic and social opportunity with subsidies, land grants, and internal improvements, the patriots left the way open to the large, if unacknowledged, role that the state as underwriter was to play in American development.

Drifting Toward Laissez-Faire

The difficulties for American republicans in reconciling increasingly deprecated state power with self-interest became painfully apparent during the war and afterward under the Confederation. The collapse of imperial controls in 1776 left the states and localities responsible for whatever economic initiatives government would take.[37] Although there was a sizable legacy of local regulatory rules on the books within each state, not all of these had been vigorously enforced before the imperial crisis. But the war and postwar economy so deranged attempts to continue regulatory efforts about prices and the supply of goods and currency that the will and the skill to continue controls were sapped. Fear of invasion, real and contrived scarcity, and economic opportunism made sorry contrasts to touted republican virtue. Stockpiling, hoarding, speculation, floods of unbacked paper issue, high costs for scarce labor, minimal willingness to cooperate among authorities at any level—these facts of the emerging national economy reduce much of recent scholarly talk about the republican virtue of the patriots to a birth fantasy of leaders trying to idealize a very troubled cause. The huge inflation was only the main symbol of squalid derangement. Old and new economic controls were tried but to decreasing avail. We are familiar with the deficiencies of the Confederation Congress in keeping good order nationally during the war as well as after, but we have no prettier picture within the states.[38] Since the Confederation had been designed not only to win the war but to keep off the terrain of the states, economic stability remained their task. There is special poignancy about the case of Virginia, since the weaknesses of its authorities were to prove so vexatious to Governor Jefferson (1779 to 1781), ironically a great idealizer of minimal and

37. Robert A. East, *Business Enterprise in the American Revolutionary Era* (New York, 1938).

38. Curtis P. Nettels, *The Emergence of a National Economy, 1775–1815* (New York, 1962).

local government. Virginia's efforts at economic controls, as well as in imposing and collecting taxes and attempting to organize adequate defense against the British, were crippled by wartime fear and confusion and the retreat of individuals and local authority to a standard of *sauve qui peut*.[39]

Similar struggles in other states to contend with war and freedom too often revealed that there was not enough effective government at any level, rather than too much of it. By 1780, two friends of fulsome government, Robert Morris, the Confederation's new finance superintendent, and Alexander Hamilton were deeply worried about the prospects for national survival.[40] But the rising prestige of the ideal of minimal government soon pointed to the repeated failure of regulatory efforts. Against the traditional regulatory state, loud voices were increasingly denouncing government controls per se as "invasions of the rights of property" and, more portentously, as inimical to the purposes of the Revolution. Price regulation, wrote one critic, will always be "impractical in a free country because no law can be framed to limit a man in the purchase or disposal of property but what infringe those principles of liberty for which we are gloriously fighting."[41] Such sentiments were expanded by the well-known businessman Pelatiah Webster and by John Witherspoon, president of Princeton.[42] Jefferson and Witherspoon's former student Madison were to join the chorus. Madison spoke admiringly of America's achieving that "very free system of commerce" in which "industry and commerce are left to take their own course."[43] And Jefferson boasted, "Neither our republic nor its ministers meddle with anything commercial. They leave their commerce free for their citizens and others, convinced that it is never better than when left to itself."[44]

Such voices were speaking of restrictive or regulatory government. The other legacy of mercantilism, state sponsorship, lingered—and understandably so, since despite continental opportunities, private capital was still small, scattered, and crudely organized. By war's end, however, individuals who had profited from the inflation and speculation had money to invest and wanted to pool it and then issue stock to attract still other investors. Imperial restrictions had prohibited pooling,

39. Dumas Malone, *Jefferson the Virginian* (Boston, 1948), chaps. 23–24.

40. Eleanor Young, *Forgotten Patriot: Robert Morris* (New York, 1950), chap. 7.

41. Morris, *Government and Labor in Early America*, 117.

42. Dorfman, *The Economic Mind in American Civilization*, I, on the movement toward laissez-faire; Pelatiah Webster, *Essay on Free Trade and Finance* (Philadelphia, 1779).

43. Madison in *Annals of Congress*, 1st Cong., 1st Sess. (Washington, D.C., 1834), I, 116.

44. Thomas Jefferson to Cavelier *fils*, July 27, 1789, in *The Papers of Thomas Jefferson*, ed. Julian P. Boyd (25 vols., Princeton, 1950–), XV.

incorporation, and stock issuance. In colonial times, organizing a business "vested with a public interest," as it was later phrased, required a special charter from the royal government. No more than a half-dozen or so of charters were issued in the colonial era, and most of those were for providing public services. The new states did continue that control over charters but with unprecedented liberality, stimulated in part by the grants shifting from the distant royal bureaucracy into the hands of popularly elected legislators. With government fully in American hands, with so many imperial restrictions gone, with "money to burn" and post-independence opportunities beckoning, venture capital turned from family and kin to the general public and to state governments for charters. Funds were assembled and charters were readily issued to incorporate and to issue stock to underwrite banks, build better roads, and produce gunpowder and cotton cloth. More than 150 state charters were given in the decade or so after the war ended.[45]

This rush to seek the state not only did not cancel but expanded colonial state intervention, especially for internal improvements. This clearly indicates that government that supported and expanded enterprise in deference to the needs and initiative of citizens was not included in the revolutionary indictment of the state. Any corruption or granting of unwarranted favors in that type of state-seeking after the 1780s was only in the eyes of the beholder. By the 1830s, however, as we shall see, the issue of special state favors was to become very tender. Adam Smith approved state investment for costly public works such as roads and better waterways and for public institutions such as hospitals and orphanages. These were necessary but could not elicit private investment because of risk and little or no profit. In America, the sponsoring and financing state was to become party to many alliances with private enterprise. From the early days of plank roads to the age of space exploration, cyclical howls against, seemingly, all state intervention would perpetually ignore government subvention. Except for the wounded in market battles who cry for justice by trying to have their oppressors regulated, the American state is the enemy only when it restricts freedom. So it was memories of imperious, restricting London that the friends of freer enterprise like Madison and Jefferson had in mind when they championed economic liberty. Generally and auspiciously, however, economic decisions after 1776 increasingly passed from the state's purview to innovative, risk-taking individuals. If they often allied with the sponsoring state through incorporation and public funding, the businessman at least took the initiative in seeking the state.

45. Stuart Bruchey, *The Roots of American Economic Growth, 1607–1861* (New York, 1968), 71–72.

At the national level after the war, the increasing propriety of linking self-interest and republicanism was also obvious in the work of the Confederation in the Northwest Territory. The decision to treat that immense swath of land not as a colony but as states in-the-making, as free and republican as the original thirteen, has been justly celebrated.[46] What is less well remarked is how the system for parceling out the public domain was at cross-purposes with republican ideals. True to ideas of unfettered enterprise, and in strong reaction against earlier British attempts to control land grants in the Ohio country,[47] the sales were to be open to all, as the ideal of freedom implied, but the big money habitually won the largest parcels. This new free enterprise created an immense advantage for the well-heeled agents of the Scioto, Ohio, and Indiana land companies.[48] They came away from the land sales with huge tracts of the best soils in their inventory for resale. In further following an ideal of free commerce, these speculators were at liberty to divide and sell their acquisitions at great profit to whatever farmers could pay the prices set by the company for choice acreage. Few small yeoman farmers, that idealized backbone of republican life, were able to afford the best parcels, but the better-off were. For generations thereafter, complaints about the inaccessibility of good cheap land for the small farmer were to become chronic in American politics.

Free enterprise and free republican ideals of virtue and comity thus were as much at odds in the frontier economy and under national auspices as they were in the wartime states. Such tensions in the very morning of independence were auguries not only of the next century of the American pandemic about land[49] but generally of ceaseless conflicts in American life between self-interest and the public good. In the 1780s, the inherent conflict was not perceived. Instead, all liberty seemed one fabric and the accumulating arguments for "free enterprise" underscored the general enthusiasm for freedom and served as a salve against memories of London's tyrannical power over colonial endeavor. Adam Smith's *Wealth of Nations* had been published in 1776 and was not well-known in America until the 1790s. But with many Americans already thinking along lines like Smith's, his ideas were "made to order" as a theory to underpin the new American enthusiasm and practice of economic liberty as part of the republican ideal.

Behind Smith's work lay almost a century of intellectual debate about

46. Benjamin Hibbard, *A History of the Public Land Policies* (New York, 1924).
47. Jack M. Sosin, *Whitehall and the Wilderness, 1763–1775* (Lincoln, Nebr., 1961).
48. Kenneth P. Bailey, *The Ohio Company of Virginia and the Westward Movement, 1747–1792* (Glendale, Calif., 1939).
49. Roy Robbins, *Our Landed Heritage* (Princeton, 1942).

stronger rights of property, freedom for self-interest, and how to reconcile that freedom with public well-being like the chronic need in Europe
for adequate grain at fair prices for the poor.[50] When the American revolutionaries took up ideas of economic freedom, they supposed that republican liberty and public-spiritedness had been intended as companions in the moral order for freedom for economic self-interest. In fact,
in republican thought since the Renaissance, the self-interest, let alone
the "moral vice," implicit in commercial enterprise was often the poi-
son that worked against the public virtue.[51] Republican thought had not
banned private economic initiative, but this interest was always suspect
for its selfishness, isolating tendencies, and breeding of "dependence"
among those subordinated by successful selfish citizens.[52]

While this republican ideology that opposed "interests" had developed over the centuries so too had a countertrend that gradually transformed the moral status of self-interest.[53] Smith's argument about the
latter was primarily moral, not economic. He not only doubted the low
estimate of self-interest but held that private interests, given freedom,
would check each other. If monopolies occasionally developed, state intervention might be appropriate to restore competition. Otherwise,
the increased division of labor from interests free to try to satisfy unmet
needs would expeditiously deploy capital and labor to produce far greater
well-being (Smith's meaning for "wealth") than under mercantilism. He
also hoped that economic liberty would bring a more moral society than
existed under the corrupt favor-granting of the mercantilist state. Indeed, by increasing its wealth through freeing interests, society could anticipate not only eliminating the vices of mercantilism but also lifting the
working class from dependence on government and charity and from a
perpetual meager existence.

Smith's emphasis on freedom for interests, rather than on cultivating
selflessness, as the path to justice and wealth ran especially counter to
that English republican suspicion that all interests, in private commerce
as well as in government hands, were corruptible.[54] By the time of Smith,
however, the moral opprobrium that still tainted the idea of self-interest in Smith's near predecessors like Mandeville (1670–1733) had virtually dropped away. If private interests, freed to compete, were led "as
it were by an invisible hand," to public benefits such as more grain at

50. Istvan Hont and Michael Ignatieff, eds., *Wealth and Virtue: The Shaping of Political Economy in the Scottish Enlightenment* (Cambridge, Eng., 1984); J. G. A.
Pocock, *Virtue, Commerce, and History* (Cambridge, Eng., 1985).
51. Albert O. Hirschman, *The Passions and the Interests* (Princeton, 1977).
52. Pocock, *Virtue, Commerce, and History.*
53. Hirschman, *The Passions and the Interests.*
54. Pocock, *Virtue, Commerce, and History.*

decent prices for the poor or a little plot of land for every American, need those interests be regarded as vices or even as suspect?[55]

In an America committed to individual rights and pursuit of happiness, neither Madison nor Jefferson adequately sensed that self-interest was intrinsically in deep conflict with republican public-spiritedness. One reason for this perhaps was the modest size of economic interests in the early republic and the strong belief that everyone should have a "stake in society" through owning property. They anticipated that the wealth of land in the New World and the small "agrarian" population would keep interests small, self-sufficient, and satisfied with simple self-sufficiency.[56] Except for rare cases of monopoly, interests would thus be far less threatening to the public good then seemed dreamable in wretched and greedy Europe. There, American republicans believed, leaders esteemed concentrated power and brought great economic groups into collusion with the state to destroy smaller ones and wreck communal harmony. Ezra Stiles caught the difference when he hailed American independence as based on "a democratical policy for millions standing upon the broad basis of the people at large, amply charged with property [that] has not hitherto been exhibited."[57] The hope gathered, fed by a strange patriotic piety that public spirit had won the war, that broadly satisfied self-interest would ally with a love of "the poor man's best country" that offered so much to commoners.

For Jefferson and Madison, however, and the successor "Jeffersonians" like John Taylor and John Randolph, there later arose the danger that the quickening and diversifying of the economy would stimulate "interests" to express themselves, not in the virtuous agriculture of smallholders, but in large-scale commerce and industry and in the growth of pestilential cities. For Jefferson, this fear was symbolized in the 1790s by Hamiltonian schemes to stimulate money-making, conducted, as in England, in collusion with government and without concern for the good of the majority. If that kind of rapacious commerce in money-for-money's-sake, in the Jeffersonians' view, triumphed over production of goods, it would lead America, as it had doomed England, to fatal luxury and vice. In all this fear Jefferson and the Jeffersonian "agrarians" had a vivid fantasy that small-scale American farming with limited ancillary commerce and simple household manufacturing were not tainted by commercial values and fevers. The fantasy censored from the Jeffersonian view American colonial "corruptions" like land and crop-price specu-

55. Hirschman, *The Passions and the Interests.*

56. Lance Banning, *The Jeffersonian Persuasion* (Ithaca, N.Y., 1978).

57. Ezra Stiles, *The United States Elevated to Glory and Honor* (New Haven, 1783).

lation, slavery, the colonial taste for luxury among Virginian planters and the great merchants of Boston, Philadelphia, and Charleston, or the prodigal abuse of the soil by freemen and planters alike. All that, so rife in colonial society, so antagonistic to virtue, and so banished from America's self-portrait, was not really traceable to England's baleful influence and certainly did not disappear with the sundering from England. If Jefferson had an arcadia to inspire him to break with English vice, it was less ancient Rome or Saxon England than virtuous, farming America as he imagined it before the onset of King George's vicious attempt to corrupt the colonists. John Adams and Madison, for all their persisting hopes for American virtue, were less sanguine than Jefferson. All interests, not merely the economic, were inherently factional and thus always potentially inimical to republican ideals.[58] Madison was to hold, however, that in a large republic, many diffused, competing interests might well check each other to the advantage of what voices of virtue there were. Adams' skeptical strain of republican thought, with its puritan and "genteel" hostility to vice, keeps government on the alert to use its powers when necessary to see that self-interest does not do unacceptable harm. America's more optimistic argument about interests adequately checking themselves if left at liberty descends to us from Jefferson and Paine via Andrew Jackson and Justice Taney and is more congenial than Adams' skepticism to now well-known and more-sweeping ideas of free enterprise.

The New Governments

What changes there were in the structure of American governments during the revolutionary era understandably emphasized the executive power. In both colonial and imperial government, the governors or the king could intrude into the legislature with the initiative, prerogative, vetoes, pro-roguing, and the informal practices of "influence." In the light of republican theory all this had violated the separation of powers essential to checking tyranny, especially of the executive. In every hint after 1776 of a strong executive the patriots saw a forbidding George III or a corrupt placeman like Lord North and vowed that power like that would never reappear in a republican America. In states like Virginia, where the acquired powers of the Burgesses and skillful colonial politicking by the 1760s had already heavily limited the royal governor's powers, the executive office was so further reduced after 1776 that frustrated Governor Jefferson called it the office of a "mere administrator."[59]

58. John Howe, Jr., *The Changing Political Thought of John Adams* (Princeton, 1966).
59. Malone, *Jefferson the Virginian*, chaps. 22–25.

For generations after 1776 the American revolutionary equation endured: strong executive implied dangerous monarchial or monocratic power. Two centuries of periodic denunciations of "dictator" presidents (those predecessors of our "imperial presidency") suggest the depth of the trauma inflicted by George III.

Historians who search for democratic intentions in the Revolution often misinterpret the changes in the governors' status, for it was less hostility to his "aristocratic" tastes and style and more to the king's political tyranny that was in play.[60] With nine royal governors gone and all London connections dissolved, the executive office that had been the great link in Anglo-American imperial politics had to be redefined. What was done was an unprecedented attack on traditional executive power. In Europe, under royal centralization, the monarch as executive had become almost synonymous with the state itself, as expressed famously by Louis XIV: "L'état, c'est moi." The Americans were convinced that George III was trying to restore such executive supremacy in England and to undo the "glorious revolution" of 1689 that had tried to put English liberty on a secure footing. To restrict the monarchial executive was thus to force the state to have a proper respect for liberty.

Revealingly, in the two self-governing colonies, Connecticut and Rhode Island, which had long elected their own governors, there were no changes in the powers of their executives or in the manner of their election.[61] Even the heavy restrictions variously placed on governors elsewhere by the patriot governments came from English republican ideas of separated powers and colonial experiences with royal officials: impeachment, annual elections or limited re-election and limited terms, election by assemblies and circumscription by upper houses or senates elected by the lower house, legislative control over a governor's appointments or loss of appointment or veto powers and prohibition against his appointees taking seats in the legislature. The effect was to destroy all chance in America for what was later known as "cabinet" or "parliamentary government," with its close links between the executive and legislature. In the decade after 1776, there was some drawing back from what turned out to be excessive limiting of the governors. This was especially the case in Pennsylvania, where many leading citizens had refused assent to the

60. The basic views are summarized in John F. Jameson, *The American Revolution Considered as a Social Movement* (Princeton, 1926). See the evidence qualifying Jameson assembled by Frederick B. Tolles, "The American Revolution Considered as a Social Movement: A Reevaluation," *American Historical Review,* LX (1954).

61. Allan Nevins, *The American States During and After the Revolution* (New York, 1924); F. N. Thorpe, ed., *The Federal and State Constitutions, Colonial Charters, and Other Organic Laws . . . Forming the United States of America* (7 vols.; Washington, 1909)

"democratic" constitution of 1776, which had abolished the governor's office. This democratic constitution was imposed, furthermore, by fiat. New laws restricting freedom of expression were also enacted. The old leaders eventually regrouped and successfully asserted their own more traditional ideas by, among other changes, reestablishing a governor.[62]

Within the Confederation government, there was another tell-tale turn against executive power. In the Articles of Confederation, no executive in our sense was created, only a committee of the Congress.[63] The figure called president was named in the older sense that Americans have forgotten because of what *president* has come to mean. The president of the Confederation was not a power or branch of government in his own right, but just a presiding officer over a committee of congressional steersmen.

The new state governments had inherited colonial forms of the European ideal of a mixed government of monarchial, aristocratic, and popular or democratic elements. After 1776 the formula changed, almost necessarily. With the "monarchial," *i.e.,* strong executive, element deplored and dismissed in 1776 and an aristocracy of the ennobled nonexistent in America, only the "democratic" element, *i.e.,* the people or the populace, remained. The Americans took up the popular element of the old mixed government and recast and broadened it by establishing "the people as constituent power" for all government.[64] This was less radical than it seemed, for in colonial America the populace already had unusual say about the choice of their leaders through broad participation in elections for legislatures and for local executives like town or county officials. The new state governments did build on and expand the people's role in providing , for example, for the popular election of governors and other officials. The executive, however, needed additional control to keep it from its "monocratic" potential; so if, for example, it had a veto, that had to be circumscribable by legislature override.

Most sentiment about a more active or immanent role for "the people" remained aloof from their charms as the principal and closely engaged element in reviewing and pressing government day by day. For John Adams particularly, power hunger and corruption were latent in all polities but especially in those democracies of the ignorant and propertyless masses that had been reviled ever since Aristotle had called them the most corrupt form of government. The American Revolution did not signal for so skeptical a republican as Adams the redemption of hu-

62. Sidney G. Fisher, *The Making of Pennsylvania* (Philadelphia, 1932).
63. Jensen, *The Articles of Confederation.*
64. Robert R. Palmer, *The Age of the Democratic Revolution* (2 vols.; Princeton, 1959), I.

man nature.[65] "Demos," like all other elements, still had to be balanced or "mixed" or tempered. Adams thus deplored "simple" government like Pennsylvania's unicameral legislature as an invitation to abusive concentrated power. Potential excess by the democratic element in any wise government had to be counterweighed by effective governors and senates of the well-to-do. But both of these also had to be elected and otherwise checked. Adams thus differed radically from Jefferson and Paine in favoring strong executives, not legislatures, as the friends of liberty.

The royal council, usually renamed "senate," was still present as a balancing element in American government after 1776, but it too was now to be elected by the people, not appointed. Ostensibly, it was to supply wisdom and experience in governing, no longer to represent the royal executive's whim about membership nor pretensions to privilege by a select few. Qualifications for the senates, however, often did specify considerable wealth.

Such checking and balancing within the machinery of the recast state and in the name of the people replaced the European emphasis on representing separately the monarchial, aristocratic, and democratic elements of society. Whatever the theory of or experience with checks and balances among the colonial governments, the assault on monarchial, executive power and the soon-to-come attack on aristocratic privilege quickly made it apparent that by jettisoning a king as the sovereign the Americans had acquired new dilemmas about the definition and practice of the sovereignty of the people.

The Sovereignty of the People

In the case for American rights, "the people" were presented to the world as paragons of virtuous liberty, but their conduct after 1776 rather than the flattering references in patriot pamphlets or the Declaration of Independence challenged the worth of that extensive investment. Warnings from the past about the chronic failure of republics from "below," *i.e.*, the tumultuous populace, seemed more pertinent and painful as the war went on and after peace came in 1783. The general lack of public spirit or willingness to cooperate for the common cause vividly contrasted with the laudatory images of patriotic republicans. By the mid-1780s, Washington, who especially knew what lack of public spirit had meant to him and his troops during the war, complained of being

65. Zoltan Haraszti, *John Adams and the Prophets of Progress* (Cambridge, Mass., 1952).

"mortified beyond expression" with the Confederation scene.[66] Many other notable leaders of 1776 were also disheartened by the squabbling and scheming, speculating and swindling in peace as well as war. Republicanism may have been accepted as an ideal, but it was not apparent that Americans could manage its demands. Some thought of the temptations in republics of the past that demagogues and a corrupt citizenry offered each other. There was recurrent chatter about making Washington a Roman-style dictator and even a small move toward a limited monarchy under Prince Henry of Prussia.[67] Others worried about easy pickings, for European powers, in the divided and quarrelsome states under a national government drifting toward impotence. No less in peace than in war could America afford to validate English wartime characterizations of the rebels as a society of slave owners and smugglers prating about their rights and virtue. If comparisons with the Romans seemed apt, it also occurred to English enemies that these backwater, republican "cives" had rejected legitimate authority in order to keep their (Roman) *latifundia* and their slaves under the protection of their own provincial politicians.[68]

In finding a suitable national plan for governing America, no question about republican ideals had more portent than fulfilling the commitment of 1776 to the sovereignty of the people. Whatever that phrase meant had to be embodied in a fundamental law clearly set off from ordinary statutes in order to provide general rules safeguarding the exercise of the power of the people from corruption by workaday politics. In aristocratic republics like Venice or Geneva, the common citizens were much further from the council chambers and deliberations of the elite leaders than was the case in America even before independence. After 1776 in the new American republic, most public officials were to come before a broad electorate, many elections were scheduled, and passage for leaders from lesser posts into the highest offices of governor and state senator was more frequent and far easier than in Europe. With such enhanced and more immediate powers for the populace, defining and expressing "the people" thus had unprecedented urgency. Steeped in republican history as the patriot leaders were, they had also accumulated their own lessons since 1776 in how time and passion and "interests," the eternal banes of republics seeking equipoise and harmony, could undermine faith in the people. Shays's Rebellion in 1786 seemed the cli-

66. *The Writings of George Washington,* ed. John C. Fitzpatrick (39 vols.; Washington, D.C., 1931–44), XXIX, 34.

67. Richard Kranel, "Prince Henry of Prussia and the Regency of the United States," *American Historical Review,* XVII (1911).

68. Pocock, *Virtue, Commerce, and History,* 163–64.

max to other follies and dangers in populistic regimes like, notoriously, Rhode Island. If after a few years some of the new state constitutions and the Articles of Confederation already seemed inadequate expressions of the sovereignty of the people, could any succeeding republican arrangement propose anything other than another imperfect machine?

We must recall, however, the recurrent optimism that the birth of the United States under popular government seemed a unique moment, *novus ordo seclorum,* one that might not come again. *Fortuna* had given "virtue" an unparalleled opportunity in republican America. In the gathering new faith that history showed linear progress—a better model for gauging human affairs than the Platonic or Polybian replayed cycles of politics—the American republican effort might not be doomed to decay and the loss of virtue. Even if any basic law proved deficient, the future lay open. As Ezra Stiles lauded popular republicanism in 1783, "We can correct ourselves, if in the wrong." And John Adams found enough optimism in 1776 to savor the idea that this time, this republican government might work. Never before 1776 "had three millions of people full power and fair opportunity to form and establish the wisest and happiest government that human wisdom can contrive."[69]

The encouraging view as peace came in 1783 was that, despite many pessimistic wartime hours, virtuous republicanism had triumphed. With England beaten, "the people," who had constituted the recast American state in 1776, now had unprecedented liberty to pursue their interests. If these interests could be made compatible with or even brought to underscore public-spiritedness, could not the old Machiavelli emphasis shift? One deeper meaning in the Florentine's work had been that human interests, being as multitudinous as they were greedy and restless, gave any government, not merely republics, only very limited chances to practice virtue. Did the patriot victory and the seeming triumph of republican virtue, its distance from the pesthouse of Europe, and so much space and natural bounty imply good-bye not only to Machiavelli but to Hobbes and Augustine as well? Aggregated *state* power in Europe had operated under the dark shadows of limited resources and staked terrain, foreign invasions and wars, and the constant pressures of a crowded and impoverished population. The American scene seemed an astonishing contrast, as Stiles had hosannaed. Society, not the state, could generate virtue spontaneously among countless satisfied republican freeholders spread out over one thousand miles from North to South and from the Atlantic to the Mississippi. Individual freedom could take prece-

69. Stiles, *The United States Elevated to Glory and Honor;* John Adams, "Thoughts on Government" (a letter to George Wythe), January, 1776, in *The Selected Writings of John and John Quincy Adams,* ed. Adrienne Koch and William Peden (New York, 1946).

dence over social control by European "orders" of nobles, burghers, commoners, and other groups, as well as over the concentrated political authority of the state.

By 1788, when Madison started to contribute to the Federalist Papers, such reiterated prospects had not negated his assumption that restless republicans would continue to have interests and to pursue them by combining selfishly in factions. But America's expanse encouraged rather than discouraged Madison's hopes for a stable republican polity. In the small republics of the past, factional strife, understandably, could quickly ruin city-states that were only a few miles in girth; but in the vastness of America, even if *only* selfish interests were in play, they would be spread over the continent and dissected by state lines. Factions would thus be so thin that any anticipated fearfully fulsome sovereignty of the people, *e.g.,* a factious majority, could neither quickly cohere nor dangerously *grasp,* as had centralized monarchial sovereignty in Europe.[70] More optimistically, Jefferson foresaw in America's newly independent popular governments powers that, being regularly dependent for election on a large, spirited, and propertied citizenry, would have to learn to be self-limiting or deferential to individual liberty. The defeat of the Federalists in 1800 seemed, to Jefferson, to ratify his hope.

The novelty of *any* sovereign, let alone a republic, catering to individual freedom and private interests instead of emphasizing authority and control was a threatening vista in the 1780s to Henry Knox, Richard Henry Lee, and even milder political skeptics. There was upset for such people in seeing what James Otis had called the "scum" rising as the revolutionary pot continued to boil. Forecasts of disaster thickened in the 1780s as some states, with Rhode Island again the worst, under pressure from voters of lesser means, authorized cheap paper-money or eased debt obligations and contracts. But for those horrified by the people gone wild, the deeper danger lay in the spectacle of the new authorities of the people that seemed to abandon restriction or caution about society itself and defer instead to a will to live by individual lights and needs. In the confused, incipient efforts in the 1780s to bring the sovereignty of the people into line with the "disaggregation" of American society that seemed under way, Jefferson saw liberty, a happy break from the European past, and limitless positive growth with, perhaps, a few cleansing cyclical thunderstorms like the Shays movement. Madison saw factions and interests clashing, but on a continental scale to the advantage of liberty. But Knox, followed by the high Federalists of the 1790s, saw anarchy and the woeful end of all authority, property, and

70. James Madison, *The Federalist* (New York, 1888), X.

order.[71] Many leaders before 1800, however, were caught between the two worlds that their revolution had vexingly juxtaposed: an old world like England, with its "command," "stations," "duties," and "authorities," and this new America of individual freedom under minimal and distant control.

History since 1776 has taught us that there is nothing inherently libertarian in the idea of the sovereignty of the people, and the following century of democratic advance was studded with observers, John Stuart Mill being the most famous liberal among them, worried about the cultural and political threats of "the tyranny of the majority." By the time of Mill's death, in 1873, a century after the Americans had declared the people as constituent and supervising power, democratic sovereignty was increasingly a fact of political life or in prospect across much of the North Atlantic world. But that was not the situation in 1776. Then the more familiar English theories of sovereignty were those of Hobbes, Harrington, Filmer, Locke, Blackstone, and others who, for all of the talk of "the people," had never anticipated a freedom like America's nor a populace in such close scrutiny of its governors. Despite the great differences among these writers about the role of the people, all had assumed that, ultimately, on all questions there had to be one clearly defined source of order and law and a final arbiter for society.[72] In rejecting the noxious claims for the sovereignty of George III, Americans like Jefferson hoped that the supremacy of the people on behalf of transcendant individual rights would somehow move the nation beyond the old pain of a powerful sovereign constantly imposing unpopular decisions. Somehow, majority rule and individual rights had to coincide. Constitution-making and subsequent American history were to show how demanding the task was to try to bring the final voice of a sovereign into harmony with both popular consent and the morality of natural rights.

Of the English writers on the nature and limits of popular sovereignty, none had more currency in America than John Locke.[73] Scholars have challenged the extent of that claim recently but have not denied that Locke's influence was great, even if he now shares a place with the Scottish philosopher Hutcheson and those English republican writers who emphasized the primacy of virtue rather than Lockean rights or the "moral sentiment" of Hutcheson. Jefferson easily cited both Locke (of

71. R. B. Morris, "Insurrection in Massachusetts," in *America in Crisis,* ed. Daniel Aaron (New York, 1952), 36.

72. Bertrand de Jouvenal, *Sovereignty* (Chicago, 1957).

73. The broadest claim for Locke's popularity is in Merle Curti, "The Great Mr. Locke," in Curti, *Probing Our Past* (N.d.; rpr. Gloucester, Mass., 1962). Contrast with Wills, *Inventing America.*

natural rights) and Algernon Sydney (of republican virtue) as sources for his ideas in the Declaration. Like Locke, he lauded the sovereign people but also anticipated their respect for individual natural rights. However, the earthly definition of rights was vested by Locke in the same "people" who were to constitute and pass on governments. Presumably, in ultimate cases, the people would also judge whether the rights they had articulated had been violated by the government they had approved.[74] In Locke, to further complicate matters, "the people" turn out to be the majority (variously construed) of society. Locke assumed the ultimate majority to be under the sway of reason, so "the people," expressed as a majority, became the authentic human voice of national public morality. The limitless power Locke finally gives to the majority to speak for the people and to define life, liberty, and property makes no sense morally unless one is as confident as he (and Jefferson) seem to be that somehow "the majority" can indeed speak for "the people" without oppressing anyone's rights and that it can even reliably define the meaning of those rights.[75] If we cannot similarly morally vindicate majoritarianism, democratic politics quickly becomes, as one line of critics since Rousseau has held, merely a version of the will of the stronger, no matter how convinced the people or its spokesmen may be that the majority defines rights properly and will never violate them when legislating.

It may not matter for the location and sweep of ultimate power in America that Jefferson's famous phrase "consent of the governed" in the Declaration of Independence was indebted primarily to Locke (as he understood him) or to others whom he had also read.[76] Whether Lockean "reason" or Hutchesonian "sentiment" or Harringtonian "virtue" ultimately animated the American people or underlay Jefferson's ideas, the Declaration, like the Constitution of 1787, did proclaim "the people" as the source and continuing judge of acceptable government. But the Declaration was a *pièce d'occasion*, an *apologia*, a lawyer's brief against a king's breach of contract, not a treatise or basic law. It did not provide details and precision about the nature and limits of the consent of the governed or of individual rights.[77]

A decade later, in the second American attempt to draft an instrument

74. Compare Willmoore Kendall, *John Locke and the Doctrine of Majority Rule* (Urbana, Ill., 1941), and Julian H. Franklin, *John Locke and the Theory of Sovereignty* (Cambridge, Eng., 1978). N.B.: No reference is made to the essential Kendall work. Richard Ashcroft and M. M. Goldsmith, "Locke, Revolution Principles, and the Formation of Whig Ideology," *Historical Journal*, XXVI (1983).

75. Kendall, *John Locke and the Doctrine of Majority Rule.*

76. Carl Becker, *The Declaration of Independence* (New York, 1922), chap. 2.

77. Bernard Wishy, "John Locke and the Spirit of '76," *Political Science Quarterly*, LXXIII (1958).

of national government, the phrase "we the people" appears in the preamble as constituent power. If we work through the text of the document to find the ultimate expression of "we the people," we arrive at the amendment process. With the articulated exception of the equality of states in the Senate, everything in the Constitution itself and any law under it is implicitly subject to "the people" acting to amend through varying procedures involving Congress, the state legislatures, or popular conventions. Only in the amending of the basic law do we glimpse finality about how the American people is sovereign.

This meaning of the sovereignty of the people, for all its seeming to express ultimate power, is immediately complicated, however, by the equally sacrosanct idea of *individual* rights, which has also been found in the American political ethos since 1776. From the outset, with both of these ideas in play, there entered into American life its deepest political tension. Two centuries afterward, neither practice nor theory has settled the relationship between the two doctrines of majoritarianism and individual (or minority) rights. More than anyone else, Jefferson bequeathed us both. He was dedicated to both, invoked both, and, typically, leaves us in a quandary about how both great glowing ideals are to coexist. Typically too, he himself tried to have it both ways by taking refuge in abstractions. As he outlined his guiding ideas on the notable occasion of assuming the presidency in 1801, "absolute acquiescence" in majority decisions is "the vital principle of republics from which there is no appeal but to force, the vital principle and parent of despotism." The typical ambiguity of the man followed, however, for although "the will of the majority is in all cases to prevail," that will, "to be rightful, must be reasonable; that the minority possess their equal rights, which equal laws must protect and to violate which would be oppression." Yet, "in all cases" the majority is to "prevail"—even, are we to assume, for a true majoritarian at least, until a minority, *e.g.,* 3,500,000 slaves in 1860 or 175,000 Japanese-American internees in 1942, converts itself into a majority or convinces the majority to change its mind? To recall such painful cases makes it apparent how popular sovereignty and individual rights were to clash far more than Locke or Jefferson foresaw in their early and fulsome investment in the rationality of majorities.

Democracy and the State

Democracy and associated words underwent notable and revealing changes after 1776. In 1776, *democracy, democratic,* and *democratical* were still unflattering words in political discourse, and the use of *dem-*

ocrat to describe a political person was not known.[78] At best reckoning, in the new nation the democracy remained, as it long had, one of the elements of "balanced government," the population of "freemen" or smallholders represented in a lower house of a legislature. But by 1776 the numbers, social achievement, and political weight of that democracy already loomed so large that it had to have a far greater place in governing than propertied commoners, let alone the huge numbers of the propertyless and illiterate, were permitted in Europe. Most patriot leaders, however, looking on the democratic element with traditional distrust or disdain, handled it gingerly. "The people," although invoked by the leaders to establish the republic in 1776, could not rule it day by day. Furthermore, as Edmund Morgan has claimed, "the people" remains perennially an abstraction that always cloaks some group claiming to speak in its name.[79]

The full history of the word *democracy* since 1776 is yet to be written. Within the generation after 1776 the "democracy" that had been regarded with suspicion when untempered by monarchial and aristocratic elements in "balanced government" began to be praised. The derivative word *democrat* was not in play in 1776 but seems to have been invoked first in the 1780s to describe, honorifically, a partisan of a republic governed not by an elite of wealthy citizens but with active participation by commoners. This shift in vocabulary did not first occur, surprisingly, in republican America but in Europe, where some of the Dutch patriots in their failed revolution of 1784 called themselves, applaudingly, "democrats."[80]

In the 1780s, leaders of the new American republic were not familiar with such usage. For the skeptics about the populace, had they known the word, *democrat* would have meant a dangerous Shaysite, an heir of the Carolina Regulators, or perhaps a wild follower of Ethan Allan of Vermont. It took the French Revolution and Thomas Jefferson to bring a word like *democrat* into favorable American usage. But to prevent it inviting the old contempt or the new obloquy connecting it with Jacobin, *democrat* was united in honor with *republic,* as in Jefferson's party named, significantly, Democratic-Republican.

Overall, we must recall that much of what European philosophes saw as America's new politics of reason in harmony with nature was already in place by 1763:[81] governors, legislatures, and courts; electoral districts roughly based on head count or geography; light religious qualifications

78. Palmer, *The Age of the Democratic Revolution,* I, 15.
79. Edmund S. Morgan, *Inventing the People* (New York, 1988).
80. Palmer, *The Age of the Democratic Revolution,* I, 15–16.
81. Echeverria, *Mirage in the West.*

for voting or holding office; elected representatives residing, like voters, in their districts; occasional reapportionment and some moves to equity in the representation of backcountry citizens; and, most of all, a widely diffused, white-male suffrage.[82]

Claims that all of this argues for an America already a democracy in 1776 ignore issues like qualifications for office, the nature of nominations, organized opposing parties and untrammeled political criticism, the availability of polling places and newspapers, the timing and frequency of elections, simplification of the ballot, and the open and confident antidemocratic rhetoric of many leaders like Knox and Lee. All of these were issues in a "democratization" that still lay ahead after the liberation of 1776. Most of all, the seemingly widespread participation in colonial elections before the Revolution should not be taken as everyman's "democracy." It was, rather, an expansion of the older English notion of liberty, construed as the right of those not "dependent" and with a stake in society, *i.e.*, the lauded English forty-shilling freeholder, to have a voice in how he was governed. Jefferson's "the people," therefore, were not Europe's "canaille," as he called them, the wretched masses recurrently gathering in mobs to sack granaries or burn chateaux. Only future fights about American democracy would involve, among other things, attempting to graft votes for the propertyless and uneducated onto the original foundation of a republic of many smallholders.[83]

That *democracy* was to be used in the future by George Bancroft and other scholars to describe flatteringly such purposes in 1776 is a distortion derived from a teleological interpretation. When Bancroft finished publishing his history in 1882, America seemed, in his retrospect, "destined" for the democracy then in vivid flower. He proclaimed democracy the eternal American ideal and identified it as the very spirit and practice of 1776. The Declaration was read with the emphasis on "all men are created equal" and not merely as a defense of independence and individual liberty against royal crimes. As we have seen, the famous phrases of 1776 about human equality, rights, and consent of the governed were implicated not in anything called democracy but in a republicanism that was moving beyond its narrow English dimensions to a wider and more active participation by the propertied populace qualified for liberty. By "all men are created equal," Jefferson meant something political, a reproof to the unjust past of kings and priests for affirming that any man or social class was born with an inherent or

82. Richard Buel, Jr., "Democracy and the American Revolution: A Frame of Reference," *William and Mary Quarterly,* XXI (1964).

83. Chilton Williamson, *American Suffrage: From Property to Democracy, 1760–1860* (Princeton, 1960).

inheritable right to rule over anyone. He also meant that human beings were not born destined to be dependent on others, even if they came into the world with unequal talent and without property. For Jefferson, land for all in America, undergirding a decent and simple life for ordinary folk, would show that dependence and subservience were not given in the nature of man.

The argument of future American conservatives about a later and alien egalitarianism being grafted illegitimately onto America's original republican purposes[84] fails to notice that for more than a century before 1776 earlier republican enthusiasts like Harrington had repeatedly warned that failure to solve the enduring "social question" of excessive inequality in wealth would continue to ruin republics. Still, English republicanism generally had envisioned a society with a fixed order of yeoman and another of an elite of leaders who shepherded the flock. Making as many people as possible propertied rather than "leveling" or abolishing private property was the republican logic. In 1776, the Declaration alluded tangentially to an excessively narrow concern about real property in earlier republicanism by broadening the traditional phrase "right to property" to the equal right of all men to "the pursuit of happiness." By that famous phrase Jefferson seems to have meant the right to acquire and use not merely land but also a skill for self-satisfaction or the right to make something of oneself in other ways and thus to become "independent" and substantiate, as it were, an inborn and equal moral worth.

Against latter-day simplifications of our early republicanism we must also note the moves after 1776 to use government to improve the status of persons whose condition seemed to contradict that "all men are created equal." Reforms with egalitarian intentions were clearly present in the new republic and did not await later radical democrats to add equality to the republican faith. Quakers and other humanitarian groups took counsel against slavery and other forms of misery and bondage, drawing upon their religion and the creed that equal rights, happiness, and justice were concerns of government.[85] In addition to the religious arguments, the principal Enlightenment idea opposing slavery was its contradiction to the republic's newly proclaimed ideal that all men were created equal.[86] Even before independence, Patrick Henry found it "amazing [that] . . . in a country above all others fond of liberty . . . we find . . . a principle [slavery] as repugnant to humanity as it is inconsistent with the Bible and destructive to liberty."[87] There are more pointed implica-

84. Willmoore Kendall and George W. Carey, *The Basic Symbols of the American Political Tradition* (Baton Rouge, 1970).

85. Jameson, *The American Revolution Considered as a Social Movement*, chap. 1.

86. Jordan, *White over Black*, 269–308.

87. Jameson, *The American Revolution Considered as a Social Movement*, 23.

tions of the insufficiency of republican liberty without equal opportunity for all in Jefferson's opposition to slavery in the rejected clauses of his original draft of the Declaration and in his later (1784) draft of an ordinance for the Northwest Territory. And to qualify more white men for participation in liberty in 1776 he proposed, fruitlessly, that Virginia grant all men who still lacked a stake in society fifty acres from the public domain. Soon, and more effectively, some state legislatures acted against the slave trade or slavery itself and also cut the influence or power of colonial grandees by abolishing quitrents and trying to deal with complaints of tenant farmers.[88] Those old bulwarks of aristocracy, primogeniture and entail, in any case more voluntary and symbolic than required or effective by 1776, were also abolished as "preferments" or "privileges" incompatible with republicanism.

Thus, despite the efforts of later antiegalitarian republicans from Calhoun and Brownson to Russell Kirk and Willmoore Kendall to deny all concerns about equality within the original republican mission, establishing the conditions for a republic of liberty did bring attention to the "social question" of unmerited station or social advantage. The emphasis here is on an accurate reading of the past as a prelude to any later disputation about the true or intended "American way." What was to be done about liberty and equality and in what spirit were and remain controversial matters, and the old question endures whether republican institutions will founder if allied with egalitarianism. Even deeper is the query whether republicanism in America can coexist with a sizable "dependent" class ready for violence to escape misery inflicted by richer persons with a stake in degrading or neglecting the less fortunate.

Where later conservative republicans have fact on their side is that the claims of and attention to equality in 1776 were limited, not broad and ideological as they were to be fifty years later. Many of the signers and other leading patriots feared "levelers" while assenting to the Declaration or worrying about slavery. Even one of the greatest exemplars of American opportunity and of the self-made man, Benjamin Franklin, had denounced "the common people who are . . . continually inflamed by seditious scribblers to trample on authority and everything that used to keep them in order."[89] Also many slave owners went over to the patriot side in 1776 in anger against royal appeals to slaves to desert their masters for freedom under the king.[90] Similarly, the common man who was a tenant often lined up with the Tories because patriot landlords were hostile to easing quitrents and thus reducing inequality.

88. Morris, *The American Revolution Reconsidered,* 57ff.
89. Quoted in Dorfman, *The Economic Mind in American Civilization,* I, 185.
90. Morris, *The American Revolution Reconsidered,* 74.

Visions that the new republic without its old authorities would be ripped apart by the "social question" of increased equality conjured up memories of the "mob" that had long haunted American and English politics.[91] But even the American mob was not made up of the wretched of the earth. What mobs there were in the era of independence, from the Regulators of the 1760s to the Shaysites and Whisky rebels a generation or so later, were overwhelmingly smallholders seeking to protect the property they already owned, not impoverished "miserables" opposing property rights.

We cannot find in 1776 the large democratic sensitivities and programs like those of the 1830s and later that Bancroft and the progressive historians of this century emphasized in defining the spirit of 1776. But the call for the state's concern about the threat of "privilege" and "aristocracy," especially if hereditary, to republican ideals came on very soon, in the 1780s against the first plans for membership in the Order of the Cincinnati. Then, in the 1790s, Jefferson's denunciations of the Hamilton program as aristocratic and monarchial invoked the "old spirit" of 1776. He believed that the rights of man and various egalitarian ideals opposed creating a privileged class by paying off the depreciated national debt at par and by establishing a national bank. These egalitarian motifs were read back to join liberty as the principal ideals of 1776.[92] The Declaration was reconstrued as opposing the hierarchical society that Jefferson discerned in Hamilton's program. The Federalist opposition, in reality no less patriots in 1776 than the Jeffersonians had been, were now discerned as betrayers of republicanism for their anglophile penchant for monarchial power and aristocracy, church and state, commercial paper, speculation, and luxury. The persistent "English" rhetoric of privilege and subordination to authority and social betters in Federalist talk further convinced Jefferson that the American Revolution had not finished its work. Benjamin Rush had already set the theme in 1787, when he wrote, "The American war is over but this is far from being the case with the American Revolution."[93] Jefferson's ultimate success in what he called the "revolution of 1800" was less to secure democracy than to purge American republican discourse of words betokening monarchy, aristocracy, privilege, or contempt for the people. The Americans had thus come a long way in fifteen years. Look-

91. Pauline Maier, "The Charleston Mob and the Evolution of Popular Politics in Revolutionary South Carolina," *Perspectives in American History,* IV (1970); Gordon S. Wood, "A Note on Mobs in the American Revolution," *William and Mary Quarterly,* XXIII (1966).

92. Vossler, *Jefferson and the American Revolutionary Ideal.*

93. *The Selected Writings of Benjamin Rush,* ed. Dagobert D. Runes (New York, 1947), 26.

ing back, Jefferson wrote, "Things have so much changed tʰ
that it is like a new world. Those who know us only from 17ʰ
can form no better idea of us now than of the inhabitants of tʰ
I mean as to political matters."[94]

Of course, unjust power and many kinds of inequality were nͦ
ished by Jefferson's victory in 1800 but were driven to more artͥ ͣͦͬͫ-
mulations. Among them was what Arthur Schlesinger, Jr., described as
a widespread Federalist-Whig rhetoric before 1840, urging the voter
of small or modest means to trust the beneficent rich.[95] But Jefferson did
complete the democratizing of our public language as part of the desanctification of the state that had been under way for generations. In
America, not only was all government to be regarded as manipulable
and human, not as a divine or metaphysical contrivance, but after 1800,
the American political vocabulary would be "middle class." Political
talk of aristocracies, demeaning of the populace, majestic titles or address, plans for a state religion, and so on, increasingly became "un-
American" or, rather, un-republican. After 1800, it was political suicide
to use such rhetoric as the arch Federalists had arrogantly done in the
1790s only to lose power to Jefferson, the champion of the people and
of what he openly called a *democratic* republic.

The People's Voices

As a practical matter, who, really, was this "people" invoked in such
lofty and abstract terms by Locke and Jefferson? However sweeping and
imposing the theory of the people's power, their direct sway after 1776
was small. Geographic isolation, hard work, and very limited leisure
were practical reasons for the people seeming to "defer," leaving politics to gentlemen purporting to speak for them.[96] If issues became hot
enough, however, the voters could turn out—as they did, for notable example, in 1787 in Massachusetts to deal with the legacy of Shays's Rebellion, or as they did in tumultuous Rhode Island in the 1780s.[97]

Since communication, travel, and the timing and location for voting
and meetings were so difficult, the sovereignty of the people meant leaving the daily workings of the state in the hands of the few. In the flattering view, these were Jefferson's "wise men," that "natural aristocracy" of talented and experienced representatives elected periodically

94. Thomas Jefferson to Benjamin Hawkins, March 14, 1800, in *The Writings of Thomas Jefferson*, ed. Paul L. Ford (12 vols.; New York, 1892–99), IX.

95. Arthur Schlesinger, Jr., *The Age of Jackson* (Boston, 1945), chap. 22.

96. Sydnor, *Gentlemen Freeholders*.

97. Morris, "Insurrection in Massachusetts," 46–47.

by the people at large or indirectly by the state legislatures or electoral college. In English republicanism, however, isolated or lethargic or self-concerned citizens not deliberating among themselves but trusting elected representatives were signs of "corruption." *All* purported representation or even instructed delegates were pernicious fictions at best. The only reliable voice of the people was from the citizens themselves. But how could that voice be articulated in a republic that extended over a thousand miles in each direction? Madison probably has more to tell us than do any of his contemporaries about such dilemmas of early American republicanism. He departed radically from the republican canon first by endorsing a representative system for the nation and then by stretching the republic over a million square miles. He boldly confounded old formulae even more by calling self-government a democracy and representative government a republic.

Despite the English teaching and its mutant version in the New England town meeting, representation seemed inescapable, given the American geography and the citizens' intense self-concern with their farms or trades rather than with public affairs. By 1776, a representative system was already established. But representation also suited the experience, interests, and ideas of most of the Founding Fathers. They believed that "the people," set too close to control of government, was too liable to be misled, was too ignorant and ill-informed, and too subject to whim and fashion. Day by day, "the people" could be vested only with a filtered or distant, ultimate voice about political decisions, as in periodic elections or in amending the basic law.[98] But saying this, one must add that the Fathers agreed that all officials of the republic had to come under general public scrutiny through free speech and a free press and be subject on schedule to the "consent of the governed." The filtered majoritarianism and antipopulistic fears in such views, so emphasized by progressive historians hostile to the "aristocratic" Fathers,[99] can obscure the latter's larger republican emphasis, that elites were no more trustable ultimately than the populace. If the besetting sins of popular majorities for John Adams were envy and ignorance, the flaws in elites were their arrogance and their hunger for power and prestige.[100] It is a large error to charge that the men of 1787 and the writers of the Federalist Papers were concerned only with limiting the power of transient

98. See, for example, the exchanges among Roger Sherman, Elbridge Gerry, George Mason, James Wilson, James Madison, and John Randolph, in *The Records of the Federal Convention of 1787,* ed. Max Farrand (4 vols.; rev. ed., New Haven, 1937), I, 48–51. Compare with Cecelia M. Kenyon, "Men of Little Faith: The Anti-Federalists on the Nature of Representative Government," *William and Mary Quarterly,* XII (1955).

99. J. Allen Smith, *The Spirit of American Government* (New York, 1907).

100. Howe, *The Changing Political Thought of John Adams.*

popular majorities. They were preoccupied with that problem as "the people" in America seemed to express themselves in the post-revolutionary upsets. The context of that specific concern, however, was always the effect of concentrated power on all men, regardless of station and class.

By 1787, the sovereignty of the people in actual decision-making had already acquired many expressions. Only distinguishing these from each other clarifies the options available and the decisions made at the Constitutional Convention. In 1776 "the people" in the Declaration and the new states were simply proclaimed the authors of their new governments by the patriot elite who had agitated against the king. As Josiah Quincy later told Tocqueville, "We put the name of the people where the king's name had been."[101] Jefferson had agreed when he described the transition to Franklin as involving "as much ease as would have attended . . . throwing off an old, and putting on a new suite of clothes."[102] Of course, this action of casting the people as constituent power rested on the prior one of transforming thirteen colonies into "states," *i.e.*, both geopolitical and legal entities. Again, however, the populace was not summoned to deliberate or approve that portentous step. The patriot leaders at Philadelphia invented or invoked two useful fictions to justify the momentous change from colony to state. Just before the Revolution, Adams, in the *Novanglus* letters, and Jefferson, in the *Summary View*, had announced that the original migrations here with charters and governing institutions had really established "states," although England called them colonies. Statehood had thus been either miniature or latent in colonial status. These pretenses encouraged the revolutionary logic that with an excrescent or incidental English tie dissolved, the proto-states came into their own with their existing laws and institutions *still* in place. No return to a "state of nature" was implied by merely putting the name of the people "where the king's name had been." The "contract of society" remained in place. Only a new "contract of government" had to be negotiated between the people and the leaders to replace the royal retinue. That Lockean logic was stretched, however, for the Second Continental Congress had not been authorized by the people or by any regular colonial government. The patriots of 1776 assumed that as delegates from the thirteen colonies whose last sitting governments had been elected by the people before being dismissed or ignored by the king, they had a mandate to sever the ties with London. Also, with

101. George W. Pierson, *Tocqueville and Beaumont in America* (Gloucester, Mass., 1969), 251.
102. Thomas Jefferson to Benjamin Franklin, August 13, 1777, in *Writings of Jefferson*, ed. Ford, II.

war under way by July, 1776, there was no chance for orderly or rapid referral back to the populace. By previous elections, by social recognition as leaders in their colonies, and by simply assuming that they were the authentic voice of America, the men at Philadelphia set to work as the voice of the people.

With the royal element expunged from the charters and laws, the colonies, now fully states, passed into American hands. During the war no state ever conducted a referendum about whether the Declaration, the Articles of Confederation, or the colonial institutions and laws still in force in most states were acceptable. The one substantially new state constitution, in Pennsylvania in 1776, never went before the voters. At first, "the people" in Pennsylvania and elsewhere could have included loyalists, so "people" was soon pared down by the expulsion of 60,000 to 100,000 Tories. Still, the now commonly accepted estimate is that a strong majority of the 2,500,000 colonists did approve of the break with England. By inference from "silence implies consent," from the driving out of Tories, from the participation in what elections there were during the war for officials and constitutional revision, the people also assented to their new governments. If we do accept gingerly the notion that silence implies assent, minimally, even the first state governments of 1776 can be said to have been based on popular consent. It was by the authority of those states, not the people directly, that America's first national government under the Articles of Confederation went into effect.

Within the state governments, the authorized voices of the people were made known as in the colonial assemblies, through elected representatives in numbers based crudely and unevenly on population districts and drawn from many ranks and classes.[103] In prerevolutionary debate about the empire and taxation there was a notion that a supreme legislature, such as Parliament, was composed of members who made laws for the good of the entire community, whatever their electoral base. In England, this idea quickly became a Tory argument not only against the need for colonists having seats at Westminster but also against electoral reform in England for the next half-century. All areas, interests, and residents were "virtually represented," even if most Englishmen could not vote for the House of Commons or if candidates did not live in a district or if some Englishmen lived overseas and did not vote. By 1776 the colonial argument about no taxation without representation had rejected virtual representation as a sophism. Besides, within the colonies, most representatives did live in their districts and were cho-

103. Jackson T. Main, "Government by the People: The American Revolution and the Democratization of the Legislatures," *William and Mary Quarterly*, XXVIII (1966).

sen by a widespread local suffrage.[104] Whether apportionment an. districts was fair was a far larger issue, especially for people in the bac country.[105]

In contrast also with England, America by 1776 was well on the way to legislative districts based on consciously contrived outlines, not on the fortuitous medieval boundaries of English fiefs or church holdings. The colonists were thus used to representation by their numbers, not by their social class, "estates," or "orders." They worked largely with the norm of one man with one vote, and soon after 1776 set themselves against what remained of plural officeholding.

Although the helmsmen of the recast state in America came from an electoral system that was remarkably "modern," they did legislate for the people with another English notion, most famously explained by Edmund Burke to his electors in Bristol.[106] In electing a representative, the people were to select not a mere delegate but a free intelligence, a man empowered to use his judgment and not bound by instructions or even by his district's needs. Chosen by those numerical constituencies and subject to the law and to regular elections, the American representatives of the people were otherwise free to steer society as they willed.

Before 1789, however, the voice of the people nationally was heard only through delegates appointed by the state governments. The Articles of Confederation expressed a "firm league of friendship" among thirteen sovereign states. The text did not declare explicitly that the document was authorized for "the people," but only for the "respective constituents" of the delegates who drafted the Articles and by approval of their state governments. The Confederation delegates were always chosen by the state governments, not by the populace. Each state had only one vote in the Congress, with nine needed to carry most laws and unanimity to amend the Articles. Not only was there no referendum for the people of any state to assent to the Articles, but in the document "the people" is mentioned only a few times in passing and never in any way to indicate that they rather than the states had any role in constituting or reviewing the national government. Nor could the Confederation enforce its laws on the citizens of the states directly. Only the states were bound to compliance and only for specified national tasks like treaty making. The Confederation could only make requests of the state governments on important matters like revenue.[107]

104. Pole, *Political Representation in England and the Origins of the American Republic.*
105. Sosin, *The Revolutionary Frontier, 1763–1783.*
106. Edmund Burke, "To the Electors of Bristol," in *The Works of the Right Honorable Edmund Burke* (6 vols; London, 1854), I.
107. Jensen, *The Articles of Confederation.* Contrast with his "Democracy and the American Revolution," *Huntington Library Quarterly,* XX (1957).

This sketch ignores the other American governments of the time but, nevertheless, makes it apparent that when the struggle came in 1787 to enhance the federal or national power, there were many notions in play about the proper expression of the sovereignty of the people, all reflecting the several versions already at work in the states and localities. Among the voices of the people available as models in 1787 were: the New England town meeting; the ballot of a wide populace-at-large for the lower state houses; the restricted electorate for state senators and executive officers; the state constitutional conventions; the "wise men of the state" (as Jefferson called them) sent to Congress with instructions from their respective state legislatures; some "consensus" of populace, leaders, and states, however determinable.

Among barbed issues at Philadelphia were whether to scrap, not revise, the Articles, whether the states as agents of the constituting people had to continue to be unanimous about amendment, as the Articles required, or whether there was some degree of majority sufficient to write and then ratify new basic rules for the Union. Beyond the basic law, in enacting ordinary legislation in the name of the people, should majorities for different purposes be seven, eight, or nine of the thirteen states, each state being equal regardless of size or strength, or 51 percent or more of those voting in both chambers regardless of their states? The deeper agreements were that the forms of government, somehow, had to be republican, with the specific forms acceptable ultimately to the populace, and that significant state and local authority had to be retained while augmenting national power. Since all thirteen states now had bicameral legislatures and separate executives, and since the Confederation without a separate executive had been too weak, a national government had to give heed to those experiences. At the national level for the first time, the practice of representing individual citizens, not states, was exemplified in a lower house, along with equal representation of the states in a national senate chosen by the state legislatures voting by head.

At every level, power was to be adequate for assigned tasks, but never so massed or unconditional as imperial government had seemed. The machine of government had to deal with the thorny issue of the meaning of sovereignty over the entire nation, but any final voice, even if it was in the name of the people, could not be hostile to individual rights or state interests. This invited tortuous exercises in trying to have a final authority and yet setting limits on it. The interests of thirteen states particularly invited attempts to square the circle of effective and yet circumscribed sovereignty. In 1787, the problem of final power echoed the ambiguities about the relation of individual rights to the collective right of the people in the Declaration in 1776 and about the rights of individual colonies versus imperial power before the Revolution. The leaders of 1787 never really escaped their conflicts over locating a final voice, and their dilemmas passed into later history with telling force. The sovereignty of "We the people" being declared, under the federal Constitution, the supreme law of the land also plays against the strong commitment to individual rights in the first ten amendments and the corollary of the states retaining all powers not granted to the national government. Behind the latter lay the myth of locality as a bastion of individual freedom. There were related dilemmas about designing the separation of powers, checks and balances, and a federal system with all officials and citizens subject to and pledged to uphold the federal Constitution. All of the twisting and turning at Philadelphia was intended to thwart corruption or tyranny. Despite such intense concern, if no state or government and no one part, especially the executive, of a forthcoming federal structure had the last voice, where, short of difficult amendment, was any clear national expression of the people's sovereignty, the ostensible final word for collective interests, let alone for virtue or for individual rights?

The principal sources on these dilemmas of constitution-making are the records of the Philadelphia convention, of the state ratifying conventions, the Federalist Papers, and a dozen other tracts for the times about ratification.[108] To read them is to be stunned by the display of political minds at work. It was never to be equaled again about any issue in our history. But reading the documents also requires forsaking some latter-day categories purporting to sort out for us the main lines of argument. There are scholars from Bancroft on who have presented the Constitution as a great act of disinterested patriots. Others, in a line extending from J. Allen Smith (1906) to Merrill Jensen (1968), have held that only the opponents of the new Constitution and those wanting only to revise the Articles were friends of the people, devotees of a democracy of 1776.[109] "Realism" suggested to some followers of Charles Beard (1913) that the "continentalists" of 1787 were, in effect, engaged in a counterrevolution of large property-owners, particularly of bonds, stocks, and other "paper," who wrote the Constitution, fearful of aroused majorities and Shaysite threats to property. In fact, the opponents of the document of 1787 were just as varied a group and just as avid about property rights as the Constitution men, and their leaders, like George

108. Farrand, ed., *Records of the Federal Convention*; Jonathan Elliot, ed., *The Debates in the Several State Conventions on the Adoption of the Federal Constitution* (5 vols.; Philadelphia, 1836–59); Robert A. Rutland, *The Ordeal of the Constitution* (Norman, Okla., 1966).

109. Morris, *The American Revolution Reconsidered*, chap. 4, on the historiography.

Clinton of New York, were at least as fearful of the populace, possibly more so, than were the continentalists who supported ratification.[110]

The Constitution emerged as a series of major tensions, a sequence of ambiguous compromises tortuous in major respects.[111] Exhausting labors produced formulas that satisfied no one completely but left few persons implacably or eternally alienated. When it deals with the issue of the ultimate authority of the people, the Constitution asserts "We the people" as constituent power, but also declares nine states, not all, sufficient to validate the new constitution and leaves the future ultimate voice of the people in that remote and complex process of amendment. The provisions for more ordinary hearings from the people involved variety and still invited complication: the House elected every two years by the same voters choosing the state lower houses; the president, by a college of popularly chosen electors every four years; only one-third of the senators chosen every two years, with a term running to six years and their choice left to the state legislatures. The document attempts to thwart direct and immediate control by any interest group. In practice, it entrusted power and authority, as in colonial and state practice, to a diverse and faction-ridden political corps that could manage periodically to get itself elected by the people directly, by the state legislatures, or by the electoral college. Those installed in Congress and the executive then had the commission to bargain and legislate, in the people's name, as "the majority."

There also remain ambiguities about everyday rule involving the precedence among the three major separate powers of national government, each in "check" or "balance" against the others. Ultimately, legislature, executive, and judiciary could not be "separated" fully, since it was apparent, despite the ideal of Montesquieu and the English republican Harrington, that full separation could invite stalemate. On the broadest consideration, taking the national and state mechanisms together as well as the varying suffrage qualifications left to the states, no interest or faction of the people that sought a voice in government was without a "check" from another voice. If the Constitution is a notable expression of Enlightenment rationalism about government as an "idea," as an analyzed and articulated system, it also echoes American Calvinism, for it reads as though all human interests and motives are forever suspect and under scrutiny for excess.[112]

110. Kenyon, "Men of Little Faith"; Jackson T. Main, *The Anti-Federalists* (Chapel Hill, 1961).

111. Max Farrand, *The Framing of the Constitution of the United States* (New Haven, 1913).

112. Richard Hofstadter, *The American Political Tradition and the Men Who Made It* (New York 1948), chap. 1.

If the intention at Philadelphia in 1787 was to enhance national powers, it was also to make them specific, counterable, and slow moving. It has been well observed that the draftsmen of 1787 sought a rationalized mechanism to deal with a history that was, they understood, not rational and always eluding the "best laid plans."[113] To deal with novelty beyond specified powers, there is an "elastic clause" for Congress that even the wary Jefferson was to accept, provided it was used for *strictly* necessary and proper legislation.[114] For Jefferson, Hamilton's future proposal for a national bank far exceeded that parameter.

Of course, conditions and prospects at the time help dispel some of the mists that "present-mindedness" may suggest about the cumbersomeness of the system. The world of 1787 could esteem at every level a politics that was intentionally slow, complex, and less geared than ours to enact programs quickly. The gathering faith, although not shared by the Federalists of the 1790s, was Jefferson's: society, not state, would take care of most problems. Also, that world of 1787 was decentralized and lacked our size and scale, our national and international industries, technology, and communications that now diversify and energize our interests while increasingly making similar the styles and tastes of every quarter of the modern republic. Even more notably absent in 1787 were our massive wealth, our galvanizing power, and our dizzying expectations from life and politics on a global scale. As the twentieth century runs elsewhere, America is still not a very politicized society, but citizens today are far more intent about enlisting or capturing the state for some need or other than they were in the America of George Washington. The sense of political time within which government did its work in 1787 was also far slower than would be tolerable to our impatience, bred as it is by our aroused needs and by the media and militants who each day espy an unprecedented apocalypse involving AIDS or child care or the national deficit, and so on, for which immediate action is required. Politics in America in 1787 was still largely about stability and order, and the regnant idea was that politics should change as little as possible in society. That small scope of the political, rather than narrow construction of the Constitution, constitutes the politics we have lost.[115]

The constitutional machine was designed to avoid clear and quick invocations, not only of "consent of the governed," however lauded, but of a rationalistic politics of despatch and precision. The implicit objective was not to obtain a swift, unclouded expression of popular will but

113. *Ibid.*
114. Dumas Malone, *Jefferson and the Rights of Man* (Boston, 1951), chap. 20.
115. Important contrasts between now and then are made clear in Richard Buel, Jr., *Securing the Revolution: Ideology in American Politics, 1789–1815* (Ithaca, N.Y., 1972).

to sustain adequate agreement to work within the new plan of government and to avoid so alienating factions that they would be willing to abandon or disrupt the system. The choice of Washington as president and the readily available promise of a federal bill of rights reconciled some opponents to try the Constitution. Thereafter, it took confidence that unpopular decisions would be reconsidered and that rejected groups would have the right to try again. Fortunately, both the Democratic-Republicans and the Federalists remained loyal to the rules in accepting defeats and triumphs in the 1790s. If separate levels of government and checks and balances did assure careful scrutiny of all legislation and adequate time to bring into play all contesting interests, an effective national government on a continental scale was conceivable. America might not become just another transient republic.

There always had to be a common will and the political talent to make the elaborate array of gears and wheels and weights of the people's sovereignty work. But "the state" in the European sense, that is, manifested in a monarch or council as the clearly embodied, exclusive source of law superior to all other powers and jurisdictions, was complicated, filtered, and hidden by the men of 1787. They devised many masks over the rarely seen, final face of sovereignty: the amendment process. Most of the time, the sovereign state would *seem* to be the Congress and the president in agreement, and sometimes it would seem to be the Supreme Court during a test of constitutionality. At other times, it would seem to be the general populace voting in a presidential year, with presidents interpreting support as a mandate from the nation. In still other views, ranging from those of Madison and Jefferson to those of Calhoun and Jefferson Davis, sovereignty would be only what the states tolerate on behalf of their people. Political realists of recent time have further contended that what the people see in any part of this machinery that purports to gauge and serve the popular will is only "show," that behind the scenes the dominant social forces work the machine to their satisfaction. But, historically, from dealing with slavery to cutting a four-trillion-dollar debt, the machinery has forced delay, frustration, shifting alliances, and compromises on many diverse factions intense about whatever program they have wanted the sovereign people to approve.

The hiding and filtering of sovereignty in the Constitution complemented the tasks of governing that emerged with the coming of political parties and interest groups. With skillful players under a Constitution that so shies away from sovereign moments, the American political game for directing state power on any issue is never finished. By 1791, the Bill of Rights added to the complexity, for it virtually guaranteed that there would be voices to say publicly "Thou shalt not," however unequivocal, majestic, or massed the voice of the people might seem.[116] On major issues especially, the Constitution and the parties make it very difficult for the sovereign American people to speak with finality or clarity. Nothing more strengthened Lincoln's hand when, ultimately, he had to act on secession in the spring of 1861. He found hundreds of artful southern politicians and bureaucrats gone from Washington rather than entrenched in Congress, the bureaucracy, and the army, ready to deny him peacefully and constitutionally the fruits of his election.[117]

In order to assure the efficacy of what national laws it could pass, the system of 1787 did abandon the earlier Confederation method of exerting the national sovereignty through the states. Instead, it bound directly to federal laws all individuals inside and outside all governments and required oaths from officials at all levels to support the Constitution.[118] It also declared, grandly, the Constitution and the laws under it the supreme law. But because it did not cancel the authority and most of the sway of the state governments, the Constitution underwrote multiple command and loyalties and thus further confounded the operations of popular sovereignty with the additional element that became known as states' rights.

That concept obviously endures despite the Civil War but was formerly more formidable an option than it is now. Although the Constitutional Convention of 1787 did not assess what would happen in any showdown between national and state power,[119] states' rights were to be invoked in every decade after 1789 and on issues that aroused all parties and geographic sections.[120] The concept cannot be dismissed as outdated or as the occasional intransigence of groups such as slave owners or segregationists at bay before federal power or even as the mere rhetoric of "ins" and "outs." The issue of the relation of federal to state power remains alive on genuine concerns like revenue sharing, oil drilling, the regulation of abortion, and control over American education. At the beginning, most leaders of the early republic did believe that the new union was as much a compact among the states as it was a contract between the national government and the sovereign people. They were as unclear about any prospective showdown tug between the states and the federal power as they were about sovereign power and individual rights.

116. On the first ten amendments, see Robert A. Rutland, *The Birth of the Bill of Rights, 1776–1791* (Chapel Hill, 1955).

117. See below, Section III.

118. Article VI.

119. Farrand, ed., *Records of the Federal Convention*, I, 176–208.

120. Arthur M. Schlesinger, Sr., "The States Rights Fetish," in Schlesinger, *New Viewpoints in American History* (New York, 1922).

The myth of locality, however, tended to compound the power of the states with the defense of individual liberties, as in the notable cases of the individual states' opposition to the Alien and Sedition Acts of 1797 and the later argument for slavery. The men of 1787 resisted a more powerful national union of states as then proposed by the Virginians or Hamilton, not merely for states' rights but out of a larger concern that clearly supreme national sovereignty could be inimical to individual rights, including that purported right to own slaves. Many did believe that liberty and rights were safer in the hands of the individual state regimes than in a distant clear sovereign power that would be too reminiscent of London.[121]

The continuing deep complexity of relations among federal, state, and individual spheres, again, puts citizens on notice that the sovereign in America can be moved to final command on a major issue like slavery only with great effort and show of common will. The full coercive power and majesty of the people for purposes of any consequence are not readily available. At rare moments of national purpose, and some would add hysteria, the voice of the people will not be denied, and World War I "slackers," pacifists, and socialists, for example, will find life painful, or Social Security COLAs will be overwhelmingly reaffirmed. But in the main, the all-powerful chance nod or decreed "nay" of a Bourbon or Romanov monarch, the dominating wish of Tudor kings over pliable Parliaments, gave way in the recast state to ceaseless negotiation, to pushing compromises through the tough resisting filters of federalism, a developing party system, and the separated but checked and balanced parts of the American machine. The highway of the state to the American dream of bliss and perfection is thus often a *via dolorosa* for idealists. But there were to be considerable costs for less intense public interests in so slowing and complicating the work of the state. Having national power readily available for large national purposes, or officials quickly equal to a crisis, would chronically be problematic, even in rare instances of wartime mobilization or a domestic debacle like that of 1929 to 1932. Revealingly too, a crisis like the Civil War or the Great Depression would rouse cries about dictatorship or constitutionality if government officials did manage to nudge the state to respond vigorously to challenges.

Virtue, Faction, and Truth

In looking at some of the basic tensions within the emerging ideology of popular sovereignty and inside the structure of the newly recast state we

121. Herbert J. Storing and Murray Day, *What the Anti-Federalists Were For* (Chicago, 1981).

are reminded of how unprecedented it was in 1787 to design consciously an entire government and to try to bring political life under a written system of reasoned, articulated controls. To say that such a machine would be challenged by unpredicted issues implies how difficult it was to transcend the vicissitudes of "fortuna" in search of republican stability, let alone to achieve virtue and maintain individual rights. Americans contrasted themselves with English vice and corruption, but it was helpful that they had drifted into a far-less-austere meaning for virtue or, rather, that they construed interests to make them appear more compatible with concern for the common good. In seeking to validate both public and private purposes, however, the Founding Fathers unwittingly accented long-contesting moralities of private profit and the public good. What the leaders of 1787 hoped they could join in virtuous matrimony, the world too often continued to put asunder.

The Americans' emphasis on their superior virtue during the birth of the republic is understandable. In 1776, during a perilous rupture with the past involving intense moralistic denunciation of once-revered authority, the patriots were under great pressure to endow their cause with the highest possible moral prestige. They divided the world between the virtuous and the corrupt. In the decade that followed, however, and from the outset of the war, very little in the new laws of the states, let alone private and public conduct, suggested that the revolutionary leaders could rely on public-spiritedness or virtue as the guiding star in republican politics. Far more attention was paid to the darker republican themes of written constitutions and checks and balances designed to keep "interests" or sin from overwhelming society. By 1787 American politics as well as the design of state governments scarcely argued for investment in virtue alone for the new government's success. Whatever leaders like Madison, Jefferson, and Washington continued to say piously or pleadingly about the need for virtue in republics and its special presence in American character, the new constitution, like its predecessors in the states, took interests organized as factions as the irreducible stuff of politics. Not only did the new charter not depend on virtue, but, exceptional for the time, it passed no moral judgment whatever on the character or faith of the Americans for whom it was designed. Instead, the Constitution implicitly validated the full play of all interests and provided all with at least the possibility of reaching the great historical goal of interests, influence, or control over the state. Had Machiavelli been available in 1787 as a consultant who knew America's setting, its history, and the character of his clients, he probably would have approved how the men at Philadelphia proposed to deal with the American scene. Given the stunning array of interests confronting the designers of the basic law, any interest proscribed or judged in advance less worthy than others would be an interest alienated and made an implacable foe of the constitutional order. A Platonic republic or Rousseauian commune with a "civic religion" would have been clear from the outset about the desired character of citizens. But republican Americans had already slipped away from the old social constraints of prescribed conduct and faith. They demanded guaranteed liberty to go anywhere and into anything that their interests dictated and to believe whatever they liked. Law and power and the state's command were to be directed to behavior, not to the making of souls. At best, virtue lingered in the background and in republican rhetoric in a vague hope that by attending primarily to circumscribing excess in the *behavior* of all interests and by giving as many interests as possible representation, virtue might have a chance for influence through the skill and commitment of public-spirited leaders. In the electoral college for choosing a president, for example, other seeming triumphs for virtue, like the election of George Washington in 1788, might be forthcoming but could not be assured or commanded. There thus lingered illusions that American politics would be freed from the corruption of Machiavellian Europe. In reality, power politics (the phrase is an oxymoron) endured in the new republic. Indeed, the struggles over the ratification of the Constitution at once revealed that there had been no transcendence of politics. Instead, an intense struggle of interest groups took place. The bargains already made in drafting the Constitution were followed by those made during ratification like that, for example, to win the support of John Hancock. No sooner was the new national government in place than bitter politicking also took place about issues such as the location of the capital, the funding of the debt, a national bank, and the nation's attitude toward the French Revolution. For or against any of these choices, there was no escaping from politics, no sweet rule of grace. The morality of honoring existing treaty commitments to royalist France was sacrificed to the seeming practical advantage of neutrality. On other issues morals and politics remained at odds, with interests taking precedence over public spirit. Federalists and anti-Federalists compromised, lied, used "dirty tricks," and vilified each other in public debate and the press.

In contrast, however, from that time also American moralistic deploring of such politics and politicians as unseemly defilements remained constant. Down to today we have a tradition of jeremiads, like those of Ross Perot and others, about the "Washington crowd." Every generation has produced a wave of revulsion against incumbent rascals who need to be thrown out of office. The politicians are cast perennially as betrayers of an innocent but put-upon citizenry. This chronic sense of besmirching should caution us that even moral ideals higher than the common politico's will not win the day without an adequate alliance with power or force. As Max Weber taught, echoing Machiavelli, the politician who thinks he can accomplish such good work as destroying slavery or defeating Hitler without dirtying his hands will learn otherwise. With equal weight against our dream of transcending politics, our history reveals that the voices periodically denouncing dirty politics often belong to citizens with their own agenda for political action. The Jacksonian coalition of the 1820s that excoriated President John Quincy Adams for his aristocratic and other corruptions may have believed that they would restore America's simple republican virtue. But they also had a hodgepodge of self-interested objectives in banking, tariff, road-building, currency, and Indian removal.

The anti-Machiavellian dream of an effective politics without sin or stain has remained so strong that mundane politicians forever falls short of our reveries of innocence. Instead, politicians like Woodrow Wilson who preach perfection but, in power, compromise on and contradict their glowing promises, seem hypocrites. But the hypocrisy is foreordained by overambitious promises about an American perfection.

The Constitution reflects Machiavellian realism in representing interests rather than striving for the expression of republican virtue. Despite the Fathers' fears of what we call party politics it was soon apparent that a politics of compromise among farming, commercial, and financial interests would be needed to get the cumbersome new machinery to mesh and work. In respect to politics as interests, the Constitution belongs to the Machiavellian world of *realpolitik*. In contrast it did reject the Machiavellian emphasis on the concentrated power of the state, especially in granting very limited domestic powers for the presidency. Under checks and balances and a separation of powers, as the executive developed toward our presidential system and as party politics rapidly appeared, the Constitution became a puzzle, our enduring challenge to all interests to make sense of the state.

In rejecting a constitution defining or depending on virtuous citizens, the Fathers also resisted two old temptations of the state before their time: the classic republican wish to keep citizens public-spirited and self-denying, and the Christian impulse to use government to make men moral and to save their souls. In 1787, neither the divine charge to Christian kings to prepare souls for eternity nor the republican dependence on self-denial would do. Instead, the recast American state of 1787 was to take men as it found them and to leave them, with the founders' fingers crossed, as free as possible to find their paths to virtue or vice, damnation or salvation. By 1791 and the Bill of Rights, not only was there no national faith under the Constitution, but the millennia-old religious purposes for the state were explicitly and fully abjured. Even more, there was no federal statement of moral (or property) requirements for citizenship, representation, or public service. If there was to be any moral or religious suasion in national life, it was left to chance and the swirling pressures of a free society or to the states. The preamble to the Constitution is at most only implicitly moral in speaking of "securing the blessings of liberty." More noteworthy is the total secularism there and in the sparse words about oaths of office. Again, no deity is mentioned, not even the "under God" or "so help me God," phrases that crept into our rituals later. All of this may reflect broad strains of Enlightenment secularism and toleration as well as the impossibility, in an already diverse society, of stipulating any creed that would not offend some group or other. What is surprising, however, is the absence of at least an articulated *moral* concern. Those Fathers who had drifted far from traditional religious commitments, or at least from prescribing any faith for others, often retained strong worries about character and principles, especially with religion no longer the publicly required bulwark of either. But the moral neutrality of the Constitution builds tolerance for vice, as well as forbearance about virtue, into the structure of the state.

In this respect the federal guarantee of freedom of religion became part of the larger strategy. The Constitution, as Madison implied in *Federalist* 10, recognizes the inevitability of human error. In leading the fight for religious freedom in Virginia he had already eloquently denounced all religious establishments and all politicized sectarianism for implying infallibility or the existence of a reliable theological "truth" to guide politics.[122] Madison's stand not only abandons to private judgment the choice of moral ideals as well as religion but implies another heterodox idea for the eighteenth century, that of accepting a society in deep conflict about ultimate beliefs and ideals.

A politics of uncensured, multiple, competing beliefs had great advantages for liberty, but the possibility lingered that, like the conflict of material interests, free ideological conflict could frustrate the constitutional system or dissolve respect for its procedures if ideals like "free soil" or "ethnic identity" become intransigent. The system repeatedly demonstrated strength when dealing with economic issues. But it was hideously strained when called upon to deal with basic "values" like slavery, Mormonism, race, and ethnicity. The confrontational politics implicit in Madisonian diversity was not to be pretty, nor would it ap-

122. James Madison, "Memorial and Remonstrance Against Religious Assessment" (1785), in *The Papers of James Madison,* ed. William T. Hutchinson *et al.* (16 vols.; Chicago, 1973), VIII, 295–306.

peal to finer sensibilities. It is often banal and selfish, sordid, messy, alternately righteous and hypocritically compromising. The reality of rough-and-tumble freedom, not the ideal, has been chronically offensive to intellectuals under the age-old spell of Plato, yearning for an escape from "dirty politics." Those wanting politics to become poetry want the state to become an aesthetic ideal, promising the finesse of truth, honor, and place for those who have been to the mouth of the cave to see the light. This perennial and tempting quest is really for the end of change and of politics itself. But not being moral or refined, the Madisonian state is open to being astonishingly free. Much of this chastened view of what republican politics could or should attempt about the character of its citizens and quality of public discourse was to be formulated fully only in time. But the basis was in place in America after 1789.

Beyond the state's definitive waning, in America, from its old tasks of redeeming souls, "truth," like virtue, was always to be at risk with citizens left free not only to develop their own ideals but also, more darkly, free to hate, to suspect or dogmatize against those who opposed their vision of the true life for man. Our state was thus fated to be ever pressed by religious and secular sectarians free to roam and rave within society but forever trying to capture the state and impose moralities like anti-Catholicism, prohibition, abolitionism, restricted divorce, and the "right to life." By leaving America so free of official dogma, the system also probably heightened spiritual tension among those at liberty to nourish deep hungers for truth. It left dogmatists not only free but often in angry despair about their limited power without their old ally the state in their ceaseless quests for certainty and for saving their brothers' souls. By forsaking an official faith or virtue, just as in setting economic interests free and thereby resigning itself far more to faction than had any previous polity, the United States also implicitly acknowledged that in civic life, zeal about virtue runs the risk of sacrificing individual liberty to the very "virtue" that classical republicans held essential to liberty's success. Soon after 1789, another republic, Jacobin France, was to show how official virtue can nourish sectarian statism. As E. M. Forster pithily put it, "Programs beget pogroms."

That the Constitution was written no later than the 1780s may have been fortunate for the future of its religious neutrality and moral forbearance. The leaders of 1787 as private individuals were remarkably indifferent or often hostile to traditional doctrinal religion. They accepted without concern opening public meetings and ceremonies with prayer, Protestant chaplains for the needs of soldiers and sailors, and Bible reading in what public schools there were. This was deferential to the guarantee of the "free exercise of religion" but hostile to endorsing any particular faith as a public standard or requirement. As public men and students of history, they were deeply antagonistic to the sectarian governments of the past and of their own time. The Fathers were also Americans who had matured intellectually in the colonial backwaters of the European Enlightenment and had felt its surges against dogmatic faith. If many remained deists, theirs was so benign and indistinct a faith that it sanctioned no orthodoxies about itself or society, except hostility to religious fanaticism.[123]

The 1770s were not afire with religion, but in the 1780s, contemporary with the move for the Constitution, another cycle of American religiosity began, a remarkably potent strengthening of religious sentiments, yearnings, and formal creeds, and of the intellectual and cultural influence of various Protestant orthodoxies. The resurgent religiosity stemming from groups like the Methodists was soon given added power and pertinence by the threats of the French Revolution to social order and to all old orthodoxies and establishments. The influence of this so-called Protestant Counter-Reformation in America was great enough to check the indifference and slow the skepticism that had spread before the 1780s.[124] The new religiosity swept back and forth, up and down the American scene for several generations. So intense were its piety and its reassertion of the importance of faith and creed, that had the Constitution been drafted in 1797 instead of only a decade earlier, there is cause to speculate about whether its guarantee of religious freedom and its almost deliberate moral indifference would have been left so broad or would have been accepted. As it was, in the 1790s Jefferson, as a son of reason and revolution and a friend of French republicanism, started to carry the lifelong brand of being the chief American servant of Jacobin atheism. Even his sponsorship in old age, thirty years later, of the University of Virginia worried many would-be supporters of the university about the faculty and curriculum that Jefferson might choose.[125]

A "godless" government (i.e., one that has left ideals or faith to the choice of the believer) in a strongly god-affirming society has been recurrently so threatening to some of the devout that, despite the separation of church and state, they have clung to any sign of public profession like Bible reading in public schools or to laws against alcohol that might preserve the republic from damnation. The chronic efforts to "save religion" in order to strengthen the republic reappeared cyclically after

123. Gustav A. Koch, *Republican Religion* (Gloucester, Mass., 1933).

124. Dixon Ryan Fox, "The Protestant Counter-Reformation," *New York History*, XVI (1935); Ahlstrom, *Religious History of the American People*, 432–37.

125. Dumas Malone, *Jefferson, the Sage of Monticello* (Boston, 1981), chaps. 18–19.

the 1790s and again remind us vividly that the recast state's restraint about "truth" remained in conflict with a society morally and religiously free enough to indulge wild flights of faith and to support spiritual nostrums and moral fads of immense variety. Historically, these seem so to pullulate through American society without a religious establishment and a formalized, obligatory belief system that it prompts the question of whether our state, precisely because it eschewed dogma, especially stimulated dogmatists.[126]

Jefferson and the State

Any discussion of American ideas of government after the Revolution must inevitably include Jefferson. His views of the nature and aims of American government have become our most esteemed statements of the larger political and moral objectives of American democracy. History is usually careless in what it takes from or neglects in famous ideas, so what Jefferson really said or meant and what Americans came to credit him with saying make quite different accounts of his life and work.[127] Debate has been continuous about the meaning of Jefferson's famous fragments and aphorisms—he wrote only one book that reached the public, *Notes on Virginia* (1784)—ever since he was "rediscovered" about 1910. It was only then that he began to become, along with Washington and Lincoln, one of our immortals. Indeed, if now we have democracy as well as republicanism in our keeping, the author of our dual responsibility is Jefferson, for it was he who brought democratic and republican ideals into tandem.

Jefferson's scattered views on government cause the historian fewer difficulties than, for example, his much-debated and conflicting ideas about "agrarianism." Through sixty years of public life and comment, Jefferson's basic major themes about government remained constant, if tension ridden. Whether he touched on majority rule or individual rights, expansive government, the fulsome "European" state, was always suspect. Infinitely preferable for Jefferson was the government that did least, especially in deference to trusting America's fortunate citizenry to fend for itself. He was encouraged in that trust not only by America's unique setting of seemingly limitless land and resources but also, after 1776, by America's ousting of the privileged and corrupting institutions of European monarchy and aristocracy, established churches and their servants or "placemen." America was no setting for a European state

126. Knox, *Enthusiasm*, on the paradoxes of freedom of religion.
127. Merrill Peterson, *The Jefferson Image in the American Mind* (New York, 1960).

forever pressed to apportion meager resources and thus inevitably to favor some citizens and abuse others. With a fresh continent and a thousand years of liberty lying before the new republic of independent and self-sufficient small farmers,[128] the state in Jefferson's America might abandon its old paternalistic pretensions of helping childlike and ignorant subjects to reconcile themselves to misery. Its activity was thus to be restricted to facilitating access for private energies to America's magnificent riches. Like Adam Smith, Jefferson lived in a pre-industrial world and could not have foreseen the immense scale of enterprise evoked by the liberty to apply large-scale technology and management to three thousand miles of virgin land. He assumed a society of small producers occasionally threatened by the abuses of an over-ambitious bank or scheming land company that might require a slap from the state. His formulae could not measure the multinational economic and governmental giants of later time.

Even the task of opening the continent to small farmers, however, was one of those Jeffersonian aims that were to imply far more work for the state than anticipated. Land policy and loans for farmers, for example, have created more problems of boom and bust, speculation and fraud, than Jefferson or Jeffersonians deemed desirable. Trying, generally, to enlarge individual liberty and opportunity by state sponsorship of roads and canals and schools led Jefferson to use government more energetically than his abstractions about its evils would have seemed to warrant. We must recall that his suspicions of the state had centered on restrictive, not sponsoring, government; the great American breakout by individual citizens beyond the cramping horizons of Europe was not always served by a passive government that refrained, for example, from building internal improvements. As president, Jefferson had to invoke stronger government and more executive initiative than he preferred, particularly in the purchase of Louisiana (1803) and in enacting the Embargo of 1807 on trade with war-torn Europe.[129] On these and other matters, the difference between his statecraft and Hamiton's was eventually a weighty matter of temperament. About the state, Jefferson's instinct was to suspect or denounce its power or to play with it cautiously, almost embarrassedly. Hamilton unabashedly used the state *a la* Machiavelli, as "a work of art," an artifice to be fashioned zestfully by will and talent. He accepted the scramble and unequal benefits that flowed from his credit, currency, and tax policies as unavoidable, "realistic" prices

128. A. Whitney Griswold, *Farming and Democracy* (New York, 1948).
129. Dumas Malone, *Jefferson the President: First Term, 1801–1805* (Boston, 1970), chaps. 16–17; Malone, *Jefferson the President: Second Term, 1805–1809* (Boston, 1970), chap. 26.

for national order, growth, and power, and for creating a strong economic base for liberty.[130] Although Hamilton's opposition did not develop workable alternatives to his scheme for funding the debt, that struggle in the 1790s and the fight over the federal assumption of state debts left Jefferson angered at Hamilton's insensitivity to equity as a measure of the new government.[131] Jefferson was deeply shocked at Hamilton's wish to augment national power by binding large financial interests to the national government, even if, unawaredly, he served "interests" of small producers no less than Hamilton served those of richer Americans.

Jefferson had introduced the enduring moral aims of rights, equality, and happiness for American government in 1776, but he failed to gauge the dependence of the "rights" of 1776 on effective power, *i.e.*, on state action. He held the "energetic government" of the great states of Europe much more poisonous, much less "natural" or inevitable than seemed acceptable or possible to Hamilton. In his first instincts, and by birth and early circumstance in the hierarchic and tightly governed West Indies, Hamilton was a "European" as well as a Machiavellian, a devotee of order and "station," a man of the state. He could worry, for example, that the Louisiana Purchase could in time remove too many citizens from the scrutiny and supervision of government.[132]

More important for the course of American history is that Jefferson juxtaposed state and society, individual freedom and political order as basically antithetical. By successfully endowing these antinomies with his own prestige and with that of the American revolutionary idea, Jefferson underwrote an enduring and misleading view of the political alternatives for Americans.[133] His times already showed that there is no meaningful liberty without an ample state to protect or foster it, even if, as Jefferson the democratic-republican believed, the state under a Hamilton was too insensitive to equal rights, popular control, and justice.

Jefferson was repeatedly offered instruction in the dependence of liberty on state power during his early terrible days in trying to govern Virginia in wartime and in his taxing labors courting French commercial favors in the 1780s. He later found a special government initiative (unspecified by the Constitution) necessary to purchase Louisiana in order

130. Gerald Stourzh, *Alexander Hamilton and the Idea of Republican Government* (Stanford, 1970).

131. John C. Miller, *Alexander Hamilton: Portrait in Paradox* (New York, 1959), 435–41.

132. "The Purchase of Louisiana," July 5, 1803, in *The Papers of Alexander Hamilton*, ed. Harold C. Syrett and Jacob M. Cooke (27 vols.; New York, 1979), XXVI.

133. The relation was discerned but inadequately developed by Herbert Croly, *The Promise of American Life* (New York, 1909).

to remove European power from the western frontier and to obtain land for those thousand years of liberty. None of these actions led him to rethink his basic views of the state. On Louisiana, he continued to avoid any deeper lessons by construing the purchase, after much deliberation, as an exception warranted for guaranteeing national security and an enduring farmers' republic.[134] But for reasons of security and because of their unfamiliarity with American rights and consent of the governed, he attempted to deny the Louisiana Creoles self-government rather than grant republican liberty.[135] That case of limiting the rights of man also seemed "exceptional" for his republican faith. He never understood how his basic tendency to invoke universal standards of morality and politics in the name of reason and nature inevitably set him up for embarrassing "exceptions." He thus missed the complex logic of liberty implicit in the need thrust upon him by the Napoleonic wars to enact a coercive embargo against Americans who pursued vaunted self-interest in commerce but to the nation's detriment. In another, greater issue of American liberty, for his own thwarted hopes for a general manumission of slaves and the expatriation of blacks, energetic government would certainly be needed if voluntary manumission failed. But he did not entertain the logic of the need for active government to remove the privilege of slave owners as slavery solidified in the South. As time tragically showed, only the great state could validate the rights of man for blacks against popularly elected local governments that enforced slavery. He thus failed also to clarify the priorities between the individual rights of blacks to be free and states' rights to maintain their own institutions like slavery as property against a "consolidation" of power at Washington.[136] That power alone, ultimately, had to wage a civil war to liberate the slaves, since democratic politics and debate could not do so.

Jefferson chronically and erroneously assumed that local and individual liberty supported each other. His widely shared call for a *federal* bill of rights in 1788 and his later ringing opposition to the Alien and Sedition Acts of 1797 invoked his habitual rationalist, universalist principles of liberty. If valid as principles, these should also have obligated the states and localities, indeed, all "states," all government, to unfiltered speech and press. But as Leonard Levy has shown, albeit invoking a later civil-liberties standard, there was a "darker side" to Jefferson's record. Although he was to be celebrated for opposition to "every form of tyranny over the mind of man," he did not extend this principle to the many common law and statutory restrictions that, despite state bills of

---

134. Malone, *Jefferson the President: First Term,* chap. 17.
135. *Ibid.,* chap. 19.
136. Jordan, *White over Black,* 430–35.

rights, the state governments used to interfere with liberty of the press. Nor did he refrain from having the faculty and library at the University of Virginia screened for objectionable Federalist ideas.[137] Presumably, he regarded the states and his university as bastions of republican liberty because they could be close to grass roots opinion and under control by anti-Federalist or Democratic-Republican leaders. In that respect, he was too at ease and too abstract about the wisdom of the "will of all" in local popular majorities, even if, in his democratic ideal, they were to be propertied, enfranchised, and basically educated. Until 1865 such wise majorities in the South supported slavery and, nationally, white supremacy.

There is a remarkable vignette of the vagaries of Jefferson's mystique about locality and liberty during his years in France as American minister (1784 to 1789). Until 1789, Jefferson sided with the so-called "aristocratic upsurge" that preceded the French Revolution. He described the Assembly of Notables as "the most able and independent characters in the kingdom."[138] Since the remnants of the old aristocracy in the French provinces spoke of liberty, as did Montesquieu, and against the royal centralized despotism of Paris, their rhetoric seems to have been for Jefferson tellingly reminiscent of the American cause of the 1770s. It is as though he envisioned the French provincial aristocrats as kin to Virginians and other Americans in defending "local liberty" in France against Bourbon centralization, with Louis XVI cast as George III. Until quite late in the French struggle he remained far less sensitive to the complaints of the leaders of the Third Estate about their exclusion from national politics. Yet those leaders of 90 percent of the nation were much closer to being counterparts to the bourgeois American patriots than were the privilege-defending French aristocrats. When he conveyed his reading of French events to John Adams, that skeptic about all power pressed him hard to understand that, behind their rhetoric, those aristocratic French friends of liberty whom Jefferson admired were often the voices of local, feudalistic privilege and scarcely allies of the liberty sought in the American Revolution. Adams deplored the "avarice and ambition of the rich and distinguished citizens" and drew the first of lifelong distinctions between his ideas and Jefferson's by noting, "You are apprehensive of Monarchy; I of Aristocracy."[139] Eventually, in 1788 and 1789,

137. Leonard W. Levy, *Jefferson and Civil Liberties: The Darker Side* (Cambridge, Mass., 1963), 42–69; Gordon Baker, "Thomas Jefferson on Academic Freedom," *American Association of University Professors Bulletin*, XXXIX (1953); Roy J. Honeywell, *The Educational Work of Thomas Jefferson* (Cambridge, Mass., 1931), chaps. 11–12.

138. Quoted in Robert R. Palmer, "The Dubious Democrat: Thomas Jefferson in Bourbon France," *Political Science Quarterly*, LXXII (1957).

139. *Ibid.*

Jefferson in France began to concentrate his hopes on the reform aristocrats at Paris who, allied with the leaders of the Third Estate, initiated the great events of May through September, 1789. Jefferson witnessed these and took a backstage, unseemly hand in encouraging the French leaders who sought his aid toward greater liberty.[140]

Almost forty years later, however, the old equation of locality with liberty still held him. At the end of his life, his optimism about their compatibility again led him astray. In defending the cause of the southern states during the Missouri admission controversy of 1819 to 1821, he seemed oblivious to the argument that states' rights and a favorable balance of states for the South against "consolidation" of national power at Washington meant, in fact, support for the very slavery that he abhorred.[141] He so still feared national power accumulating against local prerogative that he did not seem to grasp what in his earlier pleas in 1776 against slavery he had implied, that local power in the slave-owning South was no friend to democratic liberty, even for the common white husbandman, let alone the slaves.

The Jeffersonian formula for occasionally invoking the latent powers of the national state to acquire Louisiana or to enforce an embargo suggested that if, momentarily, distant government had to be energetic, less was to be feared with true "friends of liberty" like himself at the helm than with a Hamilton in power. But the European logic of liberty after 1789, *i.e.*, energetic government as the sponsoring agent of human rights, seems to have escaped Jefferson. He was not alert to the paradox shown first in Europe, but with global portents, that state power might be needed to give effect to the revolutionary ideals of the rights of man against repressive regimes that denied those rights. The insensitivity is perhaps understandable, for liberty seemed to him so much more a "given" in America than in Europe. The securing of European liberty was to involve terrible fights against priests and kings for almost a century after the French in 1789 proclaimed its arrival with Jefferson's advice and optimistic endorsement. But even in America the progress of liberty was to be threatened, not by priests and kings, but by popular resistance to equal rights for all, the ideal that Jefferson had helped set loose and to which he had given eloquent phrasing.

140. Lawrence S. Kaplan, *Jefferson and France* (New Haven, 1967).
141. Malone, *The Sage of Monticello*, chaps. 23–24.

III

TESTING THE STATE

Jeffersonian Big Government

Nostalgia about a lost world of self-sufficient citizens recurrently stirs a fantasy that America between Jefferson and Lincoln was virtually a state-less society. That view, however, considers only Washington power and maintains that what exertions there were from the Potomac scarcely mattered in daily life.

The historian's tale of the state from Jefferson to Lincoln is quite other, stressing the accumulation of government power and functions across those decades, especially, but not entirely at the state and local levels. The main theme of the story is the intrinsic, strong relationship before 1860 between sponsoring government and the securing of liberty, equal-ity, and opportunity for white men. Americans before Sumter had not done it all on their own. If we follow the clues already given to watch all levels of government, to allow for waxing and waning of functions and grasp, and to think of sponsoring, rather than only regulatory, gov-ernment, we shall move to sounder understanding. Basically, we must remain aware that an expansive capitalism on the American scale and with immense natural resources generated needs that private enter-prise could not or was reluctant to serve. We must also remember that the vaunted competitive life inflicted wounds that democratic ideals of rights and justice demanded attending.

In the year 1815 and war with England behind them, about 8,500,000 Americans were ready to engulf the continent. It is revealing that one of the first questions that confronted those moving west was on what terms the state would make land available. One of our most celebrated dis-plays of American individualism, the westward movement, at once in-volved expanding the role already played by government in disposing of the public domain. In helping citizens make good on the American dream, Washington's share in settling the West did not deny extraordinary self-reliance and self-suffiency, but it did insist that development always include a major, unarticulated premise that democratic government would do everything possible to expand opportunity for every citizen seeking a farm. Auspiciously, the logic and portents of such support for individualism are already apparent a decade earlier in Jefferson's administration.

The triumph of Jefferson in 1800 meant securing the nation from a republicanism challenged by Federalist hierarchic and authoritarian ideals. Jefferson and the Democratic-Republican opposition had repeatedly emphasized that government should not be used deliberately to confer special advantage on the rich and wellborn or on unscrupulous speculators. Left unquestioned, however, was the legitimacy of democratic government creating advantage for the majority rather than leaving *all* citizens, rich and poor alike, to their own devices and the luck of the market.

Whatever the theory, there was an underappreciated psychological dimension in pursuing either democratic state sponsorship or market freedom: state or market actions would always be construable as favoring one group or another. Freedom for all to go their way on their own without the state playing any favorites had to produce unequal results because of the natural, uneven distribution of talent, aptitude, luck, and so on—qualities, incidentally, surely separable from the rapacity habitually emphasized in attacks against laissez-faire. Indeed, part of the Jeffersonian attack on European aristocracy was that it negated the natural unevenness of human abilities, judged individuals in advance by blood or social order, and imposed artificial advantages by birth and inheritance. Jeffersonian freedom was intended to permit the commonest person to test his talent rather than be trapped for life by state-conferred privilege for any special class. It also meant that those with more talent for the great game would be rewarded proportionately, *i.e.,* unequally. With such premises, providing that the state *could* be neutralized somehow, the American contest had to produce losers as well as winners, poor as well as rich. Jefferson hoped that the great riches of nature and a rational sense of needs would minimize the numbers of excessively powerful winners. In the Jeffersonian cosmos, where the sun is always shining and the triumph of reason seems irresistible, if there had to be some losers, either their loss was temporary and they were free to find another, more rewarding opportunity or they failed because of some eccentric deficiency of character that in no way reflected adversely on the ideal of free competition.

However attractive the hope that freedom and abundance would sort things out in a more "natural" or "rational" way than under aristocracy and distorting, "unnatural" state action, Jeffersonian ideology ignored not only how people would construe their victories and defeats but a host of other historical or environmental conditions as well. Resources and opportunities, however magnificent, were *not* limitless. Even for idealized "agrarians" there were good soils and bad, high prices and low per acre bought or gathered for harvest. Access from farms to markets could be prohibitive as well as easy. Legitimate ambitions as well as damnable greed might not be satisfied by quarter-section homesteads for yeomen, and small farms could not feed a population of tens of millions. These and other lessons of the nineteenth century after Jefferson's time do not destroy the ideal but suggest that, like all "models," tested by experience it was imperfect. It is as difficult to deny the social costs of this ideal as it is to deny the immense economic growth and national power that it stimulated.

Of course, after 1776 the American tendency was not to restrict government from all intervention. The "pure" and popular version of the bootstraps ideology goes too far in dismissing the government role. Jefferson's own ideal certainly was that government should reject any restrictive regulation that would suggest the obnoxious British controls. As we have already seen, after 1776 Americans remained open to state sponsorship of enterprise, guided by their ideal that all energetic citizens should be free to incorporate and pool funds for needed projects.[1] When the new governments first started underwriting economic development in the 1780s, there was little American experience to suggest that state charters, bounties, contracts, and funding might go to more powerful petitioners who had connections or whose family name or money gave them special chance for state awards. That potential for unequal and unfair results, despite the open door of the legislature for charter seekers, was accented by the requirement for specific state action on every request to incorporate. The costs, legal advice, and savvy about the legislature were often beyond the means of many modest entrepreneurs, however ambitious. Adam Smith's awareness that mercantilist charters could lead to political corruption and rewards for the court-favored or inefficient or shabby producer made him insist that only in instances of vital but costly public works should state charters or investment be available. But in the capital starved, immensely energetic America of 1783, if there were warnings about the perils of generously awarding state charters, they were to no avail against the growing number of incorporation petitions and grants even before Jefferson came to power. By the 1820s, the sheer number of petitions required so much work that some legis-

---

1. Bruchey, *Roots of American Economic Growth*, 71.

latures gave up the system almost as much for that reason as for cries against its unfairness.[2]

Opposition to the federal charter for Hamilton's bank obscures the silence of his opponents regarding the many state charters of the time that played favorites just as it ignores the Jeffersonians in the queues for those awards.[3] Jefferson had argued that a *national* bank, at least one with the great powers Hamilton wanted, was not "necessary and proper" and that the particular charter deliberately played to the interests of disreputable citizens who would speculate in the bank shares and obtain favors from the investment capital it would have available. But this attack did not argue generally against government at appropriate levels stimulating economic development, widening opportunity, and encouraging the fruits of individual liberty. These ideals seem to have been universally felt and compelling, with Jeffersonians as well as Hamiltonians accepting a large sponsoring role for the national government in economic development. Washington may have had his Hamilton, but Jefferson was to have an Albert Gallatin to fashion his own ambitious program of state investment.

The familiar tale is to find that impetus among his Jeffersonian successors, Madison, Monroe, and Quincy Adams, and the congressional leader, the young Henry Clay.[4] But the so-called "American System," after 1815, of internal improvements, a renewed national bank, protective tariffs, and a national university had notable predecessors a decade earlier. The first precedent is well known, *i.e.,* despite his denunciations, President Jefferson did not move to end Hamilton's national bank. About his own, more positive efforts at national sponsorship, one searches in vain for signs of modesty about state action in Jefferson's second inaugural speech (1805) about applying a prospective federal surplus to "rivers, canals, roads, arts, manufactures, education and other great objects within each state" or in Gallatin's ensuing sweeping federal proposals, as secretary of the treasury, for internal improvements (1808). Even more astonishing to find in the famous enemy of centralized government and great devotee of strict construction was Jefferson's pleasure in the prospect that through the various projects, "the lines of separation [among the states] will disappear, their interests will be iden-

2. A. B. Johnson, "The Legislative History of Corporations in the State of New York: The Progress of Liberal Sentiments," *Hunt's Merchants' Magazine,* XXIII (1850); Bray Hammond, "Free Banks and Corporations: The New York Free Banking Act of 1838," *Journal of Political Economy,* XLIV (1936).

3. Bray Hammond, *Banks and Politics in America: From the Revolution to the Civil War* (Princeton, 1967), chap. 6, especially on Aaron Burr.

4. George Dangerfield, *The Awakening of American Nationalism, 1815–1828* (New York, 1965).

tified, and their union cemented by new and indissoluble ties."[5] So un-Jeffersonian a scope for the state again underscores how much restrictive regulation, not sponsorship for the general welfare, was the gist of his revolutionary attack on government. There was one cavil, however. Jefferson and Gallatin agreed that a national program of internal improvements, on the then-extraordinary scale of $20,000,000 over ten years, would require a constitutional amendment.[6] But their enthusiasm for the program, and their conviction that the states and the Congress would find it irresistible and that the voters would approve, led them to treat the need for an amendment as a technicality.

Fuller analysis of the story than given here would reveal general auguries of the sponsoring state that was to come, and not exclusively for internal improvements. It is clear even before Clay and the "American System" that where the need seemed compelling for the state to help move the nation toward great horizons, there was little talk either of the threat of big government or warnings inspired by the faith in the self-sufficient individual scornful of state action. Government funding was to be construed as *increasing* the opportunities for self-sufficiency by providing access to land, to markets, to schooling. Across the years one thinks not only of the "canal era" that was just beginning under Jefferson[7] but of other great, later projects like the transcontinental railroads, the Panama Canal, Herbert Hoover's tireless labors for Boulder Dam and flood control generally, and, more recently, the immensely expensive NASA space ventures.

But there are also in the Jefferson-Gallatin proposals signs of how even the most generous and farsighted state beneficence could stir controversy. The perception of government sponsorship would always depend on the beholder. That already became apparent when the Jefferson-Gallatin plans had to be tailored to local interest groups. These included Gallatin's former congressional district in Pennsylvania, which succeeded in getting itself located on the proposed national turnpike from the Cumberland to the Ohio rivers. Jefferson was "horrified"—the word is Dumas Malone's—that towns near the proposed route wanted a survey that would benefit them despite increasing the costs and twisting the route from his rationalist intention that it follow the most direct line.[8]

Jefferson's version of the great state, although easily approaching the

5. Malone, *Jefferson the President: Second Term*, 554–55.

6. *Ibid.*, chap. 30.

7. Carter Goodrich, *Government Promotion of American Canals and Railroads, 1800–1890* (New York, 1960).

8. Malone, *Jefferson the President: Second Term*, 557.

ambition of Hamilton's neglected Report on Manufactures, came to little after Gallatin's elaborate version, minus support for the arts and education, went to Congress. The plan contemplated spending a national revenue surplus once the national debt was retired, but the pressing foreign-trade crisis after the Embargo Act, of 1807, and defense needs precluded using even the existing treasury surplus for the program. A start was made at the time on surveying the route and on securing the approval of the beneficiary states and localities for the entry within their boundaries of the nationally funded project. The more fecund season of the Cumberland Road, as the first section of the project was called, lay beyond Jefferson's tenure.[9] Both auguries of state sponsorship in 1805 to 1808 were fulfilled, however. So popular a government project eventually went forward under Monroe and Quincy Adams, with the state thus handsomely underwriting the opening of the West. But controversy continued about whom the program favored in the award of routes and contracts.

In time, the argument against special interests heard in the 1790s by those opposing the chartering of Hamilton's bank was extended to the whole system of special charters, federal as well as those from lower governments. Gradually, between 1790 and about 1830, the record was construed to show that incorporation by legislative action and government aid generally had favored the rich and well connected. The special charters to banks and other businesses had frozen out the common man, who could not afford or understand the complicated process. More than that, obtaining charters from the state involved secret deals and bribes hostile to democratic ideals of majority rule and equal rights.[10] And special charters seemed to limit enterprising competitors like Mr. Gibbons, who wanted to get into the ferryboat business across New York harbor but found his energy frustrated by the exclusive rights previously awarded to Mr. Ogden.[11] The incorporation system, however intended in the 1780s to be liberating and enriching for all citizens, was to become a touchstone of detestable social advantage by state connivance against equal rights for all.

Emancipating the White Man

The fuel that fired the democratic struggle against state-granted privilege was discerned by Tocqueville during his visit to America in 1830 to 1831. For this young European aristocrat, America was a new society

9. *Ibid.*, 559.
10. Schlesinger, *The Age of Jackson,* chap. 26.
11. Charles Fairman, *American Constitutional Decisions* (New York, 1948), 173–86.

with startling "equality of conditions," produced by a "passion for equality." With that phrase Tocqueville meant to express a force far greater than the familiar reasoned or philosophic case for equality in various revolutionary manifestos. His words suggest a psychological power so gripping, so galvinizing that once set loose it knew no bounds. This restless passion for equality ultimately derived from the age-old dreams of justice that had been given immense momentum as worldly goals by the French Revolution. From the outset, however, that demand had been entwined with intense feelings of envy and revenge against the already powerful set off from or above their fellowmen. The passion for equality was thus morally ambiguous. Enemies of the French Revolution could oppose it for its destructive hate-filled envy, and liberals could see in it only the potential for achieving a long-frustrated respect for human beings against wolfish aristocrats. The passion could be attached to countless objectives that reassured those without power that the search for a better life for all would see to it that no one would be higher placed or more favored than anyone else. As Tocqueville viewed it, the wide-swinging zeal for equality was affecting not merely law and constitutions but all of Western culture, the arts, religion, family life, military organization, and so on, as well as politics.[12] In America, it was producing what we now call the democratic way of life.

As Tocqueville construed the half-century since 1789, promising common citizens a noble liberty that allowed them to come forth and show their worth led, inevitably, to unequal success and power. Those beguiled by the dream that liberty would bring heaven on earth might well be disappointed with their unequal or meager share of reward. The enfranchised populace might create a "tyranny of the majority," using the state in the name of equality to restrict or punish, or putting social pressure on, those who had done better with their opportunities. For Tocqueville, the great task of modern politics after the American and French revolutions was to try to bring the two powerful forces, liberty and equality, into balance and thus minimize the tendencies in democracy to envy and "level" the successful and to esteem only those easy standards of taste and behavior with which most citizens could feel comfortable.

Increasingly flattered in the 1830s by political leaders who sensed the voting appeal of equal rights, the common Americans had already been encouraged in their hopes in revolutionary days by diminishing restrictions on small farmers like the quitrent, the widened access to land, the spreading use of the ballot, and the elimination of what remained of primogeniture.[13] By about 1830, when Tocqueville's visit took place, the

12. Alexis de Tocqueville, *Democracy in America* (2 vols.; New York, 1946).
13. Clarence L. Ver Steeg, "The American Revolution Considered as an Economic Movement," *Huntington Library Quarterly,* XX (1957).

popular enthusiasm for equality had broadened and, ironically, had over-whelmed the old Jeffersonian political leaders who had prepared the way for republican ideals. Although attacking aristocracy and privilege in the name of the people ever since the days of Hamilton, they had been very chary about aroused popular majorities allied with leaders too eager to cater to popular enthusiasms like equal rights. By 1830, in contrast, the young Ohio politician Salmon Chase complained privately to Tocqueville how no leader of that day would any longer dare to oppose the folk or seem to doubt popular wisdom.[14]

By 1840 and the capitulation of the Whig Party to democratic trappings and rhetoric, Tocqueville's sense of democracy as destiny seemed confirmed. To the degree that older property and religious qualifications for voting or holding office had ever been serious practical obstacles, state by state they had been eliminated.[15] The congressional caucus system for presidential nominations had given way to the more open, or at least more visible, party conventions of popular politicians. The tone of elections had been changed into a heady populism lauding "Old Hickory" Jackson and "Old Kinderhook" Van Buren, both Democrats, as well as Harrison and Tyler, the Whig candidates in 1840, proclaiming them "Tippecanoe and Tyler Too." Many more offices were now subject to election rather than appointment, and polling places were more accessible.[16] Neither the type nor the rate of turnover of political appointees had altered appreciably since Jefferson's time, but the open championing by Jackson of "to the victor belong the spoils" as a democratic ideal helped strengthen the appetites for government jobs and favors. Such appetites, in turn, supplied the fodder of favors dispensable by full-time politicians who ran the new populistic parties and kept their ears tuned to the people's voice and needs. Fear of being out of touch with popular wishes also made administration more susceptible to political pressure from the people's representatives. Increasing literacy and the expansion of newspapers and popular literature were combining to provide a public with readier susceptibility to democratic ideology, political arousal, and campaign hoopla. And in the prospects for literacy, the power of the nascent system of free public elementary schools in the 1830s was at once sensed by democrats, as well as by the opponents of mass equality. Egalitarians thought of indoctrinating the young

14. Pierson, *Tocqueville and Beaumont in America,* 557–58.
15. Williamson, *American Suffrage,* chaps. 10–11.
16. M. Ostrogorski, *Democracy and the Organization of Political Parties* (2 vols.; New York, 1902), II, chaps. 1–2; Michael F. Holt, "The Democratic Party," in *History of U.S. Political Parties,* ed. Arthur Schlesinger, Jr. (New York, 1973); Richard P. McCormick, *The Second American Party System* (Chapel Hill, 1966).

with the democratic creeds of opportunity and of rising to the top. Moral and political conservatives hoped that mass education would teach the impossibility of reducing the limits that God or nature had placed on individual ambition.[17]

The Open Door at Home

Given the diverse and complex motives and machinations behind the march of democracy, the passion for equality created large and difficult roles for the state. In the 1830s, the growing resentment of the old system of state sponsorship through special charters as an obstacle to equal chances and fair dealing came to a head in both federal and state politics. We can now discern that economic development in the 1830s under distant federal power was largely out of keeping with the still small local and regional enterprises that dominated an intensely competitive capitalism.[18] Washington power was too far from the scene and had too many interests to consider. Corruption and favoritism put aside, it was very difficult, for example, to tune one centralized national bank to the great diversity of local needs in a vast and decentralized society. It was also more costly and unpredictable to influence Washington than county or state governments. In national programs, Washington designs, as the Gallatin proposals had already disclosed, inevitably bypassed some local interests while bringing recognition and reward to others. And whatever conditions or standards, like the layout of roads, were set for participating in federal largesse could be irritating to those left out. After 1780, five decades of state and federal charters and investment produced large congeries of such resentments against the complication and favor-playing charged to the system. Andrew Jackson, for example, shared the heavy prejudice of Tennesseeans against most banks but especially the second national bank that had been rechartered in 1816 with large powers over investment and interest rates. He was a mercurial man subject to fits and starts about policy and easily lapsing into high dudgeon and moralism when crossed.[19] Among his persistent prejudices was to favor the states over federal power and narrow over broad readings of the Constitution. On his principles, the Second Bank of the United States was built on perilous terrain, but that "principle" was tempered by Jackson's shrewd readings of popular sentiment and priorities for political

17. Michael Katz, *The Irony of Early American School Reform* (Cambridge, Mass, 1968).

18. Thomas C. Cochran and William Miller, *The Age of Enterprise: A Social History of Industrial America* (New York, 1961).

19. James C. Curtis, *Andrew Jackson and the Search for Vindication* (Boston, 1976).

action. For four years as president he temporized about the suspect bank while he tried the ground of federal retrenchment on other fronts.[20]

In 1830, Jackson vetoed national funding for the Maysville road in Kentucky because the road was to be built entirely within the state, was no better than an adjunct to the interstate, national road, and would have enhanced the prestige of his political opponent Henry Clay, whose hometown was to be the terminus of the Maysville project. Despite hostility to federally sponsored intrastate improvements, he continued to support the *mainline* of the national road.[21] Still, the Maysville veto was a signal that the decades of federal underwriting might not continue. Jackson was more forthcoming about deferring to the states when, against the existing grain of federal control of Indian policy, he gave way to Georgia's demands that it determine the fate of the Indians within its borders. With the end of federal protection, the Georgia Cherokees, who had much assimiliated to white culture, did come under the Georgia laws, and lost their lands to the many Georgians who wanted Indians of any stamp out of the way and who regarded the federal control over the Indians as an infringement of local liberty to do what was needed to speed white settlement and development.[22] Another threat to equal opportunity and majority rule was more obvious in the agitation among Jacksonian partisans to transfer the national public lands and to distribute federal surplus revenue to the states, where local promoters would have more say in their disposition than possible in far-off Washington.[23]

In all of these complex matters of turnpikes, Indian policy, public lands, and so on, any diminishing of federal roles was to mean not the triumph of laissez-faire but, often, the transfer of sponsorship or supervisory power to the states. That waning and waxing would also reverse the emphasis of the Supreme Court under Chief Justice Marshall. Before 1830, on several major matters over which federal and state purviews had clashed, the Marshall Court had favored federal initiative. The gist of the controversial decisions under its old federalist leader was that national power should be adequate for national purposes and that Washington acting to establish the second national bank or national Indian policy could preempt the powers of the states on such matters.[24] But Jackson showed himself ready to reverse the Marshall import and federal authority generally when it became apparent to him that both

20. Thomas P. Govan, *Nicholas Biddle: Nationalist and Public Banker* (Chicago, 1959), 115–21.

21. Philip D. Jordan, *The National Road* (Indianapolis, 1948).

22. Ronald N. Satz, *American Indian Policy in the Jacksonian Era* (Lincoln, Nebr., 1974).

23. Hibbard, *History of Public Land Policies*, chaps. 9–10.

24. George Dangerfield, *The Era of Good Feelings* (New York, 1952), 162–74.

were out of temper with the centripetal energies and nearby horizons of the American majority.

That national state sponsorship was biased against equal opportunity was eventually most symbolized for Jackson by the Second Bank of the United States. This powerful institution had come under early attack for bringing on the panic of 1819, *i.e.*, at the same time as the rising tide against restrictive incorporation, banking, and bankruptcy laws in the states. The bank was also recurrently attacked for being too powerful politically. Its directors and its allies among leading politicians like Daniel Webster, to whom the bank gave loans, seemed "privileged" by state connivance.[25] And the alleged aristocratic tone of the powerful eastern and big-city institution at Philadelphia, along with the imperious tendencies of Nicholas Biddle, its head, seemingly corrupted American moral fiber. Such institutions backed by government had taken the republic too far from the Edenic simplicity and severely contained government intended by the Founding Fathers. With America's fiftieth anniversary in 1826 had come calls for a general restoration of threatened republican ideals, so the aristocratic bank proved to be a ready-made victim of politicized nostalgia.[26]

Rivalries between New York and Philadelphia bankers and among banks of issue, deposit, or loan across the nation lurked behind the simplistic ideological assault on Biddle and the Second Bank for their "aristocratic" and corrupting controls over American life and enterprise.[27] Had Jackson not been dared to veto the recharter in the election year of 1832, he and Biddle might well have continued their previous four years of cool civility and restraint despite Jackson's occasional mutterings about banks generally and Biddle's bank in particular. The challenge by Biddle's Whig allies in Congress to try for recharter in 1832 provoked Jackson to focus his prejudices and impulses about banks, the people, and federal power. He vetoed the recharter and campaigned principally on the issue of threats to democracy. His election victory in 1832 reinforced the sense of the appeal of equal rights and fulsome majority rule that had been gathering strength for many years and to which the president had expeditiously attached himself. The bank was called a monster whose noxious power over the plain citizen, the states, and free and equal competition was underwritten by the federal government. It had chartered only that bank, had partly funded it, and had named one-fifth of the directors.[28] A bank that had, indeed, restrained the wilder busi-

25. John McFaul, *The Politics of Jacksonian Finance* (Ithaca, N.Y., 1972).
26. George Forgie, *Patricide in the House Divided* (New York, 1979), 49–53.
27. Hammond, *Banks and Politics in America*, 382–429.
28. McFaul, *Politics of Jacksonian Finance*.

nessmen and speculators with its large influence over the national money supply and interest rates was easily portrayed as being dictatorial and privileged and thus much like those unpopular banks and corporations in the states that had also obtained special charters.[29]

This season of the seething passion for equality also brought feelings of unfair restraint against laws that made bankruptcy very difficult, apprenticeship too restrictive, or imprisonment for debt too damning.[30] All such impediments, whether in federal or state legislation, implied to partisans of equal opportunity that the great American promise of a fair run to freedom, wealth, and success had been corrupted by state favoritism to the wealthy and powerful. It should be emphasized that these complaints were not against state sponsorship per se but against awards that seemed to violate equal chances for government largesse. Easy entry into the game seemed closed by government connivance in special charters, and running the race was unfairly affected by government giving its business to its favorites, like using Biddle's bank for the deposit of federal funds.

The widest possible and equal entry into the running and the fairest possible race were ideals already implicit in Jeffersonian freedom. They became more expansive after 1830, with their national appeal used as much by Whigs as by the Jackson followers. In fact, both parties created "Jacksonian democracy."[31] They vied with each other to prove themselves better friends of the common man, allied with his growing zest for an equal chance in the marketplace and also deferred to America's small-scale, high risk, and let-'er-rip competitive economy. In that setting, both antimonopoly sentiment and opposition to government favoritism were politically irresistible.

Politics and Equal Rights

Whether the decisions about economic policy were morally responsible or economically sound took second place to the demands of the new party politics. Given the increased potential for politicizing issues that were inherent in increasingly populistic parties, dispassionate public discussion of complex issues like currency, credit, and economic expansion

29. Hammond, "Free Banks and Corporations."

30. James Willard Hurst, *Law and the Conditions of Freedom in the Nineteenth Century United States* (Madison, Wis., 1956), chap. 1, especially on bankruptcy laws. On imprisonment for debt, see Alice Felt Tyler, *Freedom's Ferment* (Minneapolis, 1944), 283–85. On apprenticeship, see Paul H. Douglas, *American Apprenticeship and Industrial Education* (New York, 1921), and W. J. Rorabaugh, *The Craft Apprentice* (New York, 1986).

31. Lee Benson, *The Concept of Jacksonian Democracy* (Princeton, 1961).

was not in style. Nor were the finer arguments of Adam Smith and other economists. Pamphleteers like William Gouge and William Leggett were bent on vindicating Jackson and vilifying Biddle. And the Whigs responded in kind with voices like Hezekiah Niles of *Niles Weekly Register*.[32] Whatever the reasoned cases for and against the bank, not much of either will be found in such spokesmen for ideology. But it was the ideology of equal rights, not sound economic analysis, that made state policy and stirred party politics.

Jackson's veto message about rechartering the bank in 1832 was the most notable public statement of the time about allying government with equal rights.[33] Jackson contended that to achieve wealth and other distinctions was every American's birthright, but rewards should be based only on "natural and just" advantages. Disparities of wealth, like the effects of education and of innate talent, were no concern of government. Even more, equal results in the race to achievement, in Jackson's words, could "not be produced by human institutions." The state should aim instead for equal protection of the laws and "as heaven does it rains, shower its favors alike on the high, and the low, the rich and the poor." The ambiguous implication here was one with great portent for intervention, *i.e.*, that government action *is* legitimate if it "rains" evenly. Jackson's main emphasis about what democratic government should *not* do seems clear in his deprecations against the state making the rich richer and "the potent more powerful" and against "any prostitution of our government to the advancement of the few at the expense of the many." Like his reticence to amplify about the rains that should fall equally, he did not expand about the justice of advancing the many at the expense of the few, or about the state's making the poorer majority richer or the less powerful more powerful. Jackson, like Jefferson, assumed that left to themselves without "artificial" or unfair barriers at the starting line, the runners in the race would gain rewards proportionate to their natural talents and "just advantages." From such perspectives, full of unexplored complexities, he inveighed against "monopolies and exclusive privileges" from the state.[34]

Five years after the famous veto message on the bank, in 1837, Chief Justice Taney embellished the Jacksonian doctrines with his opinion in the Charles River Bridge case. According to Taney, despite the "sanctity of contracts," the government should not grant charters that restricted

32. On Gouge, Leggett, and other economic writers of the Jackson era, see Dorfman, *Economic Mind in American Civilization*, II, 608–61.

33. Henry Steele Commager, ed., *Documents of American History* (New York, 1949), 270–74.

34. Robert V. Remini, *Andrew Jackson and the Bank War* (New York, 1967).

a competition from which the public might benefit. Massachusetts' granting one company the right to collect bridge tolls, even if a contract, could not be construed as an exclusive privilege if other firms were prepared to provide similar wider, better, or cheaper services.[35] This was another blow, perhaps more potent than the Jackson veto, at special charters. Together with the sweeping success in the states of replacing the old system with incorporation by routine administrative rather than legislative action, government was moving to respect the equal right to compete by ending collusion between "special interests" and the state. Often, however, the new general incorporation laws were so hedged about with restrictions expressing antimonopoly fears that those seeking incorporation continued to look for some alternative authority from the state. How much either mode contributed to realizing the ideal of equal opportunity may matter less than the more rapid growth of corporations before 1860, albeit in what remained an economy of small family businesses and partnerships.[36]

From the point of view of laissez-faire ideals, general incorporation was intended to decrease the state's role in settling in advance who would be permitted to try his luck in the marketplace. If speculative and sleazy along with well-conceived and well-run enterprises were stimulated by general incorporation laws, the market, the game, not the state at the starting line, was to sort out the competent and cautious from the less able and the immoral businessman. This reiterated Jefferson's act of faith that the broadest possible freedom would not invite intolerable abuses or disasters like panics against which even ostensibly laissez-faire government might have to intervene. The crash of 1837 that *did* follow the death of the restraints that Biddle's bank had imposed on wildcat currency and credit was a harbinger of what reckless deregulation or government-waning on other policies might have in store for the economy in future generations.[37]

Politically and morally, however, federal waning from certain modes of sponsorship did have positive worth. Under expanded equal rights, the democratic state was not to assume virtue or vice or competence in any citizen free to take advantage of general incorporation. Similarly, those facing financial ruin might now find a second chance through easier bankruptcy, and young men could learn a craft without being beholden to establishments controlling apprenticeship. The decision about who was or was not up to participating in a more open American game would not be made by the state, but the "weaker" players would

35. Carl Brent Swisher, *Robert B. Taney* (New York, 1935), 368–74.

36. Peter Temin, *The Jacksonian Economy* (New York, 1969).

37. James R. Sharp, *The Jacksonians Versus the Banks: Politics in the States After the Panic of 1837* (New York, 1970).

be eliminated by running against the stronger, more able, more clever. Suppliers and consumers would have to decide with whom to deal and whom to trust. Ideally, the state vouched for no one. Whatever large private powers and national wealth this broader freedom led to in commerce, manufacturing, and banking before the Civil War have to be set off against the increased risks of the freer market and the high numbers and rate of business failures.[38] The harshness then, however, was less in hopeless struggles against giants than in the hard fights among what were overwhelmingly small enterprises.[39] That victories even in thousands of petty contests might come from un-Christian or illegal practices was also "denied" by moral and religious writers who poured out popular tracts and tales assuring the nation that triumphs in the American race went only to "character" and the godly and that only the corrupt or impious inevitably failed.[40]

Democratic Pileup

The fuller, more accurate view of government sponsorship after 1840 does not cancel all federal underwriting. Instead, we have another instance of government waning in some respects while it waxed in other directions. The federal government did propose to leave banking and intrastate improvements to the states and private interests. But for those economic interests whose scope or tasks were already interstate or intrinsically international or could make a case for federal help, the federal government waxed after 1830, even while it waned on banks, local roads, and, after 1833, toward lower tariffs. Only the partial view suggests a national triumph of laissez-faire in the sense of general Washington restraint. For the next generation, federal power waxed in providing subsidies and bounties for steamship companies, telegraph lines, and cod fisheries. New strains of seed were provided free to farmers. Steamboat safety rules were passed. Land surveys and maps of new territories and older areas were authorized. Army engineers were used to survey railroad routes. Imported iron for rails received a rebate. The national turnpike went on into the Midwest. Even local roads were still built with federal funds on frontiers where there were only territorial governments and too few risk-takers among private developers. Despite

38. Cochran and Miller, *The Age of Enterprise*, 76, on the rise of large private banks; G. H. Evans, Jr., *Business Incorporations in the United States, 1800–1943* (New York, 1948).

39. Edwin M. Dodd, *American Business Corporations Until 1860* (Cambridge, Mass., 1954).

40. Edward D. Branch, *The Sentimental Years* (New York, 1934), 323.

the implications of Jackson's Maysville road veto, there were still federal pork-barrel items within the states for improving rivers and harbors and constructing lighthouses.[41]

By the 1850s, with California acquired, the fever for a rail link to the West Coast grew intense and contributed to the fires of manifest destiny. By then the railroad entrepreneurs claimed sufficient competence to solve the technical problems of crossing the continent, but they alleged that the great costs of the road could not be met by private American means, even if supplemented by private foreign investment. This pressing national need found a responsive national state, and soon there began the largest state subventions to date, the mammoth land grants of hundreds of millions of acres to the railroad land-sales companies to enable them to raise capital for the roads.[42]

With a new, immense inventory of public lands under federal control after the Mexican War, Washington did not retrench but diversified and enlarged other land-disposal activities. If young men went west it was not only because they were hardy pioneer individualists but also because Washington underwrote the effort that eventually produced huge reclamation and irrigation programs, cheap and/or royalty-free grazing rights on millions of acres of public lands, crop price supports, and expert advice about farming and ranching. By 1862, there were a new system of land grants for schools and universities and increasingly liberal terms for those in the West who were land hungry. This generous federal sponsorship culminated in the much-acclaimed, if sparsely used, free Homestead Act of 1862.[43] That law, moreover, was merely one of a notable series of subsequent federal acts covering the disposal of desert, arid, and other types of acreage than the prairie lands suitable for family farms.[44] Thus, despite the Jacksonian ideology against government favors generally and federal sponsorship particularly, as the economy and "needs" grew, and when demands were national, the national state remained open to use and relentlessly expanded its activities.

Within the states the same types of local and freewheeling entrepreneurs who seemed to be decrying all state intervention in attacking the tyranny of federal support for a Biddle were increasingly active in calling on their own state, county, and town governments to increase their

41. Bruchey, *Roots of American Economic Growth*, 123. A closer view of the economy of the time is in Robert L. Heilbroner and Aaron Singer, *The Economic Transformation of America* (New York, 1977).

42. Goodrich, *Government Promotion of American Canals*, chap. 5.

43. Fred A. Shannon, "The Homestead Act and the Labor Surplus," *American Historical Review*, XLI (1936).

44. Hibbard, *History of Public Land Policies*, chaps. 19–20.

roles as sponsors and developers.[45] By using land grants, tax exemptions, bounties, and fairs, the states tried, as they still do, to stimulate enterprise and also create a better atmosphere for everyman to start a business. Within the states, capital was often too meager or too timid to plunge into meeting public needs like transport into and out of underdeveloped areas. Such entrepreneurial reluctance to take risks or low profits brought the greatest of the involvements of the individual states in enterprise. Like federal aid for the capital-shy transcontinental railroad companies, state aid in so-called quasi-public corporations, *i.e.,* joint endeavors of public funds and private effort, reached huge proportions, for the time, of hundreds of millions of dollars.[46] The state governments of the 1840s and 1850s thus played an indispensable role in what has rightly been called the transportation revolution and set the way for federal support for lines that crossed state boundaries.[47] Unlike in Europe, where the need to find markets for finished goods pushed the development of rail lines, governments in America helped open a vast continental market with roads, canals, and eventually railroads. Commerce and industry then outdid themselves to create goods and services to flow into those markets. Perhaps three-quarters of state capital funding between 1830 and 1870 went into transportation. But there is also a sizable record of individual state aid to manufacturing, banking, and insurance companies.[48]

Overall, therefore, when state and federal activities are considered together, the tide of government support already observable in the colonial and early national periods grew after Jackson, whatever the general tenets of the free-enterprise ideology about state intervention. The concentration here has been on the economy, but education and public health and safety, to mention common large concerns, were other growing fields for state and local action. The common school, public orphanages and hospitals, public police and fire fighters (when volunteers were no longer adequate), safer harbors and better docks, paved streets and roads, cleaner city water, minimal public garbage disposal, the early building codes and zoning—all such liberating and securing of the com-

45. On the political economy of individual states, see Oscar and Mary Handlin, *Commonwealth* (New York, 1947), on Massachusetts; Louis Hartz, *Economic Policy and Democratic Thought* (Cambridge, Mass., 1948), on Pennsylvania; Milton S. Heath, *Constructive Liberalism: The Role of the State in Economic Development in Georgia to the 1860s* (Cambridge, Mass., 1954); James N. Primm, *Economic Policy in the Development of a Western State: Missouri, 1820–1860* (Cambridge, Mass., 1954).

46. Bruchey, *Roots of American Economic Growth,* 128–33.

47. George Rogers Taylor, *The Transportation Revolution, 1815–1860* (New York, 1951).

48. Bruchey, *Roots of American Economic Growth.*

mon life, not only dramatic railroad building and homestead laws, put American governments on the alert, on the move, and piling up in their concerns and intervention.[49] Immigration control, a minor, relatively uncontroversial issue before the 1880s, shows the small steps, variety, constancy, and quietness of "pileup" as well as its scope beyond Washington. Federally, the import of foreign slaves had been prohibited in 1808. In the 1860s, American employers were authorized to recruit and pay the way for semibound workers from overseas. Most states continued to entice immigrants after the federal program was cut off in 1868, but as usual with intervention once begun, there remained federal requirements for an official count of new arrivals and for maintaining basic decencies on the immigrant ships.[50]

This was only the federal accretion. In the nineteenth century the states were also free to deal with immigrant restriction. The northeastern states, to which most immigrants sailed, tried restriction with boards of commissioners, largely unpaid gentry from local charities overtaxed by the immigrant flow. Even before the well-known, but far from initiatory, national restrictions of the 1880s (against the Chinese and contract laborers), there was a depot in New York City, mandatory for all arrivees, a required fee from shipowners to create a welfare fund for destitute immigrants, and a rule for a bond for any immigrant likely to require long-term charity.[51] The most well-known state efforts, California's dealings with the unpopular Chinese, date from about 1850, a generation before the rise of the notorious Chinese-baiter Denis Kearney.[52] By 1891, almost fifty years of such pileup brought about the federal takeover of immigration control.

Much of this quiet side of the expansion of state with society is obscured by histories that concentrate on the larger, national issues like the Pacific railroads or Homestead Act or, to invoke Robert Higgs's theme, on crisis in the growth of Leviathan.[53] State growth, in fact, not

49. On early public services, see Sam Bass Warner, *The Urban Wilderness: A History of the American City* (New York, 1972); Gerald Grob, *Mental Institutions in America* (New York, 1973); Barbara Rosenkrantz, *Public Health and the State* (Cambridge, Mass., 1972); James F. Richardson, *The New York Police: Colonial Times to 1901* (New York, 1970); Selwyn K. Troen, *The Public and the Schools: Shaping the St. Louis School System, 1838–1920* (Columbia, Mo., 1975); W. David Lewis, *From Newgate to Dannemora* (Ithaca, N.Y., 1965).

50. Charlotte Erickson, *American Industry and the European Immigrant, 1860–1885* (Cambridge, Mass., 1957).

51. Richard H. Leach, "The Impact of Immigration upon New York, 1840–1860," *New York History*, XXXI (1950).

52. Rodman Paul, "The Origin of the Chinese Issue in California," *Mississippi Valley Historical Review*, XXV (1938).

53. Robert W. Higgs, *Crisis and Leviathan* (New York, 1987).

only is in sudden, large, dramatic crises like war and depression, but is constant, with fluctuation. The local concerns of Americans about clean water, police, fire, and schools can escape the attention of the historian focused on Washington. Citizens in towns, counties, and states sought the state every day for problems like those just mentioned. The issues may seem small or purely local and the record, one action after another, too elusive, scattered as it is among the dull daily logs of thousands of minor legislatures and bureaucracies. To dip into such local and state lists of government agencies, functions and job rolls, the codes of laws, and the details of government appropriations after 1830 should shock anyone nostalgically invoking this time as a heroic age of ever-slack government deferential to self-sufficient individuals. Nor did this pileup of American governments come principally because of the influence of disaffected marginal groups, alien philosophies, radical protests, or "bleeding hearts." Such images as well as various conspiracy theories describe any growth of the state as due to anyone other than the principal source, those good and solid citizens whom Woodrow Wilson later lionized as the "men on the make." These were conventional folk of varying means as eager for a favor or a repair of fortunes from government as they were quick to denounce state favors for others, especially competitors. From a long, mounting, oscillating play between an immense array of interests seeking government and free-enterprise ideals that shamed it, *ad hoc,* slowly, jerkily emerged our present network of interests that so inhibits tuning or trimming the state created to serve them.

Hiding the State

Any laissez-faire ideal of vetted government after 1840 redistributed but did not lessen national or state activity. But the shame in state-seeking against the proud boasts for American individualism seems to have driven the state *as an idea* underground. What the psychiatrists call "denial" helped create a covert state by the mid-nineteenth century. Shame, secrecy, tricks, and little deals in seeking the state marked a gray market in government services for Americans of every class, even while the approved public ideology decried all government intervention. Commenting on federal expenditure in 1840, writers could already denounce government "extravagance and prodigality," but denunciatory citizens failed to mention any exception in financing their own interests. So veteran a player of the political game as James Buchanan of Pennsylvania ingenuously complained in 1852, "The host of contractors, stockjobbers, and lobby members who haunt the halls of Congress, all desirous to dip their arm into the public treasury, are sufficient to alarm every friend of his country."[54]

54. Patrick G. Goode, *A Statement of the Expenditures of Government, Exhibiting*

From another point of view, even the more stringent philosophic case against the state, often derived too quickly from Adam Smith, never adequately mentioned his contingencies like monopoly power or building the "infrastructure." Even more, general arguments against intervention were insufficiently realistic about the politics and psychology of intervention, *i.e.,* what defeats for themselves democratic citizens would be willing to accept in the behavior of the economy, whatever their ideal of self-sufficiency in freedom. Individual liberty as an *abstract* goal, however formulated, turned out in practice to be so conditioned by the liberty and interests of others and its effects so subject to expedient political intervention that the ideal gave less practical guidance than its more ardent devotees anticipated. The Smithian "model" itself, with its projected constant shifting of buyers and sellers and laborers, always implied imperfect liberty at any one time to buy and sell and to profit or to be employed as one liked. The promise of equilibrium *eventually* and thus "pay-off" from the laissez-faire system requires going through the entire business cycle, with self-responsibility and risk-taking in bad times as well as good, however painful the former.

Laissez-faire individualism and democracy have been commonly construed as natural, even inevitable, allies. In practice, they often conflicted. After every major economic crisis in 1819, 1837, 1857, 1873, and 1893, citizens refused to suffer silently through downturns until supply and demand were adjusted and prosperity returned. How a self-correcting system was supposed to operate had been worked out by one of Smith's successors, J. B. Say.[55] The model, sometimes described as "the law of markets," promised equilibrium without the distorting of "natural forces" by state intervention. In reality, at every level of government, wounded Americans facing crisis refused to go through the cycle and sought the state for relief in stay laws, changes in credit and currency and land sale laws, and so on. But between the major crises there were those less dramatic and less noticed hosts of smaller actions designed to enhance opportunity or bale out some group or other that had failed to make it. That it did not pay to advertise a successful approach to the state for fear of arousing opposition or rival supplicants helped strengthen the tendency to keep governmental machinations hidden. That most citizens' and newspapers' horizons were low also kept day-by-day favor-granting and rule-making by the distant state out of public view.

the *Prodigality and Extravagance of the Present Administration* (Washington, D.C., 1840); James Buchanan to Franklin Pierce, June 21, 1852, in *The James Buchanan Papers,* ed. Lucy Fisher West (Microfilm ed.; Philadelphia, 1974) Reel 48.

55. Joseph Schumpeter, *History of Economic Analysis* (New York, 1954), 615–25.

Laissez-faire theory had indeed taught that there would always be those who made the wrong assessment of their market interests. Their task was to try again elsewhere, in some other calling or section of the market, until they found the best niche available. The delusion of endless manueverabilty and no limit on the will and ability to redeploy has often been pointed out by critics of the market model, but more important here is how the stoicism required in downturns conflicted with American assumptions about justice and the eagerness of politicians to relieve pain. Democracy, in generosity and fear, also created excuses like "no fault of anyone" or "bad luck." More darkly, failure was blamed on evildoers like Biddle or conspirators who had no place in American democracy and who preyed on "helpless victims." Democratic culture also grew intolerant of the thought that an American should never have a second chance or should be abandoned when he was down on his luck. In such ways democratic justice and politics countered expected market behavior and created a rationale for state intervention and government growth. Of course, the strength of the ideology of self-help and the paucity of public relief still left most bad luck, suffering, and recovery to the individual; but a fuller history of state-based relief at all levels of government, beyond the mentioned familiar stay laws and currency tinkering, will probably show how across the nineteenth century, democracy's door to repair and rescue increasingly opened, and not merely after general economic disasters.[56]

In time and in the logic of the passion for equality, it would not be a great step from asking an equal and free chance to enter the game to arguing that private power accumulated even during a contest that began fairly could become unfair or unscrupulous and hurt innocent citizens. The later plaint, for example, was heard from hard-pressed small farmers against monopoly power in banking, railroads, and farm supplies. The emancipation of white citizens to enter a freer game for small producers did not at first make much of darker prospects, nor did it accompany any significant pressure for state action for those still kept out of the game like black slaves and women. Nevertheless, it was prescient of Tocqueville to catch the potential for limitlessness in the passion for equality. For the forgotten, failing, or faltering American we can foresee the democratic right to be helped *during* the race and to be

56. In addition to the works cited in n. 49 above, see David J. Rothman, *The Discovery of the Asylum: Social Order and Disorder in the New Republic* (Boston, 1971); Harold Schwartz, *Samuel Gridley Howe* (Cambridge, Mass., 1956); Robert H. Bremner, *Children and Youth in America* (2 vols.; Cambridge, Mass., 1970–74); Clifford S. Griffin, *Their Brothers' Keepers: Moral Stewardship in the United States* (New Brunswick, N.J., 1960).

protected from excessive rigors or uneven results with public redress or assistance. These portents implied a far wider role for a democratic state ostensibly committed to universal happiness and justice than the liberal capitalism of Jackson's time granted.

After 1840, need by need, state support was most justified by the claim that it enlarged democratic opportunity for all. Immense land grants to railroad promoters might not seem to square with a Jacksonian sponsorship that was to confer "equal blessings" on all. After all, the promoters profited immensely from the grants while creating some of the greatest scandals, such as Credit Mobilier, in American history. But beyond the sobering fact of the scandals was the ready argument that railroads to the West did expand opportunities for all citizens by easing transport and enlarging settlement and the marketplace. Without state subvention of some sort, building the costly lines would probably have languished. And as we can now see amid other lost illusions in socialist dreams, state control of railroad building promises no greater efficiency or honesty. About 1870, however, the readier American argument than state ownership was that if public lands were granted to one group of investors named Credit Mobilier to help construct the first line to California, that did not preclude grants to others, especially with special incorporation taken from the books. Anyone in the democracy could at least approach the dispensers of pork barrel. Although the words of Jackson in his bank veto message about government restraint did not seem to point in that direction, the politics of obtaining government aid if, as Jackson said, *blessings were kept equal* suggested that any interest group with a request for state help could make its appeal without prejudice. If some groups had already been rewarded, the logic of equal opportunity was to join the line. The race to the public till for sponsorship thus could be made to seem as democratic and open as the private race to riches. The impression of a fair shake for all and the prospect of eventual reward for persistent petitioners made it difficult to construe government as hostile to liberty or democracy. Not every petitioner could win or feel that he took home enough from the legislature to start the race or stay the course. Always, politics and resources being limited, someone was gored. But even the worst wounds seemed treatable. What was not won in railroad grants or start-up capital for an insurance enterprise or in the tariff in one season of the legislature could be sought again the next year, often with previous favors to other petitioners setting a level for successors to match or exceed.

In all of the gathering at the great American trough, selective memory about who had asked and received what from the state, the refrain of "what have you done for me lately," and memories of who had been hurt and who succored always played important roles. The state that supported and sweetened without seeming prejudiced against any citizen making another claim was not the easily discerned enemy of equal rights against whom Jefferson and Jackson had inveighed. The democratized sponsoring state was a "friend of the people" or "understood public needs" or "correctly sensed the public mood." If the state denied and deprived on any one issue there was a democratic right to denounce it and to try to correct its errors. If playing favorites or being too removed from the people were charges against Biddle, for example, or against the federal government after it enacted low-tariff provisions in 1846 that cost iron-workers jobs, the hurt lasted until the next time Washington generosity tended to those wounds and quieted howls.[57] Amid so many smaller-scale enterprises eligible for aid, so supportive a state, one seemingly so democratically sensitive to those left at the gate the last time, was difficult to portray any longer as the captive of the rich and well-born.

The Limits of Community

Of course, the rights and opportunities open to most white men by about 1840 were not yet available to the majority of Americans. Historically, only propertied white males had been fully accredited for the original political and legal community of 1776. Even for white males, however, formal rights were not marks of power or status by 1840. Many studies of mid-nineteenth-century America contest rags-to-riches claims that most white males had significant access to promising jobs or equal chances to rise from the lower ranks to comfort, let alone riches.[58] Still, by 1840, whatever limits money, class, and education placed on them, white males had more legal and political equality than they would have had in Europe. Millions of other Americans, however, remained disadvantaged in political rights, freedom of contract, movement, and employment, social prestige, and other standards of first-class citizenship. Their equal opportunities were frustrated because most white male heirs of the original community of 1776 did not regard blacks, women, Catholics, Asians, Mexicans, Indians, and others as their equals. The future of this diverse and restricted national majority constituted as much an unfinished agenda for the passion for equality as did the economic complaints of poorer white men.

57. C. B. Going, *David Wilmot, Free-Soiler* (New York, 1924), 145–50, on tariff repercussions in Pennsylvania.
58. Lee Soltow, "Economic Inequality in the United States in the Period from 1790 to 1860," *Journal of Economic History,* XXXI (1971); Edward Pessen, *Riches, Class, and Power Before the Civil War* (Lexington, Mass., 1973).

As expressed, however, the ideals of 1776 were written not for white males only but for mankind. At least they came to be seen as universals soon after the American Revolution, and, eventually, those ideals were to be invoked around the globe. In America by 1840, however, most white males were skeptical about extending equal rights beyond their circle. With the original revolutionary contract about political and legal rights for white men given impressive substance in the Jacksonian reforms, the passion for equality came against formidable racial, religious, and sexual prejudices. Nevertheless, the astonishing, peaceful successes of equal rights for white men and the ringing universalism of the doctrine of equality aroused the aspirations of those who still lived as inferiors among the heirs of 1776. Just as the Jacksonian reforms for white men were being rounded off there arose cries for the rights of slaves, women, children, paupers, the insane, the deaf, the blind, and the debtor.[59]

The history of equal rights for these groups seems to validate another Tocqueville insight: the passion for equality tends to universalism as well as to limitlessness. Each success for equal rights whets greater appetites as human beings discover new ways in which they remain unequal and thus seemingly disadvantaged. But because the new vistas for equality by the 1840s ran so against white male opposition, moving toward equal rights for other groups presaged great difficulty. Greater opportunities for white males had come about without singling them out; or rather, expanded horizons through state intervention such as easier rules for bankruptcy had, not surprisingly, most benefited white men. After the 1840s, however, it gradually became clear that state action for generalized economic advantage would be much less provocative than government proposals for dealing with what we now call the social issues of race, gender, creed, and ethnicity. If one intention of the First Amendment was to try to exclude government from acting about the beliefs and mores of citizens, it was well done. The Fathers of 1787 took American diversity as they found it. Any public action about race or religion would be left to the states. But as state actions failed to satisfy the proponents of freedom or equal rights for women and minorities, the issues could come to federal attention. Historically, the greatest bitterness our system has confronted has been over issues that have aroused conscience about "values." Our current divisiveness about affirmative action or abortion was foretold by politics connected with race, Catholicism, Mormonism, women's rights, and other social issues that began to stir in the 1840s. Most telling in that respect were the protests for millions of blacks in slavery. Their future place in the ostensibly dem-

59. Tyler, *Freedom's Ferment*.

ocratic community bitterly divided the nation and ultimately left it incapable of finding a new status for them except through war.

The fight over slavery involved not only national moral ideals but the constitutional rules for managing disputes. The system had early shown itself far more capable of dealing with economic conflicts about tariffs or banking policy than of facing cultural issues such as slavery. That was already so sensitive a question by 1787 that only the most unavoidable or least contentious of its aspects, *e.g.,* how slaves should be counted for congressional apportionment and the ending of the international slave trade, were dealt with. That the Bill of Rights denied federal power over beliefs and opinions left limts on the slavery debate to state and local governments. The growth of what we now call the free market for ideas also greatly restricted Washington efforts to posit common national standards of morality. When pressed eventually to face the moral issue of slavery, the federal system failed, as it did also on issues of equal rights for others whom society did not deem eligible. The federal system based on large, abstract, ambiguous, and clashing ideals of majority rule, individual rights, and states' rights has been intrinsically ill-prepared to intervene when basic beliefs about race, religion, nationality, and gender have been at stake. Reinforced by the constitutional system and traditions of federal continence, by the 1840s the white males of the republic whose grandfathers had created the original community lived confidently with exclusions from the democracy that would be anathema today.

We must recall the sense of paradox of European observers that as democracy in America moved on inexorably for whites, American governments maintained and even strengthened laws to continue slavery in the South and to keep blacks subordinate to whites everywhere. The southern states had legalized slavery, but the northern states had restrictive "black codes." Across the nation, many whites tried to counter the rising tide of abolitionism with its threat of making blacks the competitors and neighbors of whites.[60] If American democracy implied the end of slavery, that would be difficult enough. But the entrance of freed blacks into the American contest on the same terms enjoyed by whites was a prospect that united southerners with other Americans against a common threat, the end of white supremacy. Yet it was believed almost universally outside the South that somehow slavery would have to go. Tocqueville had written, "Slavery . . . cannot survive. By the act of the master or by the will of the slave, it will cease."[61] And Emer-

---

60. Leon F. Litwack, *North of Slavery: The Negro in the Free States, 1790–1860* (Chicago, 1961). Compare with Ira Berlin, *Slaves Without Masters* (New York, 1975), on free blacks in the South.

61. Tocqueville, *Democracy in America,* I, 381. The world of slavery has many por-

son made the point, "The inconsistency of slavery with the principles on which the world is built, guarantees its downfall."[62] Lincoln would later catch the sense of the great American contradiction and the way of the future when he proclaimed in his "house divided" speech in 1858 that America would have to become either all slave or all free. Whatever his deep fears at that time about the imperial ambitions of the slave owners, he believed that slavery was transient and that ultimately freedom would prevail. Even within the South auguries of the end of slavery were apparent in the rising notes of desperation in its defense by voices like George Fitzhugh and Edmund Ruffin.[63] Despite the southern defiance about its "peculiar institution," the growing question elsewhere after 1850 was when and how the end would come. But with the earlier faith in voluntary mass manumission a vanishing option, finding that end increasingly became the task of government. More than any other American ideal, equality beyond the world of white males portended the great state.

How could American governments manage the most deeply divisive problem they had yet faced? The growing heat of the slavery question and a sense that attempts to settle it could bring violence and disunion had led each generation of politicians after 1789 to try to evade the issue or to keep it as apolitical as possible. But after 1850, with growing agitation for and against slavery and deepening sectional truculence about it, it began to seem inescapable that politicians and government at every level could no longer contain the issue.

Ultimately, what made any government move about slavery so difficult was that the future of black Americans was indissolubly linked with the race question.[64] There were great national divisions about slavery, but there was a far clearer national stand on race. White supremacy, whatever its possible variations, seemed unsurrenderable. That stand, even more than slavery, clearly denied the national ideals of equality and freedom. Indeed, the conviction that blacks were racially inferior to whites had been a principal argument for enslaving them. But it also generated doubts about the wisdom of freeing them among racist whites

traits. The most inclusive is Kenneth M. Stampp, *The Peculiar Institution* (New York, 1956).

62. Ralph Waldo Emerson, "The Fugitive Slave Law," in Emerson, *Miscellanies* (Boston, 1878).

63. Harvey Wish, *George Fitzhugh, Propagandist of the Old South* (Baton Rouge, 1943); Avery O. Craven, *Edmund Ruffin, Southerner* (New York, 1932).

64. George M. Frederickson, *The Black Image in the White Mind* (New York, 1971); James A. Rawley. *Race and Politics: "Bleeding Kansas" and the Coming of the Civil War* (Philadelphia, 1969).

hostile to blacks, Jefferson being the great example of such skepticism. The difficulties for all white Americans, not just southerners, were implicit in the crude question, "If you did free them, what would you do with them?" Today, the logic of American equality seems clear: by the universal tenets of 1776 slavery should have ended and blacks allowed to enter American life on the same terms as the whites who had preceded them. But white supremacy, with its conviction about black inferiority, and fear of racial contamination formed the barriers by which the passion for equality was temporarily frustrated and on which all proffered political policies to end slavery peacefully and without disunion broke.[65]

The monistic atmosphere of 1850 about who "belonged" with full rights and ease in the American community is another way of explaining the failure to find a peaceful politics to free the slaves and to accept them as first-class citizens. The slavery dilemma was not an isolated instance of prejudice. The America of slavery was also a society that attacked and killed Mormons and abolitionists, burnt nunneries and abolitionist print shops, expelled and slaughtered Indians, launched anti-Catholic political parties that had startling, if transitory, successes, ignored or scorned the first women's rights movements, and treated Mexicans in Texas as racial inferiors. Even among abolitionists there were only a few like Wendell Phillips, Theodore Weld, and William Lloyd Garrison who explored beyond demands for black freedom to speak of social equality, and even fewer who formulated realistic plans about "what to do with them" after freedom.[66] Lincoln, whom history has often miscast as the nation's highest conscience against slavery, could never decide what to do about race relations once slavery ended. His equivocation during the 1850s about favoring freedom but with "the superior position" left to the white man is clear.[67] This ambivalence was in his soul and not due merely to expediency before the Illinois voters. Even as president, when he met with black leaders in 1862 he made the gloomy remark, "You and we are different races. We have between us a broader difference than exists between almost any other two races. . . . It is better for us both to be separated."[68] By 1863, with the Emancipation Proclamation behind him, Lincoln reflected the views of a gathering majority in the Union that slavery would have to go by war's end.[69] Beyond that,

65. Roy F. Nichols, *The Disruption of American Democracy* (New York, 1948).
66. Frederickson, *Black Image in the White Mind,* 126, 193–97.
67. Hofstadter, *The American Political Tradition,* 112–16.
68. Quoted in David H. Donald, *Lincoln Reconsidered* (New York, 1956), 135–36.
69. David H. Donald, *Charles Sumner and the Rights of Man* (New York, 1970), 147–52, on emancipation petitions to Congress. See also John Stuart Mill's prediction

white America faltered, not only in 1863 but for generations afterwards. It lacked the knowledge, the will, and other psychological strengths, and both the popular and politicians' persisting endorsement to support, as full equality required, a multiracial, equal-rights society. But if white *society* faltered or resisted, how could its government act wisely and well about race relations?

In Every Vista, the State

The implications that government would have to act somehow about slavery became clear after the acquisition of vast new territory from the Mexican War in 1848. Every option about the future of slavery foretold state action—a Union without any slaves or with slavery legitimate everywhere; extending a latitude like 36°30' to the Pacific to separate slave from free soil; national gradual abolition with or without compensation; letting each area of the nation decide for itself about slavery—each of these required national initiative, pervasive federal supervision, and cooperation by all other levels of government. The deeply divisive new Fugitive Slave Law of 1850, requiring all citizens in all areas not to help fugitives or hinder officials seeking or returning fleeing slaves, was a harbinger of the opposition to more extensive attempts dealing with slavery and black rights.[70]

In the next rounds, after 1850, about equal rights, two great moralities dominated schemes for ending slavery: the rights of man implicit in the free-soil doctrine, and America's other democratic commitment to the collective right of the people to decide for themselves what institutions they wanted. In their debates for the U.S. Senate seat from Illinois in 1858, Stephen A. Douglas refused Lincoln's insistence that the original contract of 1776 gave equal rights moral precedence over popular majorities. The difficult corollary for Lincoln was that government by the people had to square with what he was to call "the great proposition" of 1776 about equality. But also, because of that priority for individual rights, he contended against Douglas that a national expression of the will of the people in Congress for free soil in the territories had precedence over a local vote.[71] It is well to recall that the tension

---

about the war ending with abolition in "The Contest in America" (1861), in *Essays on Equality, Law, and Education* (Toronto, 1984).

70. Stanley W. Campbell, *The Slave Catchers: Enforcement of the Fugitive Slave Law, 1850–1860* (Chapel Hill, 1970).

71. Harry V. Jaffa, *Crisis of the House Divided: An Interpretation of the Issues in the Lincoln-Douglas Debates* (Seattle, 1959).

between individual rights and majority wishes, as well as between Washington powers and those of the states and localities, traces back to the original contract of 1776 and the Constitution. Ever since the founding, honorable men had deeply differed about how to reconcile these ideals. Indeed, national supremacy on behalf of equal rights and over local option was not amply established until the Civil Rights and Voting Rights Acts of 1964 and 1965.

Whatever the moral case for and against slavery in the 1850s and whatever the complexities of attitude, law, and constitution in which it was embedded, the answers were in the charge of the political parties. Of the options for restricting slavery, "free soil," which would forbid its extension into the territories, now seems the irresistible moral minimum against slavery. Moderate politicians like Lincoln could adopt it and at least keep the equal rights ideal viable. Yet free-soil proposals were also an option for politicians because the doctrine had useful hidden meanings beyond the restriction of slavery.[72] Those meanings dealt with the national stand for white supremacy as much as against slavery expansion. Free soil meant that when the time for statehood arrived there would be no slaves to free because Washington had banned slavery in the territories. But it also meant that there would be no blacks as competing cheap labor and no blacks as neighbors, as potential jurors, as potential voters. In sum, free soil, for all its rebuff to slavery on behalf of equal rights for blacks, also meant equal rights for white settlers to enjoy an all-white society beyond the existing states where the status of slavery was already decided.

In the 1850s, however, there was that other national policy against slavery that competed with free soil for moral prestige and that promised, falsely as it turned out, to be less divisive. Douglas was convinced that citizens in the remaining territories would never vote to permit slavery (or black neighbors) if they were allowed to exercise their democratic right to make the decision locally. In 1854, he precipitated an inflammatory federal action, the Kansas-Nebraska Act, which stipulated that the unorganized lands in those places would be brought into the Union not under free soil but with the local option to vote slavery up or down.[73]

From the point of view of national power, however, either free soil or popular sovereignty in the territories required Washington's decision to adopt one or the other. The prospects for enhanced government action, moreover, went beyond an initial decision for either policy. If vio-

72. Eric Foner, *Free Soil, Free Labor, Free Men: The Ideology of the Republican Party Before the Civil War* (New York, 1970).

73. Allan Nevins, *Ordeal of the Union* (2 vols.; New York, 1947), II, chap. 3.

lence or dirty dealing about the status of slavery occurred in the territories, as both did hideously, Washington as the governing power would have to contend with the contesting forces, keep order, and find some path to reconciliation. Washington would also have to decide eventually whether any proposed state constitution that dealt with slavery was acceptable. And all these possibilities were subject to hyper-intense party politics.

"Bleeding Kansas" showed what Washington pursuing Douglas' supposedly less divisive, more democratic option of popular sovereignty could produce in violence and political fraud in making Kansas a free or slave state. In 1860, after five years of travail, there was a new state of Kansas, with free soil and also free of blacks by local choice. But contrary to Douglas' promise, the free vote in Kansas left the nation and government officials all the more polarized.[74] For the South by late 1860, the reality of a free Kansas, John Brown's recent raid and appeal for slave revolt, Lincoln's election as a free-soiler, and the seeming sure prospect of a free-soil policy enforced in all remaining federal territories meant more than a stop to *new* slave terrain.[75] The noxious free-soil ideal would not be contained despite Lincoln's post-election promise of a constitutional amendment to respect it in the states where it already existed.[76] Backed by growing free-soil majorities in the Congress and the advent of free-soil appointees to the Supreme Court, free soil in the territories would evolve within a generation into the end of slavery everywhere.[77]

Any hope that this would happen peacefully and with the Union left intact were not fulfilled. Instead, the constitutional system broke over an intransigence about slavery, one of those "ultimates" that it was not designed to manage. War came. If it now seems that the overriding issue was the status of slavery, we also know how much complication and travail lay beyond that.

Freedom and Despotism

The question of slavery as most leaders saw it in the crisis of 1860 to 1861 was both subordinate to and inseparable from the issue of a state's right to secede.[78] Only today are states' rights usually seen as a disguise

74. Rawley, *Race and Politics.*

75. Kenneth M. Stampp, *And the War Came: The North and the Secession Crisis, 1860–61* (Baton Rouge, 1950).

76. David M. Potter, *Lincoln and His Party in the Secession Crisis* (New Haven, 1942), 105–109.

77. Jesse T. Carpenter, *The South as a Conscious Minority, 1789–1861* (New York, 1930).

78. Potter, *Lincoln and His Party in the Secession Crisis.*

for the *status quo* or reaction. The association with slavery, the bloody war, and the reconstruction debacle that followed gave states' rights a taint from which the doctrine has never escaped. Before 1860, however, states' rights had been invoked by the most diverse groups across the nation.[79] It was not yet decisively an ideology *against* liberty and equality. In the 1850s, for example, the struggle in the free states to maintain slave-free commonwealths or personal liberty laws against threats of Supreme Court veto involved as much a state's right as that to sanction slavery.[80] That after 1789 the idea of states' rights had such varied uses testifies to the general problem that the boundaries of federal and state powers had been left cloudy in the Constitution. The largest claim before 1860 against states' rights as a justification for secession was the idea that the Union had been intended to be perpetual.[81] Gradually, that idea took hold along with ideas of what we now call the living Constitution, a plan of government not limited by the mere words or circumstances of 1787 but changing to conform with the times. Along with notions of an organic union, *i.e.*, one with growing *national* ties and *national* communal bonds, "perpetual union" was invoked as the legal-historical response to a state's right to secession.[82] As defenders like Calhoun saw it, however, a state's right to secede was one of the checks against despotism when national politics failed to stop the federal government from enacting obnoxious legislation.

Not only slavery but tariffs, railroads, and much more were at stake in 1860, but these became complicatedly entwined with the future of slavery. The special depth of feeling about a state's right to maintain slavery is what the historian has to emphasize despite Lincoln's post-election efforts to calm the South about slavery where it already existed. Lincoln's election caused a "great fear" across the South.[83] Following the election, southern leaders were torn between the Union and their states and between a national party system built for compromise and local politicians threatening that compromise with Lincoln the free-soiler would be capitulation to despotic centralization. The Washington-based southerners abandoned the capital. They went home to try, mostly successfully, to retain their local power against the fire-eater challenge

79. Schlesinger, "The States Rights Fetish," in Schlesinger, *New Viewpoints in American History.*

80. Thomas D. Morris, *Free Men All: The Personal Liberty Laws of the North, 1780–1861* (Baltimore, 1974).

81. Kenneth M. Stampp, "The Concept of a Perpetual Union," *Journal of American History*, LXV (1978).

82. Paul C. Nagel, *One Nation Indivisible: The Union in American Thought, 1776–1861* (New York, 1964).

83. Steven A. Channing, *Crisis of Fear: Secession in South Carolina* (New York, 1970).

and to keep open as many options as might be available for additional dealing with the truncated Union under Lincoln.[84]

Conducting the national state under a federal system and checks and balances had always depended on the possibility of all issues being negotiable. The complexities of the constitutional system and the requirements for give and take in the trans-sectional two-party system had taught American politicians nimbleness, delay, and accommodation. Had the party system been more ideological or previous assertions of national sovereignty more rigid, the Union might have broken earlier over grave issues like the Alien and Sedition Acts of 1797, embargo, war, and peace during the Napoleonic era, or the tariff in 1832. But after the election of 1860, the southern fire-eaters believed that under the Republican, free-soil party the impending assertion of national sovereignty about slavery would be relentless. The prospect was for increasing antislavery legislation by a national sovereign whose grasp would come to equal its reach in every respect.[85] Abandoning the Union for that reason, the defiant secessionists remind us of Jackson's alleged response to Justice John Marshall's decision in *Worcester* v. *Georgia* (1832): Abraham Lincoln might make his free-soil decisions. Let the nation see if he could enforce them.

If the war between North and South arose immediately from secession as a southern response to an impending end of slavery, the nation did not at first test the slavery issue itself. Even with the South gone, slavery and the race question for the remaining Union states remained immensely complex and almost too hot to handle, especially with slave states like Maryland, Kentucky, and Missouri still clinging to the Union and no clear policy about how millions of freed slaves would live among hostile whites anywhere.[86]

The End of the Slave Provinces

In the North, and for Lincoln especially, the war began as a struggle to preserve the Union. Only gradually did that objective broaden to include full freedom for the slaves.[87] Emancipation behind the Confederate lines, moreover, started only as a promise of *eventual* liberation, when Union troops arrived at each plantation. Beyond what northern senti-

84. David M. Potter, *The Impending Crisis, 1848–1861* (New York, 1976).

85. Carpenter, *The South as a Conscious Minority.*

86. Allan Nevins, *The War for the Union* (4 vols.; New York, 1959–71), I, 6; J. G. Randall, *Civil War and Reconstruction* (Boston, 1937), 478–80.

87. Donald, *Charles Sumner and the Rights of Man,* on the evolution of war objectives.

ment had gathered by 1863 to end slavery, equal rights for black freedmen was not an objective for the North. The victory for freedom in the Emancipation Proclamation of 1863 was a victory by government decree but liberated not a single slave still under southern power. None of the thick problems about blacks and whites living together in freedom was attempted. The immediate aim was to punish and weaken the remaining rebels by proclaiming that they no longer had the right to own slaves and that they would lose the slaves when the Yankee army arrived. Lincoln also wanted to enhance the moral cause of the Union before world opinion by at last giving a show of moving against slavery.[88] If slavery did become intolerable in the North after secession, it was largely because it seemed to have led the owners to disunion and war. Antislavery and equal-rights sentiment in the North was thus interleaved with plans for chastising the rebels and for advantages for the Republican Party in restricting the southern voice in Washington after the war ended. Politically, Lincoln could not refuse to recognize the rising animosity among voters against the southern slavery that seemed to have led to so many war casualties.[89] His lifelong private revulsion against slavery was something else, as was his skepticism about racial equality.

The Emancipation Proclamation did not even free slaves in the slave-owning border states that had remained in the Union and where Lincoln in 1861 had rescinded emancipation orders issued by the local military. In the federal capital, however, and in the territories, slavery had been abolished or prohibited by the spring of 1862. The momentum of freedom for blacks at government command had thus begun to roll even before January 1, 1863.[90] In clearly visible and logical steps thereafter, Washington had ordered all slaves free by the war's end. The arrival of Union troops across the South in 1865 gave full effect to the Proclamation of 1863. The final step, the Thirteenth Amendment, came later, in 1865. But at every stage there were questions about the gap between government decree and public support for blacks in freedom. Essentially, those questions implied the larger one for all Americans: how broad was the scope of government to be when it decided to involve itself with moral ideals rather than leave a social issue such as race relations to chance or private attitudes and local ordinances?

The prominence of the slavery issue and the eventual Union victory

88. Lawanda Cox, *Lincoln and Black Freedom: A Study in Presidential Leadership* (Columbia, S.C., 1981).

89. *Ibid.*

90. Louis Gerteis, *From Contraband to Freedman: Federal Policy Toward Southern Blacks* (Westport, Conn., 1973).

in the war have obscured the wider setting of the struggle to deny the South its peculiar institution and the two-centuries-old culture with which it was so entwined. In Europe at this time, centuries of contest between the old regional and provincial powers and centralized government were also coming to a close. Although deprived by 1880 of political autonomy, the distinctive cultures of Bavaria, Brittany, Sicily, the Basques, the Walloons, and other "provinces," like the South in the United States, continued to resist a single national identity and, insofar as it was possible, control by a national government. By 1871, Italy and Germany were each politically united, so that for all Italians or Germans decisions about law, finance, foreign policy, and so on now came overwhelmingly from Berlin or Rome. The resistance to centralizing power in Europe, as in America with the South, involved momentous questions about the future sway of the state over many old regional cultures or older identities, sometimes morally odious as in the case of American slavery or Russian serfdom, sometimes more problematic like old religious loyalties to Rome or God that were hostile to the claims of the centralized state for the ultimate loyalty of citizens.[91] In America, the old loyalties included not only those to the slave South but those, among others, to the Creole culture, many different Indian tribes, patriarchal German-speaking enclaves in the north-central states, and the Mormon world in Utah with legalized polygamy.

How, and at what costs, was any one national ideal such as black freedom, monogamy, or the paramountcy of the English language to be given the force of law across so diverse a Union? Was the American people, expressing itself as national sovereign in Washington, to be supreme over any provincial mores that were morally obnoxious to the national majority? There were parallels to this dilemma of cultural uniformity within the states: for example, California's attempts after 1850 to subordinate the Chinese to white supremacy, and polygamy kept legal against a growing Utah minority opposed to Mormon hegemony.[92] If Washington had the last say about legal guarantees for slavery, did it not have

91. For a short overview of the making of nations in the nineteenth century, see John A. Garraty and Peter Gay, eds., *The Columbia History of the World* (New York, 1972), 905–17. On the dynamics of national identity, see Karl Deutsch, *Nationalism and Social Communication* (Cambridge, Mass., 1966). The tensions between nation and regions in several countries are explored in Eugen Weber, *Peasants into Frenchmen: The Modernization of Rural France, 1870–1914* (Stanford, 1976); Shepherd B. Clough, *A History of the Flemish Movement in Belgium* (New York, 1930); J. G. Peristiany, ed., *Contributions to Mediterranean Sociology* (Paris, 1968); Denis Mack Smith, *The Making of Modern Italy* (New York, 1968), documents with commentary.

92. Stanford M. Lyman, *Chinese Americans* (New York, 1974); Kimball Young, *Isn't One Wife Enough?* (Westport, Conn., 1954).

the last say about other liberties or cultural preferences? That fear, for an earlier example, had kept the Catholic hierarchy in the 1850s very leery about endorsing government action against slavery.[93]

The question of slavery in the 1850s thus involved a very complex and tender matter of the bearing of a national morality of individual freedom on a passionate but deeply contradictory "provincial" ideal. The South as a minority province included millions of citizens who favored slavery. Nationally, there were even larger millions who wanted white supremacy, even with slavery gone. The cultural questions, questions of slavery and race, eventually confronted the state, because after generations of compromise they had intruded into American politics with irreducible force.[94] Had the national state by 1860 been more clearly sovereign, had it figured larger in American imaginations, had federal power seemed more "natural" or legitimate, Washington action to stop slavery might have seemed less controversial or foreordained against local and individual interests in owning slaves. Another international perspective at this point is helpful. In England by 1880, when federal power in America had just abandoned blacks and whites in the South to their own devices, Parliament dominated local and county government. Royal veto was only a theory. The towns and shires by 1870 could only do what London permitted or tolerated, whether about voting rights or working conditions or changes in their city and county councils.[95] If there was any practice or ordinance at the lower levels of government that displeased Parliament, it could work its will subject only to support by a majority in the House of Commons and approval by the House of Lords. The English constitution was what Parliament said it was, subject to electoral approval.[96] When England abolished the slave trade throughout the empire in 1833 and then slavery itself in individual colonies, those decisions were already entirely in Parliament's hands. Unlike the American system, no lesser authority was in a constitutional position to challenge what Parliament had decided.[97]

Fortunately for England, the astonishing sweep of parliamentary sovereignty was always modulated by the strong tradition of English lib-

93. Madeleine M. Rice, *American Catholic Opinion in the Slavery Controversy* (New York, 1944).

94. Arthur C. Cole, *The Irrepressible Conflict, 1850–1865* (New York, 1938). See the critique by J. G. Randall, "The Blundering Generation," in Randall, *Lincoln, the Liberal Statesman* (New York, 1947).

95. Sidney and Beatrice Webb, *English Local Government from the Revolution to the Municipal Corporations Act* (London, 1908).

96. D. L. Keir, *The Constitutional History of Modern Britain, 1485–1951* (London, 1955), chap. 8.

97. W. C. Mathieson, *British Slavery and Its Abolition, 1823–1838* (New York, 1936).

erty. In imperial Germany after 1871, however, the new sovereignty of Berlin was soon enlisted in Bismarck's *Kulturkampf* with laws restricting Roman Catholics. In the more democratic third French Republic, Paris waged a somewhat gentler war against the influence of the Catholic Church over French life. The establishing of national political societies in these countries after 1870 did not involve rebellions on the American scale; but in losing its fight for its provincial culture, the South, like the European provinces, left itself and the rest of the nation more open to national power, certainly more penetrable than the Fathers of 1787 would have thought desirable or possible. The defeat of the southern province meant that when there would be a national will to enforce other standards of behavior like prohibition or school integration on the states and localities, that could be attempted with less impediment or catastrophe than in 1861.

The First "Health of the State"

By 1865, under wartime conditions, government penetration into northern as well as southern life went far beyond the end of slavery. Both nations felt the smack of the state as never before. After 1861 the Union government reached and grasped mightily across state and local lines. Military conscription, industrial and railroad mobilization, and dealing with disloyalty and civil liberties were major instances of federal power intruding directly into the lives of citizens who had previously little, if any, sense of federal government.[98]

In the Confederacy, between Sumter and Appomattox the stringencies of the war similarly led the Richmond government to press its member states to the utmost for supplies, money, troops, and ardor for the rebel cause as defined by Richmond. "As Richmond defined the cause" was increasingly the rub for a Confederacy hyperconscious about states' rights. Eventually, like the Union government, the Confederate government, against strong dissent, even ordered black troops into the fray. The worst and highest irony for the cause of slavery occurred at the very end of the war, when Richmond, trying to stay alive, had to contemplate the emancipation of the slaves as a desperate measure to obtain European recognition.[99] Southerners thus not only felt harsh blows as the Union troops arrived in their areas and set the slaves free but, like northerners under the Union, had increasingly felt their own government on

98. William B. Hesseltine, *Lincoln and the War Governors* (New York, 1948); J. G. Randall, *Constitutional Problems Under Lincoln* (New York, 1926), on civil liberties.
99. Robert F. Durden, *The Gray and the Black: The Confederate Debate on Emancipation* (Baton Rouge, 1972), 15–20.

their backs about wartime needs for food, arms, troops, and money.

The shock of the great state in both sections was great. Before 1860, the northern and southern states had lived with nearby political horizons. Only a presidential election or a major national event like the Mexican War or the Kansas-Nebraska Act might bring any vivid sense of a political life involving national ideas and institutions. "Government" overwhelmingly meant locality, the town or the county seat. The national flattery was that what Americans needed, they did for themselves. When Americans did seek the state, they went largely to local government or to the more distant state capital, which they did, for example, when seeking those general incorporation laws and state funds for financing economic expansion after the 1830s.

Suddenly in 1861, the scattered and even isolated communities across large regions of a continent not yet united by a rail line were called upon to come together as never before. As two nations, they were to mobilize for a war and to accept extraordinary demands from the Union or Confederate governments for obedience, loyalty, and service. In this shocking mobilization, both North and South had previews of the awesome powers of the modern, force-wielding state. Both were to experience what Randolph Bourne was later to call, satirically, "the health of the state."[100]

The "health of the state" in both North and South involved raising armies, encouraging and supporting industry, building railroad networks to move soldiers and supplies, financing the costs of war, and bringing unprecedented firepower onto the battlefields. Even more, and to recall Bourne's particular indictment of Woodrow Wilson, there was an unprecedented effort to arouse public opinion to fury and vengeance. The Union government showed what even a state "conceived in liberty" and for the enhancement of human rights could effect in pursuit of a victory in the Western world's first total war.[101] What Washington commanded from the president, the Congress, the courts, and the bureaucracy was enough to raise sharp cries about dictatorship by Lincoln's government over its own free people.[102] David Donald has shown how the Confederate government also increased its powers to fight for a holy cause with policies remarkably parallel to those adopted by Washington.[103] Both sides, for example, moved from volunteer armies to con-

100. Randolph Bourne, "The State," in Bourne, *War and the Intellectuals: Collected Essays, 1915–1919*, ed. Carl Resek (New York, 1964).

101. J. C. F. Fuller, "The Place of the American Civil War in the Evolution of War," *The Army Quarterly*, XXVI (1933).

102. Frank L. Klement, *The Copperheads in the Middle West* (Chicago, 1960).

103. J. G. Randall and David H. Donald, *The Civil War and Reconstruction* (Lexington, Mass., 1969).

scription. Both had great problems with bonuses to encourage service and with exemptions from the draft. Both finally had to use black troops. In financing the war both North and South had to resort to heavy borrowing and vast increases in paper money. By their own lights, both sides went to war for their own high goals and notions of liberty. These soon ballooned into images of two radically different ways of life, two civilizations, in deepest contest about their ideals. So both sides, to invoke Bourne again, "succumbed to the temptation to feel holy," and made pariahs and criminals of those doubtful of the cause. The North had the worse record on civil liberties, but social pressure in the South for unquestioning loyalty to the Confederacy swamped and silenced many skeptics as the cause faltered.

For the first time in American history, the hidden power and majesty of the state emerged from behind the fantasy that the use of force to coerce citizens of a free republic, and thus the spilling of family blood, had been left behind in Machiavellian Europe. War also accomplished what was impossible in the peacetime democracy, concentrated government power. Separation of powers and checks and balances were relaxed, the gears and wheels of the national state machine in the Union meshed more powerfully, and an American Leviathan, with its draft officials, contracts for war supplies, and suspension of habeas corpus, appeared on the battlefields and the home front. Although the Confederate government also tried mightily for cohesion and massed power, it had started the war far more decentralized than the North, less rich also, and less populous, less industrialized, less urbanized, and with poorer communications.[104] And the strength of ideas of states' rights within the new Confederacy and the failure also to develop political party machinery to whip recalcitrant state governments into line helped deny Davis and Lee the resources that might have led to at least a draw with the Union.[105]

By 1865, nonetheless, on both sides, an American state militant, armed, and aroused had shown how much life it could spend, how much hatred it could provoke, how it could wallow in what Edmund Wilson a century later aptly called "patriotic gore."[106] Two contesting American national ideals, one a slave civilization calling itself a Greek democracy and the other a land of a legally free and equal citizenry, served as moral justifications to find more power for each cause than any

104. E. Merton Coulter, *The Confederate States of America, 1861–1865* (Baton Rouge, 1950).

105. Emory M. Thomas, *The Confederacy as a Revolutionary Experience* (Englewood Cliffs, N.J., 1970); David H. Donald, ed., *Why the North Won the Civil War* (Baton Rouge, 1960).

106. Edmund Wilson, *Patriotic Gore* (New York, 1962).

Machiavellian despot with far fewer "modern" resources could have managed for his government. Indeed, one great difference from the world of Machiavelli was made by "modernity." Armed by modern industry, moving by modern railroads, communicating by the modern telegraph, arousing its public through modern newspapers and modern democratic literacy, the modern democratic nation-state on the field of war showed that it could be more far more formidable than the state of the Renaissance prince. Ironically, on the field by 1864 to 1865, a would-be innocent America, for all of its dreams of escaping the horrors of European history, presaged what Machiavellian Europe would do to itself fifty years later on the Western Front.

The State and Reconstruction

Since the Renaissance, war has probably been the most important influence in increasing the powers of the state as well as in accelerating social change by disrupting habit and custom.[107] The American Civil War brought another contribution to that Western record of state growth in wartime. Fortunately, the peacetime tradition of limited government, the expanse of the nation, and the accumulated American capital of individual liberty made the wartime depredations for the health of the state less than they might have been. As Morton Keller has shown, repeated proposals during the war to press Washington's claims for all-out centralizing measures were trimmed in the Congress. For both nations, American traditions of locality, personal liberty, and constrained government could not be fully downed.[108]

After 1865, the prewar pretensions of using as little government as possible renewed their swell. In the North, this earlier version of a "return to normalcy" dismantled the war machine. But the war also left irreducible strata of larger civilian government. The higher tariff and other wartime legislation endured while creating new bureaus and constituencies concerned with protection from foreign competitors, immigration control, banking and currency, land grants to homesteaders, state colleges, and railroad builders. The new federal Department of Agriculture was created in 1862 and achieved cabinet rank within a generation. It foretold a future of other "client-oriented" federal and state bureaus and departments.[109] Millions of veterans after 1865 brought the federal government into two long generations of heavy involvement in national pen-

107. John U. Nef, *War and Human Progress* (Cambridge, Mass., 1952).
108. Morton Keller, *Affairs of State* (Cambridge, Mass., 1977).
109. Leonard D. White, *The Republican Era, 1869–1901* (New York, 1958), chap. 11.

sion payments and pension politics.[110] These war-induced changes constituted those "ratchet" effects of emergencies on state growth that Robert Higgs has recently described.[111]

None of the enduring wartime accretions had the obviousness and effect of the largest peacetime effort in American history to use government power to enforce a basic social and political change. In the postwar South, government did not return to normality but assumed unprecedented powers in attempting to reconstruct the society of eleven states. Nothing in American experience had prepared government or citizenry for the massive efforts to enforce equal rights. The widening of American freedom and equality of opportunity for whites before the war had also involved laws that required new behavior, toward apprentices and debtors, for example. But those changes had been far simpler, largely because expanded rights for whites had been heavily rooted in community sentiment that demanded them. But after 1865, Americans had deep doubts about applying to blacks the guidelines designed for a free and competitive society of white men.[112] Even if opening the game fully to blacks had elicited white support, the game had not been designed for four million people who had lived for more than two centuries in slavery with its impoverishing ignorance, habits of dependence, and resentment against degradation.[113] Nor had the guidelines anticipated majority outrage against extending them to underesteemed groups.

The grim retrospect on the long and wracking Reconstruction derives from recognizing how ill-suited community feeling, the Constitution, and party system were for effectively meeting the basic needs of free blacks.[114] Extraordinary federal efforts were made to help blacks after 1867, but they were soon at variance with the will in Washington circles and among northern voters to stay the course.[115] Generally, efforts to reconstruct the postwar South in a Lincolnesque mode of good will, charity, and justice for both races asked more of Americans than they were capable of giving. For a "conquered province," a defeated American Fronde, to go willingly and rapidly from slavery at the war's end to treat-

---

110. Mary R. Dearing, *Veterans in Politics: The Story of the GAR* (Baton Rouge, 1952).

111. Higgs, *Crisis and Leviathan.*

112. Frederickson, *Black Image in the White Mind,* 145–64.

113. On black readiness for freedom, compare: Willie Lee Rose, *Rehearsal for Reconstruction* (Indianapolis, 1964); Leon F. Litwak, *Been in the Storm So Long: The Aftermath of Slavery* (New York, 1979); E. Merton Coulter, *The South During Reconstruction, 1865–1877* (Baton Rouge, 1947).

114. David H. Donald, *The Politics of Reconstruction, 1863–1867* (Baton Rouge, 1965).

115. William Gillette, *Retreat from Reconstruction, 1869–1879* (Baton Rouge, 1979).

ing blacks as equals at the polls, on juries, in the legislature, in the marketplace for labor and products, and in benefits from law required a great deal from human beings in general and from American politics in particular. More than a generation might have been needed to heal the war wounds and reconcile the two races, and the nation would have had to produce steadier and wiser policies than it had yet been able to devise for less volatile problems like the disposal of public lands or in banking, currency, and credit. Whatever the idealist rhetoric as Washington intervention in the South swelled in 1867, egalitarian change was never the solid northern purpose. For the South, so sudden and deliberate a departure from 250 years of white dominance was not tolerable.[116] There would be violence or reversal at the first available opportunity.[117]

At every level of governmental efforts to help blacks and establish race relations on a footing of equality lurked the spectacle of the state—investigating, legislating, financing, supervising, protecting, and chastising citizens as never before, yet with strong majorities in the South opposing most of those initiatives. Not surprisingly, the ventures began to collapse when the special compound of idealism, vengeance, and party advantage that encouraged them in 1867 began to dissipate.[118] That enduring, successful policies for substantial equality of opportunity, let alone equality of results, for the new black citizens could have emerged from a restored peacetime politics of bicker and bargain seems chimerical. A successful multiracial policy in the South would have required the white elite to surrender social superiority and diminish amenity, to share political power, and to pay higher taxes for education, social services, and welfare measures, and not only for the blacks but for poorer whites who would also ask a would-be broadening democracy for recognition. But substantial equality for blacks also required the great majority of poorer southerners who had never owned slaves to give up white hegemony.

In 1865, when massive federal intervention was not planned even by the enemies of the South, Washington politicians were not bitter partisans if they believed that most southern leaders and plebians had favored the Confederacy.[119] If it happened that the southern whites would not reconcile themselves to defeat by accommodation to enlarged rights for former slaves, the only chance for the latter and for the Republican Party

116. Kenneth M. Stampp, *The Era of Reconstruction, 1865–1877* (New York, 1965).
117. Michael Perman, *Reunion Without Compromise* (Cambridge, Mass., 1973).
118. Gillette, *Retreat from Reconstruction.*
119. William R. Brock, *An American Crisis: Congress and Reconstruction, 1865–1867* (New York, 1963), 42–46.

in the South might be to deal with black leaders as they could be encouraged to come forth.[120]

That surmise became stronger and clearer by 1866 as the white South, left to its own devices, organized to go as little as possible beyond outlawed slavery while returning to Democratic Party ranks.[121] Deep doubts among northern whites about the racial competence of blacks for managing their freedom[122] were subordinated in face of what seemed like southern determination to stay as close to slavery as possible. Massive federal intervention in 1867 thus came after the South used one device after another—like the Ku Klux Klan and similar groups, adaptations of northern black codes, and stringent antivagrancy laws—to control the former slaves.[123] Washington then decided to ignore state and local lines and to forsake the older American path of working with time and changing social attitudes to enlarge equal rights. Rights for the black minority would be imposed on the southern majority. If necessary, the majority of eligible southern white voters as of 1860, especially their leaders, would be tailored to eliminate resistance to a new era. A trimmed electorate, required also to take oaths of eternal loyalty, did produce new constitutions and laws that underwrote equal rights for blacks to vote, to go to school, to seek and hold jobs or farms, to travel and move about.[124] To accomplish this, however, short-lived and sporadic attempts were made to disenfranchise as a class all southern whites worth more than $20,000, to require loyalty oaths from whites seeking to participate in politics, to set specific guidelines for the new state constitutions and elections.[125] These changes and racial peace against white terror and violence were enforced by Union troops allied with federally approved local officials.

But under the surface of military occupation and restricted white liberties were deeper, contrary, powerful, and ultimately determining currents of opinion across the nation, not just in the South. Besides insistence on white supremacy over racially inferior blacks, a belief in the sanctity of private property and contracts militated against attempts to redistribute land.[126] A strong sense of stringent limits about what government should do beyond legal equality for the disadvantaged generally, not merely poor blacks, also undercut efforts like the Freedmen's

120. Donald, *Politics of Reconstruction*.

121. Perman, *Reunion Without Compromise*.

122. V. Jacque Voegli, *Free but Not Equal* (Chicago, 1963).

123. Allen W. Trelease, *White Terror* (New York, 1971).

124. Donald, *Charles Sumner and the Rights of Man*.

125. Charles Fairman, *Reconstruction and Reunion* (New York, 1971), 253–309.

126. Eric Foner, *Reconstruction: America's Unfinished Revolution, 1863–1877* (New York, 1988).

Bureau.[127] Almost three centuries of weighty American traditions were thus in play against a federally mandated reconstruction of southern society.

If there was any model in the minds of whites for helping blacks it derived from what had been done during the earlier emancipation of whites. Although some northern analysts and political leaders like Thaddeus Stevens and Charles Sumner[128] understood that former slaves without guaranteed property, ballots, jobs, and education might not make a go of freedom as effectively as whites had, most northerners wanted nothing more done for former slaves than the legal equality and the more open contest for success that had earlier been offered to whites.[129] Even black leaders like Frederick Douglass thought at first that blacks left to themselves to use Jeffersonian freedom would employ it to sufficient advantage.[130] The Constitution and the laws need only command that for former slaves there would be no political or legal impediment to make life as good as their characters, talents, private cooperation, and chance permitted. As Lincoln had put it soon after the war began, the war aimed "to afford all an unfettered start and a fair chance in the race of life."[131] This largely meant that blacks were to be free to do with their labor as they liked within the United States, *i.e.,* if they were not colonized. The war over, blacks with their lives now at their own disposal would be free to earn their bread by the sweat of their brows. They would have legal rights to buy and sell property and products and to marry their own kind and to raise families. In sum, ostensibly, like whites, they could pursue happiness up to the traditional full that the American contest allowed. Recent research has indeed shown how quickly right after the war blacks did band together in hundreds of self-improvement societies to cash in on freedom and without calls for special government subvention beyond emancipation.[132]

But the great ponderable of white supremacy that had so counfounded the prewar slavery debates had to be faced again in 1865. The war had changed that little, except to deepen it in the South. Almost four million freed blacks were not welcome as equals in the American contest not

---

127. William S. McFeely, *Yankeee Stepfather: General O. O. Howard and the Freedmen* (New Haven, 1968).

128. Fawn M. Brodie, *Thaddeus Stevens, Scourge of the South* (New York, 1959).

129. Voegli, *Free but Not Equal.*

130. Waldo E. Martin, *The Mind of Frederick Douglass* (Chapel Hill, 1984), chap. 10; Nathan T. Huggins, *Slave and Citizen* (Boston, 1980).

131. Message to Congress in Special Session, July 4, 1861, in *Collected Works of Abraham Lincoln*, ed. Roy P. Basler (8 vols.; New Brunswick, N.J., 1953), IV, 421–41.

132. Dan T. Carter, *When the War Was Over: The Failure of Self-Reconstruction in the South, 1865–1867* (Baton Rouge, 1985).

only for racial reasons but because it seemed that the millions who suddenly emerged from 250 years of bondage were woefully behind the whites in experience, education, and the know-how of managing American opportunity. It did not help the blacks that these historical, transient limits of culture were quickly and easily transmuted by national prejudice into belief in the eternal limitations of blacks as a race.[133] After northerners thus had their fill of punishing the South and a try at helping the blacks, scandals, southern white yelps of pain, and racist horror stories about black excesses brought the federal intervention into disrepute. The profound conviction about black racial inferiority was heavily available to prove that the early Reconstruction guarantees for equality were "against nature itself" and were foolish and unfair to blacks as well as whites.[134] Similarly, calls by Stevens and Sumner to redistribute plantation lands to former slaves came to nothing against deep beliefs in the inviolability of private property.[135] Generally, therefore, using government to lift up deprived blacks rather than only entitling them legally to help themselves proved unacceptable.

Politics had proposed but society was to dispose of much of the commands after 1867 to achieve equal rights in the South. Only now, more than a century later, does a newly biracial South seem to be working through the trauma that began in 1867. Recapitulating the fascinating, still not fully understood history of the decade that followed is of less concern here than noting the degree of state power needed to try to alter customs of stunning complexity in a society deeply hostile to state power concerning itself with social ideals. Contrary to the horror stories, blacks as well as whites made advances,[136] but the substantial federal grasp after 1867 that helped accomplish these gains in most respects relaxed within five years.[137] Five years still later, by 1877, massive white southern sentiment against equal rights for blacks was again in control. Most of the North was relieved, out of sympathy with the hectored whites, frustration or boredom with the limited success of once-hailed racial innovations, and prospects of greater political gain from collaborating with white leaders of a "new south" than from working with an "unreliable," irredeemable black minority.[138]

133. Frederickson, *Black Image in the White Mind,* chaps. 6–7.
134. Voegli, *Free but Not Equal,* 1–9.
135. Brodie, *Thaddeus Stevens,* 165–68, 231–33.
136. W. E. B. Du Bois, *Black Reconstruction* (New York, 1963).
137. Gillette, *Retreat from Reconstruction.*
138. C. Vann Woodward, *Reunion and Reaction* (Boston, 1951), 211–14.

Amendment and Commitment

A major revelation about the potential grasp of an American Leviathan for liberty involved the amendment process. The first ten amendments, the Bill of Rights, had been virtually guaranteed during ratification of the Constitution in 1788. So before the Civil War, amendment had really been used only twice and both times to take care of relatively uncontroversial problems that had arisen in running the constitutional system. Certainly, no amendments had proposed fundamental changes in the respective roles of the states and the national government about basic individual rights. Resorting to amendment after the Civil War testified to the difficulty of using ordinary law to assure the priority of equal rights for citizens over states' rights and of preventing the use of the latter as a cloak to deny the former.[139]

In the American system, amendment is the ultimate voice of the people and usually can be used only when a rare national consensus has gathered about an issue like slavery, the income tax, or limiting presidents to two terms. It is a measure of the difficulty of assuring equal rights for blacks after 1865 that the problem seemed to require going beyond ordinary legislation. Popular zeal for white supremacy in the South implied that ordinary civil rights legislation would be too easily countered, state by state, unless there was a national standard that could be altered only with great difficulty, *i.e.,* amendment with three-fourths of all states concurring. Since the day would come when the Union troops would end the policing of Reconstruction, only building equal rights into the Constitution seemed to give adequate promise that the South, left again to its own devices, would not again restrict blacks as in 1865–1866. If such attempts were made, blacks would have a national standard of rights and an authority beyond the states to invoke.[140]

As three new amendments came into force between 1865 and 1870, there were new howls in the opposition about "Jacobinism," *i.e.,* tyrannical leveling by the centralized state.[141] In American history, critics of egalitarianism have recurrently raised versions of the same complaint.[142] If majorities legally controlling the federal government can use the amendment process to override local custom, preference, and laws, what interests or liberties might not be threatened?[143] Indeed, it is clear that

139. Harold M. Hyman, *A More Perfect Union* (New York, 1973).
140. Herman Belz, *Reconstructing the Union* (Ithaca, N.Y., 1969).
141. Brodie, *Thaddeus Stevens,* chap. 15, "The Jacobins."
142. Kendall and Carey, *Basic Symbols of the American Political Tradition,* chap. 5.
143. The most influential discussion of "the tyranny of the majority" is in Tocqueville. Compare with Henry Steele Commager, *Majority Rule and Minority Rights* (New York, 1943).

under the American Constitution, even the freedoms covered in the Bill of Rights are not exempt from amendment. Although freedom has been enlarged by amendments ending slavery and enfranchising women, proposals have also been made for amendments to outlaw various radical parties, to severely restrict the jurisdiction of the Supreme Court, to abolish the electoral college, and to qualify the First Amendment in order to safeguard the flag. Regardless of the worth of any of these, the fact that they have been suggested emphasizes that what in law "the people" have granted, "the people" may withdraw. The Calhoun vision of apocalypse via legality recurrently presents itself: against aroused, determined majorities American liberty may ultimately have no defense.[144]

The riposte to the augury of the last days lies both in what the particular amendments to the Reconstruction period meant to do and how even seemingly so powerful a weapon as amendment could be frustrated, not by majority or minority votes in the South or in Washington as by communal sentiment that blacks would remain second-class citizens.

Most portentous about the potential sweep of the sovereign was the Fourteenth Amendment, adopted in 1868. It was a potpourri of clauses that for the first time constitutionally defined federal and state citizenship, the basic rights of citizens, and guaranteed both of these within the states as well as at the federal level. On vital matters of equal rights the states were thus made subject to federal sovereignty.[145] Despite attempts in the 1880s also to interpret the amendment as protecting corporations by treating them as persons,[146] the weight of opinion holds that it was intended to solidify the effort to protect blacks from white injustice within the states as well as under federal authority and to embed some of the provisions of the Reconstruction civil rights acts into the Constitution itself.[147] According to a broad interpretation, the Fourteenth Amendment nationalized *all* rights in the Constitution because, ostensibly, no state or local ordinance that deprived a person of any right enjoyed as a citizen of the United States would be permitted to stand if tested in the federal courts.[148]

Because the Fourteenth Amendment spoke of citizens and persons, it implied increased liberty for all Americans. The text did not limit itself to the situation of blacks—they were not mentioned—nor has it been

144. See "Postscript to Progressivism: The Health of the State" in Section IV, below, on World War I and intransigent majorities.

145. Fairman, *Reconstruction and Reunion.*

146. Matthew Josephson, *The Politicos* (New York, 1938), 49–52.

147. Jacobus ten Broek, *Equal Under Law* (New York, 1965).

148. Robert J. Kaczorowski, "Searching for the Intent of the Framers of the Fourteenth Amendment," *Connecticut Law Review,* V (1973).

used only for that purpose.[149] Nevertheless, the amendment originally was imposed on the white majority and the state governments in the South because, left to themselves in 1865 and 1866, they had refused to maintain what Washington judged to be an adequate national standard of rights for the freed slaves. Whether done wisely, morally, or legally, the amendment declared how a local majority was to legislate and behave about a minority. The amendment's language, however nonracial, did not fool southerners. They knew at once the real bite and intention. The amendment not only seemed to put the national government solidly at the service of the freedom of blacks in spite of local law but it also followed that the federal legislature and courts were to spell out the definitions of rights and to judge violations. Time was soon to show that nothing that seemed so sweeping in law could fail to contain exploitable ambiguities, including readings that would restrict rather than enlarge rights. Powerful as this amendment seemed at first, the last years of Reconstruction and thereafter showed how the rights of blacks as ostensible citizens could still languish. Indeed, for much of a century after 1877 the amendment was so narrowly construed that effective rights for blacks were reduced to mere flickers in the South and kept at a low flame elsewhere. White southern restrictions on blacks were imposed, and as early as 1876, in the Reese and Cruikshank cases, the Supreme Court severely limited the scope of both the Fourteenth and Fifteenth Amendments and thus of the intended federal protection for blacks.[150]

Given a sympathetic court, the vistas of government power opened by all three Reconstruction amendments were vast, as both civil rights enthusiasts and legal conservatives have argued ever since 1870. But those vistas could be far-off and legalistic. It is instructive that sixty years later, in the 1930s, slow successful appeals through the courts to the amendments were not sufficient to destroy segregation or restore voting rights in the South. When the nation did turn to its unfinished agenda about equal rights in the 1960s, federal legislation in 1964 and 1965, with adequate enforcement and threatened penalties like loss of congressional seats, ended much of legalized white supremacy in the South. An additional amendment of the 1960s, outlawing the poll tax, was only supplementary. The older, Reconstruction amendments, however hailed or denounced in the past, had not done the job.

What weighs most is less what the amendments themselves did accomplish than their clear implication that basic rights were national concerns, superior to local preferences and practice, and that it was the task of all governments, huge as they came to be, to see that they were re-

---

149. Michael K. Curtis, *No State Shall Abridge* (Durham, N.C., 1986).
150. Belz, *Reconstructing the Union,* 131–33.

spected. Without that resolve, equal rights could have come to little or nothing, not only for blacks, but for many minorities somewhere out there in America and often severely subject to local whim and ordinance. Left to spontaneous development of favorable consensus for them, effective rights developed slowly for blacks, women, pacifists, members of Jehovah's Witnesses and other sects, homosexuals, labor union leaders, radical government workers, and other groups that have suffered local harassment and restriction. Local leaders reluctant to provide rights for the unpopular or unorthodox have always been aware of this and have argued, often disingenuously, for peaceful evolution of majority sentiment, not government coercion, as the best path to changes in local law. The federal definitions of citizenship and rights since 1870 have at least provided a standard against leaving to time and majority pleasure the expansion of equal rights.

Whatever the purported prospects for despotism within the three Reconstruction amendments, they were not a Hobbesian assertion of the limitlessness of the national state on behalf of every conceivable right that a sovereign might grant or withdraw or choose to honor.[151] If the amendments were faulty in wording or effect, the government and the electorate remained free to change any one amendment through subsequent amendment. Prohibition was thus ended after only thirteen years. The courts could also press against abuses as well as ignore them. The Supreme Court in the 1940s thus ruled against the all-white primary election, although to little practical avail in the South.[152] Congress is also able to supplement ineffective amendments and move beyond frustrated court decisions with ordinary but forceful legislation, as it did in 1964 and 1965. The earlier portent of treating the Fourteenth Amendment narrowly was also not lost on the lawyers who induced the Supreme Court in 1876 in the Cruikshank and Reese cases to restrict national intervention rather than enjoin the states broadly to observe basic rights for blacks.

Most telling about the legalism and limits of the amendments was what southern whites, and then the country at large, showed about the resources of democratic *society* to frustrate the basic law of the democratic *state*. This resistance did not require repealing the amendment and was effective despite the constitutional standards seeming definitive. Failure to enforce, failure to supplement with adequate enabling legislation, contrary popular sentiment, an opposed electorate, tricky stratagems, and conservative judges were all effective for opponents of black rights.

151. Laurent B. Frantz, "Congressional Power to Enforce the Fourteenth Amendment Against Private Acts," *Yale Law Journal*, LXXIII (1964).

152. Fairman, *American Constitutional Decisions*, 427–33.

The conservative case at the time against both the amendments and the general grasp of federal power was marred morally in the same way that Calhoun's ideas were a generation earlier. Constitutional conservatives about race in the 1870s and thereafter continued in the Calhoun, and even Jeffersonian, vein to argue against centralized or consolidated government overwhelming both locality and liberty. In fact, the "liberty," local custom, state government responsibility, and so on invoked successfully in 1876 before the Supreme Court continued prewar aims. Local power existed to keep blacks in their places and, more broadly, to permit white grandees to maintain political control over the white as well as the black South.[153]

The arguments against federal intervention for black rights were almost as abstract, *i.e.,* an ideological cover for venal purposes, as the Jacobin doctrine of equality that conservatives had deplored in the amendments. All of their invocations of the spirit of the republic, the Founding Fathers, civilization, and mongrelization were defenses of white power at the expense of the rights of blacks. The southern elite's interest in controlling the South by weakening federal intervention could also carry further than against blacks. Restrictions could extend, and in time the threat was made, to disenfranchise other groups, *e.g.,* ignorant "poor whites" or "rednecks," whom the southern elite wanted to keep in line.[154]

None of such rebukes to conservatives as *partis pris* could have dissolved the widespread feeling in the mid-1870s that southern "redeemers" were fighting for the great principles of white civilization, American liberty, and local autonomy. Nor does it rid us of problems in government stretching itself to force majorities to respect its notions of equal rights, the issue that the opponents of rights for blacks raised. But the conservative white leaders would have had better moral credentials and would now have a better report from historians if, long before 1867, they had better tended the South's problems of liberty—and for "poor whites" as well as black slaves. Long failures as professed trustees of liberty, humanity, and Christian civilization meant, first, that the securing of liberty against slavery had to pass to federal emancipation through war. New failures followed as purported Christian friends of freedom after the war strengthened the enemies of the South, the minority of congressional, "Jacobin" radicals like Stevens, Sumner, Butler, and Wade. The southern resistance brought in the army, the "outside agitators" of the time, those excoriated carpetbaggers, and the traitors within,

153. C. Vann Woodward, *Origins of the New South, 1877–1913* (Baton Rouge, 1951), chap. 1.

154. C. Vann Woodward, *The Strange Career of Jim Crow* (Rev. ed.; New York, 1974), 85.

the scalawags. Of course, the tradition of white supremacy that the white southern elite defended had a long history. It was not a cynically devised doctrine for southerners only but a living tradition, however unattractive now. As such it had a powerful hold over the populace, not just the leaders, and was increasingly adumbrated after the war by new "scientific" race doctrines.[155] Had the white "Bourbons," the elite of the South, taken the lead in reconciling their fellow southerners to black citizenship, the misery they would have spared their section and the nation is incalculable. To say, however, what they ought to have believed or done, given America's long obsessive nightmare of "white over black," may be another howl at history for failing to move with what aftersight posits as worthy or moral.

In the first two Reconstruction years, 1865 and 1867, with South-haters contained at Washington, the white leaders in the former Confederacy had refused an all-southern initiative for racial peace and a fresh start in race relations. Instead, they sought exclusive control over a South without black influence. Caught out by Washington, after 1867, these whites flattered and cajoled the new, so-called black regimes to form coalitions with them, ostensibly for a "new departure" and for the good of all southerners.[156] With this foot in the door and sharing as much in the ensuing scandals as did the minority of black leaders, the white elite then began to lessen what was, in any case, overplayed black dominance. Ultimately, the white leaders excoriated and pushed aside the blacks who had trusted former white masters as allies for equal rights. By 1877 as they returned to top of the heap, the white leaders again went for something they valued more than racial justice, *i.e.*, political power. Their greatest failure as professed spokesmen for conservatism was in not even attempting to help staunch the wounds that can be inflicted by an ideology like race or, for that matter, jacobinical egalitarianism. The true task in 1865 for conservative trustees of the common good was to reconcile racial antagonists to each other by coming to terms with what history would no longer countenance. The war for a right to secede was lost, slavery was gone, and whites and blacks, bound in community for two centuries in Faulknerian tangle, thenceforth might have been taught to live together in liberty, without masters or inferiors. Instead, trying to find the most workable substitute for slavery and mastery and thereby bringing down on their heads the full force of the state and in the name of democracy, the southern white elite wrote the saddest chapter of that terrible time for the nation.

155. *Ibid.*, 94–96.
156. Francis B. Simkins, "New Viewpoints of Southern Reconstruction," *Journal of Southern History,* V (1939).

IV

SEARCHING FOR A STATE

The New Social Power

The extraordinary power released by science, technology, and entrepreneurial know-how in the late nineteenth century multiplied the needs for and concerns of the state. The more tightly knit national life that came from continental markets and improved transportation and communication brought greater "impingement" of person on person in burgeoning cities, giant firms on smaller firms, state government regulation on federal regulation.[1] All this growth in power, in thickening and consolidating, created immense difficulties for the faith in Jeffersonian ideals of a state-free competitive individualism. Impingement also challenged the Madison model of a continental scattering of small- to moderate-sized interests and governments checking each other's imperial ambitions as well as government power.

The original American game had been designed primarily for a decentralized farmers' republic and against the threat of distant despotic government. Of course a pre-industrial republic could not conceive how large private power was to become. In the society of the Bank of North America (1781) and of Samuel Slater's cotton factory (1790), who could anticipate a J. P. Morgan or the Homestead steelworks? It had also been impossible to foresee in the society of Jefferson's day the power that science and technology, instantaneous communication, giant weapons, statistics-gathering, and specialized bureaucracy would make available to the state.

After 1865, as it moved to meet the immense array of needs set loose in industrial society, government was not only to regulate (the hotly de-

1. For several surveys with different emphases, see: John Garraty, *The New Commonwealth, 1877–1898* (New York, 1968); Edward C. Kirkland, *Industry Comes of Age: Business, Labor, and Public Policy, 1860–1897* (New York, 1961); Zane Miller, *The Urbanization of Modern America* (New York, 1973).

bated and featured issue) but to continue to sponsor railroads, regulate defeated Indians on reservations, stimulate the growth of the merchant marine, mint silver, as well as gold, coins, and coordinate state and federal agricultural research. In considering this spread of federal intervention, we must not forget the pre-Sumter pileup at all levels of government for regulation as well as sponsorship.

Larger and more complex needs were already creating calls for state and federal intervention about farming, currency and credit, and railroads in the 1860s. Regulation of the railroads soon moved beyond the states, because those frustrated by failures there moved on to Washington after about 1880. However contrary to ideals opposing government regulation, a "permission to intervene" began to take hold and created an enduring multiplier effect. The more problems that found their way onto the list for government action about any issue, not only railroads, currency, and monopoly, the faster came the discovery of other matters for government attention. Whatever seawalls laissez-faire ideology and practice had produced were battered by intervention from all directions and in all of America's governments. No political ideology, particularly neither Marxist nor laissez-faire explanations of state growth, satisfactorily explains these changes. What may clarify them better has already been sketched here: a complex interplay between needs for growth, opportunity, and repair in a rambunctious capitalist society, the willingness of democratic authority to tend to them for a very modest price of votes and campaign funds, and an ideology for government intervention implicit in pledges like securing "the blessings of liberty for ourselves and our posterity."

From the outset of awareness in the 1880s that Washington was being asked to take on unorthodox tasks of regulation, the terms of the American debate were too simple and misleading. Even if we agree that government size can become obnoxious to freedom and efficient services, are size and expenditure or social- and dollar-effectiveness of state intervention the primary questions? And how are size, cost, and effectiveness to be measured reliably against private efforts for similar purposes? Overwhelmingly, popular and political debate early settled that "big government" and its dollar costs were the great issues. That decision marked an understandable tendency to dwell on an old trauma, the despotic King George syndrome, but it detracted from the more fruitful issues of how best to serve burgeoning needs that demanded tending, somehow, public or private, individual or in voluntary associations, by local, state or federal authority.

Historians of Europe like Tocqueville, Acton, and Burckhardt were alarmed a generation or more before 1890 about the increasing claims and power of the modern nation-state.[2] They contended that it had been growing steadily for centuries, not just in the nineteenth century. The expansion had come at the expense of the churches, guilds, "estates," towns—all those groups in whose "pluralistic" conflict they found chances for liberty. This idea echoed an old and self-serving argument of aristocracy against the growth of royal power and the loss of local privilege. Nevertheless, centuries of state expansion at the expense of old, smaller authorities had been relentless. By 1850, for those European observers, modern state power seemed to be presaging disaster, especially in new alliances with ultranationalism, militarism, and extreme egalitarianism. Some of the gloom about similar trends against both liberty and equality in America[3] is dispelled in recalling that in the nineteenth century more powerful government could also serve individual liberty, as in notable cases like the ending of slavery. Indeed, American history continued to suggest an exception to a portrait of the state based on European experience. The nation's size, thin settlement, and diversity, its complicated constitutional and party arrangements, its great suspicion of government and spirit of personal liberty made it difficult for American government to grasp as effectively as European states controlled their economies, education, and administration. Still, by 1890, in both America and Europe, unanticipated prowess was at hand for government as well as for private power. Almost every new scientific, technological, or managerial "miracle" that suggested more liberation of life also betokened an added control available to government. If a city's water supply could be effectively purified to make lives healthier, the task passed from private water companies to the state. If public education spread to increase chances for a better life, that also increased taxes and bureaucracy as well as exposure to state-designed instruction or indoctrination in "our way of life."

If America drifted toward greater state regulation by the 1880s, it did so piecemeal and grudgingly, *i.e.,* in all-too-familiar, haphazard pileup. Socialist programs that made regulation and public ownership into general principles were just one of many reasons for the failure of socialism to take hold in the United States. By far the dominant justification for regulation, as in most of the Populist platform of 1892, was to reinvigorate economic individualism and popular control of government, not to accept and civilize bigness in enterprise and government as some later progressive reformers like Herbert Croly and Walter Weyl were to urge.[4]

2. Tocqueville, *The Old Regime and the French Revolution,* Foreword and 32–72; Gertrude Himmelfarb, *Lord Acton* (Chicago, 1957), 73–87; Burckhardt, *Force and Freedom.*

3. Frederic C. Jaher, *Doubters and Dissenters: Cataclysmic Thought in America, 1885–1918* (Glencoe, Ill., 1964).

4. Charles Forcey, *The Crossroads of Liberalism* (New York, 1961).

What Americans of 1900 increasingly bewailed, in addition to political corruption and threats to opportunity in big government, were the increasing scale and complexity of all enterprises, business as well as civic, the new distances between domicile and workplace, employer and worker, officials and citizens, home and school, parents and children, teachers and administrators, and the growing relentlessness and "impersonalism" of routine and specialization.[5] In fact, these were new marks of those old American friends, money, machines, and "progress," the features of enhanced command over life. The resentment of bigness, complexity, and impersonalism was thus deeply ambivalent, however much size and complication were denounced. And no American had grasped, as Max Weber did by 1905, that these characteristics might be endemic to industrial culture, whether its guise was capitalist or socialist, and inseparable from any attempts to bring greater control over erupting industrial and technological power.[6]

Order and Control

One says "control," rather than "order," to counter some of the import of recent views about an underlying "search for order" throughout American society after about 1880.[7] Stated abstractly, a conscious search for order had been troubling Americans since the landings at Jamestown and Plymouth and was not unique after the Civil War. Whenever sought, however, "order" has often been a soft word for controls benefiting the sponsor. The "proper Christian order" enacted in Massachusetts Bay in the 1630s gave control to the elders among the "saints." Any rationalization for self-interest implicit in such efforts was no less present in the 1890s when order began to be presented in the guise of a new, beneficent, scientifically managed society.[8] "Order" started to acquire intellectual gloss and respect in the academy and among intelligent businessmen and students of business who were evolving theories of expert management and organization. The historian estimates only with great difficulty whether control over rivals, more money and power, or a guileless vision of harmonious productivity was the paramount mo-

5. Walter Lippmann, *Drift and Mastery* (New York, 1914).

6. Max Weber's essays on this theme appeared in 1906 and 1907 in *Archiv fuer Sozialwissenschaft und Sozialpolitik*. There is a translated section of the first essay, "The Situation of Middle-Class Democracy in Russia," specially titled "The New Despotism," in Bernard Wishy, ed., *The Western World in the Twentieth Century* (New York, 1961).

7. Robert H. Wiebe, *The Search for Order, 1877–1920* (New York, 1967).

8. Samuel Haber, *Efficiency and Uplift: Scientific Management in the Progressive Era* (Chicago, 1964).

tive.[9] The view here is that the new managerial order was often as much a self-serving slogan for domination as it was for improved management.[10] And disorder continued in the heralded "well-managed enterprise" far more than the publicists for order pretended or allowed the public to know.[11] J. P. Morgan claimed, in the 1890s, to be bringing order out of chaos in the railroad industry, but that did not stop him from watering the stock of roads like the New Haven. Often, too, seeming order, like F. W. Taylor's idea of contented workers on the assembly line, could be pseudorational, hiding continuing error and waste in the factories and resentment and boredom even among "well-managed" personnel.

"Irrationalities" were by no means overcome in the new political order that good government spokesmen preferred over the mismanagement and dishonesty of bosses, machines, and the spoils system. One price for a civil service system was bureaucracy with its own biases about procedures and public policy. Expert commissions of university professors concerned with public matters could also have prejudices clothed in impartial analysis aimed against corruption and expediency. Blue-ribbon panels could become dodges to substitute a study for action. Nonpartisan civic administration and city-manager systems could be very naïve about avoiding or minimizing "politics." Impartial experts were chronically partial to their own views and interests and scornful of popular wishes. The direct primary could be held at times of the year convenient for the in-party and with registration and nomination and ballot-arrangement procedures designed to blunt the challenge of the people or party interlopers.

By 1910, such lessons about reputedly rational management were not adequately clear. The enthusiasts for a nonpartisan or up-to-date management ideal for government wanted to freshen American democracy rather than accept the drift toward a diseased nation of increasingly large and corrupt organizations of bosses and tycoons.[12] But had the optimistic reformers appreciated, at the outset, the subtlety of political power and the play of interests within all government machinery, new as well as

9. William Miller, ed., *Men in Business* (New York, 1962). On enlightened leaders like Harry Varnum Poor, see chap. 10. Allan Nevins, *Study in Power: John D. Rockefeller, Industrialist and Philanthropist* (New York, 1953), especially on "vision" versus power.

10. Alfred D. Chandler, Jr., *The Visible Hand: The Managerial Revolution in American Business* (Cambridge, Mass., 1977).

11. The classic study of the play between capitalist rationality and disorder is Joseph Schumpeter, *Capitalism, Socialism, and Democracy* (New York, 1942). See also Morrell Heald, *The Social Responsibilities of Business, Company, and Community, 1900–1960* (Cleveland, 1970).

12. David P. Thelen, *Robert M. La Follette and the Insurgent Spirit* (Boston, 1976).

old, there might have been fewer lessons to be learned and less disappointment, let alone cynicism or political reaction, when progressive reforms came to little. Unsuspected variables, unanticipated results, as well as the old Adam, were to confound many hopes for a cleaner politics as the search for order moved from glowing premises into actual confrontation with industrial America's political and social disarray.[13]

Information about industrial America as much as rationalistic impulse and ideology helped launch the new managerialism in politics. The alleged facts came in exposures of the wealthy and powerful that began with books like Henry Demarest Lloyd's *Wealth Against Commonwealth* (1894) and continued later with the muckrakers.[14] Whether in Rockefeller empire-building, Harriman railroad shenanigans, Morgan takeovers, machine politics, or the sprawl and filth of slum and city, the new social power running amok threatened to wreck or corrupt or infect the daily life of democracy. This threat argued for an end to graft and special favors and for no patience generally with waste, excess, and defying the public good as in earlier days when population was smaller and more scattered and the power available to the unscrupulous more limited. Appalled by what they saw and heard about corporations and bossism, men like the university professors Ely and Commons who gathered around Governor Robert La Follette in Wisconsin in the 1890s, were convinced that something like their "Wisconsin idea" of drawing into public life impartial experts would help restore good government. Only the recently pathological parts of American democracy needed to be cut away to leave the rest of the republic free to respect individual rights and popular consent as had been intended by the Founding Fathers. The boss and ignorant nonprofessionals would be replaced by nonpartisan leagues of concerned citizens, the direct election of senators, city managers, the referendum, initiative, and recall, and "efficiency" everywhere.[15]

Unlike the programs of socialists and anarchists for public ownership or for small, confederated communities, the enthusiasms of progressive reformers were attractive for seeming to be fully compatible with traditional American ideals of individual liberty, equality of opportunity and competition, the rule of law and the Constitution, and uncorrupted majoritarian government. But with the rare exception of a Walter Lippmann, neither the socialists nor the progressive liberals understood that the new social power was so vast, so unprecedented, and so complex in its impact on individuals that it might require decades of impartial

13. Samuel P. Hays, *The Response to Industrialism, 1885–1914* (Chicago, 1957).
14. David M. Chalmers, *The Social and Political Ideas of the Muckrakers* (New York, 1964).
15. Thelen, *Robert M. La Follette.*

study just to understand its fast-changing and many-sided nature. It was even more risky to be confident about progressive-backed alterations in American institutions, particularly in the newly envisioned tasks and techniques of the state.[16]

Some of the best analysts of the malaise of the Progressive era were also led astray because they misread the past. In 1909, Herbert Croly posed a now-famous opposition across American history between Hamiltonians, who openly enhanced state power to build a strong economy, and Jeffersonians, who emphasized individual liberty and deprecated the state.[17] Croly failed to discern how the former had always been an unacknowledged adjunct to the latter, how the Jeffersonian individualism that he suspected and the Hamiltonian state intervention that he embraced had complemented each other historically, despite their professed hostility to each other in political rhetoric and ideology. For example, as emphasized previously, ardent Jeffersonians never abjured the state as sponsor of freedom and enterprise, and Jefferson as president found large internal improvements and Hamilton's bank and bureaucracy useful for his own purposes.

Not Croly's history but his doctrine placed his brilliant book outside the mainstream of reform. Croly did not put most Americans at ease with enhanced government, let alone with the excessive admiration he had for it. Nevertheless, the threatening pileup of the powers of *bad* government in alliances with monopoly and flooding immigration pushed alarmed citizens to search for a state for their time with which they might at least live in good libertarian conscience. Jeffersonians such as Louis D. Brandeis and Woodrow Wilson were particularly blind to the fact that much of the pileup and corruption they denounced had emerged from freedom for initiative for self-fulfillment, including seeking state favors. The flattering ideology of self-help as well as the astonishing successes of vaunted individualism obscured how much Americans themselves had built and invited state power. The following series of vignettes about the generation or two after 1880 will reveal how widespread and respectable the search for a state was, however much against the Jeffersonian grain it may also seem.

VIGNETTE: SLIDING FROM SPONSORING TO REGULATING AGRICULTURE

Given the dominance of agriculture in the American economy in the nineteenth century, it is not surprising that it was the first major calling to

16. James Weinstein, *The Corporate Ideal in the Liberal State, 1900–1918* (Boston, 1968).

17. Croly, *The Promise of American Life.*

seek and find the state. Ignoring here the great government aid in disposing of the public domain and what individual states were doing to aid their farmers, as early as 1836 an agriculture section in the Patent Office collected simple statistics and also began to make available, at no cost, improved strains of seeds.[18] Waxing of federal and state services for farmers slowly continued over the next generation. By 1862, at the same time as those other notable federal sponsorings, the Homestead Act for free farms and the Morrill Act for land-grant colleges, all federal dealings with farm life came together in establishing the Department of Agriculture, the first federal client department. In 1889 the department was moved from bureau to cabinet level. By that time a large and impressive array of leading scientists and experts had joined the agency. Initially, they came to expand sponsorship, not regulation, *i.e.*, to use federal-funded research to improve the quality and volume of production. The experts also increased liaison with their counterparts in research in the state governments, leading to a nationwide system of agricultural experiment stations under the Hatch Act of 1887. The federal experts also took leading roles in various national associations and meetings to promote better farming. In the now-mythic heyday of a once-passive Washington, the 1880s, this was no tiny, sleepy bureaucracy isolated from the ordinary farmers it was to serve. By 1893, for example, hundreds of Washington personnel and 10,000 members in a department field corps worked with 150,000 volunteer farmers to supply the crop statistics that Washington needed to help farmers plan.[19]

Such burgeoning activities suggest how approachable Washington was to serve new needs. A little earlier, one of these needs, research into plant and cattle diseases and improved breeds, became increasingly important as the national and international market for meat and grains expanded. Without political battle or public uproar, these research and information sponsoring activities about diseased animals expanded into federal inspection, purchase, and destruction (1880). By 1884 a new Bureau of Animal Industry was authorized to go into the field and suppress disease in livestock, and by 1890 federal controls were extended to all livestock for export. None of this suggests effective regulation, with grasp equaling reach, but it shows how more publicized actions like the Meat Inspection Act under Theodore Roosevelt in 1906 can obscure a previous, sizeable pileup of government rules and agencies and under eminent and respectable auspices within and outside government. Like other headline-making changes, the 1906 action created the impression

18. White, *The Republican Era*, 238–39.
19. Alfred C. True, *A History of Agricultural Experimentation and Research in the United States, 1607–1925* (Washington, D.C., 1937).

of a sudden intrusion of the state and a dramatic, controversial shift from laissez-faire to federal regulation. Instead of a great reversal after 1906 from leaving ranchers, butchers, and the public free to choose, compete, and take risks, federal intervention in agriculture precisely to reduce the risks of farmers had been continuous for seventy years. Sponsoring of better breeds had expanded easily into regulation. Presumably, as scholars have suggested about other regulatory acts, regulation was welcome when it made state power available for the healthier cattle that ranchers on their own could not guarantee for the millions of head pouring into the shipping towns of Abilene, Dodge City, and Ogalalla. In all realism, the cattlemen also acted to forestall an even less friendly and less influenceable government intervention.[20]

VIGNETTE: FROM THE PEOPLE'S TO THE PROFESSIONALS' SCHOOLS

Given the appeal of the American evangel about education and the great growth of free public schooling, by 1870 the school already had immense tasks, from the familiar three R's to creating righteous men and women and saving the republic from sin and immorality. The number and variety, as well as awesome, missions of the schools had already created by 1870 a new corps of professional educators ready to monitor how the great American commitment was being met. Although jobs for those educators trained in the so-called normal schools were for public pay and under government or quasi-state controls, the professionals and citizens soon clashed about teacher qualifications, school administration, and that opiate of the educator, the curriculum.[21]

The contest became especially clear in growing cities that were absorbing adjacent enclaves.[22] With expansion, local wards or districts began to lose their earlier control of school matters. Local boards used laymen, *i.e.,* common citizens, who might be grocers or butchers or saloonkeepers with no professional competence in education. Often, members of the ward boards were tied to the city machine and ambitious for pelf and higher offices. Eager professionals easily regarded such grass-roots control of the temples of education as amateurism and ignorance. They also noted the corruption in who was hired, reasons for

20. Two studies with contrasting political biases move on the path traced here: Samuel P. Hays, *Conservation and the Gospel of Efficiency: The Progressive Conservation Movement, 1890–1920* (Cambridge, Mass., 1959); and Gabriel Kolko, *Railroads and Regulation* (Princeton, 1965).

21. Lawrence A. Cremin, *The Transformation of the School* (New York, 1961).

22. David Tyack, *The One Best System: A History of American Urban Education* (Cambridge, Mass., 1974).

firing, contracts for schoolbooks and supplies, repairs to the buildings, and other constant concerns. The professionals found allies in citizens who were high-minded about childhood, schooling, and democracy and who were appalled at what they perceived as the ineptitude, crassness, and vulgarity of the bartender or undertaker on the local school board.

The religion of education thus inspired the need to increase enlightened public intervention. The grossly uneven quality of an entire city school system was traced not only to the excessive independence of the ward boards but to the many conflicting authorities and standards across the city. Professionalism and democratic-humanitarian pleas for saving "the little ones" as well as the promise of more value for money made a strong case for citywide boards of education. Of course, these boards would be responsive to professionals who wanted to run the system. The professionals and leading citizens made common cause.[23] Slowly but steadily the neighborhood boards with ordinary citizen control gave way to larger city and county systems, promising the lowly a better education and the more affluent and concerned citizen better schooling for their children, control over the offspring of the masses, more honesty, possibly lower costs and taxes, and greater efficiency.

By early in this century, large school systems already included a wide range of problems of control and financing that Americans now like to think belong only to later, distant, and large-scale government. These shifts in the level and tone of government authority about school matters suggest an important way in which, generally, the scope, level, and power of governing passed to ever-higher and more inclusive authority.

VIGNETTE: FROM THE OLD POLS TOWARD THE NEW POLIS

More weighty than, but analogous to, the changes in the schools was the shift under the banners of municipal reform from ward-based representation to citywide candidates.[24] Those elected would increasingly have to compete with the enlarging corps of professionals to run increasingly centralized services like the schools. The move to citywide candidates was supposed to produce better public servants and promised a more honorable expression of democratic suffrage and representation. Supposedly, electoral appeals to an entire city would have to cut across, and thus diminish, class and other special interests. Those elected would be

23. Troen, *The Public and the Schools*.
24. Samuel P. Hays, "The Social Analysis of American Political History," *Political Science Quarterly*, LXXX (1965), 383. This article is especially useful about the general tendencies and dynamics of government growth and reorganization.

free to consider the general interests of the city rather than the small, provincial views of the ward. As intended, this reform did gradually decrease the street-corner pol's ties to a ward nabob, but it also diminished the voters' will to ballot for outsiders or strangers from downtown politicos to uptown goo-goos. The reform also marked a shift from grassroots controls and a politics of favors for local voters to larger, centralized policy-making and citywide plans not only for schools but for sewers, water supply, firefighting, street building and maintenance, and so on.

From the point of view of better control over safety and public health, more effective use of resources, marshaling hard-to-find professional talent, and better pinpointing of responsibility, such changes in constituencies and the scope of improved urban management seemed irresistibly reasonable. It is difficult to overstate how much government growth in the recent century of the state has come not only from respectable citizens priding themselves on their self-reliance and skepticism about the state but in the name of reason and expert management.[25] In small as well as large cities after 1880, explosive growth of population and enterprises and the greater impingement of inhabitants on each other had aggravated older, already appalling living conditions. But a heightened sense of unacceptability of these conditions came from the promise of control through new ideas like the germ theory of disease, antisepsis, pasteurization, and water purification. With the health and lives of millions at stake, how could one deny a scientifically based case for government intervention as well as for programs for citywide economies? The analysis of the cause of a polluted water supply was correct, but organizing to eliminate it, one of the stunning achievements of mankind, was difficult to separate from the political manuevering that went into creating citywide water-supply systems. "Rational solutions" were subject to what have by now become familiar limitations. Each round of claims for better order, larger units, higher funding, and new expertness in running government produced its modicum of intellectual faddishness, moralistic arrogance about programs, ideological and professional association loyalties in personnel policies, bureaucratic caution and red tape, and less value for the dollar than promised for the new program. Foul water disappeared, and petty corruption gradually shrank at the ward level but did not disappear as promised in the new citywide systems. Politicians now operating out of city halls still lined up votes and promised favors. Businessmen now sought the larger, citywide contracts for creating the reservoirs and giant water lines as well as for paving, subways, sewers, trolley lines, textbooks, and school construction.

25. James Weinstein, "Organized Business and the City Commission and Manager Movements," *Journal of Southern History,* XXVIII (1962).

VIGNETTE: WAXING AND WANING ABOUT GOOD ROADS

Few needs spawned by America's population and economic growth have been more constant than the demand for roads, and few feeling those needs have been more aggressive in seeking the state. Despite the historic role of federal and state governments in building turnpikes as well as railroads and canals, most road construction before the gasoline-engine age was in the purview of localities and reflected simple requirements, like farmers who needed to get to town.[26] Longer roads beyond a village or county crossroads depended on whatever cooperation various governments could muster. But the continental marketplace of 1890 and the coming of the automobile and the truck soon led to decrying both the meagerness of American roads and the chronic disorder in building and maintaining them. The need to take a larger view of supplies and distribution for an industrial-urban economy quickly became linked with the old ideal of Jefferson and Henry Clay, an "American System" of a national network of major routes.[27]

Rural America was more divided than hinterland-dependent big cities on shifting local powers over roads to higher and wider authorities. But evermore distant raw materials and markets put localities in a position analogous to city areas that had to abandon using neighborhood wells and communal taps in order to gain the advantages of a single dependable urban water system. Economic advantage clashed with the established suspicion of distant government power. Rural citizens feared not only loss of local control but also higher costs and taxes for larger systems. They also resented insufficient say about routes and maintenance, especially about the connections from the major routes to the local roads. Small contractors feared loss of construction and upkeep contracts, and business interests with only local horizons also resisted the calls of reason and the taxes for larger and better systems.

The proponents of improved highways for the national marketplace argued not only for statewide road plans but for centralizing and systematizing the power over roads at the state capital. The old American waning and waxing and struggles among authorities and interests were very evident about road modernization. The nearness of a major good road could deeply affect a community, and competition for places on a route was, as Jefferson had been shocked to learn, a political, partisan concern. Higher construction standards as well as building costs tended to favor the larger, better-connected firms and edged out small

26. Edward C. Kirkland, *Men, Cities, and Transportation: A Study in New England History, 1820–1900* (Cambridge, Mass., 1948).
27. Philip P. Mason, *A History of American Roads* (Chicago, 1967).

local contractors. As the states began to lay out new routes, that too involved encroaching on the *status quo* by subordinating local jurisdictions and property lines to the state's layouts and administration.

These transportation difficulties at the start of the twentieth century were compounded after about 1905 by that godsend for producers and shippers, the gasoline-engine truck. Its light weight, sturdiness, speed, and easy servicing for even small businessmen and farmers had irresistible advantages over horse-drawn vehicles. Road building quickly became more urgent and more contentious, since the truck required more expensive, smoother, hard-surface roads than those that were adequate for horses and wagons. The gas engine also complicated the politics of road building. What rural areas lacked in argument or money against modern road policies they compensated for by their favorable apportionment in state legislatures. Relentlessly, the new roads appeared, but not without many delaying fights against particular road appropriations and taxes, inadequate benefits for a town or county, and payments for roads that heavily favored larger businesses and the cities. Among rural Jeffersonians who pleaded for more economic opportunity for "the little people," their leaders in state legislatures often balked at costs and unacceptable roads or routes and they used their political power to thwart the modernizers. Local liberty was thus posed against ostensibly liberating opportunities to come from government sponsorship and regulation of better roads. Recurrently, economic growth conflicted with political assumptions about virtuous local power and untrustable distant, big government.

One escape from the roadblocks in state legislatures was to turn to the federal government. With the increasing national scope of industry and commerce and the certainty of much higher interstate traffic because of the gasoline engine, Washington's old concern with national turnpikes had a new, powerful stimulus.[28] Soon after the truck appeared, a wide variety of transportation interests with needs frustrated by local and state boundaries and politics clamored for federal involvement, ignoring any prejudices they might otherwise have against state intervention. Washington aid for highways most notably increased in the landmark Federal Highway Acts of 1916 and 1920. These laws established national standards and regulations, but they also directed money to those states with established highway commissions, which encouraged confidence that national dollars would be well used. State government stymied or stunted from within about roads found itself in a position analogous to that of its jealous localities. The nascent federal highway

28. John B. Rae, *The Road and the Car in American Life* (Cambridge, Mass., 1971); Charles L. Dearing, *American Highway Policy* (Washington, D.C., 1941).

program did provide a bypass around the obstructionists in the states. The price, however, was that the enlarged initiative in road building that state governments had been wresting from localities would now have to be compromised in deferring to federal standards in order to obtain Washington funding.[29]

We must note a passing-the-ball-up-the-line effect in this aspect of state growth that is also discernible in other interventions like railroad, livestock, and education policies. An underlying zeal for growth created a demand for funding and a more sensible system that pushed the responsibility for roads ever upward from hamlets after the 1880s to Washington, D.C., only a generation or so later. Local and state powers were gradually eclipsed by the economic expansion that very few citizens wished to restrict, even if they were upset about losing voice about better roads. The push toward ever-wider and ever-larger roles for government in improving highways left go-getting citizens eager for greater opportunities more open to the dependence on and intervention from state and federal government that they feared. Federal conditions for distributing other pork-barrel money show many similar dilemmas in policies for waterways, flood control, and conservation.[30] Economic growth increased state-serviceable needs, but in seeking the larger jurisdiction able to satisfy them, successful programs included higher levels of government to see to it that sponsorship funds were properly spent.

VIGNETTE: MUNICIPAL LEVIATHANS

The dilution of political control within wards and localities in order to raise the standards of politics or increase economic growth should not imply that small towns and minor cities lay supine before the new social power. It is appalling to return to the records of the 1870s and 1880s and read about the blows that growth created for unprepared and crudely governed communities. There was not one aspect of daily life from birth to burial, and for rich and poor alike, that was exempt from greater "impingement." It was the rare older community, whether town, county, or state, that had developed up-to-date services before the beginning of America's great leap forward into the industrial-urban world. But as the blows came, the localities began to act.[31]

29. Fredrich L. Paxson, "The Highway Movement, 1916–1935," *American Historical Review,* LI (1946).

30. Hays, *Conservation and the Gospel of Efficiency.*

31. For suggestions about the expansion of cities generally, see Sam Bass Warner, *Streetcar Suburbs: The Progress of Growth in Boston, 1870–1900* (Cambridge, Mass., 1962). On two vital matters of civic concern, health and public order, see Rosenkrantz, *Public Health and the State,* and Richardson, *The New York Police.*

Traditionally, citizens bred on individualism and self-help professed to expect little from government in what we call social services. When they did turn to the state it was likely to be to nearby government first. By the 1890s, the prospect for better controls over daily life rose as much for localities as for higher authorities. Both vistas were implicit in the new social power of science, public health studies, and the emerging gospel of management. We have noted that the turn to national regulation after 1890 came less from ideology than out of frustration with local and private inability or unwillingness to act adequately. But that many small communities, nevertheless, continued to try to do better about health, safety, schooling, housing, and so on, is abundantly clear.

Raleigh, North Carolina, and Oakland, California, two small cities at opposite ends of the nation, had greatly different economies, sizes, and locations within their states. Raleigh is 150 miles inland, but Oakland is on San Francisco Bay. Neither had much industry. Nevertheless, for all their differences from industrial cities and from each other, they show remarkable similarities in government patterns between 1880 and 1910. In such locales, population growth and pressures for better control over living conditions, not industrialization, seem most responsible for seeking governments that could master the challenge of being up-to-date and better managed. Large factories, wicked bosses, and tens of thousands of massed immigrant workers were not necessary to tempt small localities like these toward more inclusive government.

In 1880, Raleigh had about 10,000 people and by 1910 almost double that (19,000). In those years Oakland's population more than tripled, growing from about 34,500 to 116,400.[32] In the later year, only 1,200 people in Raleigh were employed in few small mills, and the proportions for industry in Oakland were only slightly larger. That more officials for old challenges like crime were added in both places in thirty years is not surprising, considering the growth in population. More revealing is the remarkable increase in new, specialized civic functions, the growth of support staffs, the hiring of professionals, especially in health services, and the renaming of old functions with words that also suggest a more professional and larger compass for officialdom. In Raleigh, "constable" and "chief of police" gave way to "police department" and "police commissioners." A Board of Audit replaced a single auditor, and new positions like Board of Health, Sanitary Inspector, City Physician, and Superintendent of Health had been added by 1910. Overall, not only

32. *Raleigh City Directory, 1880* (Raleigh, 1880); *Raleigh City Directory, 1910* (Raleigh, 1910); McKenney, *Oakland City Directory* (Oakland, 1883); Polk-Husted Directory Co., *Oakland City Directory* (Oakland, 1913).

had the number of officials doubled in thirty years but new functions were added and citizen-volunteer officers were joined by paid professionals.

In Oakland by 1913, a single "police judge," a constable, and a clerk of police court of the 1880s had evolved into a group of ten officials covering two judicial "departments," each with a prosecuting attorney, bailiff, and official court reporter. The constable of the 1880s had given way, as in Raleigh, to a police department. But far more than smaller and less-bustling Raleigh, Oakland had also added these new titles and activities by 1913:

Building Inspector
Fire Chief
Police Chief
Price Expert
License Inspectors (2)
Market and Food Inspector
Poundmaster
Purchasing Agent
Superintendent of Electrical Department
Supervising Architect
Board of Education (with a Business Manager)
Civil Service Board
Board of Library Directors
Board of Playground Directors
Board of Park Directors
Board of Woodyard Directors

The differentiation by function in this array was also reflected in changes in the Oakland City Council. The seven-man body of 1883 had become only five persons. But smacking of the rising penchant for at least seeming to be professional and up-to-date, councilmen were now called commissioners and were elected to tend to specific functions: public affairs; public works; streets; revenue and finance; public health and safety.

VIGNETTE: LEVIATHAN IN THE STATE CAPITALS

What happened in small cities like Raleigh and Oakland also occurred in the state capitals. Executive administration and legislative committees grew and became specialized in order to tend to new needs. In 1875 there were only eleven elected or appointed officials in state administration at Raleigh. They were served by a total of five secretaries, clerks, and tellers. In 1910, major state officials included new commissioners of agriculture, labor, and insurance.[33] Also new were a Department of Labor and Printing, a Board of Health, a Corporation Commission, a Department of Insurance, and a Board of Examiners. Single officials with simple titles gave way to collective bodies with corporate, more abstract titles. Even the "State Geologist" was now part of a "Geological and Economic Survey." Within older offices like that of Secretary of State, there now was support from four clerks and a stenographer; the auditor had added three clerks and the treasurer seven, along with a stenographer. Within the more recently added state offices, education now required not only a Superintendent of Public Instruction, but under him, a Superintendent of Teacher Training, an Inspector of High Schools, a Supervisor of Elementary Schools, a clerk, an "agent" and a stenographer. Within the Department of Insurance, besides the commissioner, there were now three deputies, two clerks, a bookkeeper, a stenographer for the commissioner, an actuary, a license clerk, another bookkeeper, and clerks all now on salary.

The increase in state regulation since the 1880s implicit in such changes is also suggested by the functions of the North Carolina Corporation Commission, a replacement in 1899 for the earlier Railroad Commission (1891). It had the power to regulate not only railroads but telegraph and telephone companies, street railways, steamboats, canals, and "all other companies" exercising the powers of eminent domain. Similar new sweeps for the state are to be found in the tax commission, in novel functions connected with public health, and in the tripling, over thirty years, of the number of standing committees in both houses of the North Carolina legislature. Specialization in the latter is apparent. Railroads, for example, had been split from the older, broader Internal Improvements Committee.

Parallel developments in California state government are striking.[34] Since 1880 these boards and specialists replaced the individual laymen who had been used previously:

> Accountancy Board (with secretary)
> Agriculture Board (with secretary)
> Board of Architecture (with secretary)
> Building and Loan Commissioners (with secretary)

33. *The Legislative Manual and Political Register of the State of North Carolina for the Year 1874* (Raleigh, 1874); R. D. W. Conner, ed., *A Pocket Manual of North Carolina for the Use of Members of the General Assembly, Session 1911* (Raleigh, 1911).

34. "State Officers," in Langley, *San Francisco Directory* (San Francisco, 1880), 1095–96; "Officers of State of California," in Crocker-Langley, *San Francisco Directory* (San Francisco, 1910), 48–50.

Debris Commissioner (with secretary)
Board of Dental Examiners (with secretary)
Board of Examiners (with secretary)
Department of Highways
Commissioner of Horticulture
Labor Statistics Bureau
Registrar of Voters
State Veterinarian
Veterinary Medical Board

By 1913 there were also dozens of new officials for expanded older concerns and institutions like prisons, ports, harbors, pilots, hospitals, special schools and "homes," insurance, health, mining, railroads, normal schools, and the state university.

Spot checks of the records of other localities and other states from about 1880 to 1910 strongly bear out the tendencies sketched here for such different places as North Carolina and California.[35] Not only had bigger government arrived below the federal level, it was also more diverse, more specialized or functional, literally more bureaucratic, more corporate, more professional, more costly. But it was not necessarily the "good government" wanted by progressive reformers nor the effective government hawked by the mongers of scientific management. Perhaps our myth that the locality is a state-free garden of innocence and the difficulty of investigating government changes within more than forty diverse, relatively insular states account for American amnesia about where big government first appeared. Suffice to say that it had already come to America long before New Deal days ushered in the fixed idea that big government is a federal phenomenon and alien to the rest of national experience.

VIGNETTE: CONGRESS AND FEDERAL FUNDING

As the localities and states tried their experiments to control the new social power before the 1890s, federal regulation, despite the steady, slow accretion suggested earlier, seemed small. The scope of enterprise, suspicion of distant power, and the constitutional division between state and interstate matters limited moving toward Washington until problems or needs could no longer be contained at lower levels. But even in the decades before 1890, when federal regulation increased, there had been the sizeable Washington sponsorship we have already noted. There

35. Based on sampling of records for New York, Connecticut, Illinois, and the state of Washington.

also had been stronger portents of a wider, regulatory role in that ceaseless fretful upward movement from local or private authority. Our vignettes have shown some of the paths of control from localities to counties to state capitals. Seeking the state at Washington for railroad regulation was thus within an established logic—almost, it seems, an inevitable step. Justice Brandeis' description of the states as laboratories for social legislation was meant as flattery. But we must also note how often experiments with regulation failed or ran against obstacles like inadequate jurisdiction over an interstate business like Standard Oil.

We cannot rest with the conventional view of the acceleration of federal regulation that concentrates on dramatic, scattered major legislation like the laws establishing the Interstate Commerce Commission (1887) or the Sherman Anti-Trust Act (1890). It is more fruitful to go beyond these publicized actions and look also for quieter, changing functions like those smaller ones we have traced in the Department of Agriculture. Below the department level we find a long pileup of federal regulation in concerns like steamboats and ocean vessels, Indian affairs, mining, land policy, and immigration. All of these presaged the better-known and more hotly debated intervention late in the century.

One problem for historians who want to sail into the murky waters of administrative history has been posed by the dean of that scholarship, Leonard D. White.[36] His trailblazing work heavily emphasizes the executive departments and administration. Within that scope he maintains that overall growth in federal activity before 1900 was overwhelmingly proportionate to population, and that significant changes in federal functions like regulation still lay ahead. This view contrasts with the emphasis here on slow accretions of tasks other than those in the dramatized, new regulatory commissions, the growth of nonfederal government functions and, as will now be suggested, in Congress and the national executive.

If, as White has claimed, a larger national officialdom, a generation after Ulysses Grant, was working on more of the same tasks and with little change in horizons, how does one account for the growing sense of the importance of Washington that ambitious men like Mark Hanna were acquiring in those years?[37] Washington by the 1890s was pulling into its service not only lifelong politicians but lions from the private economy like the banker William Whitney, John Wanamaker the

36. Leonard D. White's principal work is in four consecutive volumes on national administrative history: *The Federalists* (New York, 1948); *The Jeffersonians* (New York, 1951); *The Jacksonians* (New York, 1954); and *The Republican Era, 1869–1901* (New York, 1958). The last covers the period dealt with here.

37. Herbert Croly, *Marcus Alonzo Hanna* (New York, 1912).

merchandiser, and Hanna the coal and ironmonger.[38] For such men, Washington could speak louder than the states about needs and interests that required national tending. Washington and its power were also less boring than office life in Cleveland or Philadelphia. Generally, the tide of makers and shakers, of favor seekers and relief seekers was increasingly toward the Potomac for the larger view or more substantial aid than could be found at the statehouses.

In stressing changes in government activity within the executive, White overlooks many indications about government scope on Capitol Hill.[39] Like his works, the influential histories of the United States have been national histories, not histories of the states. And national histories tend to emphasize the presidencies while ignoring changes in Congress except at big moments or in great clashes with presidents.

The enormous growth in national population and states in the nineteenth century meant larger political constituencies for the House and Senate, more senators and congressmen bringing to Washington more and increasingly diverse interest groups, like those after 1870 in the rapidly expanding businesses of ranching and mining. By 1913, all but two of today's fifty states had been admitted to the Union. After 1911, the enduring cap of 435 members had to be put on the number of congressmen seatable under the Capitol dome. It is, of course, speculation that the total in 1820 of 213 congressmen, each answerable to 40,000 citizens, without the aid of railroad travel, the telegraph, or telephone, became less responsible or less responsive as the constituency steadily climbed to about 135,000 by the 1870s and to 235,000 citizens by 1911. In 1908, the press of business led to authorizing personal staffs for the congressmen and constructing a new office building for them. Even 435 House members could not be accommodated in the existing chamber, so in 1913 the traditional desk space for each member was removed and the current system of seats without desks was installed.[40]

To get mounting and more diverse work done and with increasing emphasis on specialized knowledge, investigation, and statistics, Congress, like the states, had to diversify its committees long before 1910.[41] Between 1789 and 1870, over four generations, Senate and House

38. Josephson, *The Politicos*, 422–26.

39. The following analysis is based on various tables in U.S. Department of Commerce, Bureau of the Census, *Historical Statistics of the United States: Colonial Times to 1970* (2 vols.; Washington, D.C., 1975), II, 1067–85. See below for specific tables.

40. On the cap of 435, see De Alva S. Alexander, *History and Procedures of the House of Representatives* (Boston, 1916); on the facilities for the House, see Neil MacNeil, *The Forge of Democracy* (New York, 1963).

41. George B. Galloway, *History of the United States House of Representatives* (New York, 1961), 66–67, 273.

together had created 38 standing committees. But in the forty years after 1870, and only half of the previous fourscore years, standing committees increased by 50 percent. By 1913 there were 61 House committees and 74 in the Senate, a total of 135.[42] The tendencies in this growth are clear and parallel changes in cities and states. In the House, novel and larger and more demanding interests had led to new specialized committees like Mines and Mining (1865), Alcoholic Liquor Traffic (1893), and Irrigation and Arid Lands (1893). By 1886, a young scholar named Woodrow Wilson had already noted that not only had the federal government become "congressional government" but that the latter had become, in effect, committee government.[43] In the national legislature, therefore, as in city and state governments, the federal machine tended to more structure, more and newer functions, and more complex organization and procedure. This glimpse at historical tendencies may lessen the shock of learning that a century later, in the 101st Congress of 1992, there were 300 committees and subcommittees. They had become so specialized that 30 committees and 77 subcommittees had voices about the defense budget and 40 committees and subcommittees worked on the Clean Air Act. There are other striking facts to ponder when we survey other aspects of earlier congressional organization.

In the years 1829 through 1831, during the 21st congressional session, 213 congressmen and 48 senators, a total of 261, introduced 856 bills, of which 369 became laws with 143 of those being "public acts" and 217 "private acts." Whatever the early system for controlling traffic, each senator and congressman on the average presented between 3 and 4 measures in the two-year session, with slightly better than a 40 percent chance of enactment. In the session of 1909 through 1911, 391 congressmen and 93 senators, or 484 legislators, were a little less than double the 1830 number. They brought in 44,363 bills, a fiftyfold increase over 1829 through 1831, for an average of about 92 measures for each legislator. This was almost thirty times the individual average in 1830; constituencies, however, were only six times larger. Probably because of the traffic controls demanded by such an avalanche, only 595 public acts and resolutions and 289 private acts resulted. Was much of the flood of bills "more of the same," as one might infer from Leonard White, and thus concerned with similar interests and needs as in earlier Congresses? Or were the subjects of the bills and the scope of the legislation so more diverse and so novel that we can infer that

42. George Goodwin, Jr., *The Little Legislatures* (Amherst, Mass., 1970), 3–6.

43. Woodrow Wilson, *Congressional Government: A Study in American Politics* (1885; rpr. Baltimore, 1981), chap. 2.

while Congress did do more of the same, it was also asked to act about subjects that it had previously ignored or had not even existed in 1830, like railroad problems. Clearly, only a content analysis of bills and laws with adequate awareness of the control system on Capitol Hill could unravel the conundrum about this vast increase in legislation.

Other ponderable statistics also bear on the sway of the federal state by 1910. These concern the size and distribution of the federal job corps and the costs of national government. From 1861 to 1910, twelve additional states had been admitted, making about a 30 percent increase in number in fifty years. The federal cadre in 1861, all of which was party patronage, stood at about 37,000, excluding the military. Only about 3,000, or 8 percent, worked in the national city. By 1911, with 30 percent more states and triple the population, gross federal employment numbered 396,000, more than ten times that of 1861. Still, only 10 percent were on service in Washington, and even that Washington figure represented a small decline from a previous high. Breaking down those figures of 1861 and 1911 among the three branches of the government and then, within the executive, among defense, postal, and "all other services," shows that in 1861, while 83 percent of employment under the executive was in postal service, by 1911 that figure had shrunk to 53 percent. The number under the executive classed as "other" (not military or postal) had more than doubled from 13 percent to 29 percent. (Throughout this fifty-year span, 94 to 98 percent of all federal jobs belonged to the executive branch.) These signs around 1910 suggest, abstractly, not only growth but new tasks and goals. But had such changes occurred in all the executive departments? How many jobs were created for new functions, and how many persons dealt with expanded established services? Did the increases clump in a few departments, like Agriculture or Interior, so that the growth there could be classified as "exceptional"? These questions, like others in this foray, remain to be fully researched.

Budget, appropriation, and expenditure figures are equally intriguing. Here we consider what the record calls federal "outlays."[44] In 1860, these came to about $63 million, of which almost $32 million, or about 46 percent, went for all services other than armed forces, veterans, and debt. Over the next thirty years, changes in the value of the dollar and in methods of calculating outlays came into play, but by 1890 the indicated total annual federal outlays had more than quadrupled, reaching about $318 million, of which more than 67 percent was for "all other services." By 1910, the outlay for the year stood at $693 million (dou-

44. *Historical Statistics,* II, 1086–1134. N.B. the cautionary notes on p. 1089 about the criteria for use of the statistics about expenditure.

ble 1890), with $359 million, or just over 50 percent, for "other services." If these changes only represented increased costs for simple items like office supplies, typewriters, or harnesses for horses, such figures might deflate any easy assumption that more outlays imply more government roles.

Because of the lack of a settled system for recording the information in the late nineteenth century, when the term *expenditure* is used it appears as a figure for all American government rather than for federal activity alone. Also, expenditure was recorded over different spans of time than used for "outlays," "budget" or "revenue." Still, if our thesis is viable that government functions piled up at every level, expenditure as recorded for all levels can test that idea. By 1869, 4.2 percent of all national income is traceable to wages for all government workers, excluding defense. With some dips over the years to 1909, this had increased about 30 percent, to 5.5 percent. Within the productive work force in 1869, 3.5 percent were in government service at all levels. This figure only inched upward until about 1890 and then took flight, so that by 1909 it had reached 4.8 percent of the work force, an overall change of 37 percent in two generations.[45]

Two complicated categories that invite a little further speculation are the national gross and net dollar expenditures by the federal government per person in the population. In 1861, all federal government expenditure for each American in the census of 1860 was $2.12 a year, but when we exclude military, veterans, and debt service the outlay was only $.86. By 1911, each American required, as it were, $7.50 annually of gross government expenditure, an increase of more than 250 percent over the steady upward path since 1861. With military, pension, and debt service excluded, the net expenditure per American by 1911 had increased to $3.84, or 450 percent from 1861.[46] Within this, so-termed "public welfare" programs in the United States cost $318 million in 1890, divided two to one for state over federal items.[47] By 1913 a generation had passed in which public provision for social services had risen with increasing urbanization and immigration, the rise of social work, and reform agitation. Whatever the explanation, by 1913 the nation's welfare expenditure over 1890 had more than tripled, while national population in those years since 1890 had grown by 50 percent. Total government outlays for public welfare in 1913 had reached $1 billion, but still at a ratio of about two to one for state government over federal aid. What we do have in *Historical Statistics* to help refine the figures toward more

45. *Ibid.*, Tables F259–260.
46. *Ibid.*, Interpolated from Tables Y308–317, Y335–338, and A6–8.
47. *Ibid.* Based on Tables H1–31.

subtle analysis reveals that as a percentage of gross national product, the welfare costs did not yet represent the immense needs that were later made legitimate for public action. Over a generation, they had remained at about 2.5 percent, and as a percentage of all government expenses they had even dropped slightly, from 38 percent to 34 percent.

These figures about bills and laws, outlays and percentages are a gross retrospect intended to move us beyond speculation to fuller investigation. They do not validate contemporary complaints nor, even more, stand as available statistics to score points in political debate or to stir scandal or supper-table moralizing about socialism or to arouse government to more intervention. As gross figures, however, they can help us understand the growing concern by 1910 about the size of government, its costs, and the legitimacy of the tasks Washington had taken on. The important questions, nevertheless, are less whether net growth in functions, costs, and bureaucrats had occurred over 40 years than about the dynamics of the growth and the effectiveness of expanded state services.

From all these vignettes a sketch of common dynamics of government growth emerges. Private enterprise and initiative, perhaps encouraged by government sponsoring of programs like free public schools or research into animal diseases, lead to a variety of problems in efforts to expand business or to police it privately. The responses by groups such as the cattlemen need not be immoral or illegal. The high capital costs of transcontinental railroads, for example, were probably beyond the supply of private funding. Inspecting millions of head of cattle was beyond private organization, especially across state lines. Beset by difficulties often traceable to their own growth and ambitions, the interests organize and approach the state, often at the lower level of state governments at first, but government nonetheless. Government responds with at least a minimal or symbolic gesture of aid or repair, such as research into breeding and diseases or granting the earliest railroads difficult rights of way. Opposition may be spirited or proposals may sail through. Indeed, much of the pileup of government seems to come quietly, in small, easily passed proposals for cattle inspection. The reasonableness of the need and its broad acceptability for most ranchers, the prestige and persistence of the big-rancher supplicants, the modesty of first government support, the minimal public hostility to the initial and slight regulatory thrust, allow it to find a base in government. But another all-important permission to intervene has been established. Who cannot agree with the need to safeguard the national cattle herds? Self-interest dictates that the ranchers seek the state. A specific regulation soon develops a constituency of hundreds of thousands of voters across many states, ready to make alliances with other favor-seeking groups. What happens for the cattle industry is not lost on others, in forestry and mining for example, let alone on other farmers upset about the boll weevil or inadequate grain storage. The political context is the approachable, democratic state, and all is subject to the constant search by democracy's politicians for new issues, favor-granting, and votes. With varying degrees of opposition and consent and with politics always in play, the pileup of functions and agencies and funding proceeds. This also creates the vested interests of increasing numbers of specialists in programs among bureaucrats and congressmen, like "Silver Dick" Bland for the silver mining interests. There are also aspirants for office and constituents who want the cattle interests or other groups to be even better taken care of. From some moment in the 1880s wholesome meat will thus remain a growing public concern, and taking chances on market forces alone to improve the quality of meat will be repeatedly abjured. It is discovered that better city schools, the national road system, farm credit, or immigration control are other issues vital for the nation that also must be tended. Progress or justice is hailed as each program begins. So the country moves toward a widening sweep of possible state concern and activity. Once the permission to intervene begins to gain general legitimacy, where on the horizon of the public good can interest groups or aggrieved parties not espy something that cannot be declared remediable by enlisting the state? There appear virtually self-propelled cycles of bidding, receiving, and upping the ante for the state's action. As Robert Wiebe has observed, economic problems like railroad rates thus become political ones of influencing the state. Those first in line for a new type of favor, *e.g.*, free seeds, or for a new redress of grievance, *e.g.*, tainted hamburgers at Jack in the Box, will become those already "on board" with a favor or a regulation. They will learn to seek added state servicing of needs whether stimulated by fresh changes in the market or by the fact of regulation already obtained.

This capsule model of state intervention is not the old story of good reformers fighting bad capitalists to bring a better life or social justice for "the people." Close study denies any simple moral tale about the growth of government regulation.[48] In a more refined saga, reformers and their opponents share capitalistic ideas of enterprise and profit. Business, like reform or radicalism, is not a monolithic world.[49] All interests are divided within, with little superior virtue clearly dividing the small businessman, yeoman farmer, or honest workingman from the great en-

48. Hays, *The Response to Industrialism.*

49. Robert Wiebe, *Businessmen and Reform: A Study of the Progressive Movement* (Cambridge, Mass., 1962).

trepreneur. Some groups welcome and others oppose state intervention, depending on the issue and propects for success. All groups, however, have interests to protect, with the small ranchers' needs no less nor more moral than those of the big powers they deal with that are winning market games in cattle raising. For other farmers the issue may be warehousing grain or improving windmills or the costs of twine, insurance, or grain shipping. Reformers seeking regulation often fly idealistic banners like "save the family farm." But they are interested parties, *i.e.*, not impartial servants of justice or order. They speak for changes in railroad or bank regulation that their followers need. Or, if unwanted reform seems inevitable, as in 1913, the portentous first year of Woodrow Wilson's administration, its opponents play politics to be sure that the state throws only the smallest bone to the yapping hounds of morality or fair dealings about monopoly or the banking system.

Many needs for regulation actually taken up by government are not intrinsically or uniquely concerns of the state, but they become matters for the state's attention when private restraint, trade association regulation, and other controls without a government role fail to do the job adequately. There always remains the problem of impatience in a democracy increasingly afire to satisfy all needs and end all pain. And that fire is fed by the seeming permeability of democratic government. The pulse of American needs and the notion that government exists to serve them are at the heart of most of state growth. Docile citizens in adversity who would let the business cycles run fully while tightening their belts would have far less need to seek the state. Tightening belts and taking it on the chin have never been the effective chants of democracy in pain. The better motto has been, If the shoe pinches, seek the state.

The deep drive toward expanding government is not fully explained by citing catapulting capitalism, worried ranchers, enthusiasts for state intervention, or self-aggrandizing bureaucrats. John Stuart Mill, early in the industrial era (1836), pointed out how what he called civilization, *i.e.*, the larger-scale, more organized, and harmony-needing society of his time and ours, increasingly crowds in on itself.[50] Innumerable, more closely knit interests touch and clash with each other and demand adjustment. Citizens who wish less conflict in daily life and ever-higher standards of living as well thus make the state, in the name of democratic justice, another contributor to what Max Weber discerned as the systematization or "rationalization" of life over many centuries in Western culture. Mill's friend, that state-obsessed observer Tocqueville, had also read the early auguries. Again, for this French aristocrat, all

---

50. John Stuart Mill, "Civilization—Signs of the Times," in *Prefaces to Liberty: Selected Writings of John Stuart Mill*, ed. Bernard Wishy (Boston, 1959).

seemed fated for America as well as Europe: "It is easy to foresee that the time is drawing near when man will be less and less able to produce by himself alone, the commonest necessaries of life. The task of the governing power will therefore perpetually increase, and its very efforts will extend it every day. The more it stands in the place of associations, the more will individuals, losing the notion of combining together, require its assistance: these are causes and effects that unceasingly create each other."[51]

With a deepening sense of unfinished tasks and enhanced possibilities in government action, radical protests or elaborate ideologies like a search for order were not much needed to evoke regulatory bureaucracies. Only deep-dyed skeptics about most ideals like William Graham Sumner sensed the watered stock in the company named "rational reform" whose work he pessimistically termed "the vain attempt to make the world over." He was as alert to the statism in tariff favors for the plutocracy as in the socialism aimed at the plebs. But whether the concern was to drive buccaneers out of the railroad industry or banking or to bring poor and rich alike clean water in the cities, all controls involved that larger, more intrusive, more distant government that, as an idea, Americans scorned. That the dreaded Leviathan was nurtured for generations by their honored expansive, individual, private enterprise and in the pursuit of happiness remained one of the most difficult lessons that twentieth-century Americans had to learn.

Laissez-Faire in Retreat

The word *state* appeared frequently in the stream of reform proposals that swelled out of the 1880s. Impressive scholarly commentary about the nature of the state and the history of American government also added to the flood. Ideas ranged from libertarian notions of anarchists and Spencerians to socialist and Hegelian visions of the state as the supreme sponsor of human freedom.[52] Most writers with a program for American government were restorers and sought a state that would be able to bring back individual liberty and cleanse a democracy stained by corruption.[53] Even restoration, however, implied intervention and policing. A government that would do better at protecting small enterprises

51. Tocqueville, *Democracy in America,* II, 108.

52. Barry D. Karl, *Charles E. Merriman and the Study of Politics* (Chicago, 1974), deals with these intellectual crosscurrents during Merriman's early career.

53. Lewis L. Gould, ed., *The Progressive Era* (Syracuse, 1974), lays out the variety and the tensions within progressive reform.

and political life against robber barons, monopolists, and city bosses would require far more power than most Americans understood. But Americans also wanted to profit from economic growth, and the path to that goal for an industrial nation clearly required much more bigness in both government and enterprise than in the past. It seemed difficult to grasp that whether controlled by a Charles Francis Adams or by a Daniel Drew, a major railroad line, as well as a modern steel industry and a national supply of petroleum, were, intrinsically, large-scale businesses and also would need active state supervision if they were not to be run in the excoriated Rockefeller manner.

In many respects, therefore, the search for the state involved deep tensions and contradictory tendencies, the deepest being enhancing state power in order to strengthen individual freedom, choices, command of life. Finding the formula that could strengthen both authority and liberty preoccupied almost two generations before 1914. The search drew on that new flow of philosophic ideas about the state but turned out to be far more remarkable for its intellectual stir than for deep reforms. Nor did the search for the right kind of state end in 1914, as President Wilson thought it had. The search continues today.

To characterize the pileup in state intervention after 1880 as a retreat from laissez-faire is misleading, since it is abundantly clear that there has never been a time in American history that the state stayed out and thus needed to be brought back from Jeffersonian somnolence. Any attempt to restore a society in which the state *had* stayed out was to pursue a chimera. But persisting loyalties to that ideal of minimal government chronically undercut attempts to use government more effectively.

Failure to enact effective antimonopoly or railroad regulation, for example, can be traced to inadequate knowledge of railroad economics, a simplistic reading of American history, and ideological hostility to the very state proposed as regulator. Beyond these important failings and explaining the general limits for most major reforms were the limits of the American constitutional and party systems. However strong and informed presidential leadership, both systems worked to accent at Washington the role of separate and conflicting interests. Whatever the cogency of reform schemes, on major matters American politics at Washington demand trading among interest groups. As reforms such as federal antitrust legislation moved through the triple filters of the federal system of governments, checks and balances, and the party system, the provisions tended toward the most widely acceptable formulae and lowest possible costs to all contending interests. Almost a century of reform morphology was thus prefigured in one senator's riposte to the interminable debate about the Sherman bill in 1890. All that the Senate needed, he said, was only "some bill headed: 'A Bill to Punish Trusts.' "[54] Especially on major domestic matters, our political system has put a premium on safe, or minimally alienating, legislation and, at that, for only those larger problems that could not be evaded. Even before 1890, the powerful role of *gestures* in the generations ahead was apparent in the Pendleton Act (1883), the Interstate Commerce Commission (1887), and the Sherman antitrust legislation. In these three laws commonly said to mark the birth of federal regulation, only whatever was agreeable to the coalition that formed the majority could pass Congress and gain the president's signature. Diluting and filtering to impede rapid, sweeping action by a consolidated national majority was clearly James Madison's intention. We can only speculate, however, about what Madison or Jefferson would have thought about the fate of their original design that, by the 1890s, so hindered bringing national power to bear on the distress of millions of Jeffersonian small businessmen and farmers who felt beset by the trusts. In contrast, there were also those who relished the going system of arranging political compromises, especially if they profited from being masters of the intricacies. And there always were rare Thoreauians who wanted nothing more from the state than that it leave their needs alone—except, perhaps, to preserve the wilderness.

In both the economy and in recourse to government, the enormous potential for massive individual power inherent in industrialization pierced all horizons that Jefferson or Adam Smith or even Hamilton had envisioned for the scale of both private enterprise and state action. But even before the era of industrial giants, the long record of rush-about expediency of American democracy in need from both the hopes and pains of laissez-faire gives some credence to Smithian theorists of our day like Milton Friedman. They rightly observe that free enterprise in its full sense of minimal recourse to the state has never been tried but has continually been compromised by unwise, hasty, wavering, and politically expedient government intervention about, for example, land speculation, the gold standard, or interest rates.[55] But if political realities of American democracy have so militated against the full run of a laissez-faire system, their power implies that the very supposition of a self-correcting, pure economic system that will work, eventually, *if only* citizens would forego seeking the state, is chimerical, even utopian. The tenets of strict laissez-faire are too abstract for ambitiously needful or wounded Americans urged to await ultimate beneficent results by trusting market forces. In 1932, after four years of depression and with a

---

54. Josephson, *The Politicos*, 460.
55. Milton Friedman, *Capitalism and Freedom* (Chicago, 1962).

25 percent unemployment rate, Americans bet that, ultimately, they would all be dead before the system righted itself.

But at any time, not just in a crisis like 1932, what was the best reading about the nature and role of competition and monopoly? That light was essential for Americans to determine how and when government or private power should be deployed or whether to learn to live with big business or to move to restore and maintain competition. In the decades of investigating monopoly that preceded the famous Pujo inquiry by Congress in 1913, Americans did not believe that efficiency and productivity, rather than competition or consolidation, might be the key questions. Nor could they have learned from the many shortsighted investigations that capital and labor, kept out of the enterprises dominated by the trusts, were going into many new small and medium enterprises so that, *overall*, competition was not only lively but growing. Indeed, one recent student contends that by 1910 competition was excessive.[56]

For all-important questions of fact as well as for understanding the limitations of laissez-faire theory, Americans at that time were ill-served by strong moralistic tendencies that obscured major issues in debating regulatory policies as well as by reforms that were only gestures. As Richard Abrams has observed about Louis Brandeis, one of the deans of the antitrust movement, "His opposition to big business . . . had more of the qualities of a prejudice than of a conclusion founded upon coherent analysis."[57] Intense as they were about their ideal of a small producers republic, Americans had very little patience with any case for a Rockefeller or Morgan, even if, as entrepreneurs, their own machinations had amounted to what Schumpeter was to call the "creative destruction" of edging out smaller firms and scrapping the inefficient and less productive practices in the firms they controlled. The chief perception in the investigations of monopoly was of the unprecedented and unjustified powers of the trusts to close the marketplace to the little man and buy off the state. The trusts and financiers were not patiently and dispassionately studied. They were castigated and their leaders were damned by public opinion voiced by denunciatory and exhortatory politicians led by candidates like Woodrow Wilson in 1912.[58]

A major part of the indictment of big business was that it consistently bought the political support that it needed and that it had pushed its own

56. Naomi R. Lamoreaux, *The Great Merger Movement in American Business* (New York, 1985).

57. Louis D. Brandeis, *Other People's Money and How the Bankers Use It*, ed. Richard M. Abrams (New York, 1967), xxviii–xxix.

58. Woodrow Wilson, *The New Freedom* (New York, 1914). See also Arthur S. Link, *Wilson: The Road to the White House* (Princeton, 1947), chaps. 14–15.

political program for the American economy. In fact, ever since the Civil War, "business" had been divided about major public policies as well as about turning to the state for protection, and it seldom remained consistent about what it wanted, in what degree, and when.[59] Some producers of iron and steel from domestic ores wanted protection from imported ore or rails. Those who might be producing specialty steels requiring the import of alloys like tungsten or who were running out of domestic iron favored imports and, consequently, wanted little or no tariff on foreign ore. In time, a firm might shift from favoring a high tariff to wanting a low tariff as its operations required raw materials from foreign mines or sugar fields. But, again, accuracy about the variety and relative weight of the tariff interests was not the issue for those outraged by tariff rates or the politics of tariff making. The answer to injury from the tariff, "the mother of trusts," was not a counsel of reason or of citing evidence from meticulous inquiry but, as with the issue of competition, indictment.

In the fuller view of how business-operated, the indictments neglected to note that if a tariff rate was the large favor for some big businessmen, a municipal license or low assessment on a house or store were typical concerns of small capitalists. Like the larger entrepreneurs in Washington whom the small businessman denounced for corrupting the republic, the latter sought their own favors but from city hall, not higher up. Business at all levels thus helped set examples for other American groups whose developing needs required buttressing or salve from the state. Despite labor union hostility to unfair laws and court decisions against unions in the 1890s, the American Federation of Labor and other labor voices had their own political program, including federal restriction on contracts made overseas to lure immigrants willing to work cheap when they arrived in America, thus undercutting established workers.[60] By the 1890s many small farmers, organized in "Alliances," "Wheels," or the Populist Party, called on the state for radical measures like government operation of the railroads, state-sponsored credit and warehousing, and allied steps to protect the little man against market forces as well as to bail themselves out from their own unacknowledged follies, like speculation.

Simple, gross categories like "industry," "workers," and "farmers" thus do not help in understanding the patterns in the retreat from whatever laissez-faire Americans had practiced. Enough of American enter-

59. For the Civil War splits in business and the implications, see Stanley Coben, "Northeastern Business and Radical Reconstruction: A Re-examination," *Mississippi Valley Historical Review,* XLVI (1959).

60. Oscar Handlin, *The Uprooted* (Boston, 1951), 289–90.

prise of various stripes did seek the state, and with sufficiently enduring and intense interest, that we can only agree with those students of capitalist development for whom the notable moments in the decline of open competitive markets are when capital itself, not radicals, rejects competition and also tries to use the state to shore up its position.[61]

Politics as Free Enterprise

Decentralization, competition, and hostility to regulation were as characteristic of professional politics as of the economy before the 1880s. To the victor belong the spoils was the political version of may the best competitor win the largest share of market. In the famous observation of Max Weber, the professional politicians lived off as well as for politics. Before the advent of federal civil service in 1883, the cutthroat job market in politics was much like that in the business world, with one notable exception: loyalty to the party leaders counted more than honest performance in the job. The costs of doing business for favors with the politicians entrenched in fortresses of patronage like Tammany Hall and the New York Customs House of the 1870s alienated enough players of the old game in the business community. They moved into reform in order to limit the costs of that arrogant individualist, the boss. His banked pelf from payoffs and skimming and inflated charges by the 1870s had made his party secure enough to raise prices unconscionably for his favors.[62]

The rhetoric of civil service reform was heavily elitist and skeptical of popular democracy.[63] The professed need to restore virtue to a republic debased by an excess of democracy was a lofty ideal, but it was combined with a more venal desire to cut the expense and frustrations of the current system for seeking state aid. Both ideals and interests created the turn against the spoils system and ushered in the Pendleton Act, a gesture toward a federal merit system that put about 10 percent of federal jobs on the civil service lists.[64] That marked another heavily business-endorsed retreat from an excessively disorderly free market for selling favorable tariffs, property assessments, or police and fire protection.

Civil-service reform at least had the great virtue of recognizing that

61. Schumpeter, *Capitalism, Socialism, and Democracy;* Gabriel Kolko, *The Triumph of Conservatism* (New York, 1963).

62. Thomas C. Reeves, *Gentleman Boss: The Life of Chester Alan Arthur* (New York, 1975); Seymour J. Mandelbaum, *Boss Tweed's New York* (New York, 1965).

63. John G. Sproat, *The Best Men: Liberal Reformers in the Gilded Age* (New York, 1968).

64. Ari Hoogenboom, *Outlawing the Spoils: A History of the Civil Service Reform Movement, 1865–1883* (Urbana, Ill., 1961).

the affairs of the modern state could not be conducted by will-of-the-wisp marketplace standards. Public services and government jobs could not be sold to the highest bidder if Americans really wanted an unbuyable and skillful government rather than a "for hire" system staffed by casual laborers. But with the large covert roles in granting favors that the state had played in the economy, what group wanted or could afford clean government as, for example, in an extensive and incorruptible civil service? Had the gesture of the Pendleton Act of 1883 been stronger and properly supplemented, American public service might have come to much more than resistance to payoffs.

The long-range results of civil service remain ambiguous. If corruption slowly declined, the federal merit system led eventually to that fourth branch of American government, the professional bureaucracy, with which presidents and Congress have had to struggle in order to make their policies effective. A century after the Pendleton Act, the now thick and diverse histories of bureaucracies suggest excessive emphasis among early civil-service enthusiasts on codified procedures and incorruptible personnel. In addition to the alternating tendencies of professional civil servants to either Mandarin arrogance or Prussian servility before the political leader, the American civil service never gained the weight that "the expert view" requires to counter the politicians' ignorance or expediency. The civil service ideal was inadequately augmented by salaries, pensions, or marks of honor and place to attract the best and the brightest to government service.[65] Nothing in America has come close to matching the top talent that in England, France, and Germany finished university training with highest honors and then entered government service in the principal ministries.[66] Their performance, of course, was another matter. American civil service at all levels of government remained low paid, underesteemed, and underpowered, and the public learned to expect little from civil servants in devising imaginative major policies to deal with the problems of modern America. Honest competence was the conventional standard.[67] Business and the professions, not government, were the roosts for bright and energetic Americans. Also, the top, nonelective policy-making positions in Washington never became civil service jobs with prestigious permanent undersecretaries who know the ropes

65. U.S. Senate Committee on Government Operations, *Confidence and Concern: Citizens View American Government* (Washington, D.C., 1973).

66. Hans Eberhard Mueller, *Bureaucracy, Education, and Monopoly: Civil Service Reform in Prussia and England* (Berkeley, 1984); U.S. House of Representatives Committee on Post Office and Civil Service, *History of Civil Service Merit Systems of the United States and Selected Foreign Countries* (Washington, D.C., 1976).

67. Samuel J. Eldersveld et al., *The Citizen and Administrator in a Developing Democracy* (Glenview, Ill., 1968).

and help guide the politically appointed department head through the maze of the system.[68] Like other societies, America received no better bureaucracy than it deserved, paid for, or could tolerate, especially considering that our civil servants are to staff a government that few Americans trust, let alone want to enhance or honor.

If government in the 1880s needed more decorous servants than those who might be chosen by a Platt or a Conkling, lest they bite too hard, one impulse was to let them look moral while remaining figureheads.[69] And inexpensive, also. In the first generation of shift toward touted federal regulation, what happened in public service provided another major portent about reform for the next century, *i.e.*, starving the state of the resources it needed in money, personnel, and "bite" to accomplish its assigned regulatory tasks. Those opposed to regulation but forced to accept a gesture like the Sherman Antitrust Act gradually learned how easily constituencies aroused for reform could be satisfied by such moral moments and how easily the state's seeming new bite could be minimized by starving it through meager staffing, vaguely worded laws and regulations that the courts would disfavor, harassment of the enforcement bureaucrats about favors for constituents and threats about agency funding, contradictory legislation, slim salaries for agency members, skillful lobbying against regulation, and infiltration into the bureaucracy of the point of view of the very interests it was supposed to regulate.[70] The great pity was the meager public capacity that gathered to deal with the explosions of the new social power. Here and there were exceptions, like the previously mentioned cadre of experts in the Department of Agriculture with Chief Chemist Wiley, not a legislator, drafting the essentials of what became the Pure Food and Drug Act of 1906 and the U.S. Commissioner of Labor playing a similarly large role in the meat-packing act of the same year.[71]

Although the size of their needs pressed business and labor and eventually farming to organize their enterprises on national lines without being bound, as Washington was, by state borders and constitutional limitations, the deployment of even expert federal power would have been far more difficult. What one hundred Wileys and a string of strong presidents could propose to confront the new social power was constantly at risk against those constitutional limits, state boundaries, and

68. Hugh Heclo, *A Government of Strangers: Executive Politics in Washington* (Washington, D.C., 1977).

69. The brilliant but coruscating contemporary image was by Henry Adams in his novel *Democracy, an American Novel* (New York, 1880).

70. On starving the state, see Weibe, *The Search for Order,* 196–223, and Kolko, *The Triumph of Conservatism,* 159–70, 285–86.

71. White, *The Republican Era,* 244–45.

party politics as well as the tradition that Washington had better not act at all.[72] There was thus a dramatic disproportion between the gathering sense of need by the 1890s for some sort of national action about the new social power and how seldom the federal government was able to grasp for all of its growing reach. Of course, ample recognition must be given to the fact that this was the first generation that asked Washington to address simultaneously so many needs welling up from both the release of vast economic powers and the limitations of governments below in dealing with them.

One particularly formidable force in starving the pretensions of governments was the federal courts. By 1910, many judges had matured in an America unused to regulation and unlike the industrial-urban world whose problems the courts were asked to adjudicate. Regulation under antimonopoly laws like the Sherman Act was also not helped by the intrinsic complexity and slipperiness of its key phrase, "restraint of trade," or in other regulatory criteria to follow, like "fair rate of return" or the "rule of reason." Soon after the Sherman Act, its opponents sensed that leaving action against monopoly ultimately to the courts, rather than to the Justice Department or a special agency, would eviscerate the new law. And so it proved in most cases for the next twenty years.

By 1910 if citizens worried that all lines for intervention by the state might lead to Washington, the federal government, generally, was not prepared to accept intervention in the fulsome, expert way that Walter Lippmann would soon call "mastery." America had not caught up with its history. It suffered from a national dearth of dispassionate, expert public servants who understood railroad management, the imponderable economics of farming in an international market, or the equally great intricacies of corporate finance. Even impressive analysis was too often colored by prejudices. That did not mean that a Brandeis could not get the facts straight about the Morgan-Rockefeller collaboration for spheres of influence over American corporations. But the evidence in his work for the Pujo investigation confirmed the chicanery he had expected to find.[73] His deductions from those facts, to break up big business and restore competition, did not *necessarily* follow, however, as Herbert Croly's, Walter Weyl's, and Walter Lippmann's criticisms of his brand of laissez-faire suggested.[74] For Brandeis, again, competition in freedom

---

72. Keller, *Affairs of State,* emphasizes the persisting institutional and ideological limits on federal action.

73. Richard M. Abrams, Introduction to Brandeis, *Other People's Money.*

74. Forcey, *The Crossroads of Liberalism.*

was a political and moral faith, not primarily an economic technique to be tested by practical consequences.[75]

Apart from the intellectual errors of expert opinions and tendencies to scold and denounce, informed minds from the social Darwinists to the socialists were at odds with each other and even within their own camps about economic policies. Some who favored a restoral of competition did not want government policing the market. Other Jeffersonians did. Brandeis and Wilson, who held each view at different times, eventually agreed to policing. But the political world, not the bureaucracy or seasoned investigators like Brandeis, counted. There, in a politics much less rational than the expert views, in the torrent of problems and proposals about matters like rural credits, currency, tariffs, and monopoly, time and care in evaluating almost 45,000 bills annually could only be selective or sporadic. Democratic elections as a control over the provisions of antitrust or tariff policy were even less dependable. What "the public" or "farmers" as national groups thought about their large issues was often as contradictory as the ideas of the experts, with competing enthusiasms for this nostrum or that for controlling rural credit, for example. It is difficult to imagine, as early as 1910, a political atmosphere in a capital city less calculated to help get a giant industrial democracy's work done well, let alone to have it adequately defined.

By 1912, the many recent victories in localities and states by progressives against "the interests" did suggest that American government, however corrupted and secretly dominated it seemed, remained permeable to reform. The nation was open not merely to the recently combined interests of Morgan and Rockefeller but to a countervailing "voice of the people," as progressives liked to put it.

Unfortunately, "the people" in America remained inchoate or hydra-headed about national policies and ambivalent about their own attraction to the new money, power, and success that could be found in the industrial-corporate world. Progressive leaders railed mightily against money and power-mongering during moral moments like the presidential campaign of 1912. But the multiple efforts of progressive reform were much less effective in delivering America back to the man on the make than one would have expected from the evangels of Woodrow Wilson or Theodore Roosevelt.[76]

On most issues, most of the time, the great nation, the people at large,

75. Melvin I. Urofsky, *Louis D. Brandeis and the Progressive Tradition* (Boston, 1981), chap. 4.

76. Christopher Lasch, *The New Radicalism in America, 1889–1963* (New York, 1965), 231–33, 253–56.

lived day by day not as political creatures or under the sway of what was in the public interest but in the time-honored conviction that in America private interests alone deserved citizen attention. Indeed, it could be said that the nation was dedicated on principle to the supremacy of the private life, for how else should commonsense interpret "life, liberty, and the pursuit of happiness"? How many Americans had been taught to care about "the state," except in disdain? What solid citizen could take seriously the fripperies and inanities of public life with its "dirty politics"? Occasionally, many Americans could be stirred to reconsider the republican creed of a virtuous concerned citizenry. In every generation or so, "the system" made many citizens feel fed up. Too often, however, such times became a mere moral moment to look at horizons of public-spiritedness beyond the farm or job or business and to take a spin with American ideals or to vote against popular images like the wicked Rockefeller or the unspeakable J. P. Morgan. Like the bracing moral moments of 1800, 1828, or 1865, that of 1912 passed. The altars of democracy had been revisited and honored. "Normalcy" returned, with the private life of family, church and birth, marriages and funerals, and money making.

The usual apathy and limited knowledge among the public as government piled up and problems of legislation became more complex meant that expedient alliances of bureaucrats and legislators could confront most issues as they saw fit once they had held hearings on unavoidable controversies. By 1913, on the major issues like the tariff, the banking system, and monopoly that had come to the fore since 1890, an extraordinary play of interests, and not just those of idealistic reformers, clamored for a hearing as a new Democratic Congress and new Democratic president went to work. In 1933 Franklin Roosevelt was to declare that his generation had a rendezvous with destiny. He believed that the time had come for Americans to meet the challenges of the new social power to democratic ideals inherited from preindustrial times. He did not note how often in the past similar motifs had been sounded as earlier leaders faced the contrasts between their ideals and current behavior. From the Jeremiad preachers in Massachusetts Bay in the 1660s through the pamphlets and speeches against the threats to American liberty in the 1770s and to Lincoln's warnings about the threats to freedom in the 1850s, a common theme in almost every generation was the need to make momentous choices, to meet America's destiny. So it was also in the years 1912 to 1914. The failures then do not reveal merely the contrasts among Wilson's, Theodore Roosevelt's and E. V. Debs's summonses to great purposes and the thin returns in answering the calls. Those years of revivalist campaigning and notable legislation provide deep instruction about chronic limitations in modern American government that have continued to make it so difficult for the nation to control the great problems of a giant industrial society. Not since the Civil War had the pledges and prospects for thorough reform seemed brighter than in 1912, but never had the underestimated accretions of the political system been thicker against deep or effective changes.

Whither, Christian Soldiers?

The presidential election of 1912 came not only after waves of reform proposals that dated back to the Populists of the 1890s but after longer years of pileup of state intervention in local, state, and federal efforts to contend with needs created by industrial culture. Much might have been learned from this record of pile-up, including lessons from previous reforms, about the way to go if a national effort at reform was to succeed.

The presidential election of 1912 was the first of the industrial era in which both respectable citizens and radical or regional groups seemed open to ideas of federal intervention to put the country right. All four candidates, Taft, Wilson, Roosevelt, and Debs, proclaimed that they would "do something" about the trusts and other ills as proof of America's capacity to put its house in order against the derangement of powers that had taken place during the previous generation. The sense of a decisive moment in American history engendered by the campaign may have made 1912 into the first twentieth-century "rendezvous with destiny," but the destiny was not clear nor the rendezvous heavily fruitful. The promise of great changes or redemption was, nevertheless, implicit in the recent auguries of reform in many states and in the redemptionist lingo, including the campaign songs "Onward, Christian Soldiers" and "There'll Be a Hot Time in the Old Town Tonight." There was, however, no clear consensus about the precise source of national difficulties, the priority among them, or remedies for them.

If 1912 gave the middle classes an opportunity to vote without shame or fear of being dubbed radical for a president pledged to restore the republic to health, it was also a chance to endorse someone—Wilson or Roosevelt—whose words and record encouraged belief that he would be a strong president. As an antimachine governor of New Jersey, Wilson had inveighed mightily and had acted with enough selective vigor against "the interests" to be dubbed a reformer. He also was a new face, an idealist professor, untainted by politics, who had taken on the bosses and beaten them. Wilson had adopted from his scholarship the idea that executive power had to be brought into play forcefully to check the normal drift and particularism of congressional politics.[77] Since the twentieth century was to show repeatedly how much strong presidential leadership mattered in attempting to break out from the usual government norms of impasse, gesture-ism and pileup, study of Wilson provides many ideas and important evidence about the tactics of a strong president in moving the state toward cohesive and substantial reform.[78] We also need to understand, however, those "presidential moments" since 1912 that have set the conditions for the successes and failures of would-be strong presidents. In that respect the years 1912 to 1914 were especially a trial run for the twentieth century of the type of strong president who might do well if he enjoyed a presidential moment.

Wilson's reform record before 1912, his character, training, writings, and experiences as a leader, make it apparent why his supporters anticipated that he would use every possible resource to sell his program to both the Congress and the electorate.[79] The record even before he entered politics in 1910 also shows Wilson's limitations on entering the White House, *e.g.*, an underlying skepticism about reform and energetic government, tendencies to run away from a fight, to seek disciples not colleagues, to reverse policy suddenly and abandon allies, and failure to carry through when "guts" and clarity of purpose might have won more.[80] How far he was likely to go with reform and in what ways he might disappoint those who expected much from his presidency were, in the campaign of 1912, important but unfeatured questions.[81]

In the 1880s, Wilson was among the leading young academics proclaiming the need to search for the facts rather than be content with fashionable "essences" like "sovereignty" to describe law and government. His first book, *Congressional Government* (1885), was fresh light on old subjects. It abjured pious and legalistic descriptions of federal power and gave a realistic account of how Congress had taken the significant role in Washington from the chronically weak executive. Wilson also showed how, within its broad command of the terrain, Con-

77. Wilson, *Congressional Government*, chap. 5.

78. E. Pendleton Herring, *Presidential Leadership* (New York, 1940), is a classic statement for the case. The view is continued in the several works of James McGregor Burns. Strong dissent against "presidentialism" is expressed in Willmoore Kendall, *The Conservative Affirmation* (Chicago, 1963).

79. Arthur S. Link, *Woodrow Wilson and the Progressive Era, 1910–1917* (New York, 1963), chap. 1.

80. Edmund Wilson, "Woodrow Wilson at Princeton" in Wilson, *The Shores of Light* (New York, 1952); James S. Kerney, *The Political Education of Woodrow Wilson* (New York, 1926).

81. See, however, a contemporary view of Wilson's Princeton years in Harold C. Syrett, ed., *The Gentleman and the Tiger: The Autobiography of George B. McClellan, Jr.* (Philadelphia, 1956), 314.

gress's vital machinery, the committee system, operated. But such scholarly respect for fact in Wilson had been grafted onto the vibrant religiosity he learned from his minister-father and from the Protestant moralism of the American South of the 1860s and 1870s when Wilson was at school.[82] From those sources he had learned to pose too neatly good versus evil in human affairs and to take excessive satisfaction in high-mindedness and lofty denunciations of the wicked. Throughout his professional life, Wilson gyrated between fact and great abstractions like "the spirit of this nation." He never seemed more at ease and more pleased than when he could leave the facts behind him, speak of American ideals, and sermonize about "lifting the veils" of ignorance or selfishness and "marching forward into the promised land." Since he never really understood the complexity of the great issues like monopoly power or world peace that he was to confront, mere forays against sin too often seemed larger victories. Of course, he was also encouraged by substantial victories like those over Boss Smith in New Jersey in 1911 or the high-tariff forces in Washington in 1913. But they were not unambiguous or irreversible triumphs, and settling too early or too cheaply in those cases and others led Wilson to a buoyant ignorance about the limits of what he had really wrought. He could be shocked if allies in a good fight, like the struggle against monopoly in 1913 and 1914, were bitter about his compromises and contradictions. His denunciations of the trusts were flights into absolutist scolding that did not change the facts about the American economy, just as they did not indicate what might work in coping with them. Wilson was a great orator and lecturer in a pulpit fashion now out of style, but his moralism enabled him to strengthen the American belief that politics could realize immanent truth and that great leaders were master-workers against sin and corruption in the vineyards of the Lord.

Wilson was particularly weak in economic analysis. His ideas were not beyond the going, merely intelligent, Jeffersonian tenets.[83] Such conventional views, as we have seen, ignored the logic and facts by which laissez-faire itself had stimulated business consolidation by encouraging individual interests to master their markets. Instead of grasping that, Wilson in 1912 had voiced the common American mystique of restoring opportunities open to everyman and the ability of common citizens to create without state intervention both prosperity and social justice.

82. John M. Blum, *Woodrow Wilson and the Politics of Morality* (Boston, 1956).
83. William Diamond, *The Economic Thought of Woodrow Wilson* (Baltimore, 1943). Arthur S. Link claims other severe limitations even in Wilson's own academic specialties, history and political science. See his *Wilson: The New Freedom* (Princeton, 1956), 62.

Even though his presidential actions during his two terms took him light-years away from these Jeffersonian premises, he never assented to the *general* proposition that whatever future there was for economic individualism might require constant and thorough state support. As early as the 1912 campaign, Roosevelt drove him so hard on his sentiments about free competition and minimal regulation that under his still-flying Jeffersonian maxims, Wilson the candidate had already created, or revealed, a muddle before he had won the election.[84]

Like Roosevelt, however, Wilson wanted government freed for good works by a president rallying the Congress and nation to respond to its new challenges. As the only nationally elected official of the sovereign people, a forceful president might accomplish what Congress, left to itself and to checks and balances, could not achieve. The strong president would use a broad construction of the Constitution, constant and wide publicity about presidential initiatives with Congress, ceaseless direct political pressure on House and Senate to fall in with the president, and periodic "going to the country" to seek or renew mandates. Following such paths, the president should be able to wring from the rest of the political system what the country needed. *Wring*, however, is the right word to describe the Herculean tasks that Wilson's idealism created for himself.[85]

Despite an undercurrent of unease about this newcomer to the world of politics and reform, an unusual Washington scene in March, 1913, added a unique presidential moment to his gifts and determination. The Democrats had their first sweep of the White House and Congress since the Civil War. Insurgent Republicans, particularly in the Senate, would join the many Democratic newcomers in reform measures. Wilson was then a Jeffersonian in a party whose veteran congressional Democrats from the South were of the same stripe. They were happy to have in the White House not only a son of the South but someone who carried no signs of agrarian radicalism—a stigma that had marked their old hero Bryan as a greenhorn. Wilson's stands in the campaign used all the touchstones of southern faith: restoral of competition, states' rights, opposition to big government as much as to monopoly, and adequate insensitivity about the rights of blacks and women.[86]

Other details about Wilson's opportunities in 1913 are less important than the strong general impression of a splendid presidential moment, one promising meaningful reform. Even at this distance and with Franklin Roosevelt and Lyndon Johnson behind us, Wilson seems as-

84. Link, *Wilson: The Road to the White House,* chap. 14.
85. Link, *Wilson: The New Freedom,* chap. 1.
86. Woodward, *Origins of the New South,* chap. 17.

tonishing in his legislative leadership in 1913 and 1914. Theodore Roosevelt's energetic presidency had started the new style; Wilson added personal appearances before the Congress and special sessions, and he worked directly on the legislators out of the long-unused "President's Room" on Capitol Hill. He also went to the people directly via press conferences, interviews, and speeches to bring pressure on Congress.[87] These great gifts make it all the more painful to doubt that Wilson knew what was really needed in coming to terms with monopoly, the tariff, or the complex currency and credit conditions in the nation. He thought he could distinguish between businesses that achieved power fairly and the trusts that had broken laws and had violated standards of fairness in amassing their powers. But the facts and logic that undercut such simplistic distinctions did not help when the moment for making definitions into antimonopoly law arrived in 1914. His shifting pressure on the Congress then simply did not have behind it subtle, detailed, and mastered ideas about the economic maze of 1913. And for want of that nail, the shoe, more effective legislation about business conduct, could not be shod despite his unusual presidential moment.

There is no doubt that Wilson worked on the intricate intellectual challenges of the monopoly analysis that Brandeis and others brought to him, but such tasks were not as congenial as sermonizing. His announcement of great moral victories on the Underwood tariff and the Federal Reserve system were denials that he had made political deals and lost some hard fights in Congress and that he had already had to yield to weakening compromises with the excoriated "interests." Unfortunately, his redemptionist rhetoric in 1912 had led to impossible expectations. A modest 10 percent reduction in tariff rates, albeit the first since the Civil War, was scarcely, as events soon enough showed, the death knell of protectionism. Each of his three great fights in 1913 and 1914, on the tariff, the currency, and monopoly, is a tale of shining surface victories with underlying basic problems left unattended. We concentrate, however, on the antitrust legislation.

By 1913, a generation of investigations, legislation, debates, and court cases, as well as volumes of exhortations and exposures, offered as trained a mind as Wilson's the outlines of what might work. An instructed leader should first have recognized the relative novelty of large-scale enterprise and of effective federal regulation, the complexity of both, and the need to go steadily but thoughtfully through the muddy waters. The uninstructed but strongly opinionated public needed guidance from its president about differentiating among industries that were intrinsically large

---

87. Link, *Wilson: The New Freedom.*

scale, like steel, and those more productive when operating in modest size, like tableware or clothing manufacture. Pilot programs could have been started for each type with effective regulation by watchdog agencies to maintain boundaries of business size and fair practices. Experience with the ICC for more than twenty years also suggested safeguards against infiltration of the agencies by appointees tepid about regulation. Such lessons would have avoided the tendencies to simplistic absolutism within both Wilson's New Freedom and the Roosevelt-Croly evangels of 1912. It is irksome to recognize then and now that politicians will not even try to trust citizens to understand and approve well-presented ventures in complexity rather than confirm them in the layman's tendency to oversimplification. Wilson, like Bryan and Roosevelt in this respect at least, was an appropriate leader of that time because he reflected and reinforced strong tendencies of national character. All three tended toward that old American pietistic absolutism that Ralph Barton Perry characterized in "the moral athlete" engaged perpetually in contests to make right prevail in the world that was God's arena. But the moral athletes fighting for laissez-faire in 1912 needed to understand that economic competition could not by itself inhibit monopoly—indeed, could even set the stage for it—and that, henceforth, the part of the Adam Smith formulae that had heavily deprecated the state was no longer adequate. It was a fearful irony that to save laissez-faire, Americans might now have to invoke federal power in unprecedented degree and constancy.

A Strong State for Laissez-Faire?

Brandeis' ideas of regulated competition, despite his disclaimers, implied a state no less interventionist in maintaining economic competition than Theodore Roosevelt's proposals for a state that would accept but police big business by distinguishing between good and bad trusts. But whether under the Brandeis or the Roosevelt criteria about bad trusts, what were the prospects of reducing billion-dollar U.S. Steel to several multimillion dollar businesses? Wilson's New Freedom speeches of 1912 encouraged the hope of a return to a Jacksonian world of small enterprises in which a citizen who wanted to could get started on his own. The modern steel industry, however, with its huge Mesabi mines, heavy transport, and giant furnaces and mills was no enterprise for small capitalists, whether they were as good as or as bad as J. P. Morgan or Elbert Gary. For key capital enterprises like steel, moreover, not small or large but efficient production for national well-being was the proper criterion.

Laissez-faire logic, nevertheless, could conceivably dictate that ten large independent steel firms be carved out of U.S. Steel to enhance competition or to punish Morgan, who had assembled the firm in 1901. Of course, there might be unacceptable adverse effects on the economy during any attempt at breakup, but that aside, policing those firms to prevent recombination could easily frustrate one important market test of competition, whether a firm could measure up to its rivals. Insisting on competition or a set size for a firm as an unsurrenderable imperative could imply some type of government support for survival of inefficient firms. The imperative after breakup, ostensibly in the name of laissez-faire, would be that ten steel firms in market contest not be reduced to nine and that the nine, given likely poor performance of some, should not shrink to even smaller numbers.

We may now be more adequately complex in making judgments about business organization, efficiency, and productivity.[88] But even in 1914 as the congressional debates about the monopoly legislation began, Rooseveltian progressives were at least trying for realism about the huge capital costs of modern industries, the inherent tendencies of competition to consolidation, and the potential of consolidation in some cases for greater production and efficiency. If Adam Smith's idea that the free market would produce consumers and business rivals to inhibit monopolistic tendencies did not work, then the state watching for movement toward excessive combination, punishing those who combined to bad effect, and tolerating law-abiding large firms were at least logical aspects of Roosevelt's monopoly policy. But, again, both this and Brandeis' wish to break up monopoly implied a far larger role for the state.

Wilson first tuned to that part of the clamor about smashing the trusts that emphasized better definitions of monopolistic practices to warn the businessman and for the courts, rather than a new potent bureaucracy, to enforce. He recognized that the principal task was to inhibit future monopoly rather than undo existing damage. As the antimonopoly battle in Congress began in 1914, he championed the original Clayton bill explicitly forbidding a long list of defined depredations, especially "interlocking directorates." That particular technique used the same directors to serve on many boards. The Morgan and Rockefeller empires had recently employed the device to coordinate their interests. It seemed that prohibiting it would cut off the worst heads of the hydra of monopoly.[89] Wilson gave the Clayton bill strong support, but there were

88. Chandler, *The Visible Hand,* on the paramountcy of efficiency. Compare with Martin J. Sklar, *The Corporate Reconstruction of American Capitalism* (New York, 1988). On antimonopoly as a faith and its fate, see Richard Hofstadter, "What Happened to the Antitrust Movement?" in Hofstadter, *The Paranoid Style in American Politics, and Other Essays* (New York, 1965).

89. Link, *Wilson: The New Freedom,* for the details of the antimonopoly legislation that follows herein.

other antimonopoly bills adopting different tacks than Clayton's, which relied on better definitions of business practices for court action. The alternatives included telling criticisms of Wilson's definitional approach and of his favoring punishment for individual businessmen who ignored the definitions. One plan that quickly gathered force was a trade commission bill that involved strengthening the information-gathering work of the recently established Bureau of Corporations (1903) and giving it effective policing and enforcement powers through "cease and desist" findings.

Debate on the Clayton bill increasingly revealed the virtual impossiblity of defining "unfair competition" or "restraint of trade" with adequate precision to guide the courts and without encouraging corporations to find a way around what was explicitly prohibited. The trade commission proposals that were the principal alternative to the Clayton bill moved in directions that had become clearer since the passage of the Elkins Act (1903) and Hepburn Act (1906), dealing with railroad regulation. Both of these were thoroughly familiar to Brandeis, but his switch in 1913 to 1914 to some sort of regulatory commission for industry was momentous.

The Clayton bill may have begun its legislative course as the Wilson administration's antitrust effort, but that effort ended, months later, as a law with much less force and less importance for Wilson than the Federal Trade Commission Act of 1914.[90] In midstream Wilson lost most of his once-high interest in court-enforced detailed definitions of "restraint of trade." To try to placate the angry but still vibrant New Freedom and insurgent voices of laissez-faire, Wilson contended that the weakened Clayton Act that he signed really did fulfill his campaign promise of 1912 for an all-out assault on monopoly. It was widely apparent, however, how far the act really was from Wilson's ringing promises. In final form, the Clayton Act still ostensibly aimed at definitions of some unfair trade practices, particularly interlocking directorates, but as Hebert Croly said, with pleasant surprise, the legislation emerged "contradicting every principle of the party which enacted it."[91] In the other act, a new Federal Trade Commission, not Congress or the courts, seemed to have the power to act pragmatically about business combination, i.e., the FTC was not to enforce a specific list of congressionally prescribed unfair trade practices but to define them itself.

What Jeffersonian insurgents wanted, in any case, was something better than the Sherman Act that only looked like a law to control the trusts. But insurgents like Senators Norris, La Follette, Borah, and the south-

90. *Ibid.*, 425–44.
91. *Ibid.*, 444.

ern Jeffersonians had anticipated from Wilson's phillipics about the trusts a significant attack on concentrated industrial and financial power. They were dismayed not only that he capitulated to the final form of the Clayton Act but that he seemed as enthusiastic about the trade commission in 1914 as he was denunciatory in 1912 and 1913 in rejecting such statist ideas. Not only was Herbert Croly happy about this unexpected enhancement of federal power but his view of Wilson's apostasy was scathingly endorsed by a Croly opponent, Senator Reed, a bitter-ender for a stronger Clayton Act: "The people were led to believe that the Democratic Party, now in full possession of all branches of the government, by this bill intended to make private monopoly . . . both unprofitable and dangerous. . . . In its finality [the Act] is soothing melodies of 'peace on earth, good will towards the trusts.' "[92]

Passing both the FTC and the Clayton Acts, however different in philosophy, was a portentous triumph in *both* cases of expediency over good policy and an augury about effective reform generally in this century. Interest group and party bargaining and Wilson's needs for victories and "face" qualified not only the Clayton Act but the ostensibly stronger FTC bill. To placate die-hard laissez-faire progressives, a great limitation was inserted at the last moment that helped curtail the commission's prospective effectiveness. The fear of too-powerful and too-independent an agency among both business conservatives and the antistatist progressive reformers crept into the heart of the bill by making key parts of the "cease and desist" orders of the commission subject to court review. In effect, this left most of the say about monopoly in the courts where it had been and where it had for so long frustrated the antitrust forces. But Wilson accepted that also, despite his newly discovered need for an effective commission that would lessen reliance on the courts.

Together, the two laws from such different reform perspectives represented not effective, reciprocal wisdom but the power of wheeling and dealing over the promising combination of a strong president, a unique presidential moment, and the deliverable votes of a coalition of diverse reformers for one clear and effective national policy for which the president should have given unwavering leadership. If the nation in the 1912 campaign was confused about the monopoly debate and had been insufficiently instructed by the president thereafter about the complexity of antitrust policy, it was not helped by obtaining two acclaimed laws, both flawed, with contradictory intentions and neither one, nor both together, able to do what was thought to be needed in bringing business before the bar of reason.

Wilson may have regretfully concluded from Brandeis' and others'

92. *Ibid.*

urgings that the case for a special enforcement agency was, despite all hopes voiced in 1912 to avoid it, undeniable. He also may have learned much about business combinations in the year or so since the presidential campaign. When the FTC legislation seemed likely to pass, Wilson also may have found an incentive to gauge the problem of monopoly control in what appeared to be a more realistic light. On the other hand, he may have wanted to associate himself with a suddenly popular bill that was going to win even without his support. But the strong stand Wilson had taken so recently against both big business and big government, to the delight in 1912 of many supporters of laissez-faire, might be thought to have precluded an equally certain endorsement of the opposite policies a little more than a year later.

The obvious questions about a strong president follow: strong how, for what? An insufficiently instructed leader who, nevertheless, announces too quickly and too sweepingly just what is wrong and exactly what is needed and who soon reverses himself with equal fervor creates skepticism about his intellectual grasp and seriousness, as well as about his loyalty to any principles. But Wilson's principles and his steadfastness had previously been called into question even before the antimonopoly debates had gone very far. His post-Princeton, anti-big-business coating had already cracked when he made conservative, business-approved nominees not only for the ICC but for his new Federal Reserve Board. La Follette denounced Wilson and these appointees for triumphing *over* the progressives, and the antimonopolist Senator Hitchcock remarked that he would not draw up antitrust bills and then put into office "men who make trusts."[93] Perhaps because of an economic downturn in 1914, Wilson also took direct steps to reconcile himself with big business by meeting with and reassuring leaders like J. P. Morgan and Henry Ford.[94] In that light, his subsequent switch in 1914 to limited steps against significant business combination is not surprising, however much it dismayed the veteran foes of monopoly. The big-business interests Wilson had excoriated in 1912 were much more persevering and could afford to look beyond just another president, "mere party politics," and moral moments for aroused citizens and politicians. The latter two were easily indulged, and a moral moment would quickly pass.

Wilson was also too quickly satisfied by the sin of monopoly, like bossism and corporate power in New Jersey, *seeming* to be on the run. The successful tariff and Federal Reserve fights had already given the moralist in him deep satisfaction in appearing to have driven his generation of money-changers from the temple. Wall Street financiers and

93. *Ibid.*, 455.
94. *Ibid.*, 449.

Pittsburgh and Gary steel producers thus appeared stymied or contained by the crusading leader of the democracy even before the two antitrust bills came to their final stages. A rare presidential moment had strongly implied that Wilson might have whatever antitrust policy he wanted, short of nationalization. Wilson did not need to moralize or strike poses as much as he needed to think and to get free of both Brandeis' and Roosevelt's higher cant about the trusts. And if the best themes in the existing volumes of antitrust debate warned that good policy about the trusts, within the limits of what was known about them, involved trade-offs, not "truth," so strong a president could have done invaluable work in launching a new style of well-conceived presidential reform initiatives with announced general plans for "next steps," depending on the success of the first ones.

The moral moment about monopoly in 1913 and 1914 was symptomatic of the years ahead as regulatory government continued to pile up after the Clayton and FTC Acts. It was increasingly difficult to remember Wilson the New Freedom candidate of 1912 in the president after 1914, fearful of electoral reverses and successively approving laws about the railroad workday, seamen's working conditions, farm loans, warehouses and education, highway construction, compensation for injured federal employees, and rules against child labor.[95] Each of these represented responses to genuine needs. But like the antitrust legislation, were the needs met adequately? Regulatory legislation continued to come from Wilson with pretensions to finality and rationality about "at last" solving this or that American problem by establishing another program, rule, or agency. The underlying tendency of American politics from then to today, about the big issues at least, has been what radical critics have repeatedly charged: to settle cheap, with lofty rhetoric about wars against the money changers in the temple, poverty, and racism.[96] Ironically, by the 1960s settle-cheap gestures came into play to limit the big government that had piled up to fight those wars.

The pressures to speak loudly but use only a little stick have chronically affected strong presidents like Wilson searching for answers to the great problems of the industrial era. But why does mastery chronically elude the democratic leader? One painful probe into a progressive politics like Wilson's may suggest that mastery in American politics is an illusion. Mastery may be a compound of fantasies that problems of the magnitude of monopoly power in a nation of our size and complexity can be adequately analyzed and definitively legislated for. In retrospect,

95. Link, *Woodrow Wilson and the Progressive Era*, 223–41.
96. Lasch, *The New Radicalism in America*; Kolko, *The Triumph of Conservatism*; Weinstein, *The Corporate Ideal in the Liberal State*.

none of the major proposals of 1912 to 1914, neither Wilson's, Roosevelt's, nor Deb's about the trusts, now seems even an adequate analysis of the dimensions of the economic and political difficulties. Roosevelt and Croly were as wrong in their faith in state power under benign regulatory experts as Wilson initially was about finding clear and workable definitions of monopolistic practices for the courts, not bureaucrats, to apply. The terms all parties used in 1912 in the national debate of the issues were the ultimates of American public discourse: liberty, individualism, opportunity, progress, justice, fairness, righteousness, purity, character, and "standing at Armageddon and battling for the Lord." Opponents of the reformers, like Taft, used many of these words to obverse effect. They foresaw stultifying increases in government intervention and predicted that the election of either Wilson or Roosevelt or that reforms like the income tax or the Clayton Act would mean the death of American freedom and the advent of dictatorial socialism. If reformers chronically suggested the resurrection, the phrases of the opposition too often implied apocalypse—unless they were elected. With leaders on all sides in 1912 generally rousing such grandiose expectations for victory or for the death of American democracy we may well wonder whether any foreseeable reform legislation that had to go through the mills and moralizing of American politics could come up to the glowing phrases of the political leaders.

Neither Wilson nor the Roosevelt intellectuals had the truth about controlling monopoly because there was no truth. The accurate portrait of the facts and alternatives suggests only dilemmas about policy. Vaunted competition itself had led to the trusts, but effective antimonopoly policies would only lead back to the temptations and frustrations in competition. And effective regulation in either the Brandeis or Roosevelt mode would create a host of political-administrative quandaries. The principal dilemma, in any case, was political, not economic. As such it was a riposte to both Wilson and Roosevelt. How much could self-interested factions be entrusted to maximum liberty if their competition created unacceptable private power and social costs even while, *pace* the radical analysis, also increasing opportunity and the general standard of living? If the state needed adequate power to keep such factions in bounds, especially as their competition led to massive consolidation, how could regulatory government itself be prevented from becoming a faction of experts and politicians more fallible and more open to pressure groups and infiltration by weak appointees than their gloss of undefiable expertise may have suggested? Secretary of Commerce Herbert Hoover, Louis Brandeis, David Lilienthal, to recall three very different but splendid public servants, were all strongly partial to their own views of the economy and of proper regulatory policies. The limitations of even such state servants may encourage Americans to trust individual freedom rather than officialdom. Citizens then remain with the dilemma implicit in a century of Jeffersonian liberty that encouraged entrepreneurs to amass as much power as possible only then to turn toward monopolistic practices against the competitive ideal that had nurtured them. What we confront in the attempts of 1913 and 1914 to tame the trusts are rehearsals of now-chronic difficulties. As yet, no party or program, including the socialists, seems able to transcend the tension between private markets and overbearing regulatory power. Mastery is the eternal promise of all parties. But pretentious, piled-up government as well as arrogant private power continue, whatever policy about big business seems to be the reality.

The failure by 1914 was not only political. Increasingly, the cash-in-pocket interests of common Americans depended on their lusty industrial culture; but about the new mills of abundance, they felt no better than ambivalence or confusion. The world of 1914 increasingly gave America its daily provisioning, *i.e.,* its wages and jobs, its business opportunities, assembly lines, and organization, its small-town Ford and International Harvester agencies, its vaccines and hospitals, electric sewing machines, and home telephones, its instantaneous wire and soon wireless communications, nascent, up-to-the-minute "mass media," and overnight trains from New York to Chicago. All this had congealed into "modern culture" in only a few decades after 1865. Walter Lippmann warned that in managing this new world the horizons of families, the expectations of youth, the moral standards for men and women, the sense of community and of its proper size and sanctions, had remained "horse and buggy." The American metaphysic of 1914 was still largely that village Weltanschauung that Mencken would soon be assaulting with his own imperfectly transcended moralism. And that *mentalité* took its toll on the quality of what state intervention there was, *i.e.,* starving the state even after seeking it, vetting both the Clayton and FTC laws before they began to operate.

But the 1914 Lippmannesque faith in experts excessively deprecated the sentimental and "ignorant" resistance to the new corporate, managed world. Fumbling and at cross-purposes though the folk may have been about the new America, it rightly distrusted the growing anonymity of massed power, the increasing transitoriness of fads and fashion, the impersonalism of the organized and managed life, the alienation from unrelenting and routinized factory and clerical work, the jargon and blah in justifying the scale and suzerainty of organization leaders and skillful bureaucrats, the invitation to callousness and hectoring intrinsic to all giant enterprises, however ostensibly rational they pretend to be and however much they might pay off in salaries, wages, perquisites, and leisure time. On the other hand, the marshaled facts that came from many investigations by muckrakers, social workers, and the new social scientists increasingly showed the old folkish ways of conducting business, the home, the school and government, medicine, law, charities, not right or wrong but gone or rapidly disappearing. Spokesmen like Lippmann wanted an America that was to be more skilled, more plentiful, more democratic, more honest, less hypocritical about morality and religion, and generally more humane. They could plead their case in 1914 with confidence and optimism because they were leaving a Jeffersonian world with little experience of, but high hopes for, a democracy controlling the mass society that was going to replace it. Minimally, they asserted that America would not go on as it had earlier in its history. And they were right in that respect. Like it or not, everything had been called into question, and American society was so adrift that almost any change might seem for the better. Maximally, during the birth of American social engineering only lovable and robust progeny were foreseen once the birth pains passed.

On deeper historical perspective, the difficulties in achieving effective reform in that fast-changing American life of 1913 had been endemic in the constitutional and party systems since their beginnings. Madisonian pluralism accepted interest groups or factions as unavoidable in any free society. All groups could seek power and exert it as effectively as governing coalitions could manage. But government by representatives, checks and balances, and the federal system were intended to force delay and compromise and to avoid quick and easy victories by overzealous factions with governing power. The hope was that whatever government policies emerged would be less extreme than under a centralized and plebiscitarian state. The limits of the tariff, banking and business regulation reforms of 1913 and 1914 were hallmarks of the compromises forced by the traditional constitutional and party system. Such limits on effective governing were already manifest in earlier struggles over slavery, the currency, and the tariff. Wilson also confronted not only antireform opposition to all his proposals but the factions within the reform majorities in both houses. Faction remained omnipresent and manifest in questions such as whether controls over banking would do as much for rural credit as for the industrial world, what specific lower tariffs on what imports, what degree of laissez-faire and of regulation in corporate enterprise. Factions in Congress and among reformers across the nation might have watered down whatever clearer views Wilson might have had, quite apart from the deeper question of whether there was any ideal tariff, banking system, or business regulation. A definitive answer to the problems of monopoly power was a chimera, but a better answer than what emerged depended on more informed, consistent, and persistent presidential leadership.

The enduring limits of our democracy on effective government, however, were rooted in society and in American ways of looking at the world. As Lippmann understood, before they even turn to "politics" Americans remain excessively evangelical. Citizens are encouraged to dream impossible dreams, most famously, life, liberty, and the pursuit of happiness. Low or high tariffs or credit for beleaguered farmers become matters of gospel. Politicians come out of that citizenry and play to and reinforce salvationist fervor: elect the Democrat or the Republican and all the nation will be redeemed or saved. This evangelical political culture looks to golden horizons, but the national system of government was designed to frustrate over-intense dreams. The ambitious refomer, especially on larger issues such as the rational conduct of business life or adequate provisions for health care, cannot really deliver overtouted goods. And citizen frustration with, ironically, their abstractly much-vaunted anti-absolutist system of government remains chronic. If Americans in 1912 had begun to learn to expect less from reform politics under the system of 1789 they might have been more content with what modest but effective changes the system could yield. Instead, the Wilson years revealed how even more difficult than in the past "mastery" would be in the modern era of massive social power. Drift remains the national political norm. The power needed to make modern America work well is probably far more concentrated and noisome than a society dedicated to individual rights and representative government could tolerate.

Within a decade after 1913, events in other ostensibly open societies such as the constitutional monarchy of Italy, Kerensky's Russia, and Weimar Germany would show what disgust and despair about ordinary democratic politics could produce in the name of various versions of mastery championed by Mussolini, Lenin, and Hitler. America was to be spared such a fate but not similar voices from the KKK of the 1920s to the Minutemen and Aryan Nation of today. Such groups rail against democratic mess and disorder and promise solutions for citizens in uproar about their America. Too often these embittered Americans have evangelical fervor that politics be guided by and aim for moral and religious absolutes. In 1913 and 1914 we had the first national test in the industrial era of how constitutional government can limit the effectiveness of even rational reforms. The tensions in 1913 and 1914, between America's larger ambitions and its political realities, remain to vex most hopes for meaningful change.

Postscript to Progressivism: The Health of the State

To the degree that Americans of 1914 believed as Wilson did that what reform had called for had been completed, that the price for change had been modest, that no further national travail was needed, America may have seemed delivered back to Wilson's "man who is on the make."[97] Such optimism about the future of democracy lay behind the enormous shock brought by the outbreak of World War I in 1914 followed by the role of the state as it prepared for and managed the war in 1917 and 1918. The fight for reform in 1913 and 1914 reveals how little of what a managerialist might think effective could get through the peacetime constitutional system. The new scientific managers had to await the world war for their first big innings. Americans have forgotten the full record of their attempt to mobilize the economy in 1917 and 1918. The tale could have been immensely sobering in understanding prospects for command economies and planning bureaucracies later in the twentieth century.

The war emergency made it possible for business, technocrats, reformist intellectuals, and government officials to bypass many of the checks and balances, the antitrust laws, the Bill of Rights, the courts, the political parties, and the other filters of the peacetime American system. The men of 1787 had built that system to contain swiftness and certainty, to frustrate what we call reform as well as reaction. But as moments of crisis like 1917 and 1918 have shown, the system can be gallingly at cross-purposes even when many of its filters are put aside. Starting during "preparedness" and accelerating during the war, there was an impetus in the corridors at Washington to push toward planned, coordinated, and more expertly managed policy in national mobilization "with Americanism their only motive."[98] That search for order that had begun a generation earlier thus picked up speed within the federal halls.

By the war's end, however, much of what in the modern-management ideology had seemed demonstrably rational or objective had often turned out to be half-baked, heavily subjective, and unexpectedly coercive, for all the talk of reliable scientific opinions and voluntary, democratic cooperation to achieve efficiency and order. World War I thus provided the first large national test of an inclusive and trained rationalism applied to American public policy. What peacetime slack could not produce in mastering American sprawl, wartime discipline and fervor might accomplish. The customary crossfire of Washington politics, national

97. Link, *Wilson: The New Freedom*, 469–70.
98. Grosvenor B. Clarkson, *Industrial America in the World War: The Strategy Behind the Line, 1917–1918* (Boston, 1923), 21.

traditions of voluntarism, habits of expediency, and the profit motive did not subside. They proved to have superior strength over patriotic pretensions that manifestly rational plans would elicit assent and compliance without dictatorship.[99]

At first, Washington at war did try to attain the mobilization goals through cooperation and consultation among agencies and with industry.[100] That not working, confused steps toward centralized command were taken and reached their apogee in the Overman Act of the spring of 1918, one year after the war began. Its record was almost as bad. By November, 1918, the real message was clear: both voluntarism and command had high prices, including dismaying failures in reaching objectives for an efficient war effort at top speed. There was no painless way to more rational controls and certainly no escape from dilemma and difficulty, at least with basic liberties intact, as in the visions of rational planning among Veblenesque "engineers." It was also apparent that there was an unacknowledged authoritarian imperative lurking within the ideal of democratic planning that was difficult to contain if one really wanted reason to triumph over disharmony and waste. A command economy meant obey and deliver; but "obey," with bureaucracy and citizens still allowed to protest and petition, meant delay and confusion. Here then was one of the great dilemmas of political economy in this century. The elusiveness, even in a time of high patriotism, of "rational order" while trying to retain significant freedom of debate and manuever to correct error, is what makes the wartime experience so instructive. If 1913 and 1914 was a trial-run for piecemeal reform for the industrial economy, 1917 and 1918 was a test for centralized planning both without and with coercion.

To the degree that planning failed even under the alleged "dictatorial powers" derived from the Overman Act, that fate does seem inseparable from Bernard Baruch's and Wilson's hesitation to institute fully the authorized dragooning government.[101] By war's conclusion, the managerial dream of planning under freedom had turned into the lesson that democracy might, but only *might*, obtain huge production under centralized controls if it was resolutely clear about production priorities and standards and would guarantee industry a premium price for delivering the goods. The last point was also underscored by Herbert Hoover's im-

99. Robert D. Cuff, *The War Industries Board: Business-Government Relations During World War I* (Baltimore, 1973).

100. Robert D. Cuff, "We Band of Brothers—Woodrow Wilson's War Managers," *Canadian Review of American Studies*, II (1974).

101. David M. Kennedy, *Over Here: The First World War and American Society* (New York, 1980), chap. 2.

mense success in enticing farmers to grow food and fiber by abandoning market prices, by government setting a premium price and leaving stimulated self-interest to do the job.[102]

How especially ignominious it was by Armistice Day to those progressive intellectuals who had reluctantly joined the war effort to find that their villains of 1912, the industrialists and financiers, had virtually stolen the wartime state from them. They had forged an immensely profitable marriage of their own planning ideal of privately managed markets and money-making with government power. Various appeals to the profit motive were the carrot and government production standards were the stick that led to an average climb in wartime profits of 30 percent annually, but ranging as high as 800 percent for Bethlehem Steel.[103] American producers learned that the old bugaboo of free enterprise, the state, was not always or even intrinsically an enemy. Valuable alliances with it could be made and, as the 1920s trade association movement and infiltration of the bureaucracy showed, in peace as well as war.[104] What emerged by war's end was a very crude version of a state-coordinated capitalism that created inflation to pay high profits to farmers, workingmen, and businessmen to win the war. Even so, with the exception of Hoover, no major government manager of railroads, ship building, coal mining, and so on, could point honestly to success in either the quantity or quality of goods. On the battlefields, American manpower, not our machines, turned the tide. The Allies' victory, however, converted the facts of a planning mess at home into a myth of a miracle of American management. It was symbolized, for example, by the changed view of Baruch from his prewar reputation as the wolf of Wall Street speculators into the wizard adviser to presidents.

We cannot understand the wartime dismay about the state-business alliance and we can miss aspects of rightness in the protest of a minority of progressives like Randolph Bourne if we forget the extraordinary investment they had made before 1914 in optimistic visions of a reformed America. Traveling on various paths laid out by their intelligentsia, the followers of Croly and Lippmann especially had argued for a more rational politics that would be freed from myths and falsehood and would find supreme activity in a freshened and stronger democratic state. Just before the war, the young and newly declared pragmatist and socialist Bourne joined a gathering chorus about what John Dewey, his teacher, would later call the "new liberalism." That liberalism was skeptical about laissez-faire, dedicated to social action informed by science, and allied

---

102. Bernard Baruch, *American Industry in the War* (New York, 1941).
103. Kennedy, *Over Here*, 117–23.
104. *Ibid.*, 139.

with an activist state. America organizing for preparedness and war taught Bourne how much the confident theorists of enhanced state power, including his fellow socialists, had neglected in their eagerness to show how pragmatic intelligence could use government to enlarge liberty, equality, and justice.[105] But in contrasting the progressives who had sold out with their idealism in 1912, Bourne had missed the darker, censorious side of peacetime progressivism, the campaigns against dance halls, the movies, prostitution, and, most of all, the zeal for prohibition—all reform measures intended to make private life more moral by public action.[106] And humane cosmopolitanism before the war had grossly underestimated the force of patriotism, "gloire," godly mission, racism, and revanche that were to resist the claims of reason and drench all the powers in blood starting in that "fateful, beautiful summer" of 1914. In America as well as Europe, the "atavisms" (if such they were) shook or shattered the peace movements, socialist solidarity, and other efforts at international good will. They shriveled the "great illusion" that modern economic interdependence of nations made major wars in the twentieth century impossible. Peace, not war, was to be the great illusion of the century.

In America, as the conflict began, and especially in Wilson, there lingered the belief that in time a neutral United States, uncorrupted by the Machiavellian diseases of war and diplomacy, could bring its great power as a disinterested nation to bear on the mad Europeans.[107] As the blood bath continued, some progressive intellectuals like Dewey began to think that if the country entered the fray, American wealth and moral superiority to the imperialist nations might convert a war that had begun for profits and colonies into a world struggle for democracy and social justice. That would enlarge, not diminish or cancel, domestic progressivism.[108] Bourne was honest and acute enough to discern even during America's unneutral neutrality and "preparedness" (1914 to 1917) that the country, including many of its progressive intellectuals, was "succumbing to the temptation to feel holy." They not only accepted augmenting state power for preparedness but they agreed to and helped direct a crusade that unleashed the latent oppressive force of the war-state clothed in righteousness. The growing muscle of industrial society

105. George H. Soule, *Prosperity Decade* (New York, 1947), 138–41.

106. Bourne, *War and the Intellectuals.*

107. Kennedy, *Over Here,* chap. 1; John M. Cooper, *The Vanity of Power: American Isolation and the First World War, 1914–1917* (Westport, Conn., 1969).

108. John Dewey, "The Social Possibilities of War," in *Characters and Events: Popular Essays in Social and Political Philosophy by John Dewey,* ed. Joseph Ratner (New York, 1929).

in alliance with crusading fervor brought what Bourne had sarcastically called "the health of the state" into full bloom after 1917, thus showing how callous, even perverse, the republic could become in pursuing its ideals.[109]

The painful, but too often missed, irony was that greatly augmented power had been sought for the state by progressive reformers like Bourne for one good peacetime purpose or another. In war, that greater state would also use those powers to try to silence dissent at home while professing to enlarge reform abroad in a crusade for global democracy and an end to war. Never did the American republican moment confront the Machiavellian eons to greater frustration and disadvantage of liberty as in 1917 and 1918. Aware of it or not, Bourne and his reformer allies of 1912 had worked to enhance not only government power but the moralistic politics that the war deflected from progressive causes of individual liberation and liberal nationalism to wartime order and discipline for war's holy cause. There was a strangely terrible path from the high idealism of 1912 to the wartime assault on the "slacker," the jailing of the pacifist and anarchist, the ousting of the socialist lawmaker who had been legally elected. If, as Richard Hofstadter contended, there has been a persistent "paranoid style" in American history to divide the nation, as many progressives had, between saints and sinners and to use the state against sin, that style has not been limited to the right-wing or backcountry evangelicals.[110] In larger compass, it is the more ragged edge of a general American propensity for preachment, a style that knows no one party or cause. The moralism that turned so vindictive after 1917 was embedded in America's old penchant for exhortation that had flourished in camp meetings and stump speakers, in pulpits and professors. Tragically, it tainted many reformers, including Wilson himself. For the intellectuals who helped George Creel's war propaganda mill, the moralism produced an American version of "the treason of the intellectuals," showing the danger of an overindulged idealism that obscures hunger for power. Too many reformers before the war had bathed in respectable versions of the paranoid style, giving it objectives like controlling the trusts and closing the nickleodeons. Having sharpened the public appetite in 1912 for a politics of purification, that moralism was easily turned against antiwar moralists who could not hasten with Wilson to even larger visions of a world made subject to American truth.

For all of his accuracy about the armed moralism of the modern state, Bourne himself was never weaned from the denunciatory style used by his jingoist opponents during the war when they banned *Masses* and ar-

109. Bourne, "The State," in Bourne, *War and the Intellectuals*.
110. Hofstadter, *The Paranoid Style in American Politics*.

rested Debs. Bourne died in 1918 as he had lived, full of a just but futile moral fire against the state whose "health" he had brilliantly excoriated but whose claims he had, nevertheless, unwittingly invited to increase.

V

THE AMBIGUITIES OF THE STATE

Ritualistic Jeffersonianism

If wartime statism was radically at variance with Jeffersonian ideals of individual liberty and minimal government, those ideals were confounded in other ways in succeeding decades. The facts about America show an ever-larger, more corporate, more complex, and more tightly knit national life. The bearing of these changes on the great American ideals of liberty and equality provoked intense debate. It is patent, however, that when ideals are in excessive conflict with facts, disarray or even a disaster like 1929 may follow. Invoking Jeffersonian ideals of a small-owner's capitalism and limited government to describe an increasingly corporate society after 1920 transformed those revered economic themes into ritualistic abstractions. These so distorted both American interests and institutions that the workings of neither state nor society could be understood adequately. As a guiding ideology, however, Jeffersonian individualism under passive government was to be undercut less by opposing socialist or welfare capitalist ideas than by the growing dependence of all Americans on a large-scale economy with expanding productivity, growing bureaucracy, and ever-greater seeking of government assistance.

Despite the great leap forward toward bigness and bureaucracy during the war, comforting experiences with bigness were still not common for most Americans by 1920. For all the new ideas about large-scale corporate life, none could rival the prestige of Jeffersonian beliefs in individual effort and small-scale competitive enterprise.[1] Scientific management, trade associations, government-business cooperation, public planning, expert bureaucracy, "industrial democracy," and social-democracy were still fresh faiths. They were difficult to accept because all were invoked against purported limits of the abiding faith in Jeffersonian lais-

---

1. On Jefferson's reputation in the 1920s, see Peterson, *The Jefferson Image in the American Mind*, chaps. 6 and 7.

sez-faire enterprise and passive government. Jefferson's ideals of political freedom and popular control of government were other matters. After the war, economists in the Croly vein like Simon Patten, W. T. Foster, and Waddill Catchings retained Jefferson's ideals of happiness, political rights, and democratic control while jettisoning his faith in limited government, economic individualism, and competition. They were confident, however, that the political ideals were reconcilable with extensive government intervention, including centralized planning.[2] This democratic statism as well as the Jeffersonian laissez-faire that it tried to supplant would both be severely tested ideas in the decades ahead.

But the basic problem of government intervention could not be settled ideologically. Given the increased meshing of daily interests with the corporate world and the promise in the 1920s of the new "people's capitalism" for a consumers' paradise, Americans increasingly found, issue by issue, that they could not afford to live with small enterprises, all-out competition, or minimal Jeffersonian government. Caught in the clash between the old ideology and their burgeoning collective interests, their principal psychological escape was moralizing against bigness or against Bolshevism. Seeking the state while shaming it grew increasingly contradictory. Nostalgic Jeffersonianism alternated with halfhearted moral moments of reform like Prohibition on behalf of lost worlds and restored values.[3] Neither contended with the real national agenda.

Despite such widespread posturing, the range of American government after 1920 grew in line with large-scale organization in the economy, the professions, the churches, education, and national voluntary associations like the Red Cross, YMCA, and Boy Scouts. If there had been any hope that the Wilson reforms of 1913 and 1914 would tame or halt the drift to giantism, the war that followed was to the contrary and revived the prestige and hold of the huge organizations. Wilson had railed against them in 1912, but they soon helped win the war after 1917. Although the war also stimulated the rise of many new small entrepreneurs seeking profits in the expanding economy, the large firms of 1914 like U.S. Steel and General Electric were notably more powerful by 1920 and gigantic by 1929.[4] The war had also revealed the potential for moving regulatory government along lines congenial to the most powerful interests in industry and agriculture as well as for pushing society to-

2. Simon Patten, *Essays in Economic Theory,* ed. R. G. Tugwell (New York, 1924); William T. Foster and Waddill Catchings, *The Road to Plenty* (Boston, 1928).

3. The diversity of such postures and fantasies in the parties is shown in David Burner, *The Politics of Provincialism: The Democratic Party in Transition, 1918–1932* (Cambridge, Mass., 1967).

4. *Recent Economic Changes in the United States* (2 vols.; New York, 1929), I, 217; Soule, *Prosperity Decade,* 158–86.

ward bureaucracy in education, labor, and the professions. After 1920, the entrepreneurs in the "romance of American business," and under slogans like Harmony, became the production heroes of American consumers and of boys dreaming of becoming an Edison or a Henry Ford. Dismaying though most of the experience with wartime planning was, it brought home to a wide range of interest groups what a confirmed and constant influence over government could mean in corporate America. After the end of the war crisis, its "ratchet effect," as described by Robert Higgs, left government, all levels considered, more deeply involved than ever before in railroads, farming, mining, shipping, labor, and industrial policies.[5] As the stakes of the national game for money and power and comfort climbed higher, the state was increasingly involved in wider concerns about sponsorship, regulation, and social justice. What farmers, electric power producers, education or highway enthusiasts now wanted from government went far beyond their lists of 1914.

If shaming the state in the 1920s was more strident, it was as though the more Americans succumbed to the novelty of bigness, the more they fulminated against this "fate." The fervid Jeffersonianism in popular books like Herbert Hoover's *American Individualism* (1922) lessened chances that public policy would accept important revisions of laissez-faire theory that were becoming available. The 1920s was a period of momentous ferment in economic theory, not only in America but across Europe, from Cambridge through Vienna and into Italy.[6] Sharp battles among subsequently famous economists involved contests not only about the different economic systems inherited from the last century but about new, increasingly recondite methods of economic analysis, *e.g.,* "institutional," mathematical, inductive. Overall, economics was moving away from grand theories that the educated and concerned layman might at least approach. Complex and specialized subjects like business cycles and mathematical concepts in matters like monetary theory were soon to put key issues in economics beyond the merely intelligent understanding of even the banker, broker, or businessman who had to make the practical decisions about the economy. The gist of the debate about general economic theory was expressed in Keynes's iconoclastic Oxford lecture of 1924, "The End of Laissez-Faire."[7] The talk would not have pleased any stalwart Jeffersonian, for it dealt with the collectivist and interventionist implications of World

5. Higgs, *Crisis and Leviathan.*

6. Karl Pribram, *A History of Economic Reasoning* (Baltimore, 1983), chap. 28 and notes, on surveys in the 1920s of new economic doctrines.

7. Reprinted in J. M. Keynes, *Essays in Persuasion* (New York, 1932).

War I and the postwar managed industrial economies: a much different economic analysis was in order than that of the prewar years. In America a scintillating symposium of this new economics was edited in 1924 by the young Rex Tugwell.[8] The excitement in the clashing views, however, was matched by their groping quality with about-to-be famous figures like F. C. Mills, Sumner H. Slichter, and Tugwell himself trying as much to define the complex and cloudy present as to divine the future. Implicit throughout the book was the question Keynes raised at Oxford, even if there was no agreement about how most economists answered the problems. Was the modern, large-scale, highly technological capitalist economy able to fulfill its task efficiently, especially if it fancied itself operating under the old model, here called by the shorthand expression "Jeffersonian"? Three years later Tugwell published his own response. He stressed that America's now "mature capitalism" required not an outmoded small-scale competition but "national economic planning."[9]

Tugwell was a very intelligent critic of Jeffersonian assumptions but not the equal of the more "technical" economists like Wesley Clair Mitchell or John M. Clark. In the main, these rising students of imperfect competition, monetary theory, or business cycles were not socialists or planners, as Tugwell professed to be. They were trying to make adjustments in theories of capitalist enterprise to take account of giant and dominating firms, managed markets, inelastic demand, sluggish prices, reluctance to invest, mass unemployment, as well as a more openly active state. We can only speculate if such ideas had passed into wider lay debate or, even more, into public policy whether much of the grief and disarray of the years ahead might have been avoided. Throughout the 1920s, in the highbrow reading that did not reach the laymen, research and analysis mountingly showed how neither free competition among small firms nor state restraint marked the basic dynamics of the economy. Many bellwether professional studies for redefining capitalist theory in this or that respect pointed toward two more general works at the end of the decade. Both *Recent Economic Changes* (1929) and Berle and Means, *The Modern Corporation and Private Property* (1932), for all of their different biases, found little of a Jeffersonian marketplace or passivity in government policies. Instead, ownership in major industries was both increasingly concentrated in fewer firms and increasingly separated from management while the state was growingly sought as an ally in establishing a sound business climate.

The spreading role of large firms and their networks of dependent,

8. R. G. Tugwell, ed., *The Trend of Economics* (New York, 1924).
9. R. G. Tugwell, *Industry's Coming of Age* (New York, 1927).

smaller enterprises was quite other than in the favorite portrait of competitive private enterprise. But the older picture was repeatedly and admiringly invoked in the 1920s by businessmen and their spokesmen like Dr. Julius Klein or Owen D. Young of General Electric in magazines like *The Saturday Evening Post* or *Colliers.* Despite the persistence after the war of the Brandeis strain of hostility to monopoly and of hopes of presidential candidates like La Follette in 1924 to restore competition,[10] the industrial giants were not congenial to competition from aggressive newcomers thinking of establishing themselves among the mammoth firms in automobiles, steel, aluminum, insurance, or transportation. Touting their increasing share of market and other powers as proof of their hard work and their honesty, efficiency, and productivity, big businesses played a complex game. In some markets, competition from new firms intrinsically was minimized by the huge cost of capitalizing a steel mill or automobile factory. Competition was further and deliberately restricted by mergers or takeovers of existing firms, as Chrysler took over Dodge in 1925. A growing repertory of methods evolved to beat back challenges, plan markets privately, and encourage a friendly government by more intensive and permanent lobbying or by "infiltrating" the Federal Trade Commission to assure favor for the business point of view.[11] In contrast, when small businesses, small farmers, or nonunion laborers asked government for help in the name of antimonopoly or against unfair or illegal practices, their big-business opponents not only denied their charges about rigged prices or other "market stabilizers" or about hostility to labor but warned against state encroachment against the proven productivity, efficiency, and innovation of privately operated businesses.

In the fullest assessment of competition, however, it is by no means clear that the growth of giant firms reduced competition overall in the economy, whatever those firms did in dominating their own fields.[12] Mass production in automobiles, for example, stimulated many new small- and medium-sized firms in plate glass, tires and other rubber components, electrical equipment, gas stations, automobile servicing and supplies, road building and repair, highway signals and signs, and so on. An energetic, self-styled Jeffersonian small businessman might not have been able to set up in automobiles or dynamos, but that did not imply he could go nowhere except into the ranks of embittered proletari-

10. William E. Leuchtenburg, *The Perils of Prosperity* (Chicago, 1958), 134–35.

11. D. M. Keezer and Stacy May, *The Public Control of Business* (New York, 1930).

12. The complexities in evaluating the changes are apparent in *Recent Economic Changes,* I, 181–90.

ans.[13] Similarly, the continuing battle against monopoly in the 1920s should not imply that would-be entrepreneurs were completely ruined by monopolists rather than being pushed to invest elsewhere. And moral indictment of monopoly, like La Follette's, continued to ignore that frustrated small capitalists, given their chance in steel or oil, might have been just as monopolistic or ruthless in market behavior as were Sinclair in oil or Schwab in big steel.

Action by federal and state regulatory bodies, increasingly imbued in the 1920s with the business point of view, was more and more welcomed by businessmen to enhance price domination, orderly production, stabilized markets, and standardization of products in their enterprises. As government intervention widened after World War I in activities like conservation, power generation, mining, and road building, the regulations included ideas that had been lobbied for by weighty firms and trade associations willing to have government sympathy for how they thought the marketplace should be run.[14]

Nevertheless, business attitudes overall toward state intervention remained as divided after 1920 as before the war. For the advantages of alliance with a friendly and powerful government one had to confront irritating red tape, undertake full-time and expensive lobbying, or submit to government specifications for products like nuts and bolts and machine tools. The same industry often split on what stances its operators wanted from government on tariffs or other regulation. Domestic tobacco, textile, fruit, and sugar interests might favor high tariffs on foreign imports, while investors in Cuban sugar and tobacco and Central American bananas and pineapples would favor the lowest possible tariffs and the least possible inspection of products imported from their overseas haciendas. Smaller-scale oil producers might want federal help against big oil's drive to dominance, but big oil might want the government to set nationwide quality standards like octane ratings for refining gasoline or their versions of controls over pipelines or refineries that would raise production costs for smaller operators and thus limit the challenge from competitors.[15]

In *popular* attitudes toward government in the 1920s one senses a profound stiffening against "the state" even while alliances with or seeking it increased. George Babbitt's fulminations in Sinclair Lewis' novel,

13. Harry W. Laidler, *Concentration of Control in American Industry* (New York, 1931), a respected socialist judgment that ignores shifts enhancing competition and emphasizes the growing, crushing power of the giant corporations.

14. Louis Galambos, *Competition and Cooperation: The Emergence of a National Trade Association* (Baltimore, 1966), makes clear the origins of such changes before 1920.

15. Harold F. Williamson *et al., The American Petroleum Industry* (2 vols.; Evanston, Ill., 1959–63), I, chaps. 13 and 14, and pp. 463–532.

the Amercian Legion warnings about radicalism, and the Jeffersonian views reported in *Middletown* were all hostile to government intervention. Certainly, Harding and Coolidge, as well as Democratic candidates like John Davis and Al Smith, played to sentiments against big government. In the populace, a host of bad memories of and experiences with government and reform drove back many citizens to the American bedrock, the seeming virtues symbolized by a quiet president like Calvin Coolidge and the old certitudes to which Coolidge knowingly played, of family, village, and clan, of money making, church going, and distant, cheap, and restrained government.[16] These verities from the last century, however compromised, had never been dispelled by flirtations with progressive or wartime ideals of a large-scale and bureaucratic America. Indeed, since the 1890s a work-a-day materialism was always intricately braided with many of the reform idealisms. One test of effective reproof to the monopolists and financiers for followers of La Follette in 1924, like those behind the New Freedom of 1912, was to be a restored chance for making money, euphemistically called in the 1920s "getting ahead." The easy and genial ways of a Warren Harding seemed a welcome recoil against both progressive earnestness and the big state with its recent, wartime dragooning and directing of citizens. Years later in his memoirs, Harry Truman incidentally symbolized the postwar reaction against the "big parade" of the war government: he complained that the Follies Bergère in Paris, which he visited in 1919, was "a disgusting performance."[17]

But return to a now-profitless family farm in Missouri or a struggling haberdashery shop or other ways back to civilian "normalcy" also meant pain and dislocation for millions of Americans. Vaunt though both Jeffersonianism and the new-era capitalism did "the American way," prospects were bleak in the coal mines and on overexpanded farms on the fields of the republic. For such American enterprises there was precious little gold in the golden 1920s. In those parts of the economy, as well as in cotton textiles, forestry, and railroading, if there were jobs there were thin wages for hard work, no matter the patriotic affirmation of its virtue.[18] Constitution-worship in the 1920s[19] put no money in the hands of the more marginal farmers who had eagerly profited from the state-encouraged wartime expansion of acreage and who were now caught by the shrinking world market, as well as by their chronic dis-

16. Donald R. McCoy, *Calvin Coolidge* (New York, 1967).

17. Harry S. Truman, *Memoirs* (2 vols.; Garden City, N.Y., 1955–56), I, 132.

18. Soule, *Prosperity Decade*. On soft spots in the economy of the 1920s, see 124–25, 175–82, 215–17, 232–34.

19. Leuchtenburg, *The Perils of Prosperity*, 204–205.

position to take risks and expand production and debt in hopes that good times would continue.[20] Given these veins of brass in the midst of the gold of the 1920s, the wounded now turned to government at every level, much more readily than before 1914, for aid or support for farm prices, easier rural credit, better inspection and work conditions in the coal mines, and more sympathy for welfare and social legislation. Assorted discontents brought La Follette's Progressive Party of 1924 just under five million votes, an all-time high for an American third party. The pained yelps for repairs by the state in his platform and in lobbying in the 1920s were signs of the slow legitimation of calls for intervention against the wounds inflicted by high-powered corporate "individualism." The response by government was complex. Across all tiers of American government, the state became an even more open, even hailed partner in promoting enterprise.[21] In a contrary direction, in national legislation like the Railway Labor Act (1926) and Agricultural Marketing Act (1929) Republican administrations moved toward becoming at least a more readily conceived healer of free-market wounds. Especially in state legislatures, limited remedial legislation about working conditions continued to mark the way for the federal repair efforts in the depression decade.[22]

The nation's growing stake in productivity and its mystique and a mounting aversion among Hooveresque engineers and "modern managers" to waste in unstandarized, over-inventoried, or foolishly spoiled goods also enlarged the scope of federal intervention. As we shall see, the Hoover husbandry for a now massive industrial economy aimed at greater state-sponsored rationalization of production and enterprise against wasteful or underproductive small-scale competition. But for all the Jeffersonian rhetoric, the new benign interventionism betokened a business world far from the horizons or purpose of a Jefferson or Jackson.

We must emphasize that this turn in public policy toward cooperation with the state, like the first effective calls for federal regulation a half-century earlier, came not from radical critics of capitalism but from its doyens, its great figures in industry, science, and corporate life. They were relentless not merely to enter and exploit private markets but to master them and now, if necessary, with the help of government. Those parts of the capitalist world that sought closer alliance with the state

20. Theodore Saloutos and John D. Hicks, *Agricultural Discontent in the Middle West, 1900–1939* (Madison, Wis., 1951).

21. Herbert Hoover, *American Individualism* (Garden City, N.Y., 1922), the classic statement for the new cooperation.

22. Clarke A. Chambers, *Seedtime of Reform: Social Service and Social Action, 1918–1933* (Minneapolis, 1963).

were thus tacitly the "statist" allies of radical critics who wanted control of big business transferred to the state or the "public," not to the workers and not broken up to restore competition. Technocrats and socialists favoring state ownership, like Hoover, their erstwhile opponent, foresaw enlarging economies of scale bringing improved mass production deeper into the lives of more Americans.[23] For radicals, this meant lifting the standards of life for the lowly. Ostensibly, public operation would end senseless gluts or scarcities traceable to selfish and ignorant entrepreneurs. The hopes of both private and public planners contrasted, however, with one of the most underappreciated general tendencies of the 1920s. Bureaucracy and size within private, as well as public, organizations already showed the potential to frustrate both productivity and effective public services. If planners of the 1920s could realize fantasies about riding the dinosaurs of industry because their size suggested so much power and speed, time would show that many of the behemoths had grown too clumsy or were too small-brained to be able to move quickly and skillfully over the terrain that they seemed destined to dominate.

Hoover's Happier Days

No public figure in the 1920s tried more to have it both ways with the Jeffersonian tenets than Herbert Hoover. In his cosmos, large-scale organization of state and society, efficiency, and productivity seemed reconciled with economic individualism and minimal government. Some of the most instructive lessons for our century about the state and the economy derive from Hoover's work as Secretary of Commerce in the 1920s.

Hoover had come out of the war with an immense reputation and was commonly regarded by 1920 as one of the outstanding citizens of the day. To secure his services as Secretary of Commerce, Harding even agreed to the broad charge Hoover requested before accepting: he was to participate in all important government economic decisions, regardless of department lines. This unusual sweep makes clear Hoover's larger purposes to rouse all government to a new style and pitch of intervention in his years in the Commerce Department (1921 to 1928).[24]

23. Stuart Chase, *The Tragedy of Waste* (New York, 1925); Alfred D. Chandler, Jr., *Strategy and Structure: Chapters in the History of Industrial Enterprise* (Cambridge, Mass., 1962).

24. This material about Hoover draws on these works unless otherwise footnoted: David Burner, *Herbert Hoover: The Public Life* (New York, 1978); Herbert Hoover, *The Cabinet and the Presidency, 1920–1933* (New York, 1952), Vol. II of *Memoirs;* Evan

When Hoover took over the department in 1921 he found an odd accumulation of regulatory and information services in a lethargic agency. When Hoover left Commerce in 1928, it was the most expanded and modernized department of federal administration and the most active and diverse agency concerned with the national economy. All this growth and intervention, we must recall, came under Republican leaders extolling Jeffersonian ideals of a minimal and passive state. Department employees grew in number from about 13,000 to almost 16,000, an increment of about 23 percent, and appropriations went in annual steps from $24,500,000 to $37,600,000, or about 53 percent. These percentages not only outstripped those for other departments but would have been higher had not Congress and a Coolidge often vexed with his expansive "wonder boy" resisted Hoover's endless agenda of unmet national needs. Hoover practiced one of the big tricks for getting government to do something desirable: to suggest that intervention was friendly sponsorship rather than outright, unwanted, coercive intervention. This formula helps explain why the growth of the department could not only be tolerated but extolled by Hoover himself and other fans of a government that gave private enterprise maximum freedom.

Hoover's activities were so diverse and they so transformed old tasks for government, as well as added new ones, that the highlights alone are astonishing. But the condensed record also reminds us of the extant, longer-term patterns of government pileup. The Hoover chapter is a telling account of evermore, ever-faster, but now consciously coordinated government growth. His record also makes apparent the multifold activities into which the modern state can spread without fanfare and when it comes as a friend, not a foe.

Overall, Hoover thoroughly reorganized the department, recast the principal existing offices, created many new ones, and brought in "top talent" to head the more technical bureaus. He greatly expanded the activities of the officials handling Foreign and Domestic Commerce, Standards, the Census, Fisheries, Lighthouses, the Coast Guard, and the U.S. Employment Service. Hoover was the first administrator to regulate new American industries as they were being born, the fledgling aviation and radio businesses. He expanded earlier federal roles in conservation, petroleum production, the national highway network, railway labor re-

B. Metcalf, "Secretary Hoover and the Emergence of Macroeconomic Management," *Business History Review,* XLIX (1975); Joan Hoff-Wilson, *Herbert Hoover: Forgotten Progressive* (Boston, 1975); Ellis W. Hawley, "The Discovery and Study of Corporate Liberalism," *Business History Review,* LII (1978), and *The Great War and the Search for a Modern Order* (New York, 1979).

lations, and inland waterways. He took the lead in creating the interstate Colorado River Commission that started work on building Boulder (now Hoover) Dam. But that was only preparatory for similar plans for the St. Lawrence, Mississippi, Missouri, and Columbia river systems. Hundreds of national conferences were sponsored to bring together the leaders of various interest groups concerned with problems like unemployment, agriculture, foreign loans, radio, and aviation. The most publicized of these meetings were called White House Conferences. One of Hoover's favorites was on child health and protection. The publications, reports, and statistical services of the department can only be described as an increasing torrent. Some, like *Commerce Reports,* are still appearing and are highly regarded. Hoover-sponsored books like *Recent Economic Changes* (1929) are standard sources about the American economy in the 1920s.

Nothing in the history of the peacetime growth of American government matches this stunning Hoover record. Many may be astonished and puzzled to learn that Herbert Hoover happily sought this swell of government and that he regarded it as only a prelude to what he wanted Coolidge to do elsewhere and planned to do himself as president. The deep incentive lay in his Quaker horror of waste and excess, which was reinforced by his immense success as an engineer famous for efficiency and despatch. Both led to a master vision for "reconstructing" America—the word was his—to perfect modern capitalism under state-prodding and state-coordinated private and voluntary initiatives. We can only speculate about what President Hoover might have accomplished in mastering and modernizing the state had the Great Depression not so shockingly confounded his assumption that America was destined only for abundance, not for disastrous dearth.

But what Hoover did not understand or foresee involves more than his management of the great depression that started only a half-year into his presidency. Despite fine studies of Hoover by David Burner and Ellis Hawley, we still have much to learn in taking the deep measure of the ideas of this extraordinary man. Hoover's type of political rationalism goes far beyond his particular program and still colors much of American proposals and policy making that disguise increasing intervention and control through "industrial policy," for example, as more rational management and sensible, coordinated growth.

Hoover was so dedicated to his goal of bringing about a scientifically managed economy of abundance under private enterprise that he never recognized how much new power he actually brought to the state in the name of "merely encouraging" entrepreneurs to help build the new capitalism. By 1920, insightful capitalists like himself had openly acknowledged excesses of both profligacy and selfishness in the free-market system. They traced depressions, bankruptcies, strikes, glutted inventories, uneven flow of raw materials, and duplication of labor, products, and services to the growing pains of youthful industrial enterprise that a more mature but still private capitalism could eliminate.[25] Hoover believed profoundly in the *ultimate* rationality of the market under enlightened private management. All irrationalities traceable to earlier "selfishness" in capital, labor, and finance alike would lessen as self-interest, "in time," yielded to science, Quaker-like meetings, consensus, and documented experience. That "in time" many irrationalities in both industry and government change form rather than give way to wisdom and to "the spirit of service" was not Hoover's thinking. The altruism or service that Hoover extolled as his goal for the nation's economic leaders was too easily a pious cover for self-interest in business and government alike. And even when "men of good will" wanted to do well, overlarge ambitions and excessive organization, ignorance, complication, and chance could bring havoc to the best-intentioned plans. Disequilibrium, excess, and stubborn irrationality may be inescapable in all private as well as public organizations, however intended for serving science and progress. As for the state providing only a forum for business discussions and for eliciting consensus without coercion, Hoover did not seem to grasp that a government invitation to businessmen to collaborate voluntarily with the best expert views could be strongly manipulative. Washington "merely" sponsoring an idea at a Hoover conference could carry great weight, especially, as some evidence indicates, the conferees did not include confirmed skeptics or obstructionists.[26] Hoover's solicitous government, however, often went beyond calls to science and reason and set standards for its massive purchases of products and services. For one notable example, the dollar worth and volume of the government orders for millions of Hoover standardized nuts and bolts also set limits for production for private purchases. Businesses could not afford to forego such government orders and then continue to produce several versions of the same screws or to create multiple inventories. Similarly, if the Commerce Department "merely" collected and issued information about favored projects for flood control or airline expansion, those facts then heavily supported what government wanted to do.

In these and many other respects, the ostensibly liberty-loving Hoover seemed oddly cordial to ideas of a peacetime nation marching in ranks to fulfill a technocratic faith. In his earlier great work in relying on moral

25. Hoover, *American Individualism.*
26. Burner, *Herbert Hoover,* 161.

suasion for compliance with his food-saving programs in 1917 and 1918, we already find innocence about suasion as coercion. Time after time in the Hoover gospel of cooperation we hear echoes of Edward Bellamy and portents of the militaristic potential of all erstwhile benign and hortatory social rationalism carried to excess.

Implicit also in Hoover statism is the insistent question of whether stimulating the economy or encouraging rather than regulating entrepreneurship is any less "state intervention." By classical versions of laissez-faire, if entrepreneurs of the 1920s were failing on their own to eliminate waste and inefficiency and undue costs, they should have faced the penalties that the market could inflict, *i.e.*, going under before more astute or energetic competitors. What was new, therefore, in Hoover's initiative to avoid waste was not state sponsorship of growth but rather thickening the state's role to avoid potential distempers or disasters that business, left to itself, might bring on itself and the nation. In that light, the crash in 1929 was a terrible reproof of Hoover's faith in volunteered rationality.[27] But it was also another temptation to radical critics to believe that even more planning with more government and more bite in it was the logical path beyond Hoover's imperfect vision of a self-taming capitalism.

Republican Husbandry

Considering the strength of the myth of government continence in the 1920s, it may be tempting to regard Hoover's imperium as an exception. A quick look at the overall figures for growth in federal employment in the 1920s can indeed suggest temperateness.[28] But deeper analysis shows the continuity with earlier pileup. In the last peacetime year, 1916, federal civilian employees numbered about 438,500. By 1922, the purely wartime expansion seemed flushed from the system. The low point for federal employment in the 1920s was about 537,000, in 1923. That, however, was an increase of 22 percent in seven years. By 1930, *i.e.*, even before the spurt in state activity that came in the depression, that 1916 figure of 438,500 had increased to more than 601,000, a growth of 37 percent, although only a more modest expansion of 7 percent for the 1920s. Outlays for 1916 for all functions, excluding the armed forces, debt interest, and veterans, were only $193 million. By 1922, with those three "special" expenditures put aside and with war left behind, the fed-

27. James W. Prothro, *The Dollar Decade: Business Ideas in the 1920s* (Baton Rouge, 1954), 216, 225–26.
28. The information below derives mainly from Solomon Fabricant's study, *The Trend of Government Activity in the United States Since 1900* (New York, 1952), and from *Historical Statistics of the United States*, II, Ser. Y, "Government Employment and Finances."

eral outlays were about $1.111 billion, more than five times beyond the 1916 figure. Even adjusted for inflation, the increase was huge. The 1930 federal outlays of $1.601 billion were up 44 percent over 1922 despite the only 7 percent increase in federal employees, but the 1930 outlays were more than 700 percent beyond the 1916 peacetime amount of $193 million. The 44 percent increase in outlays from 1922 to 1930 rather than the 7 percent growth in workers may be the more revealing indicator, since it points to the expansion of federal functions not only in Commerce but in Agriculture, Interior, and Labor, in old and new independent agencies like the Budget Bureau, and in congressional staffs.

Even more telling about government growth in the ostensibly anti-big-government 1920s are the figures for state and local employment and outlays. Excluding education, merely because it was an established task with already ceaseless growth, from 1920 to 1930 state government employment grew from 183,000 to 279,000, or more than 50 percent. City, town, and county employment increased from 664,000 to 1,047,000, or more than 57 percent. In this decade, however, national population grew by only 16 percent. An especially dramatic index of growth, developed by Solomon Fabricant, displays the book value of the capital assets (buildings and facilities) of the states and localities. In 1922, these stood at $16.7 billion, in 1929 at $31.9 billion. This not only was an increase of 79 percent in seven years but includes a drop in the federal share of total government capital assets from 18.4 percent to 16.4 percent. Infrastructure for continuing urbanization—the expansion of streets and sewers, growth in dwellings and schools, public health measures, hospitals, welfare, licensing, and building inspection—help explain these leaps beneath the federal level. The automobile alone brought dramatic changes in the tasks of local government involving new needs about roads, parking and garaging, safety, servicing, and traffic crimes. For those without cars in the cities, population and industrial growth meant deepening problems of moving ever-larger thousands of citizens to and from work by public transportation and further increases in the onerous daily tasks of feeding and otherwise provisioning urban dwellers. Recreation needs in off-hours, restaurant inspection, playgrounds, forays into public or quasi-public utilities or housing, the spreading of the electric power grid above and under ground, and increased regulation in social legislation against sweatshops and child labor were also on state and local agendas. In some states, incipient old-age and widow funds and provisions for accident and unemployment income were preparing the way for the federal social security and wages and hours legislation of the 1930s.[29] As more cities adopted reforms like

29. Chambers, *Seedtime of Reform;* Roy Lubove, *The Struggle for Social Security, 1900–1935* (Cambridge, Mass., 1968).

professional city managers as counters to the excoriated waste and corruption of boss rule, the irony we discerned after the 1880s continued: the attempt to rationalize government increased its corps of bureaucrats and their costs. Skilled urban administration required not only more money and more officials but more office space, more information, more costly analysis, typewriters, file cabinets, better articulated rules to guide the added inspectors, and more supervisors with better "follow-up." The advent in the 1920s of that most pretentious of conscious social controls, national prohibition, and the concomitant growth of the illegal liquor trade in alliance with prostitution and gambling, especially contributed to the buildup of government needed to advance the "noble experiment."

The paradox of "modern administration," intended to simplify and improve services but making government grow and cost more, is also obvious in federal waxing in the Harding-Coolidge era, an illustrative case being the Bureau of the Budget and the General Accounting Office (1921). The former was aimed at improving executive control over the generations of pileup in federal appropriations and the latter at better congressional supervision of how federal agencies used their funds. Each of these reforms of 1921 brought a new bureaucracy, its own budgetary needs, and a widening scope of intervention. Sometimes, bureaucratic growth had other guises than the attempt to reduce government costs and personnel, *e.g.,* agencies that were reorganized, like those at Commerce so dramatically under Hoover. Often, new agencies inherited, while consolidating, tasks from older ones, as in the establishment of the Veterans Administration (1930), or new agencies absorbed older, smaller agencies in their entirety, as was the case in many of the amalgamations in the Commerce Department.

Recalling the torrent of new agencies that appeared during the "Hoover New Deal" and the Roosevelt years, it is instructive to look back a bit beyond 1920 and recall the continuities with previous growth under *both* parties in the generation before the New Deal. During the second term of the Wilson administration (1917 to 1921) and separable from the needs of war, or if launched for wartime purposes, continuing during "normalcy," came diverse major agencies like the Alien Property Custodian (1917), Woman's Bureau (1918), and the Federal Power Commission (1920). After 1921, under the Republicans there appeared:

> Bureau of the Budget (1921)
> Railway Labor Board (1921)
> General Accounting Office (1921)
> Bureau of Home Economics (1923)
> Battle Monuments Commission (1923)

Board of Tax Appeals (1924)
National Capital Park and Planning Commission (1924)
Bureau of Dairy Industry (1924)
Railway Mediation Board (1926)
Food and Drug Administration (1928)
Mount Rushmore National Memorial Commission (1929)
Federal Farm Board (1929)
Veterans Administration (1930)

Every one of these represents a success for a coalition of pressure groups that increasingly sought Washington for its involvement and for far less traditional subjects than the tariff. Hoover's conscious efforts at streamlining the Department of Commerce and what conscious planning came with the Bureau of the Budget and the GAO were exceptional. Waxing, waning, and pileup remained the governing norm in growth. What problems or needs across the continent should be left to private initiative and which aspects of regulation, if any, should be delegated to local or state or federal authority remained murky and partisan matters. And ideologically, prestige and myth still heavily supported leaving all overseeing to private forces. Also left unattended or in haze was the deepening problem of the compatibility of the traditional systems of federalism and checks and balances with the increasing size and impingement on one another of the economic and social needs of a continental capitalism and of Washington sway over the old geographic and governmental boundaries. By 1930, it cannot be said that the country was governed better than in 1900, although it was clearly increasingly subject to government intervention.

By 1933, the record amply documents the ability of the American political system not only to avoid big issues, such as effective control of monopoly beyond mere gestures, but to frustrate hailed initiatives for better governance, like the Budget Bureau and increases in congressional staffs. What changed with the depression were the unprecedented proportions and great dangers of untended needs and the immediacy with which tens of millions of threatened lives and emaciated interests affected each other. America's starved state was not prepared for such a challenge. The federal system that Franklin Roosevelt inherited in 1933 also had all the warnings accumulated in the fifty years since the Pendleton Act gave the signal that regulatory pileup might fail to cope adequately with government dysfunction let alone disasters. The New Deal did not create the "mess in Washington" in confronting a perilously sick society. It received from the past most of the inadequacies of the state in diagnosing and treating. By 1933, professional students of public administration had already raised many of the basic questions about the efficacy of the short-range thinking and political expediency that had gone into many twentieth-century endeavors at "governing" the United States better.[30] Gesture-ism, starving the state, short-term financing for long-term projects, haste and carelessness in legislating, prosaic, weak, or hack political appointees like, notoriously, the "Harding gang," buck passing and end runs by career bureaucrats to frustrate unwelcome initiatives, vetting an established program that had been too popular to resist when first proposed—in sum, an immense weight of government irrationality and pseudorationality was in place before Franklin Roosevelt tried mightily for both recovery and reform.[31]

New Deal Lore

The lore of more fervent liberals and of conservatives agrees on one thing, that Franklin D. Roosevelt and the New Deal decisively and dramatically altered the role of government in American life.[32] Conservative views trace back to the efforts of Herbert Hoover and the Liberty League in the 1930s to defeat FDR. By 1935, they decried "the challenge to liberty" in Roosevelt's statism and berated his administration for a radical rejection of individualism, localism, and voluntarism. For them, after a century of golden freedom from government, Roosevelt created *ex nihilo* an oppressive centralized American state on the road to dictatorship. A near-apocalyptic tone is apparent in such landmark criticism of Roosevelt as Hoover's *The Challenge to Liberty* (1934) and F. A. Von Hayek's *Collectivist Economic Planning* (1935).

In liberal legends, dogmatic hostility by Republicans in the 1920s against social legislation and aid to the distressed on farms and in the mines encouraged the depredations of powerful economic groups that brought on the disaster of 1929. Failure to use government to limit speculation and to increase, instead, general productivity and purchasing power also prepared the crisis. When it came, an out-of-touch Hoover fearfully fretted about saving American character and the traditions of individual and voluntary effort while millions faced starvation or bankruptcy. The sense of deliverance in partisan discourse about the debut

30. J. M. Gaus and L. D. White, "Public Administration in the United States in 1933," *American Political Science Review,* XXVIII (1934); Louis Brownlow, "The New Role of the Public Administrator," *National Municipal Review,* XXIII (1934).

31. Discounting the partisanship in the account, much of the disorder by 1932 is well portrayed in Arthur Schlesinger, Jr., *The Crisis of the Old Order, 1919–1933* (Boston, 1957).

32. The evolution of the FDR image is traced in William E. Leuchtenburg, *In the Shadow of FDR* (Ithaca, N.Y., 1983).

of intervening and compassionate government under Roosevelt is suggested in books of the 1930s like Rex Tugwell's *The Battle for Democracy* (1935) and George Soule's *The Future of Liberty* (1936). The theme of hope following disaster continues in later liberal scholarship like Schlesinger's *The Crisis of the Old Order* (1957) and *The Coming of the New Deal* (1959).

Read carefully now, the full range of serious ideas in the 1930s about the prospects of American government shows great diversity.[33] But policy makers working in the midst of battle in those days could not read everything nor care much about cautionary, qualifying, and conflicting arguments about the dangerous directions or unperceived portents of New Deal efforts to save homes or put food on family tables. As the New Deal thickened in the 1930s, however, popular opinion about it increasingly polarized. In the Sunday news supplements, editorials, letters to the editor, and radio broadcasts by commentators like Lowell Thomas, Raymond Gram Swing, H. V. Kaltenborn, and Gabriel Heatter there was a war of ideas about the growth of government.[34] Hoover could be denounced as a reactionary or fascist and Roosevelt and his purported mentors Stalin or Keynes as statists, Communists, or dictators.

However simplistic Sunday newspaper ideas were during the heady Roosevelt decade, the debates did force Americans to a painful consciousness about state intervention that still burdens us. The growing sense more than fifty years since 1933 is of government irritatingly and ineradicably intrusive, with every major decision about American society increasingly seeming to depend on what government does or will not do. But for 1933 the impression is inescapable that so many problems that desperately needed tending to save homes, jobs, and bank accounts would have remained largely neglected had Roosevelt not intervened as he did and with initial hurrahs from business leaders who were soon to excoriate him. After the three years of steep slide since 1929, individual liberty did not seem assuredly self-correcting or self-repairing. When the White House announced at midnight on March 3, 1933, that it was at the end of its rope, much more was implied than the calendar running out on the Hoover tenure.

The degree of the crisis of 1933, as well as the persistence of depression throughout the 1930s, dramatically expanded the agenda for federal government activity from the earlier more circumscribed, quieter,

---

33. A good sampling is in Arthur Schlesinger, Jr., *The Politics of Upheaval* (Boston, 1960), chap. 21, especially the notes and 690–93. A broader and later reprise is in Otis L. Graham, *The New Deal: The Critical Issues* (Boston, 1971).

34. Of many notable debates by intellectuals reaching the general public, read Keynes versus Laski in "Can America Spend Its Way Into Recovery?" *Redbook*, December, 1934.

and sporadic intervention. A historian may now make his claim that before Roosevelt there is a long chronicle of growing state intervention and never more rapidly than in the Republican decade before FDR. But the basic model for intervention had been developing at least since Jackson's time a century earlier. Government at all levels existed to serve constituencies that were sufficiently aroused and organized to feel entitled to action. Politicians who did not meet needs could be dismissed in elections. As beliefs and practices these remain hallmarks of democracy, whatever the wisdom about what government does. In the New Deal years the old democratic seeking of the state was enlarged to include groups such as labor unions and recent immigrants, who now learned how to play the American party games at the Washington level, often after training in the cities and states. But scholarly claims about how much state-seeking was already under way before 1933, and, incidentally, thus "determined" how expedient and roughhewn so much New Deal intervention would be, falter before the national denial that government had played much of a role and that in fact it had been growing in line with the general expansion of American economy and society. The denial, coupled with the sense of the limited access that millions of humbler Americans had previously had to Washington, produced the shocking sense of the state that came with the cascading Roosevelt intervention.[35] It seemed from the furor of the Liberty League in the mid-1930s as though the federal government had never passed a benefit for farm credit or a regulation for banking, monopoly, or the railroads before 1933. Forgotten also was how much Hoover's sizable intervention after 1931 had already broken significantly with government reticence during earlier depressions.

The extent of the New Deal intervention "blew the cover"—that was its shock—of the covert state. It brought Washington and government generally from the distant horizon into the full view of citizens with such undeniable, tangible evidence as federal checks in pay envelopes for construction workers and small farmers. The New Deal thus greatly stimulated the contest about the role of government to encourage spending, provide social security, and advance the public welfare when private endeavor failed. In the half-century after 1933, if Americans came increasingly under the shadow of state protection and regulation for mighty purposes, many found it difficult to be at full ease even with what government did for middle-class farms or mortgages, let alone what it did for lowly groups on relief or for post-office-mural painters. Guilt, anxiety, and anger increased quickly about the "alphabet agencies" and the hundreds of programs that revealed the state looming ever-larger in

35. Lewis W. Douglas, *The Liberal Tradition* (New York, 1935).

American lives. Unskilled, casual, and marginal wage-earners, the aged and infirm, tenant farmers, migrants, poor students, actors and artists, and, very unevenly, blacks came under the umbrella of the national state, or at least its edge, for the first time. Even more weightily, the so-called solid citizens who had lost jobs and businesses were told not to feel shame about aid from Washington. Gradually, therefore, many groups that had only tenuous connection with government became conscious political constituencies anticipating state services. Actually, most citizens on relief received money from Washington for short periods but their vacated places on the relief roles were taken by others. For however long, millions thus received at least a whiff of the state, but millions also became permanently involved with the social security system, wages and hours legislation, collective bargaining, and mortgage or crop insurance. Great numbers discovered new friends in the Democratic Party, which quickly replaced the Republicans as the normal political affiliation of groups like blacks and farmers.[36] And as the voting power of previously neglected groups increased, the political parties had to find places for leaders who spoke for workingmen, union leaders, teachers, social and government workers, a wide range of "ethnics," and a scattering of blacks.[37]

In emphasizing, as many studies do, the economic crisis and political pressures that forced both Hoover and Roosevelt to act as peacetime presidents never had, we can miss the profound psychological and cultural change that New Deal intervention wrought in Americans. This lay less in their formal ideology than in how they actually assessed their needs and in their expanding sense of expectations and entitlements from the state. Despite the unceasing pileup of government intervention before 1933, it is astonishing, from today's perspective, how much most citizens were still left on their own in daily life. Finding a job or making do without one, bargaining individually with a boss, banker, or crossroads merchant, putting aside money for dark days and old age, owning a savings account or home mortgage, financing medical care, paying for food raised without crop subsidies and controls, finding cash for most purchases—all such daily provisioning required choices and incurred risks without any or significant federal involvement. Despite the century of government involvement before the 1920s, the common belief of Middletown in 1927 was that Americans stood on their own legs and that it

36. William E. Leuchtenburg, *Franklin D. Roosevelt and the New Deal, 1932–1940* (New York, 1963), chaps. 4, 7.

37. *Ibid.*, 184–90; Samuel Lubell, *The Future of American Politics* (New York, 1952); Raymond E. Wolfinger, "The Development and Persistence of Ethnic Voting," *American Political Science Review*, LIX (1965).

was un-American or showed weakness of character to do otherwise.[38] Generalizations about actual self-sufficiency may be risky, but popular slogans before the 1930s set off those times from what followed: Sink or swim; God helps those who help themselves; The race belongs to the swift and strong; Only the fit survive; Grin and bear it; and so on. Of course, ever since at least the 1890s there had been calls for government aid against the worst rigors of the economy, but it is revealing that from Coxey's Army and the Populists of the 1890s down to the Bonus March of 1932, the dominant theme of protest was that the state merely help get self-respecting and hard-working Americans back on their feet. Government would then retreat from public works or the easier credit temporarily needed to reinvigorate individual effort.

No ideal of self-help or the limited aid available to get through dark times anticipated the depth of the debacle after 1929. Ruin went shockingly beyond the circles of traditional victims of hard times. An unemployment rate of 25 percent and a 50 percent drop in national income by 1933 made unprecedented assaults on the livelihood and pride of millions, many of them used to a life of modest comfort and self-built security. Not only were the number and variety of the stricken hideously large but relief from limited public or private sources was exhausted after four years of downturn. Roosevelt understood that in such disaster millions of citizens who had traditionally taken care of their own needs were against the wall through no fault of theirs. "Character" may have provided some citizens bank accounts and insurance policies and small stock portfolios, but it could not replace lost wages or control what the managers of the American economy did with entrusted funds. At first, Roosevelt anticipated that a few more billions of direct government aid beyond Hoover's emergency provisioning would prime the pump to make enterprise resume running under private auspices. But priming, as much under Roosevelt as Hoover, did not get the pump going. Up to 1939 and then with defense and war expenditures, government stimulus became habitual and more diverse. Slowly, if controversially, expectations of state aid became engrained. What were once private needs, such as providing for old age, were politicized, and intervening government gained voter support despite warnings from both right- and left-wing opponents of the New Deal.

No one better anticipated American disquiet about these changes than Roosevelt himself. He had campaigned in 1932 predominantly with attacks on Hoover spending, deficits, and bureaucracy. At the beginning of his own budget-busting in 1933 he repeatedly assured citizens that his broader recovery programs were born of the emergency and that

38. Robert S. Lynd, *Middletown* (New York, 1929), 413–27.

he sought only to strengthen individual responsibility and spending power and restore vigorous private enterprise. Even a permanent public program like, notably, the Social Security Act of 1935 was not to be a budgeted obligation or a dole financed from revenue but was to be based on employer-employee contributions to a state-administered social insurance "trust fund" to provide a minimum for old age. Beyond that first thin safety net, as it was later named, Americans still had most to do on their own to take care of themselves through savings, life insurance, and family care. Few people seemed to note that not even the contributed funds to the social security system were guaranteed for repayment. Similarly, when FDR uneasily accepted federally mandated wages and hours in 1938, they, too, were presented solely as a floor to counter extreme unfairness in the labor market.[39] The professed intention was to help assure an absolute minimum wage of 25 cents an hour in interstate commerce and then to leave Americans, aided by recently guaranteed collective bargaining, free to take care of financing their lives as they saw fit rather than rely on the state to guarantee them an adequate income.[40] Still, the expectation arose that the state would underwrite a basic minimum of life sustenance. But as the years passed, the logic of this most recent and large wave of the permission to intervene led to a growing alertness about other unmet needs. The politicians' ceaseless search for popular help programs drew millions to expect ever-broader coverage. Already in the original Fair Labor Standards Act of 1938 the hourly minimum was to rise over seven years from 25 cents to 40 cents.

Traditionally, "entitlement" was only a technical clause in legislation establishing who was qualified for the government benefit; but over the decades entitlements were to become a synonym for rights, and the annual battle in Congress called to arms all those expecting entitlements to continue and expand. Together, the complex play between expectations and entitlements amid the setting of American interest-group politics came to provide much of the dynamics of domestic politics and government growth down to today. As war, cold war, and the sensitivities of minorities came to the fore, these created additional layers of expectations and entitlements so that, for example, a military base or weapons system should not be cut back and deprive local merchants of their entitlement to a livelihood. For American ethnic groups, aid for foreign cousins would be taken to be an entitlement, and many blacks would come to feel entitled to "set-asides" and percentages of jobs and contracts.

39. James McGregor Burns, *Congress on Trial* (New York, 1949), 68–82.
40. J. Joseph Huthmacher, *Senator Robert F. Wagner and the Rise of Urban Liberalism* (New York, 1968), 246–49.

Often, large changes have small beginnings. In the 1930s, the traditional business world beneficiaries of state action had been in line for decades for aid in tariffs or the metal backing for paper currency. As the line began to grow to include supplicants from every class, Roosevelt also went far beyond Hoover in channeling federal money from tax revenue directly into pay envelopes, not through the states. Who of the millions working for the WPA or PWA or on a run-down family farm had ever received Treasury checks? Federal money brought them into unprecedented intimacy with the state for meeting the commonest needs for food, clothing, and shelter. The state was thus embarked on underwriting not only the traditional chance for the energetic to prosper but now for the defeated to survive or to begin a comeback from disaster. But every new program, for poor as well as rich citizens, whether successful or not, was a signal for others to join the swelling queue seeking the state and to raise their previously private expectations to political horizons.

Whatever Roosevelt's first intentions that most New Deal aid would be temporary and would be reduced in future budgets, the expectations about state action went far deeper than for relief job payments or farm income. New Deal intervention played to a growing conviction, strengthened by the creeds of social engineering, that American society in full sweep presented a vast series of specifiable needs for which there were satisfactions devisable by experts and depending for success on government action and funding.[41] Politicians on the hustings and the new bureaucracies easily caught the import of the expanding possibilities. Pie in sky became a featured item on menus offered by politicians, along with denunciations of rivals who would take it away if elected. Those opposing the new cuisine denounced the big spenders who were squandering hard-earned tax dollars on the lazy and dishonest or, from another perspective, spending for "big bucks" citizens rather than on "my constituents" with genuine needs.

We do not have to judge the worthiness of programs or the needs of the petitioners but, rather, to mark the political expectations that the pileup of New Deal programs engendered and their galvanizing effects on party politics. If private, local, or voluntary group activity to serve needs seemed ineffective, the vaulting legitimacy after 1933 of turning to government to service them and fulfill expectations encouraged speaking out, organizing, lobbying, making contacts, and securing a benefit. If citizens begin to believe that only government action stands between them and making good on the American dream of happiness, what limit

41. Richard J. Kirkendall, *Social Scientists and Farm Politics in the Age of Roosevelt* (Columbia, Mo., 1966).

can be specified for government involvement? What costs and inefficiency and scandalous bureaucracies, to use Jimmy Carter's repeated phrase, will not be borne because democratic government must always show that it "cares"?

New Deal programs shifted some of the responsibility for meeting needs not only from the individual but from the stunned or exhausted local authorities and charities of 1932. Later in the thirties, as cities and states revived from the depletion of their "poor funds," they too expanded social services and other intervention to correlate with or supplement federal programs.[42] As Washington took the lead in providing funds for mass public housing in the 1930s, the cities and states also had their own programs for low-rent housing as well as for a widening array of social services.[43] Historically, there had been joint programs like state-federal agricultural research, highway building, and some of the Hoover initiatives like flood control and expanding the electricity grid in the 1920s. After 1933, federal construction of airports, hospitals, and other public facilities, and federal work relief were increasingly coordinated with state and local activity. This made the web of all government thicker, but it also encouraged the other tiers of government as well as individual citizens to anticipate a larger federal role backed, as that could be, by the immensely larger funds from national revenue. In that perspective, the habit of looking to Washington and the increase of little New Deals in states like New York, Michigan, and California jointly increased expectations about what government generally could do.

If the states in the past had experimented with activities that the federal government subsequently adopted, in the depression period a strong pattern in the opposite direction developed. Between 1932 and 1938, total federal funds going to revenue-shy state and local governments almost quadrupled.[44] Federal action thus gave the localities the cues or required responses with local money to qualify for federal aid. In activities like low-cost public housing, to cite a notable example, federal dollars grew from $3 million to $106 million, a 35-fold increase from 1933 to 1938. As local finances and economies were juggled to come back from the trauma of 1933, and after the powerful push from Washington, their own funding for housing and slum clearance went from $3 million in 1938 to $230 million in 1940 and even maintained itself when Washington retrenched in the war years.[45] In contrast, while

42. James T. Patterson, *The New Deal and the States* (Princeton, 1969).

43. John Braeman *et al.*, eds., *The New Deal: The State and Local Levels* (2 vols.; Columbus, Ohio, 1975), II.

44. See *Historical Statistics of the United States* for the data on housing, health, welfare, police, etc., as indicated in the following citations.

45. *Ibid.*, II, Ser. Y, 605–37.

federal expenditure for hospitals waned about 20 percent from 1932 to 1938, funding from the other governments for hospitals waxed by 15 percent within that period. This reflected tasks and funding that were still left or returned to local governments, especially for health. Pressed by old unmet needs and the depression-era sicknesses of those without food or doctors, the lesser governments increased their expenditure for health by 41 percent.[46] National totals for "relief," eventually to be known as "welfare," also soared, with annual state and local outlays going from $444 million to more than $1 billion from 1932 to 1938, a jump of 141 percent. In that period, direct federal expenditure for relief rose at an even higher rate, about 163 percent, with some of the federal funding again compensating for the shrunken revenue bases of thousands of localities and states.[47]

Looking at the longer swell and beyond depression economics, by 1942 when Roosevelt commented that Dr. Win the War had replaced Dr. New Deal, citizens or newspapers mentioning "the government" probably meant Washington, not the nearer authorities.[48] This new horizon and change in the sense of which government was important was patent not only in U.S. government checks in millions of mailboxes but in the construction, after 1933, of the first "federal buildings" in many cities, as well as in the federal standards and financing in older local concerns like parks and playgrounds and "little theatres." In towns and county seats, store-front branches of new federal relief and security agencies opened and made the grass roots even more aware of Washington officialdom and nourishment and of finding "your government" on Main Street.

In all of this after 1933 there was no concerted threat to subvert America. Despite the zealous ideas of the small numbers of party Communists and larger numbers of fellow travelers in New Deal agencies[49] or remarks like that of the irrepressible planner Rex Tugwell, "We are going to roll up our sleeves and remake America," America obtained no planned economy, let alone much of the planning so vaunted in the 1930s. It did experience a concentrated and accelerating version of its historic, just-grewed, pileup of government. As for power-mongers, the expansive state always stirs an enlarging bureaucracy's ambitions for jobs, promotions, salaries, higher funding, and new projects, but this occurred

46. *Ibid.*

47. *Ibid.*

48. *Complete Presidential Press Conferences of Franklin D. Roosevelt* (25 vols.; New York, 1942), XXII, items 246–48.

49. Irivng Howe and Lewis Coser, *The American Communist Party: A Critical History* (Boston, 1957), 361–62.

largely because of the growing public willingness, however troubled, that untended needs should now be met by the state. Of course, the growth in budgets and officialdom was not only for taking care of the underdog or "relief cheaters" but also in response to the capitalist farmer's or banker's or rancher's lobbying for what the state could now do for his respectable needs.

A history of the use of the word *rights* since the 1930s would reveal not only the increased expectations of Americans but a sense of how, and how easily, the new state-backed advantages came to be regarded as unsurrenderable parts of the order of nature or of the God-given promises of 1776. Beyond their classic rights of "life, liberty, and the pursuit of happiness," citizens under the New Deal became more sensitive to other "rights" that they might now legitimately invoke. The list expanded steadily with calls for rights to jobs, social security, a "living wage," for labor to organize and engage in collective bargaining, to a home or decent housing, to as much education as wanted, to adequate health and hospital care, and on and on. By today, this fifty-year tendency is marked by "rights" that include bilingual education in schools, publicly financed child daycare, and the unrestricted power over one's own body for any desired form of sexual pleasure. The columnist George Will cited several court actions in the 1990s that suggest how even more detailed the claims for rights had become: the right of a seven-year-old to be free from dirty language on the school bus; the right not to be exposed to sexual graffiti on a restroom wall; the right of the homeless to safe zones on the streets where they can perform "life-sustaining acts" such as cooking, sleeping, and defecating free of police action; the right to disability payments because of stress suffered by a woman working alongside large black males; the right to state benefits if 10 percent of personal anxiety is job-related; the right of a baseball player to play because his chronic use of cocaine was due to the hyperactivity of the game; a prisoner's right to be free from the cruel and unusual punishment of being in a prison that did not prohibit smoking. The ultimate metaphors that describe the tendencies in this proliferation of rights derived from the abortion debate: the rights to "choice" and to "life." Both of these, however, were complemented by the right to die either by suicide or by being disconnected from life-supporting food, medication, and machinery.

Forty years after the New Deal, the case of the Tennessee snail-darter illustrated the degree to which this politicizing of expectations and entitlements could reach, and in good logic. New TVA projects, it was said, threatened to decimate this small, rare species of fish. Ultimately what was weighed was what had happened to Americans to bring them to such passionate recourse to the state to save a fish. Those merely moralistic in demeaning petitioners for "yet another government program" misconstrue the situation. The needs of the threatened snaildarter (as far as we can tell) and certainly the concerns of its devotees are not spurious or laughable. Both derive from an increasingly voiced American ethos of "reverence for life" and "respect for environment." Although such notions are often dismissed as the concerns of "bleeding-heart" radicals and liberals, they know no party lines, and liberals generally have yet to gauge the profoundly conservative implications of the so-called environmental issues. But at that level of minute and intense concern about public action for the snaildarter or more recently the spotted owl, like the aspiration to make all American children healthy and happy, the needs that came to seem state-serviceable seem infinite. Who, if not the state, can save all threatened species?[50] In the four generations since Theodore Roosevelt of pileup of government conservation efforts to save bears and bison, the effort for the snaildarter may seem inevitable. Beneath it, however, lies that stunning theme that has fired so much state intervention since the New Deal taught us about the insufferability of pain or disaster: let no American suffer; let no one die, man or beast.

Beyond this single suggestion of the strength of our expectations for the state-serviced life is another story, also long after the New Deal, but suggesting how quickly and solidly an entitlement could become embedded in the lives of citizens. In 1979, Washington began to underwrite low-interest loans for tuition costs. Democracy being reluctant to draw pejorative distinctions, the money could be used at the greatest universities or at the commonest school of cosmetology or bartending. The federal loan program was offered at first without any test for family income. Almost at once, it was criticized in both parties for ignoring ability to pay and freeing affluent families to take the cheap loan to pay for college costs while using their own capital for profitable investments. But the two years of the new entitlement were enough to raise a national hue and cry against the tightening of standards as a violation of student and family rights. Court actions were filed against the government for retrenching on so vital a national program.[51]

Although the partisans of the New Deal came to speak admiringly of the unconcerted expansion of American rights as democratic experiment

50. On the snaildarter's plight, see *Time*, October 8, 1979. On the still-later extent of protecting all endangered species, see "Bill on Rare Species Passes," New York *Times*, July 24, 1988.
51. "New York Law Students Sue Over Eligibility for Loans," *Chronicle of Higher Education*, April 14, 1982.

and well-conceived pragmatism, critics on the left as well as the right have emphasized expediency, confusion, waste, and a liberal façade for capitalist failure and fraud.[52] But in the severe crisis of 1933, Americans lacked reliable experiences with activist government to confront such unprecedented domestic disasters even for what rights were already recognized, like the sanctity of contracts or receiving mortgage payments on time. There were few tested priorities about what interventionist government could do well or poorly. There was no secure base of well-run government agencies like a powerful and efficient Budget Bureau to which additional powers could confidently have been added. With, instead, so much mere pileup and the economy at the verge of collapse, improvisation was preordained. On any one of the major matters affecting recovery or reform, moreover, there were many conflicting expert opinions accompanied by research to prove the incontestability of printing more money, abandoning the gold standard, or of limiting crop planting.[53] The sense of new challenges but with inadequate experience was best expressed in Harold Ickes's famous response that the government would not know what to do with the mines if it did nationalize them.[54] Had the sense of emergency lessened in the 1930s and had the Roosevelt experiments in both recovery and reform been more successful in restoring vibrant private enterprise, there might have been more chance for an official to do more in one day than to get through the mail about new needs or disasters that were reported almost every morning.

There may be too much temptation here to trace the failures of New Deal government not only to the emergency and the inherited thinness of effective governing but also to what more "mind" and deeper reflection and coordination among the New Dealers around the president might have accomplished. Other major world powers in the 1930s did have deeper traditions of energetic governments staffed by the best-educated public servants but these traditions gave no significant advantage in combatting the depression.[55] Energetic and fulsome governments in Germany, Italy, Russia, and Japan, moreover, were creating political disasters with their elites, and democratic England and France, despite the service of the best from Oxbridge and *les grandes écoles,* remained mired in depression, despair, and disorder. But this overseas record does not imply that greater American conversancy with well-managed active

52. Norman Thomas, *After the New Deal, What?* (New York, 1936). A perspective from the left thirty years later is Barton J. Bernstein, "The New Deal: The Conservative Achievements of Liberal Reform," in *Towards a New Past: Dissenting Essays in American History,* ed. Barton J. Bernstein (New York, 1968).

53. Elliot Rosen, *Hoover, Roosevelt, and the Brains Trust* (New York, 1977).

54. Frances Perkins, *The Roosevelt I Knew* (New York, 1946), 230–31.

55. Charles P. Kindleberger, *The World in Depression, 1929–1939* (Berkeley, 1973).

government would not have provided a gyroscope to better steer through the storm. Instead, both the Hoover and Roosevelt administrations never stopped scurrying to plug countless leaks in the dikes of private enterprise.[56] The ceaseless sense of crisis also frustrated the calls of academics and the learned for general, basic reform of public administration.[57] In the political world, with its habitual insensitivity to "crackpot" or ivory-tower schemes, the Democratic politicians in control of the system put the best possible face on New Deal "experiments." The word *pragmatism* was to be abused to describe contradictory and ill-informed actions without well-considered general hypotheses. The only opposition that had a chance for the White House, the Republicans, failed even to begin to articulate a realistic alternative to New Deal pileup of state agencies and programs. Instead, with former president Hoover taking the lead, they denounced the entire range of state intervention as subverting all American institutions and ideals.[58] So between Democratic defensiveness and Republican defamation, neither party produced a workable analysis, *i.e.,* beyond "campaign oratory," of the future of big government. Nor did either party admit how much time and experience, patience, and criticism would be needed to provide the much-vaunted "pragmatic test" for a "big democracy" doing its mounting work well.

Among the Democrats, it was a rare long-range program, like wages and hours legislation, whose details were not subordinated to the overwhelming need, in a favorite Roosevelt word, for "action." But "action" that was too hodgepodge, too partisan, too quickly come and gone, and too influenced by constant emergency could not do much more than staunch wounds. Band-aids, popped from a box, quickly peeled and easily applied were the favorite dressing. Some of the greater disorders were even worsened by New Deal precipitous "pragmatism," like the government stimulus to big business hegemony under the National Recovery Act. Similar political thrashing about and veering hither and yon in farm policy, the international economy, antitrust measures, and currency management were chronically worsened by the complexities and ambiguities inherent in all such challenges and regardless of what party dealt with them. Despite that rich brew of neocapitalist theories about business cycles, fiscal policy, monetarism, and so on, that had been sim-

56. Jordan A. Schwartz, *The Interregnum of Despair: Hoover, Congress, and the Depression* (Urbana, Ill., 1970).

57. Paul Appleby, *Big Democracy* (New York, 1945), summarizes the optimistic case for big government in the American setting and with the view of so much still to be done after the dozen years of the New Deal. See especially chap. 12.

58. Herbert Hoover, *The Great Depression, 1929–1941* (New York, 1951–1952), Vol. III of *Memoirs.* See also his views in the 1930s in *American Ideals Versus the New Deal* (New York, 1936).

mering for more than a decade, there was little reliable consensus about what government policies could be confidently constructed about any major public problem.[59] Keynes, for example, did not even round off his general theory until 1936, and he never intended heavy state investment as a permanent supplement to private resources. To the extent that New Deal "pragmatists" or Republican policy formulators hawked old truths, like breaking up big business or upholding the gold standard, they were chasing chimeras from the outset.[60] Joyfully presiding over the contest of hot, flashing ideas that he invited as signs of action and optimism, Roosevelt played the indispensable role of showing that democratic government was not immobilized and could move beyond the Hoover limits. But we particularly miss in Roosevelt a strong urge as well as the ability to think less immediately, less politically, and with sharper focus about the future of American government. Again, the word *pragmatism* is abused to describe so much flippant expediency and partisan deals.[61]

When the administration in 1937 and 1938 was again pressed by some of its brighter brain-trust members to try for the longer view of government and a general analysis of the big business economy, Roosevelt agreed to reorganize some agencies and, later, to establish the Temporary National Economic Committee. Politics and ideology made a shambles of the reorganization bill of 1938.[62] For the TNEC there was the vivid promise from the White House about what the nation could expect from so serious a venture, especially one heralding a long-delayed start on a general blueprint for the economy. The TNEC did produce some of the most careful investigations of business concentration and suggestions for policy at the time. But for Roosevelt it became another exciting foray with brainy people, a passing enthusiasm, a bow to a group of advisers who held his attention long enough (on an overnight train ride from Atlanta to Washington) to convince him to open yet another front on the future.[63] He also appointed as trustbuster Thurman Arnold, who fell to with vigorous prosecutions, but these did not halt business concentration. All this presidential "action" *looked* good; it *felt* serious, it associated the president with good and thoughtful people. But it was only one of too many bright schemes tried simultaneously, often at cross-purposes and without coordination. TNEC recommendations for vigorous antitrust activity became, under Arnold, largely price-policing.

59. Seymour Harris, ed., *The New Economics* (New York, 1947).
60. Alvin Hansen, *Full Recovery or Stagnation* (New York, 1938).
61. Schlesinger, *The Politics of Upheaval*, 653–54.
62. Leuchtenburg, *Roosevelt and the New Deal*, 278–90.
63. *Ibid.*, 257–59.

It is impossible to believe that Roosevelt ever took the TNEC studies as seriously as the effort warranted and as its partisans and members of the investigation deduced he would from his words when he launched it.

By 1939, it was clear that the depression was still unconquered. One of the president's favorite advisers, Maury Maverick, remarked, "We have pulled all the rabbits out of the hat and there are no more rabbits."[64] But the state was far freer to act, and there was now a visible momentum and at least a vastly enlarged, if contested, legitimacy for it to grow. Gradually, millions of Americans were moving into alliance with big government and to become Democratic Party interest groups. Had better government been as central a concern as more government, Americans might have felt less ambivalent about what Washington was doing. Neither faith nor confidence about the benign purposes of bureaucracy appeared despite all the votes for the Democrats, all the billions spent, and the president's encouraging of citizens to use "your government."

Those policy experts after 1933 who left the academies and research groups to serve the New Deal did so because they welcomed the chance to put into practice their ideas for specific problems like soil erosion, utility regulation, or rural electrification. The broader-thinking recruits like David Lilienthal, Benjamin Cohen, and A. A. Berle remained scattered, uncoordinated, even contesting voices. For notable example, the regionalism and decentralization of policy making devised for the TVA, for many the most praiseworthy and innovative of major New Deal programs, was not brought into play in legislation for other public works. Instead, New Deal policies were largely drafted for the nation at large. "Slum clearance," *e.g.*, blanket bulldozing for New York's decrepit brick tenements, was largely the same as slum clearance in other cities with smaller, wooden structures on less-crowded acreage. And the insensitivity to the sense of community within neighborhoods whose squalid conditions appalled middle-class housing experts helped lay the groundwork of the future impersonalism, decay, and crime in what were sincerely intended as decent habitats for former ghetto dwellers.[65] Such "continentalism" in New Deal programs created the strong tradition that comes to us of regarding complex and vast national problems like homelessness or infant and child daycare or long-term nursing-home stays as requiring a Washington plan with thick national criteria about every conceivable contingency and centralized public expenditure.

The inherent difficulties of legislating for a continental citizenry in-

64. *Ibid.,* 284.
65. Robert Caro, *The Power Broker: Robert Moses and the Fall of New York* (New York, 1974), 520–25.

creasingly attracted to the idea of no need without a satisfaction, no problem without a solution, leaves little room for normal human dysfunction. Every problem soon gets hawked as a crisis, *e.g.*, the savings and loan crisis, the deficit crisis, the Persian Gulf crisis, the drug crisis, or, by skeptics, as a plot, and elicits countless interest-group views about what to do. The problem with clarity in the American setting is suggested in the New Deal years when diverse alternatives to federal schemes such as the Townsend, Huey Long, and Coughlin plans for social justice were too rigid and too narrowly conceived. Together with other plans to redistribute wealth and increase equality, they did not reveal a common, workable basis for dealing continentally with the depression's dearth and dysfunction. With consensus about long-range, effective policies so difficult to discern on the hustings or in Washington, large government spending for the short term on specific needs of farmers, union labor, stock investors, and everyone else thus became America's "quick fix." In full compass, a problem like farm income is often so complex that it may elude a solution. The easy way out is to appropriate enough money for one year and thus temporarily assuage the many separate constituents, whose diversity seems to suggest only two common needs, less risk and higher profits. Spending, not governing well, seems the inescapable highest incentive of the piled-up service state with continental tasks.

We cannot forget that the political limits on effective national policies were already obvious in the Wilsonian legislation of 1913 and 1914 and are probably intrinsic to pluralistic, interest-group politics. The limits against effective governing were so much thicker by 1933 that there is something appalling in the bravado of attempting, amid the frantic Washington turmoil and crisis, national programs on hundreds of fronts for a continent of 130 million citizens in direst need and to fund and administer those well. Is our hubris any less today as the national agenda of expectations and entitlements has reached gargantuan proportions?

Surely, there was cogency to Roosevelt's *initial* decision, and even more in his temperament, to defy dogma and abstract scruple and to act. Banking had to be stabilized, people fed, jobs created, farm produce moved. But the emergency and the obsessive Roosevelt imperative for action continued too much of the 1933 immediatism in the years ahead. For the future effectiveness of government that lay beyond the crisis legislation of the "hundred days" after March, 1933, the president, the politicians, and the nation were all swamped by their history, trapped by their styles of gesture and slap-dash, and hemmed in by the poverty of the institutions of a state that had never learned to govern.

In shaping the state as in other human action, there is great weight in what men do not or cannot know even when they act thoughtfully in ways that history *will* applaud. This is apparent even in an enduring achievement of the New Deal like the Tennessee Valley Authority. When it began, and for decades afterward, it was widely hailed for rescuing the region from degradation and ravishment and for its heterodoxy of trying to administer a program within the region and in consultation with local citizens.[66] Only time would reveal that TVA would become largely a power project rather than a blueprint for the region, that it would use strip mining to exploit coal deposits, build coal-fired powerhouses that polluted far and wide, and later switch precipitously to creating the nation's largest concentration of nuclear plants that were to be cited countless times for violating nuclear regulations. TVA's praised working with the local citizens in planning rather than imposing its ideas was too often show-window and *pro forma* consultation. Like most bureaucracies, TVA innovations hardened into constricting formulae based on self-congratulation about presumed previous successes.[67] Even those "environmentalists" hired by TVA in the 1930s who knew about contour plowing, deep-root grasses, and wind belts of trees did not then plan for smoke-free power plants in the valley or ask for methods to dig coal that would not ruin the terrain. However sincere or gifted they may be, policy makers for great projects like TVA have their limited horizons, biases, and resistance to other views. From the TVA days to our times of *Challenger,* Hubble telescope, and drug interdiction radar fiascos, "systems" that seem splendidly planned chronically suffer from one of the besetting illusions of twentieth-century ambitions. Great needs translated into huge enterprises for satisfying them will not necessarily be served effectively by the incorruptible high talent essential to install, control, and improve the dams, nuclear plants, or space rockets. The more complex and ambitious a system is planned, the more caution is dictated that it not turn into a Three Mile Island, a farm support monstrosity that cannot find storage for the surpluses it is supposed to avoid, or a Medicare reimbursement swamp. Most of such messes can be explained by what planners and politicians forgot or neglected or denied or underplayed or covered up.

Most experts who do the work on the great projects that capture the headlines are narrowly trained. Very few possess wider-ranging minds than those of the humanist professors who often deride them as mere technocrats. Nor do they have great curiosity about alternatives to their schemes. Most rarely know enough that is reliable or that is needed, for

66. David Lilienthal, *TVA: Democracy on the March* (New York, 1944); Philip Selznick, *TVA and the Grass Roots* (Berkeley, 1949).

67. Selznick, *TVA and the Grass Roots,* 69–82. Also "Troubled Times for the TVA," *Newsweek,* January 27, 1986.

example, to launch a program for migrant workers or to tender an existing wound of filthy tenements within the lights of what they have been taught. But this is as true of bureaucracy in business, the professions, and the universities as it is of government. In the TVA, as in so many large-scale "modernization" projects now dotting the globe, what the experts did not know, what they had not been trained for, what they had not been sensitized to, all were in play as much as the talent that did deliver the Tennessee valley from despair and disease and death.

What happened with TVA warns of the unforeseen, inherent limitations of much of large-scale policy-making as the state increases its social engineering. A generation after TVA, one of the most successful and hailed programs of the 1960s, Head Start, revealed in time how overlarge many of its pretensions had been. The criticisms that accumulated were not against the idea of giving preschool children the chance to do better by the time they entered first grade but against the excessive promises and major contingencies that seem endemic in many public efforts to meet social needs. Important friends of Head Start found that after a generation of the program the beneficiaries performed no better in the primary grades than nonrecipients, that the claims for the better health and improved social services for the children had been exaggerated, that the teachers and buildings were often inadequate, that, in sum, about 25 percent of the programs were only marginally effective and another quarter did not help the children at all.[68] Still, like TVA, the needs endure, the beneficence of the goals remains unchallenged, and the stake of administrators and recipients in continuing and enlarging the program virtually guarantee that it will continue. The new promises are not about more modest hopes and cautious investment but about what more money, wider and longer coverage, and less "carping criticism" will accomplish.

The Republican Alternative

If there was error or excess in the New Deal and twenty years of Democratic control, alternatives in 1952 depended on how the Republicans perceived what had happened to American society and how they understood the role of government in coping with economic policy and institutional reform. Even more challenging was their response toward the politicizing of needs that had traditionally been met privately.

Forming alternatives to the New Deal was complicated by its increasing

68. "Sharp Criticism for Head Start, Even by Friends," New York *Times*, March 19, 1993.

popularity and diverse appeal. The diversity was accented by 1940 by the congressional Democrats being divided about spending, deficits, and more New Deal programs. Some Republicans were willing to accept such measures as unemployment insurance and farm price supports. Governor Alfred E. Landon of Kansas, the 1936 moderate Republican nominee for president, had thus found more in common with New Dealers who came out of the earlier progressive movements than with a conservative Republican like Senator Reed of Pennsylvania.[69] Such tensions within both parties were recurrently to lead to cries for realignment of the Democrats and Republicans into liberal and conservative parties.[70] But failing that, in runs for the presidency, how could the Republican amalgam define itself against the amalgam of successful Democrats?

Being denied both the White House and Capitol Hill for twenty years after 1932 bred frustration and ideology-mongering among most Republican leaders rather than a realistic coming to terms with New Deal America and Democratic victories. Gradually, a minority position against the dominant Hooverism emerged and was called "modern Republicanism." But the regnant, orthodox Republicans favoring low taxes and freedom from regulation saw Roosevelt win four national elections in a row, maintain Democratic control in the Congress, and create a national Democratic majority. By 1953, with the majority of voters regarding themselves as Democrats, the Republicans were left with a minority of voters with which to start a presidential campaign. Still, against the tide of New Deal programs and votes, leaders like Roosevelt's favorite Republican targets, Congressmen Martin, Barton, and Fish, chanted old-time remedies of limited government, self-help, and balanced budgets to stop the New Deal disasters. When it came to presidential candidates, however, starting in 1936, the Republicans nominated a series of men far more moderate in record and words than could be inferred from the Hooverian attacks on the New Deal as a "challenge to liberty." Jeffersonian freedom was one thing, counting the probable votes another.

The party was thrilled to capture the 80th Congress in 1946.[71] After that, both Republican wings worked together erratically on whatever program they could create against the threat of Truman vetos. When it came to winning the White House in 1948, the moderate Republican candidate Dewey labored in vain. He was opposed by the thick Democratic grain of the electorate and Truman's slam-bang warnings about

---

69. Otis L. Graham, *An Encore for Reform* (New York, 1967), on the later paths of the old progressives.

70. James MacGregor Burns, *Deadlock of Democracy* (Englewood Cliffs, N.J., 1963); Leuchtenburg, *Roosevelt and the New Deal,* 266–74.

71. James T. Patterson, *Mr. Republican* (Boston, 1972), 313.

Republicans turning back the clock and doing nothing except taking away benefits. Whoever the president, conservative power in Congress had been augmented because of the Democrats' split. An informal coalition had formed about 1938 between most Republicans and Democratic conservatives leery of spending and of Washington power. Even the Congress restored to the Democrats in 1948 denied Truman's Fair Deal about public housing, health care, and civil rights, despite the upset presidential and congressional victories of that year.[72]

The next chance to undo the "national shame" of the New Deal came in 1952. By then, the generation of momentous intervention by Washington and within the states was creating a national psychology of statist expectations and spreading federal entitlements. Regardless of Republican denunciation of big government and "creeping socialism," the New Deal style of vigorously intervening government was becoming history, including a Democratic dominated bureaucracy and federal judiciary.[73] Voters were increasingly used to an energetic Washington.

By 1952, however, there was a new, momentous fact in defining either party stance on big government. World War II and the Cold War had fashioned an immense federal presence and expenditure against totalitarian threats.[74] However debated the portraits of Cold War America as a garrison state sustained *principally* by war or defense production,[75] billions of dollars annually for the armed forces, for the NATO allies, and for new, developing nations would have forced Americans to accept the great state if only for defense purposes. Democracy on the ramparts meant mounting billions of dollars in defense contracts and jobs, training camps, air and, soon, rocket bases, and so on. These very quickly became new entitlements serving the needs of hundreds of communities from Boston with its navy yard to desert towns near the bomb-test sites in Nevada and New Mexico. Legislators like Senator Bricker or Congressman Rivers of South Carolina who spoke boldly of cutting bureaucracy and government welfare costs while also cham-

72. Alonzo L. Hamby, *Beyond the New Deal: Harry S. Truman and American Liberalism* (New York, 1973).

73. Charles D. Hadley, *Transformations of the American Party System: Political Coalitions from the New Deal to the 1970s* (New York, 1975).

74. Richard Polenberg, *War and Society: The United States, 1941–1945* (Philadelphia, 1972); Roland A. Young, *Congressional Politics in the Second World War* (New York, 1956).

75. This emphasis is clearest in Gabriel Kolko, *The Limits of Power: The World and United States Foreign Policy, 1945–1954* (New York, 1972). Variants of the garrison-state theme as described in Robert J. Maddox, *The New Left and the Origins of the Cold War* (Princeton, 1973). The best riposte to the claim is Adam Yarmolinsky, *The Military Establishment: Its Impact on American Society* (New York, 1971).

pioning the strongest possible defense budgets failed to understand how defense on the Cold War scale implied a bureaucracy and expenditure that might have made even the avid New Dealer of 1939 gasp. The total federal outlays for that year were just under $9 billion, including all defense costs of $1.8 billion. Although total annual spending in the 1950s under the Republicans varied and there had been much inflation since 1939, federal spending was never less than $68.5 billion annually and peaked under the Republican Eisenhower at $97.2 billion in 1960, almost 50 percent beyond the last Democratic budget, in 1953. Trying to end the Great Depression had put Americans further than ever under the shadow of the state, but war and defense alone since 1939 spread and darkened those shadows immeasurably.

Fear of renewed depression after the flush times of the war years pushed Americans to vote for politicians pledged to underwrite full-employment and to see to it that the immense national plant and enforced savings created during the war would be used for peacetime ease and affluence.[76] The hopes of 1945 for a life beyond the mean streets of the depression years inspired the Employment Act of 1946, a solemn gesture obligating the government to avoid depression and act constantly for full employment. The Republicans never could afford to repudiate that commitment.[77]

Overall, by 1952, the Democrats in control in Washington had momentous changes in state and society behind them. Success in politics, however, blunted (as it will) the party's self-criticism and its awareness of errors and confirmed most of the Democratic Party in formulas for government action that had been designed for dealing with crisis in depression and wartime. These policies favored Washington over state and local initiatives, public over private action, and large appropriations for nationwide programs over, for example, small, experimental, easily monitored projects. Although the word *conservative* was very seldom used at the time, the Republicans had the opportunity as 1952 approached to play one of the great historic roles of conservatism, to resist sweeping ideologies of reform or revolution, and to administer the extant government well. After the generation of almost unmeasurable New Deal and wartime pileup, there was much for the Republicans to do to refine, pare, purge, and prepare the post–New Deal state for such national tasks as sustaining economic growth with social justice, fulfilling the civil rights promised blacks almost a century earlier, repairing and enhancing the

76. Joel Seidman, *American Labor from Defense to Reconversion* (Chicago, 1953); Norman D. Markowitz, *The Rise and Fall of the People's Century: Henry A. Wallace and American Liberalism, 1941–1948* (New York, 1973).

77. Stephen K. Bailey, *Congress Makes a Law* (New York, 1957).

national "infrastructure" and landscape, and administering the immense international responsibilities of the world's greatest power. Few of the fresher domestic goals, *e.g.*, health insurance, such as Truman had proposed, *automatically* dictated exclusive federal jurisdiction or funding. The needed sorting-out by both parties of what really had been a half-century of government pileup since Theodore Roosevelt would have also reexamined what the lesser governments and private, voluntary effort might once again do despite the dominant federal presence during the depression and war years. Instead, Republican antistate bombast encouraged Democrats to continue to invoke depression-era formulas, such as many of Truman's Fair Deal proposals, and to play their old anti-Hoover themes, not to transcend them.[78] Rather than reconcile themselves to enlarged government as historic fact, most Republican leaders obsessively maintained most of the Hoover line about the radicalism of the New and Fair Deals with their threats to American character and liberty and the need to undo the enormous damage inflicted on the nation since 1933.[79] The repeated casting of the next presidential election as a golden opportunity to stop "creeping socialism" was politically suicidal against the sustained tide of Democratic presidential voters indebted to that party for their entitlements. Hoover himself had become the largest living symbol of an immense Republican failure. What national majority in 1952, being reminded of his limits in 1932 and indoctrinated with the Democrats' anti-Hoover lore, could afford to sacrifice the interests in social security, savings insurance, and federal home mortgages now served by the New Deal state? Still, voters were also nostalgic about Hooveresque incantations of individual responsibility.[80]

What most blighted Republicans as an alternative government was that, unlike European conservatives, they had never developed any ease with the state, any significant and sufficiently varied skills with well-run political institutions that could successfully counter the assaults of all-or-nothing ideologies and expedient power-mongering. Most American "conservatives" were, after all, only private-enterprise enthusiasts. Ideologues of profitable markets as a model for all political effort are strangers to a political husbandry based on moral ideals rather than on money making. Too many of the mere business-as-usual conservatives in both Europe and America in the 1930s thus thought that the greatest threat of Communism was to private property or that they could "do business" with Hitler. They tolerated or dismissed "all that racial rot" and "just

78. Patterson, *Mr. Republican.*
79. Herbert Hoover, *Addresses upon the American Road, 1948–1950* (Stanford, 1951).
80. The Republican dilemma in coming to terms with the New Deal is well stated in Emmet John Hughes, *The Ordeal of Power* (New York, 1963).

literary ravings" in *Mein Kampf*. They could not appreciate the force of ideas in politics compared with their conviction that in a world that was only a marketplace, everyone has his price and would make a dependable deal if the price was right. Market conservatives from business backgrounds like Neville Chamberlain or Joseph P. Kennedy could not understand the connection between the state and the defense of traditional morality, justice, and other communal ideals that had inspired European conservative leaders from Burke to DeGaulle and that so formed the sensibility of writers in America such as George Kennan and Hannah Arendt. By 1952, New Deal programs, with their almost automatic mode of Washington intervention and funding, did need skepticism, honest review, careful embellishment, or realistic honing. In activity like massive public works, good husbandry suggested federal retrenchment and a return to local or private initiative or, with "welfare" costs still so modestly priced, to diverse subfederal and nongovernmental programs by labor and credit unions and rich corporations, perhaps within general national guidelines for minimums and equity.

In such work in 1952 lay the great tasks of the Republicans as the alternative party. But most Republican leaders, like most Democrats, lacked the sensitivity to "community," as well as the ease, the tested abilities, the secure sense of prowess in knowing how to govern. These qualities were essential if one wished to create a viable alternative to decried or formulaic New Deal statism. The Republicans of 1952 constituted only another prosaic political party. Like Democrats, they welcomed boosters, rooters, and joiners of Rotary and the Lions or the Chambers of Commerce. They were "eminently club-able" people, as Dr. Johnson had said about the need to be congenial. The party lusted after votes and overall was no more talented or insightful than the denigrated Democrats they wanted to supplant.

The valuable motifs in the Truman-appointed, or first, Hoover Commission on Organization of the Executive (1947) could have represented the start of another Republicanism. In the report, Hoover and Hooverism were at their forgotten best: the engineer, the irreverent reorganizer of enterprises, the enemy of waste, the tireless, innovative administrator. The bipartisan report under Hoover's insistent chairmanship took two years to prepare and was published in 1949. It made some 275 recommendations, of which 200 were put into effect by Truman within the executive branch. That Hoover's excoriated New Deal was now history, and in the main a running if ungainly machine, did seem to have meaning for the old engineer when he was off the rostrum and laboring very hard to make a going system work better. It is difficult to believe that the two Hoovers, defeated politician and efficiency engineer, had anything to do with each other. The 1949 report, however, presented so very little to even begin to shrink the executive that one is surprised at Hoover's enthusiasm for it. Indeed, one major judgment of the report implies that by enhancing the president as manager and by lessening congressional roles, the Hoover Commission actually strengthened federal power.[81] Nevertheless, the prestige of the report and of the renewed luster it gave Hoover led President-elect Eisenhower to call on him again in 1953 to the larger task of refining the full machine of the great state.

The second Hoover report, of 1954, certainly took that charge seriously. But it aroused much more political resistance than had the recommendations in 1949 for the executive branch. For all the verbal assaults on the New Deal state, the political costs of the 1954 call for across-the-board rationalization of most federal activity were telltale not only about the Eisenhower years but about all regimes after him. The electoral price of disentangling and trimming the bureaucracies serving increasingly politicized needs seemed too risky.[82] Too many interests felt threatened. Too many voters might be alienated.

The by now virtually forgotten episode of the second report in 1954 gave a clear augury about significant government reorganization and retrenchment by either party down to today. The second Hoover report was, in effect, "filed" by the Republican administration that sponsored it, for it played the specific costly notes in the songs attacking big government. The report, nevertheless, did reveal what a genuine conservatism concerned about institutions and their viability could have given American government. Instead, not acted on, the report became another cyclical gesture to wisdom and virtue-serving, that increasingly familiar, painless dodge against genuine change in government and bureaucracies generally. The flood of such assays about America and its problems was to become a characteristic reply to organizational dysfunction: when confronted by telling arguments against disarray within foundations, the university, the larger charities, banking, the criminal justice system, and race relations, by "the failure of the schools," the breakdown of the family, "competitiveness and productivity," and so on, assuage anxiety by creating a prestigious commission or fact-finding committee. Staff it with top talent and revered names, declare it free from all pressures except to "tell it like it is," and give it good funding, adequate office space and help, and, especially, all possible honor. When it presents its findings to the president in an Oval Office ceremony, long

81. Bradley D. Nash and Cornelius Lynde, *A Hook in Leviathan: A Critical Interpretation of the Hoover Commission Report* (New York, 1950).

82. A contemporary assessment is W. R. Divine, "The Second Hoover Commission Reports," *Public Administration Review,* XV (1955).

enough after its establishment that most people have forgotten it and the heat that forged it, file it or give it minimal "implementation." Proposals like the Hoover reports, similar to *Recent Economic Changes* (1929) or the TNEC findings a decade later, were inexpensive ways to pretend to settle accounts with the rational and the ideal while really threatening no one's interests.

By 1952, long before Ronald Reagan's recitals of his little horror tales of the state, there already were many real-life vignettes about the half-century of growth in government. One story of 1952 drew a comparison. During his second term (1893 to 1897), President Cleveland had vetoed $25,000 for seed corn for drought-stricken Texas farmers because he did not think it a proper government concern; but in 1949, a small-scale program of disaster relief for snowbound ranchers in the Dakotas and Wyoming grew in just over a year to a $31 million program involving 26,000 loans across thirty-five states and with both parties helping farmers not merely against blizzards but in repairing ravages from the boll weevil in the South and windstorms in New England.[83] Such sagas of the state were not just illustrative anecdotes about the politicizing of needs, the currying of favors, or the growing compassion of government. More deeply, their increasing commonness suggested how much the statist style had caught on in the twenty years since 1932 and how many indubitable, respectable needs, like countering the effects of severe storms, were becoming concerns of government. Citizens and the state were increasingly allies, however tacit and uneasy they were about big government. Attempts to trim significantly unworthy as well as worthy needs were to become as fruitless as Quixote's charges against the windmills or Canute's words against the waves. By 1952, the great issue about the state for modern America was similar to the one that Lippmann had pleaded in 1914, but it was now stunningly larger: to tame it, to domesticate a mindless burgeoning into a useful power, to help government deliver what only government might deliver, but efficiently and fairly.

The real Republican task was thus to come to terms with a half-century of pileup of state functions to which both parties had contributed. By 1952, however, whatever the worth of in-place programs, they were formidable challenges electorally. The Republican's "nonpolitical" national hero, Eisenhower, promised a crusade to tame government. Although installed in the White House in 1953 and with a Republican Congress, he could not undo most New Deal achievements, however, because of an opposing array, issue by issue, of politicians from both parties with constituents who felt entitled to their own government program.

83. Fabricant, *The Trend of Government Activity*, 4, 9.

Of many revealing cases that showed how the state was becoming stymied by entitlements, the controversial Dixon-Yates proposals of 1953 for a new private power plant for Memphis aroused too many vested interests in the nearby government-run TVA. That sense of unsurrenderable entitlement and some minor corruption in the proposed deal made it impossible for Congress to accept a private plant for Memphis.[84]

By the Eisenhower years, the accumulated sagas of the state do not chronicle a slow, fits-and-starts half-century of growth. *Explosion* or *wild effusion* are more appropriate terms, as Solomon Fabricant's astonishing study at the time revealed.[85] In the half-century since 1900, total American population had increased 100 percent and total private and public employment had grown 120 percent. All government employment—federal, state and local—however, rose more than 500 percent while private employment rose only 100 percent. In 1900, 1 in 24 American workers worked for government. By 1950, 1 out of 8 did so. The businessman's stake in the state by 1950, despite his chronic state-shaming, is equally impressive. By mid-century all levels of government purchased 33 times more in assets and services from private industry than they had in 1903. The gross figures in sales to government had risen from about $750 million per year to just under $25 billion annually. What this represented as a percentage of total national private sales is available only after 1929, but in the next twenty years, to 1949, government's share in peacetime national purchases doubled, going from 4.4 percent to 8.7 percent of the national total. When estimates are made for the effect of changes in the value of the dollar, government purchases of assets and services rose more than 450 percent for the period from 1903 to 1949. When total "inputs" (labor and capital) used by government are calculated, the sum, exclusive of national defense, grew about 350 percent between 1900 and 1949. With defense included, the sum lies beyond 500 percent. In the same period, total national input more than doubled, so that the rise in government inputs as part of the national total was more than twice as large.

Another startling way of depicting how embedded in government American life had become shortly before the election of 1952 can be derived from a 1947 study, *Inventory of Governmental Activities in the United States*.[86] This analysis listed four hundred broad government activities within fifteen major groups. One of the traditional and once-sim-

84. John P. Diggins, *The Proud Decade* (New York, 1988), 132.

85. Fabricant, *The Trend of Government Activity*.

86. Population statistics in this section derive from *Historical Statistics of the United States*. Carl H. Chatters and Marjorie Leonard Hoover, *An Inventory of Governmental Activities in the United States* (Chicago, 1947).

ple concerns of government, an adequate police force, included the familiar tasks of "police protection and law enforcement," but that activity as such was only one among eight major items. The police functions themselves now included specific services about records and statistics, crime control, vice and morals, detention and custody, traffic control, international border control, and fish and game protection. The "vice and morals" services within the police functions broke down into prostitution, liquor and narcotics, dance halls, poolrooms, censorship of books and motion pictures, supervising athletic contests and racing. All these tasks had piled up over many years.

The *Inventory* of 1947 also presents an analysis of how government penetrated the common life-cycle. From birth to death, citizens had moved under an ever-broader, ever-thicker cover of state services, all, by current standards, probably "unsurrenderable" to those involved. The full list of only major government services in the *Inventory* runs from prenatal clinics and birth certificates to death certificates, surrogates' courts, and the morgue. Such accounts of life-long encounters with the state were also arranged in the study according to profession, region of the country, day versus night services, and services at different seasons of the year. However arranged, the two studies suggested the thickness of the fabric of government with which political leaders and citizens serious about the quality and size of government services already had to contend.

In such circumstances, 1952 rather than 1932 was the crossroads for twentieth-century American government as well as the test for the announced Republican alternative of getting the government out of citizens' lives. Hooveresque wails about the dangers of all big government were at least suggesting the approach of threatening limits—of size and scope of funding, of administrative competence, of adequate review and of control over thousands of contradictory and sometimes counterproductive programs. Along with the fifty-year record of big government at all levels and in many modes, specific proposals for reform abounded by 1952 in professional and concerned citizen circles and went in many directions other than in the more publicized Hoover Commissions reports. Experts in public administration, scholars from research organizations like the Brookings Institution, public policy groups like the Council on Economic Development,[87] and reflective veterans of the great state like Lilienthal and Berle had much, if conflicting, advice to offer post–New Deal leaders determined to make better sense of the state.[88]

87. Major varieties of advice about government economic policy are analyzed in Robert M. Collins, *The Business Response to Keynes, 1929–1964* (New York, 1981).

88. Adolph A. Berle, *The 20th Century Capitalist Revolution* (New York, 1954); David Lilienthal, *Big Business: A New Era* (New York, 1953).

To many in 1948, Dwight Eisenhower already seemed a man for such tasks. As a political general he had long been concerned with creating consensus among competing powerful military and political figures. He had intimate knowledge of bureaucracies here and abroad. He had spent his younger years in the War Department of the 1930s in Washington and was, in fact, a scion of that bureaucracy. He knew well its foibles as well as the ins and outs of the Washington game, most of which he detested as a West Pointer dedicated to an ideal of patriotic national service. His roles as head of the wartime and NATO coalitions had broadened his perspectives on power, and he thought of himself as far beyond the narrow partisanship of "mere politicians." Some of his devotees seemed to envision him as a modern Cincinnatus, a selfless foot soldier's general from Abilene in the uncorrupted provinces and outside the fashionable and power-hungry Washington circles. Above all, the Republican regulars sensed in him a sure winner for the presidency over an unglamorous but able Republican senator like Robert Taft. The party presented Ike as a highly dedicated great American who, untainted by "dirty politics," had known and mastered great power and had saved Western civilization.[89]

Although it now seems that Eisenhower was a brighter and shrewder man than many disappointed with him during his presidency thought,[90] he misjudged what low-keyed and veiled acuity could accomplish if he used his power behind the scenes. Eisenhower was no cynic about his reiterated campaign pledges of leading a crusade to clean up America. He was on to important themes when he denounced "stop-and-start planning . . . [to] mobilize and then hurriedly remobilize or swing from optimism to panic." He had promised to "plan for the future on something more solid than yesterday's headlines" and to obtain "the best level of business management this nation can produce to help us run this government."[91]

Once in power, his ideas and will for "real politics" proved to be too prosaic and too thinly developed. So too were the political talents of some of his top managers recruited from industry, like Charles E. Wilson of General Motors. The myth about such types from Wendell Willkie to Ross Perot endures: that the powerful successful outsider, being uncorrupted by Washington and politics, is better able to tame both. Eisenhower, however, was never an outsider and had actually played the Wash-

89. Charles C. Alexander, *Holding the Line: The Eisenhower Era, 1951–1961* (Bloomington, Ind., 1975), chap. 1.

90. Arthur Schlesinger, Jr., "The Ike Age Revisited," *Reviews in American History,* XI (1983).

91. Stephen E. Ambrose, *Eisenhower* (2 vols.; New York, 1983) I, 567–68.

ington game about defense appropriations, strategies, and promotion in rank for most of his military career. But that had made him not a battler but a temporizer and compromiser. He disliked the raw political life of daily wheeling and dealing that lay beyond what little could be accomplished by presidential urgings for good will, by personal charm, by shows of reasonableness, and by quoting American homilies about God-fearing individualists. Moralizing against selfish interests and other evils was often enough to satisfy him. Ultimately, Eisenhower, the hailed crusader, had too much deference to the system, an excessive sense of presidential propriety about not pushing Congress hard, and too much reluctance about upsetting the citizenry or the economy with frank and clear words in the press. What strong beliefs he did have about government and party politics had developed from fit-and-start intuitions, hunches, prejudices, and personal preferences. These reduced to a conventional but vote-winning piety that government should do as little as possible, with the president especially setting citizens an example of calm decency and moderation.[92] He fueled rather than countered the chronic nostalgia about cutting down government to size even while maintaining entitlements. Once uttered, sincere words, like his notable warning about the "military-industrial complex" relieved his worries and fulfilled a duty to speak moral truth. But he had found no sizable stick, no coherent proposals, to give his warning effect. The famous words, moreover, came at the end of his tenure when his recommended military expenditure far exceeded the funds appropriated in his first years in the White House.[93]

In deeper realism, for most of his time in the White House he was also limited by a Democratic Congress allied with some anti-Ike Republicans, by a federal bureaucracy of almost 3 million workers, and a federal judiciary filled largely by Democrats and New Dealers. The presidential electorate "liked Ike" but liked even more their accumulating stake in the New Deal state that Ike shamed for them while the benefit checks and paving and defense contracts continued to arrive.[94]

Despite his reiterated remarks about the old American verities regarding self-sufficiency and limited government, Eisenhower developed his own commitments to state intervention in order to maintain economic prosperity, *i.e.*, Keynesian federal stimulus confusedly mixed with tax cuts, control of money supply, interest rate manipulation, and

92. Arthur Larson, *Eisenhower: The President Nobody Knew* (New York, 1968).
93. Robert Griffith, "Dwight D. Eisenhower and the Corporate Commonwealth," *American Historical Review*, LXXXVII (1982).
94. Gary W. Reichard, *The Reaffirmation of Republicanism: Eisenhower and the Eighty-third Congress* (Knoxville, Tenn., 1975).

public-works programs.[95] What there was of intellectual grasp in Eisenhower on such complex matters was too often diluted by his being open to the daily winds of doctrine among disagreeing advisers.

In 1961, with Eisenhower's presidency at an end, the Republicans had not been able to launch a significant and concerted attempt to reduce government. More important, they had not brought order to the federal sprawl that they had so long deprecated. Budget cutting early in the Eisenhower tenure helped bring on a slump that forced countercyclical steps on the White House. The minimum wage was raised, and millions in previously uncovered categories of workers, including even the armed forces, came under social security and with expanded benefits. For that already powerful entitlement group, the farmers, electrification and loans for ownership and improvement continued, but far more lucrative and enduring were the new federal financing of farm surplus exports and making surpluses available at home through the food-stamp program.[96]

Some of these enlargements of Washington roles came when Republicans controlled Congress, others under Democratic control or initiative; but there were always Republican as well as Democratic votes for them, and all were either signed into law or proposed by Eisenhower. Although the rate of growth in federal employment was slowed, the gross numbers had not declined by 1961. Federal expenditure was almost 50 percent beyond the last Democratic year. Deficit spending with unbalanced budgets had been tolerated. Deficiency appropriations signed by Eisenhower continued to hide functions and expenditure that had not dared to appear in the regular budgets. Such tricks as off-line budgeting and the use of unofficial advisers were other ties to his Democratic predecessors and Republican successors. No major New Deal bureaucracy was eliminated. Indeed, ironically, Eisenhower created the very department, Health, Education and Welfare, that would soon symbolize fresh and deeper incursions of Washington power into the lives of citizens and the lower tiers of government. Eisenhower at the time thought of HEW as a sensible and economical regrouping of programs and officials at Washington,[97] but even by the end of his presidency it was apparent that HEW was becoming the base for expanded Washington intervention in the virtually limitless needs implicit in the words *health, education,* and *welfare.* Another sign of the future in that respect was Eisenhower's own, if unsuccessful, proposals for government help in financing health insurance. Similarly revealing of the statist forces at

95. Herbert Stein, *The Fiscal Revolution in America* (Chicago, 1969).
96. Alexander, *Holding the Line,* 39, 163–64.
97. Sherman Adams, *Firsthand Report: The Story of the Eisenhower Administration* (New York, 1961), 62, 306–307.

work in America and in Washington, whatever the political rhetoric, were forty-eight states accustomed to not spending their own money in hopes that Washington would. Those expectations were encouraged by Eisenhower's enthusiasm for completing the St. Lawrence Seaway and a new, giant, federal interstate highway network. Again, the road system represented a genuine and very large need, but how to build it with no increased federal role seemed an insoluble problem. Collaboration among forty-eight states reluctant to tax and spend their own money when Washington might or should was another heritage of the New Deal. Eisenhower was willing to back the interstate highway program because the roads ostensibly enhanced national defense, but 90 percent of federal funding for the new road system further enlarged Washington's voice about previously local matters such as billboards, abutting construction, rights of way. However contrary to his skepticism about Washington wiles, Eisenhower had responded to familiar dynamics of government growth: a "crying public need" for better highways, contracts for communities and construction companies along the way, improved access to supplies and markets in an increasingly integrated national economy, communication and easy movement for the military, and extraordinary lobbying by many interest groups for the roads. Similar powerful incentives for internal improvements had been making mush of the antistate pronouncements of leaders from Jefferson to Eisenhower. The real motto of the nation seemed increasingly to be In God and the state we trust. The government that sponsored growth for private enterprise was still regarded as helping all of America. If Eisenhower's HEW was "dime-store New Deal," the interstate highway system was Tiffany intervention.[98]

So much in the Eisenhower years that began in a mystique against the state thus foundered in the politics of "undeniable needs"—and votes. The Eisenhower presidency, precisely because his was the only alternative party that had a chance for the White House, revealed most of those enduring structural and political obstacles that were to inhibit either party from effective governing. America was becoming a society so vast and had grown so pluralistic in its freedom for entrenched and politicized interest groups that it could veto almost any major change that seemed to threaten someone's existing or prospective entitlement. The years 1953 through 1961, all antigovernment rhetoric notwithstanding, thus witnessed the emplacement of an embarrassed Republican statism under the post–New Deal Republican presidents, who start with Eisenhower. Jefferson's famous inaugural plea "We are all Republicans;

98. *Ibid.,* 250–51, 326, 527–28.

we are all Federalists" needed revision. By 1961 Republican policies clearly meant "We are all New Dealers; we are all statists."

The patterns of the next thirty years thus seem ordained. It is not surprising that the future Democratic presidents Kennedy, Johnson, and Carter would be champions of New Frontiers and Great Societies. These leaders, like Democratic voters and the party coalitions, were accustomed to New Deal entitlements. The leaders were also at ease with the Croly faith in using the state to serve the unmet needs of citizens. Of course, although big government never gained general moral legitimacy nor put Americans at ease, by 1960 the old traditional stance of shaming while using the state had been intensifying for more than a generation. The more government was used, the more its expansion was attacked. As for using it even more, Kennedy's call in 1960 to "get America moving again" meant that citizens' wishes for wealth, comfort, power, and justice were not being met fast enough or well enough and that it was government's task to tend such expectations. A complex combination of economic growth, Cold War demands, higher standards of living, growing habituation to entitlements, and hawking of favors by politicians had been raising political expectations for government action for many years. By 1960 it also seemed that local and state authorities had not been moving sufficiently to meet those swelling needs. Many of these governments were also not full-time, experienced, or expert enough to meet new or expanded demands for services. From Virginia to Texas, state governments defended segregated societies against rising black leaders. There also, as well as in many other states, legislatures still favored rural areas over growing cities and suburbs. Nearby low horizons for rising needs in housing, schooling, and health care for the elderly and the very young pushed frustrated voters and their Washington representatives to move toward the Potomac for action rather than toward state capitals or city halls. Getting America moving again after 1960 thus meant another major cycle of waxing and waning. Washington would grow and the older purview of smaller authorities over traditional concerns would lessen. Despite the ensuing wails against bigger federal government, funding from Washington was welcome. It promised to keep state and local taxes low while, for example, older citizens might now get basic health-care insurance. But more waxing in Washington was to bring federal functions, offices, and money on greater scale. That implied more national review, control, and budgeting that complicated fifty state and tens of thousands of county, state, city, and town systems. If the new tasks were well done at Washington the growth might be justifiable, but the record was to be very cloudy. The new departures under Kennedy and, even more, his successors in both parties immensely complicated the 1960 challenges of serving needs tended by Washington.

Kennedy's actions toward getting America moving were far more limited than his youth, "vigor," and fine words in 1960 had suggested would be the case. When he took office, that informal coalition of Democrats and Republicans that had so long constrained "boldness" (another Kennedy exhortation) was still in place. Indeed, it had not found all of Eisenhower's proposals uncongenial. But that power, along with Kennedy's distaste for or boredom with the dull, grungy political dealing with Capitol Hill, made his achievements very modest, despite the later Camelot myth of his brave, unstinting, selfless service of great causes.

His successor, Lyndon Johnson, had no such inhibitions as he faced those increasingly aroused, diverse needs in housing, health, transportation, education, and so on, which were unmet because of the conservative coalition in Congress. Johnson's zest both for causes and for the caucusing to win them was radically different from Kennedy's standoffishness. The difference between Johnson and his predecessors was the zeal and skills that he used to bring Congress to support him in the wars he launched for rebuilt cities, civil rights, Head Start, and ending poverty. Goals on the Johnson scale of eliminating poverty in one generation brought giant leaps in American expectations of what "caring" government could do and in creating greater entitlements. The break in the logjams of the Kennedy and earlier years was made even larger by Johnson's presidential moment after his huge victory over Goldwater in the election of 1964. Goldwater was the first major party candidate to feel confident enough about voter anger against big government openly to call himself a conservative and to expect to ride the anger into the White House.[99] Johnson's strategy was to let voters hear from Goldwater himself what the price would be of anger against entitlements such as social security and against obdurate Soviet power. What was already apparent in the Eisenhower years a decade earlier worked to defeat Goldwater. However great the ire, there were not enough votes to endorse sacrificing the entitlements that seemed threatened by Goldwater's conservatism. Those joyous about Johnson's stunning majority were even more heartened by the coattail effect that brought into Congress enough new, younger, and liberal legislators to fracture the conservative coalition. The new lawmakers in the House and Senate had been raised in the style of going to Washington if private effort or nearby governments would not meet needs for affordable housing or preschool education. Those legislators in his presidential moment gave the voracious Johnson almost every major program that he championed.

99. Barry Goldwater, *The Conscience of a Conservative* (Shepherdsville, Ky., 1960).

More portentous than the Johnson victories on economic issues was the expansion of federal entitlements from traditional New Deal concerns about jobs, housing, and utility rates to the far more touchy needs based on race, ethnicity, and gender (see below). The passion for equality now meant that hurt feelings of honor and place in society were to be state-tendable. The logic in the passion for equality remained relentless, as Tocqueville had foreseen, and Johnson rode that tendency to limitlessness. By the end of the Johnson presidency, the vistas for state-service of needs were becoming horizonless. An often-used, revealing response to complaints about such sky-high goals was that if government could send men to the moon, why could it not triumph over mundane problems like poverty or racial prejudice.

The election of Richard Nixon as president in 1968 encouraged some conservatives to believe that spiraling statism would at last be halted and reversed. In twenty years in politics Nixon had worked hard to become the leader of Republican stalwarts. From Orange County, California, to the small towns of New Hampshire, his conservative followers had good reason to regard him as their man. Ever since he had entered politics after World War II he had been a keen fighter against the New Deal, combining a conventional opposition to government growth, higher taxes, and deficit spending with a vigorous anti-Communism. Still, by 1968 he had not gone to the extremes that had so disabled Goldwater. Nixon did not speak of dismantling the social security system nor of threatening the Soviets with nuclear annihilation. Whether adopted for expediency or as principles, his safer conservatism gave true-blue Republicans hope that as president Nixon would effectively counter the size and costs of the post–New Deal state. They had misread their man, the times, the electorate, and the dynamics of entitlement politics. Nixon was not a conservative ideologue, but he was politically shrewd in sensing that power in American presidential politics and policy-making lay largely on the middle-ground on various issues and that there was no national electoral majority for extremes. By polled preferences, moreover, most voters still regarded themselves as Democrats but could be wooed to vote Republican, as suggested in Kevin Phillips' book, *The Emerging Republican Majority,* and by earlier positive responses by Democratic voters to Republican anti-Communism. The complex dynamics of expectations and entitlements that had already checked Eisenhower thus had even more force for Nixon. By 1968, many more Republicans, whatever their rhetoric, had sizable stakes, such as the oil depletion allowance, in the state. And post-Johnson Democrats had even more to defend. For all of the talk of state trimming, it was always meant for other constituencies and needs than one's own. The antistate rhetoric was familiar, but the expansion of state services since Eisenhower greatly raised the stakes of the old game of whose ox was to be gored if it came to cutting appropriations and agencies.

The complex dynamics of congressional action along with Nixon's acuity about a cullable national Republican majority tempered whatever conservatism he had preached while out of office. Although he cut funds for health care and rural electrification, the degree of his temporizing on other issues surprised liberal Democrats as well as the Nixon conservatives. One general symbol of his compromising was that Nixon was the first Republican president to announce that he was a Keynesian, ready to use the state for fiscal stimulus of a sluggish economy. But the specific initiatives by Nixon that encouraged government growth are even more impressive demonstrations of the temptation to make politics out of needs. It was Nixon who established the Environmental Protection Agency and revenue-sharing between the federal and state governments. The latter especially made the states even more dependent on Washington for both the money and the guidelines for using it. It was Nixon who backed the Family Assistance Program devised by his Democratic aide on urban affairs, Daniel Patrick Moynihan. Despite all Nixon's words over the years of the bane of welfare, he now accepted the idea of federal guarantees of a minimum income. As presented to Congress, the plan probably doubled the number of eligible poor who could receive federal largesse and for whose basic sustenance Washington would now assume responsibility. Democratic carping left the proposal dormant while conventional welfare payments approved by Nixon continued to climb. Far more popular was the Nixon initiative to add annual cost-of-living adjustments to the social security benefits for retirees. Ominously for the future of that massive entitlement, it was also under Nixon that the social security payroll tax was not adjusted adequately to fund fully the new federal obligations. On the increasingly sensitive issue of affirmative action (see below), it was Nixon who approved the "Philadelphia plan" that federal funding for construction projects in that city would guarantee 10 percent of the contracts for black-owned firms even if they submitted higher bids than other suppliers.

Of course, what Nixon added to federal programs was sometimes called conservative, for he professed to be helping Americans become more self-sufficient and ultimately less dependent on government. The Family Assistance Plan, for example, purported to cut the overhead and bureaucracy in the welfare system. There was great irony, however, in now needing to use the state in order to check the state. Overall, the Nixon initiatives did not diminish federal activity nor the general weight of government in American lives. Indeed, revenue-sharing produced ripples that enlarged state and local governments as they expanded to use the new funds and to comply with Washington guidelines. And when one recalls Nixon's imposing the price controls that he had explicitly foresworn, Republican dime-store New Deal had grown into something far more costly.

The auguries for government growth readable in the Eisenhower years were steadily fulfilled. The politicizing of newly discovered needs and the growing eagerness of politicians to advance and protect them seemed to be ordained regardless of presidents being liberal or conservative, Democratic or Republican. Whether the needs of the world's richest society were well served for all the hundreds of billions spent or whether the needs generated by an expansive capitalism might be better met by quasi-government or cooperatives or private efforts were less featured questions than the ritual of bewailing state growth as such while voting for expansive programs. If the partisans of needs could show adequate strength politically, especially if they had strong appeal for the comfortable classes, foreseeable needs such as child care, health insurance, and parental leave from a job would eventually be served, whatever the cost in dollars or effectiveness. Of course, not every articulated need could be met, and Washington politics had to sort and juggle constantly in doing as well as it could for the most powerful voices or skillful lobbyists. But, generally, the signal from the Potomac that needs could be met by going to government steadily increased the struggle and the momentum to service as many of them as politics and funding would permit. The political scene in the thousands of other governments that make up the totality of the American state was no less a scramble for benefits than the one along the Potomac. As for needs or problems that might be intrinsically intractable, such as poverty, or had portents for limitlessness, such as aging or good health or ethnic or racial honor, the illusions mounted that they could be, in Lyndon Johnson's word about poverty, "eliminated."

For more insistent conservatives, the winds toward limitlessness grew both higher and more chilling. Already faced by a rising flight to the state within their own party under Eisenhower, Republicans on the right like Goldwater had more difficulties within their own party than with liberal Democrats. They became increasingly shrill about liberal domination of *both* parties and about *all* presidents as captives of the state, the eastern establishment, the Washington crowd "inside the beltway." By 1960 conservatives with new journals for their views like *The National Review* and *Modern Age* moved volubly, almost desperately, from one issue to another, seeking reversal of the latest surge of tide toward centralization.[100] They had small, if symbolic, victories in enacting structural limits like restricting the presidents to two terms by constitutional amendment, but there was also support for or silence before Senator Joseph McCarthy or for the proposed Bricker Amendment to limit presidential powers in foreign policy or to impeach Chief Justice Warren. If it was apparent even by 1960 that, for worse as well as better service of expectations and entitlements, "bigness" had burgeoned toward irreversibility, the so-called modern Republicans like Nelson Rockefeller and Charles Percy at least did bring reason to bear against the old pileup. But most of the political conservatism that emerged against Eisenhower as much as against liberal Democrats was often as abstract and doctrinaire, *e.g.*, in idealizing the free market, as the liberal statism it would repeatedly denounce for grandiose ideologizing about poverty or urban renewal or the welfare state.

From the presidential election of 1968 to the balloting of 1992, the platforms of third parties reveal growing sensitivity to citizen anger and alienation from politics as usual. These feelings in the electorate had no boundaries of class, status, region, education, race, sex, or gender. Nothing other than anger against government seems to unite followers of George Wallace (1968), John Anderson (1980), and Ross Perot (1992). Millions of Americans seemed increasingly to resent the price paid for the ordinary politics of entitlements and bigger, bossier government. Under the indignation, however, was always—and it remains—the compromising fact of their own farm price supports or pork-barrel items or social security benefits from the system they excoriated. That stake in the state was also one reason why reforms, especially for deficit and debt reduction, would come to less than seemed implicit in the shrillness against the state. From the New Deal on, however, as the net of entitlements was spun and became permanent, its political, social, and monetary costs became too obvious to be ignored. Periodically, the net provoked voter rebellions using broad phrases such as the threat to liberty or the road to serfdom that implied that all state intervention was suspect. These phrases gave little clue as to which voters the angry words would catch. Why individuals voted as they did remains a record of separate histories. Not all poor southerners, for example, voted for Strom Thurmond in 1948 or for George Wallace in 1968, despite strong feelings against desegregation. Overall, the issues that drove some voters to third parties and that eventually also confronted the two major parties gradually created an indictment that was clear by the 1970s: a welfare

100. George H. Nash, *The Conservative Intellectual Movement in America Since 1945* (New York, 1976).

system that seemed to encourage permanent dependency, idleness, illegitimacy, and fraud; affirmative-action programs that seemed to be replacing a national ideal of equality of opportunity open to all with merit with an ideal of mandated equality of results for women, blacks, and other minorities; a compound of taxes, deficits, debt, interest rates, and fuel prices that seemed to sap initiative or destroy the fruits of those who had worked hard for their pay, savings, homes, and businesses; busing and other race-related changes in the public school system; rising crime rates and less-effective crime controls; radical assaults against the worth of American ideals at home and abroad and against symbols like the flag, the military, and the national anthem; increasingly costly and intrusive government that seemed more dysfunctional the more it attempted in meeting needs with arbitrariness, paternalism, and telling Americans how to live; ungrateful allies in Europe and third-world leaders such as Khomeini, Castro, and the Chinese Communists who insulted the United States with impunity. What counted in all such indictments was not the real, complex record but the individual citizen's perceptions of the dimming or befouling of American dreams. As time passed, these complaints and a nostalgia about a forsaken American Eden spilled beyond specific irritations about a failing family farm or quotas in hiring to a floating general style of hostile alienation. The sense of disgust was already implicit in the Republican slogan of the 1950s: Had enough? Vote Republican. The force of accumulated resentment eventually touched those Democrats who had remained loyal to the party when others had deserted it for third parties or for the Republicans. It was the Democrat Jimmy Carter who featured notes of "scandalous" and "outrageous" in his 1976 campaign as a common citizen and an outsider. Carter's failure in office to reverse the tides he denounced seemed to heighten the anger he had articulated. With Carter frustrated by both Washington gridlock and Iranian intransigence, the anger that had sought him for relief was ready to go elsewhere.

The Reagan Walk-On

In analyzing the recent Reagan-Bush years, scholarship must be laced with journalism, even if it begins safely by observing that no president since the New Deal seemed more passionate about government retrenchment than Ronald Reagan in 1981. Seldom did it seem clearer than in 1980 and 1984 that millions would cross political lines to vote for a spokesman who had a clever formula of being sunny about American horizons while also lashing out at government itself as America's besetting problem. One of Reagan's more thoughtful early advocates, the conservative George Will, wrote about a sense of bullying by Washington that Reagan helped articulate, especially on what became known as the "social issues." As a presidential candidate, Reagan repeatedly opposed using federal power to establish national, liberal standards of behavior against local or more conservative preferences about sexual conduct, pornography, abortion, police and court procedures, school prayer, busing, and so on.[101] These were the same issues that Reagan's successor, George Bush, was to summarize in extolling "mainstream" America in 1988 against his "way-out" challenger, Michael Dukakis. The battle lines were important for liberals. If they let stand mainstream local ordinances about race relations, sex discrimination, pornography, dealing with criminals, or prayer in schools, the federal government would have agreed to what liberals regarded as infringements on individual liberties and violations of constitutional safeguards.

Whatever the facts, the law, or the justice in these conflicts between mainstream America and individual liberties, in appealing to the wide variety of feelings of outrage against Washington intervention, Reagan rode that rising tide of shame on the state that had accompanied America's wider seeking of government entitlements. His all-out attack that Washington itself was the problem helped enlarge the tendency of many former Democrats to cast Republican votes. That shift had been apparent since the 1950s; but by 1984, only 38 percent of white males voted Democratic, and in the once solid South only 28 percent of the same group voted for Mondale. The shrewdness of Reagan's instinct about the votes to be found in American anger became clear after his election. The Democrats tried to recoup by stressing their own sensitivity to the "social issues" or to threats to "family values" from crime, drugs, abortion, sexual license, and other increasing pathologies. Beyond that, however disturbed or dismayed as they were about the spread of the state, few Americans could consciously admit how much they themselves had done to admit the evil spirit of statism into the national home. As already clear under Eisenhower and Nixon, their unacknowledged alliance with government for economic entitlements set strong barriers against any anticipated Reagan revolution to undo big government.

By the 1980s, most citizens lived daily lives suffused with the state, whether as businessmen habituated to Washington favors or as welfare recipients consciously dependent on government. Each citizen spent

101. George F. Will, *The Morning After* (New York, 1986), 249. There is a larger portrait of these and less ideological fears about the nation in Alice M. Rivlin, *Reviving the American Dream* (Washington, D.C., 1992). See her bibliography especially for many studies of popular anxieties and frustrations since 1980.

his day with the great state from the morning moments when he washed his teeth with state-delivered, purified, fluoridated, and taxed water to lights out as he turned on an electric blanket built to OSHA and other government standards, heated by a supply of electricity whose delivery and price were determined by some regulatory agency. To go through the rest of a citizen's day in the 1980s was to pass far beyond Sidney Webb's "monstrous list" of unacknowledged services and activities that government in England had quietly assumed a century earlier in the supposed heyday of laissez-faire. As the common householder headed for the bank, like tens of millions, his FHA or VA mortgage payments and savings account balance were backed by Washington. If his "savings and loan" bank failed, Washington paid the giant price to protect each account up to $100,000. His costs for consumer credit on his Visa card and the interest paid on his deposits and mortgage traced back to Washington controls over the money supply and other decisions by the Federal Reserve Board and Treasury. When he arrived at work, the floor under his wages and hours and his net monthly salary after FICA and FIT deductions had been set by Washington. His basic social security was decisively federal, however much he may have supplemented it with a private pension plan. But that too was within federal tax guidelines. If he had an IRA, its existence and tax status were set by Washington. When he read the bill in the mail for a recent hospitalization, even the uninsured portion he had to pay derived heavily from the giant weight of Medicare/Medicaid reimbursement for covered citizens because that level of huge government payments helped establish the "usual and customary rates" allowed for all reimbursement and billing. The splendid diagnostic and treatment facilities at his favorite hospital, like the CAT scanner and kidney dialysis machine, may well have been paid for by federal funds as a needed community system or provided under government guidelines to prevent proliferation of such machines in his locality. His children in college, at a 1985 average annual national cost of $7,000 each, often depended on a U.S. guaranteed tuition loan or some form of government-funded campus aid for student jobs in libraries, offices, and laboratories. Food bills at the supermarket were directly affected by tens of billions of dollars annually in price supports for the farmer who grew his provender. Whether during his lunchtime break he could buy a small foreign car at an affordable price depended on government auto-import policies toward foreign manufacturers, just as more than ever of his clothing came from foreign countries like Taiwan or the Philippines and with prices that would have been dearer were it not for U.S. tariff favors for developing nations. The mounting cost for his gasoline, his sixpack, his liquor, and cigarettes picked up on the way home reflected climbing federal and state taxes. If he dreamed of getting away from such horrid facts and visions by taking a vacation, he might well travel on the interstate highway network, 90 percent of whose costs since Eisenhower days had been paid by Washington and thereby also provided construction work for his blue-collar neighbor and a contract for his relative's paving firm. Federal pollution standards affected the air he breathed as well as the water he drank. And when he went to sleep at night, his remarkable freedom from the knock of a secret police at 2 A.M. or from the devastation of war and revolution that wracked the rest of the globe depended on a visible $300 billion annual defense expenditure and much more funding for defense that was not visible. And each year that passed and every new presidency left him that more deeply caught in the gigantic web of "governmentalized" society. So it was that by 1980, citizens resenting the state's intrusions decided to call in Reagan the exorcist to rid them of their devil. However, their sense of entitlement took its toll from the outset of the Reagan administration and blunted the powers and will of this indignant American president.

Historically, before 1910, when pileup and government generally were less obvious, a politician's railings against interventionist government were mere rhetoric without costs. Only a minority of citizens would have been affected by curtailing, for example, existing federal harbors regulation. By 1980, when government seemed to drench all of American society with regulations and services, state-trashing might still have been ritualistic, but it also implied pain for most citizens if taken seriously. Once entitlements were cut for the least powerful or politically marginal groups or for more-questioned programs like Amtrak, the surgeons would be close to such vital tissues of middle America's statist interests as social security increases, Medicare expenses, farm price supports, and the sacrosanct (for Reagan) needs of national defense during the costly Cold War.

Such limited options were not foreseen or weighed enough in 1981 as Reagan went to work with a will to begin to deliver on his promises by aiming principally at welfare costs. With federal taxes and some federal services cut as promised in his first year, there were at once fears of fewer funds or diminished increases for other entitlement programs. Middle Americans who had come to depend on government funding began to growl. As Reagan seemed to move toward further besting of the state by cutting, for example, revenue-sharing with the states, that did not lessen the aroused national demand for money for medical care and welfare. When funding for such needs waned on the Potomac they waxed at the state capitals still accountable for Medicaid for the poor or for education. One response in the states was to raise taxes and fees for programs formerly funded by the federal government. This shifting of burdens, as well as increasing the FICA tax, meant that by 1989 total taxes as a portion of gross national product had actually risen in the decade. The federal portion remained at about 21 percent.[102] When states followed California's lead in the 1970s and reduced homeowner property taxes, aid for schools and libraries had to wax in towns, cities, and counties.[103] Politicized needs like welfare, especially, would not die either at Washington or in those states beset by problems of poverty, unemployment, massive school drop-out rates, and swarms of poor immigrants. The Reagan revolution against big government thus quickly became a game played with mirrors or, rather, another version of the old American pattern of waxing and waning. To cover government costs, particularly for the defense buildup that could not be met by abhorrent taxes, despite the historic Republican excoriating of deficits and of borrowing from the future, Reagan sent the federal debt soaring. It tripled in his eight years and moved a trillion higher under Bush. Meanwhile, the lesser governments and consumers also increased their borrowing as well as their taxes. If there was prodigality in increasing debt, the problem was not merely governmental or federal, for as middle-class income flattened in the 1980s not only did more women enter the work force but credit card use and other forms of borrowing ballooned.

The federal retrenching in welfare and social services was often only a slowing of anticipated increases, in part because each budget line started with a base in every previously appropriated dollar. Limited increases as well as cuts were bewailed as "uncaring" or as the destruction of "vitally needed services." Retrenchment had ironic effects on a few million citizens, many of them black, just below or just above the poverty line. One ostensible purpose of the Reagan cuts was to stimulate more self-help. The customary piety had been that aid to poorer citizens or service-meager communities was intended to help lift them to self-sufficiency or at least greater independence. For Reagan to cut aid just after

102. Ferrel Guillory, "Legacy of 1980s helps explain no-tax decision," *News and Observer* (Raleigh, N.C.), July 6, 1990.

103. As Reagan cuts and any demythification of the service state moved in tandem, there was news that cities, states, and citizenry were finding alternatives to federal action for coping with their problems, despite a generation of their own protests about their limitations and continuing needs for Washington aid. See, for example, John Herber (New York Times News Service), "Counties Gaining New Responsibilities as Reagan Shrinks Federal Aid to Cities," *News and Observer* (Raleigh, N.C.), November 10, 1985. Also Spencer Rich, "Study Finds Cities Fared Well Despite Recession, Reagan Cuts," Washington *Post,* September 28, 1986. The "new voluntarism" is the theme of another encouraging report of citizen activity, "How to Track Down Toxins," *Newsweek,* May 6, 1985.

they crossed the line in income to disqualify them for benefits might well deny the "little extra" in a government support such as rent supplements that they would need for a while to sustain their recent more-adequate level of life. Cuts in welfare also warned the poor away from the dangerous borders of higher income where one lost benefits. The cuts could seem most punitive for those furthest from the border, in the so-called permanent underclass, who seemed mired in joblessness, poor health, and minimal education. How they had come to that and how they might move up provoked very hot and confused debate. Even some liberal black writers like the anti-Reagan columnist William Raspberry joined conservative blacks like Thomas Sowers in denouncing the "drug of welfare" that created a psychology of dependence and infantilization.[104] Disregarding here the deeper, tender, and complicated questions of defining poverty and how citizens became or remained poor, the expectations of support and the fear of slipping back into dearth with diminished government funding in AFDC, food stamps, legal aid, rent supplements, and so on, had become weighty psychological facts but not as potent politically.[105] The poorest voted least and had the least influence, despite many middle-class spokesmen. Beyond these considerations, the chemistry of expectations and entitlements had so developed that at any margin of support, high or low, there were going to be groups in all classes and income levels who would feel politically offended by reduced spending.

Even families with the 1985 national average annual income of $12,000 were scarcely living in luxury or security beyond the safety net, especially if, for example, the local factory in a northern rust-belt state closed or moved to the Sun Belt. The "fairness issue" was also invoked by better-off voters with entitlements that included the aforementioned college student loans, mortgage interest deductions on vacation houses, or federal payments for old farm acreage turned into lawns or woodland. These angry fatter cats had called upon Reagan the exorcist but had not calculated the full price of effective retrenchment. There were rapid portents starting in 1981, Reagan's first year, of the costs of cutting regulations or benefits for middle and corporate America. The airlines suffered grievous financial losses from the return of competition as well as from chronic poor management. With lower profits they had to lower

104. Outstanding examples are summarized in William Raspberry's "Breaking the Code," *Newsweek*, October 21, 1985. Other issues and very contested assertions about state action worsening American poverty are in Charles Murray, *Losing Ground: American Social Policy, 1950–1980* (New York, 1984).

105. Even before Reagan, the sensitivities and the mare's nest of political problems implicit in public concern for the family were apparent after the controversial Moynihan Report. See Lee Rainwater and William L. Yancey, *The Moynihan Report and the Politics of Controversy* (Cambridge, Mass., 1967).

costs, so service and maintenance had to be cut. The annual prospects of the end of Amtrak sent congressmen and senators from along the routes scurrying to make sure that their towns and cities would, at worst, be the last to be eliminated from the service. Conversely, the auto, shoe, steel, textile, and clothing industries pleaded with the free-enterprise president not to permit his free-market, free-trade ideals to slash government protection against overseas competition.

The earliest major augury of political limits on Reaganesque trashing of big government came even before the first Reagan victory in tax cuts in the spring of 1981. Increasingly confident about obtaining Reagan's tax slash and other "honeymoon" measures to reduce federal power, the administration considered limiting some of the benefits that over the decades had crept into monthly social security payments. The proposals floated around Capitol Hill during the late spring amid howls of pain from all sides. The mere prospect was denounced by the Senate in May by an advisory vote of 96-0. That was the vivid sign marking the limited turf that Reagan and all others might expect to control if they tried to cut the big-ticket items with large constituencies.[106]

As noted, the grotesquely complex political phenomena of expectations and entitlements had been building up for decades, so by the 1980s economic and political judgment about managing them better was very complicated. Government retrenchment in order to encourage market forces could ruin industries like shoes or textiles, hard-pressed against Asian or Latin-American products. Chrysler and Lockheed might close, should the state defer to the market pressures against them rather than guarantee private loans to shore them up. Bankruptcy, a classic market test for competitiveness, would not only produce tens of thousands of unemployed voters but lessen competition further in the auto industry and wreck the economies of the auto and aircraft plant towns. Their congressmen and senators held as axiomatic that state services such as the proposed federal guarantees for repaying Chrysler's private loans did not contradict free-market ideals of risk in an open competition.

Neglected variables in all program planning generally involved a consideration that was at the center of the ambitions of the welfare state. Far better and more disinterested thinking was overdue, problem by specific problem, about what *only* government might do, and do reliably, for what were intolerable conditions of housing, health, income. All too well, American governments had learned the lesson that when in difficulty, whatever the ambiguities in your situation, act; the increasing ques-

---

106. David A. Stockman, *The Triumph of Politics* (New York, 1986), 192. The entire book chronicles its title's implicit plaint about the surrender of Reagan principles to his political advisers' "pragmatism."

tion about "running to Washington" was whether Washington could act well or better than any other force. When action turned out for the worse, as in bulldozing vast acreage for urban renewal that then remained undeveloped, congressmen, senators, and bureaucrats tried to save face and not admit mistakes. This seemed to support Reaganesque criticism of government programs as reckless or as boondoggles. Rabid protection of "turf" ranging from university research grants and their overhead charges to subsidized computer-chip production certainly did not help clarify any national stock-taking about government intervention that Reagan had promised. But dogmatism about the positive worth, let alone the inviolability, of programs for space ventures, super-colliding atom smashers, or nuclear submarines was matched by those opponents of food stamps or free cheese who denied that they were really needed because, allegedly, recipients of food stamps bought candy and junk food or, as Spiro Agnew had charged, the beneficiaries were bums or deadbeats.

Dogma and anger along the spectrum of political opinion about entitlement society thus dulled the edge of the gathering argument that there seemed to be limits to what government could do to succor American needs for risk-free lives. However pressing some needs were, especially in health care and education, how might they be met other than in the post–New Deal mode of uniform nationwide programs devised in Washington and relying on a quick-fix of spending? How ample, how quick could other answers be? For all the fashionable talk of limits in the 1970s, the difficulty was to make limits tangible and specific for policy purposes. For whom in a rambunctious democracy, overaroused about expectations and entitlements, would limits on both be invoked first?

Equally revealing of limits on Reagan was the fact that, despite a host of cuts in services for the poor and a slowed rate of growth in some other outlays and personnel, the Reagan budgets overall remained very close to Carter's. Calculations by the Congressional Budget Office and Reagan's Office of Management and Budget in early 1986 showed that government spending in 1980 was 22.5 percent of GNP.[107] Reagan had originally projected a reduction from 1981 to 1986 to 19 percent. Instead, by 1985 federal spending had climbed to 25 percent of GNP, largely sparked by increases in mandated, "sacred," or too-difficult-to-cut items like debt service, social security, veterans' benefits, military and civil service pensions, and Medicare. Above all was Reagan's massive military

107. Robert D. Hershey, Jr. (New York Times News Service), "Despite Budget Cuts, Federal Spending Continues to Climb," *News and Observer* (Raleigh, N.C.), February 2, 1986.

buildup, especially in more glamorous and more debatable items like giant aircraft carriers, stealth bombers, and an antimissile defense shield. Where spending was "discretionary" and cuts theoretically possible for both major parties, *i.e.*, in the "all other" categories beyond those mandated items listed above, five years of the Reagan revolution had cut the portion of "all other" as a part of GNP from 9.4 percent to 7.7 percent. In that slice were the welfare trimmings but also the snips and slashes at nonwelfare expenditure like Amtrak. In any case, and ignoring the immensely important matter of the perception, psychology, and politics of "cutting," a decline of 1.7 percent for "all other" scarcely suggested any return to the good old days of Calvin Coolidge, whose portrait Reagan had brought into a more inspirational location in the White House.[108] Overall, entitlements by 1985 for all Americans had doubled under Republican as well as Democratic presidents in the generation since Lyndon Johnson. In 1986, the director of fiscal policy studies at the conservative think-tank the American Enterprise Institute aptly summarized a realistic view of the much applauded Reagan cuts in social or marginal programs: "It makes for a lot of noise, but that's not where the big bucks are." If the last Carter spending-level policies in January, 1981, had been continued, the Carter outlays would have been only $1.2 billion more than Reagan's proposals for 1985.[109]

The Reagan pledge to maintain a safety net was another implicit limit on his sweeping shaming of the state. Even what he proposed to keep in the safety net maintained a degree and cost of federal intervention that would have shocked both Dwight Eisenhower and Franklin Roosevelt. By 1985, however, even if all welfare services were somehow swept away, the remaining discretionary outlays and mandated costs for debt service and pensions, for example, dictated a federal government in a far larger universe of concerns than that of the expansive Lyndon Johnson.

It was thus apparent that in the middle or longer term and against the deeper tides of the American political economy, any Reagan revolution against big government had died early, easily, and predictably, killed by "politics." As in the timid Eisenhower trial run for retrenchment a generation earlier, the Reagan advisers would not risk losing the voters who wanted cuts—but not in "my backyard." Ironically, Reaganism dried up on the sands of the self-interest that Reagan had praised for private endeavor but had excoriated when it allied with the state. During

108. Andrew Shonfield's comparative study of Western democracies claims that the 1.7 percent put America far in the rear of the Western democracies on welfare outlays. *Modern Capitalism* (New York, 1978), 69.

109. Hershey, "Despite Budget Cuts, Federal Spending Continues to Climb."

a half-century of state-sousing, American self-interest had attached it-self as much to its government entitlements as to private profits, and of-ten the two dovetailed as, for notable example, in the loudly denounced tax shelters or in the huge part of farm benefits that went to the largest producers. Proposed presidential budgets alone revealed that at the end of the Reagan-Bush era, services and budgets were still waxing, all lev-els of government considered. If Washington restricted funds for the poor or the Small Business Administration, it increased them for other irre-sistible needs such as Medicare, the AIDS or drugs crises, or for man-dated insurance for failed savings and loan banks.

In response, negative gestures came into play, the obverse of so many gestures since the ICC and Sherman Anti-trust Acts that expanded state intervention. Negative gestures included those cuts of 1.7 percent from 1980 to 1985 in the budget's "all other" discretionary items, however trumpeted as major Reagan triumphs. Given the gap between Rea-gan's encouraging words about retrenchment and the small deed, the ballyhooed cuts were gestures to what the country wanted in electing Reagan, not what it needed to cut, if indeed cutting rather than rede-ployment, redesign, and better quality of services was the recipe against the failings of big government. In any case, the impression was that the Reagan bureaucrats by his second term were walled-off politically from further substantial cuts in appropriations. The trimmed safety net now seemed minimal and the benefits of comfortable citizens inviolable. As for the minorities whose skillful politicking since the 1960s had brought great victories, the tide had turned. The needed votes of allies in Con-gress were not there, and the threat of vetoes also lowered prospects. Shaming the state at their expense, however, had served to discharge some of the general moralistic resentment against big government.[110]

If the Reagan revolution in state-shrinking ran dry, measurement of its thin achievements in dollars and percentages may well be of secondary importance. The primary consideration was whether Reagan had seri-ously dampened that common national habit of seeking the state, that uneasy legitimation of alliance with the state that had been strengthen-ing since World War I. One sign of the effectiveness of the Reagan anti-state rhetoric, as well as the weight of the Reagan deficits, was the re-luctance of Dukakis, the Democratic candidate in 1988, to indicate what taxes would be needed to fund new programs, talk as he did of Ameri-can wounds, ills, and unmet needs. Similarly, Dukakis' Republican op-ponent, George Bush, promised significant action about drugs, educa-tion, and environment, but both the $3 trillion debt and his reluctance to enlarge the Washington role, even were funding available, kept his

110. Robert J. Samuelson, "The Politics of Escapism," *Newsweek*, October 22, 1984.

legislative proposals as president modest and often financed by juggling or combining existing programs. This could seem like increased funding without adding the new taxes that he had repeatedly foresworn.

Sensing the potency of the anger that Reagan had articulated, several dozen so-called boll-weevil or conservative Democrats in Congress had joined Republicans to provide him with some of his victories or to increase his margins of support in the House and Senate. On the hustings, increasing numbers of Democratic candidates starting in off-year elections in 1982 and 1986 already tried to distance themselves from big government, big spending, and big new programs. The turn-abouts of so-called new Democrats such as Bill Clinton, the young governor of Arkansas, along with the formation of the Democratic Leadership Council to work for fiscal continence, welfare reform, a strong national defense, and the aforementioned "family issues," strongly suggested that Reagan had made legitimate and politically profitable, at least, a rhetoric against spending and for cutting those programs that cost the comfortable classes nothing. He had achieved enough trimming to seem to give substance to his rhetoric and to vindicate himself for the anti-Washington voters whose COLAs and crop payments, nevertheless, continued to arrive.

Beyond symbolic action, the actual status of needs and of the politics of needs were quite other matters. Against prospects for substantially attacking the existing state-serviced needs of mainstream America, one recalls the warning of another, perhaps more luminous conservative than Ronald Reagan, Edmund Burke: it is one thing to grant people new rights, but to try to deny rights and privileges that are already widely enjoyed is to run one of the gravest political risks. Making government bigger and more "caring" after 1933 gradually brought to millions in all classes benefits they had never imagined they might possess. Finding and serving their needs or expectations through the state had become a right. Denying those needs by cutting the entitlements of tens of millions threatened voter rebellion. To recall another appropriate saying of Burke, "You cannot indict a whole people." The politics of retrenchment implicit in the absolutist antistate Reagan rhetoric presaged an indictment, not just against the poor or Texas oil millionaires with depletion allowances, but against the American people, all classes, who had learned to seek and to take from the state. Room for maneuver for post-Reagan politicians would be no more and probably less than his as he approached those perilous shoals of respectable entitlements. Every dollar cut and every dollar borrowed in vaulting deficits moved government nearer the point where, politically or economically, it would be able to cut or borrow no more. That foreseeable limit would frustrate hopes for retrenchment that big talk about state-taming or mandated balanced budgets had aroused.

There were some critics who contended that Reagan had remained relatively unengaged about the mounting debt because it was not the kind of issue that immediately concerned most voters who did not watch the government bond market. Reagan may also have foreseen a large national debt as an effective limit on domestic spending. But giant debt could also affect Reagan's cherished trillion-dollar defense buildup. As the Cold War clouds began to dissipate, the cost for defense and the debt and the mounting calls for Washington to meet neglected domestic needs were effectively used by Reagan opponents to begin to trim defense outlays by 1986. Reagan was forever quick to explain deficits as due to the "Democratic big spenders" in Congress, but in all his years as president he never submitted a balanced budget nor one in which the added deficit for a year was less than $100 billion. Several times he had to accept tax increases to meet outlays. Furthermore, many Republicans had voted with the Democrats on spending items not only for white collar entitlements for farm aid and for the Pentagon but also for indispensable strands in the Reagan-approved safety net of social security, welfare, and health benefits. Reagan's and Bush's piety was that more private and local effort, more aid from those "thousand points of light," not government at Washington, should take care of housing, health, the arts, transportation. And although, selectively, in the Reagan years private funding and other nonfederal initiatives for serving such needs did increase, the proportions of problems like housing for the homeless, the ill-housed, and would-be householders had not stimulated the degree of needed private or local efforts or the home-purchase funds. For private developers to put venture capital into building "experimental" multiclass apartment houses or rehabilitating low-return and migraine-producing inner-city housing was against the self-interest that Reagan thought so beneficent a force in American life. And if states and localities, not Washington, were to tax more or float bonds to pay for public housing or for subventions to "young marrieds" priced out of the housing market, was that any less government intervention or did it bring lower taxes or did it decrease the *total* American public debt that far exceeded the "mere" $3 trillion (1989) federal burden?

If the fifty years a'knitting interest net was too thick and knotted by the 1980s to permit serious trimming, more gestures about debts and deficits were in order to escape from the intractable difficulties. Several were forthcoming. The first and much-heralded was the Gramm-Rudman-Hollings Act of 1986. It was never a debt-cutting plan, but a deficit-growth-restriction formula. Questionably setting annual dollar schedules for permissible *new* deficits in budgets over five years, it foresaw a balanced budget at the end of that period. It did nothing about the $2 trillion of debt already on the books and would actually increase the total debt by 1992 en route to an imagined balance of revenue and outlays for that year. If future Congresses could not meet each year's stipulated, highly hypothetical, lower deficit target, then across-the-board cuts equal for all discretionary items would be made. By placing, at first, the responsibility for cuts on the controller-general, the politically vulnerable Congress tried to escape the electoral price for potential cuts that might anger voters. Overselling the plan, Capitol Hill seemed to sense that what the country really wanted was only something called a law to deal with deficits while mainline entitlements remained secure. Each year thereafter brought a new round of White House and congressional dodges, tricks, and deceits to seem to reach the Gramm-Rudman deficit reduction targets. Tax receipts were overestimated, real costs were masked, projected "savings" were misleading, federal services and assets were sold off, obligations were postponed or stretched out, federal payments in the last month of the budget year were postponed until after the start of the next year, taxes were called fees, and existing fees were raised. And the law itself was quietly revised to extend the time to reach the cherished balance. No sooner had this theater seemed to have reached its nadir in mid-1990 than it became apparent that the projected savings of some $40 billion for the year were highly questionable and that the actual deficit for the year—it was variously calculated—was beyond $200 billion.

This mangling was compounded by another trick to avoid voters' wrath, the final actions in 1986 (to be repeated in 1987) on the appropriations for the year. Instead of voting on each agency's requests for funds, Congress lumped together all appropriations in a single giant bill about eight inches thick. The Democratic Congress presented the Republican president with a take-it-or-leave-it choice to sign or veto—if he dared to tie up the entire government. But the monster as it left Capitol Hill also permitted legislators to claim that they were forced to vote for or against specific programs because the decision to abandon the old piecemeal appropriations had somehow been taken from the hands of the individual legislator. Next year, during his State of the Union address in January, 1988, Reagan held aloft a copy of the 1987 appropriations volume for the eyes of the American public, dropped it to the desk to show its portentous weight, and then offered another round of state-shaming solutions for national ills like a line-item veto power for the president and a constitutional amendment requiring a balanced budget. His own submitted budget for that year, however, was again seriously out of balance.

That the difficulties were structural and no less for the Democratic Party than for the Republicans was made clearer when Clinton became president in 1992. The Democrats now controlled both the White House and Capitol Hill for the first time in twenty years. The gridlock between a Republican president and a Democratic Congress had supposedly prevented adequate action on many matters. But that proved to be less the problem than the gridlock in entitlement society. It limited a Democrat-controlled Washington as much as it had Reagan confronting the Democrat-controlled Congress. Whatever the entitlement and whatever party had enacted it, it remained the manna for the sponsoring senators and congressmen, whoever was president. As the Clinton budget in 1993 moved through Washington, older citizens, welfare recipients, defense industries and towns, cattle growers, energy producers, and forest loggers all worked to whittle down the modest Clinton proposals to deal with deficits and stimulate the economy. Reminiscent of the campaign of 1912, all the bright serious talk of an America at the crossroads and of the need for sacrifice turned into yet another round of gestures in Congress. There was a very small increase in the gasoline tax, some increases for the uppermost brackets in income tax, and another five-year plan full of hypothetical assumptions that the deficit could be reduced to zero with the budget balanced. The disastrous floods in the Mississippi Valley in the summer of 1993, with total damage of about $10 billion, also brought to mind other unforeseen costs that could seriously skew any five-year plan. It was a foregone conclusion, however, given the especially deep sense of entitlement about disaster relief, that government would pay heavily for lost crops and destroyed homes and businesses, regardless of party lines. Had even a conservative Republican been president, Washington would have been ready to offer massive, deficit-defying funds. The established dynamics of the politics of entitlement and interest-group democracy suggested that it would be a rare moment when senators and congressmen would accept significant cuts in their particular entitlements in order to heed presidential pleas for the national interest in deficit reduction. Presidents come and presidents go, but constituencies and the need to satisfy them extend beyond a mere four or eight years in the White House. In any case, Clinton's "serious" proposals for the deficit, like those of his predecessors, did nothing to reduce the trillions of dollars of national debt costing hundreds of billions of dollars a year in interest that would actually grow while attempts were made through deficit controls to slow it. If all targets proposed in mid-1993 by the president were met and $500 billion in deficit reduction was accomplished, the debt would still have grown by almost another half trillion dollars in five years because of the deficits that were not controlled in anyone's plan, including the draconian proposals of Ross Perot. The limitations on all parties were not only political, *i.e.,* what party politics would permit, but were deeper, more than a century in growing and intrinsic to the modern democratic system. The century had repeatedly shown, especially since the trial run of 1913 and 1914, how gestures of reform were about the best the Madisonian machinery could produce, failing only the severest crisis.

The new moral moments and gestures about cuts in spending under Clinton strongly suggest that the billions of entitlement dollars were the basic difficulty. Over fifty years, however, adding or cutting money had become too easy a formula for managing deeper aspirations confronting both New Dealers and conservative opponents. Dollars were only the costs of encouraging the growth of the interest net that ultimately derives from the immense and pressing needs generated by a continental capitalist society increasingly insistent on having those needs served by the state.

Reagan had challenged the faith that government programs could master virtually unlimited concerns about poverty, health, education, environment, and so on. But he and other fiscal conservatives had tried unsuccessfully to substitute another magic for the New Deal formulae: that less government taxation, regulation, and expenditure would expand private energies. Under supply-side economics, large tax cuts would meet both individual and public needs. The income and the comforts and freedom of at least the middle classes would rise. Investment would grow, and higher productivity would increase jobs, gross domestic product, and thus tax revenue. But the tax benefits went heavily to the richest, with large social costs in low capital reinvestment, savings and loan failures, increased homelessness, vast but unproductive leveraged buyouts, and stagnation or loss in middle-class purchasing power. The most valuable lesson from these adventures could be for Americans to understand that if Reagan, a conservative and a charismatic challenger of the going system, could not do the job, they were stuck with the state. They had best get around to the long-neglected tasks of running big government better, rather than continuing to indulge the chimera of a return to the good old days of a state-free nation, a time that had never existed.

The State Was Never "Out"

One besetting question about American big government has less to do with the advisability of new programs or the attraction of old principles of hostility to the state than with the politics that will decide about either. The spreading state now succored all Americans in some way or other, but it did so with great unevenness, decreasing dollar effectiveness, degenerating services, and increasing skepticism about government's ability to provide decent schooling, safe air and water, reliable and inexpensive mail service, passenger railroad service, air travel safety, debt reform, high quality medical and hospital care, assured benefits from the social security system, to name a few.

Aside from the old and misleading rhetoric of shaming while seeking the state, there appeared in political circles many ideas for more effective government policies. On the surface, at least, some had cogency beyond the sloganeering versions of ideas like a new "industrial policy" (once called planning). There was talk cyclically about a revived federalism through augmenting state and local revenue while reducing federal funding; for semipublic or fully farmer-run corporations to take care of grain marketing; for interstate, not federal, public authorities for various purposes like PATH for trains and busses in the New York area; for wiser tax systems and higher quality of services at the state level to permit the states to tend to their own problems with less recourse to Washington; for incentives to encourage insurance companies, cooperatives, corporations, and pension funds to use enormous reserves to underwrite nongovernmental or local governmental efforts to deal with health care, support for the arts, schooling, environmental problems, or the degradation of America's aging infrastructure of roads, sewers, water supply systems, and transportation lines. In a culture in which ideas had themselves become marketable commodities, there was no dearth of prescriptions nor of conferences and colloquia about the "plight" of American government. The problem underlying all proposals was that, however wise they were, their fate was largely political. The ultimate paradox was that it would now take the state, *i.e.,* new bureaucracies, to trim or restrict or reform the state, as in, for example, the rules and administrators needed for so-called sunset laws to review annually all programs and agencies starting with the first dollar of appropriation.

How would effective legislation or administrative action for reform or retrenchment be launched against the grain of entitlement politics? Even more, what citizens in the nexus of the great state would pay or suffer—and how much—for enacting a "new federalism," for a "new voluntarism," for a "new competitiveness"? Given the huge tentacles and tenderness of the government octopus, the easier answer was not to deal at all, or at least not for the long term, with "structures" like the budget system or Pentagon procurement or the administration of welfare or farm support but to shame all state activity in the Reagan style while cutting mostly programs in which the political damage was least for both parties. If chance and politics permitted anything more sweeping than trimming welfare or Amtrak, they brought popular "across-the-board" or "something-for-everyone" tax cuts, as in 1981 and 1987. Both disdained the worth of skillfully targeted and testable tax policies to increase investment, productivity, jobs, and research and development with any tax relief claimable only with proof of reinvestment for higher productivity. Instead, under Reagan both parties cooperated in enacting general income tax reductions. These provided more money for general consumption, including unproductive take-overs, mergers, and so on, and for indiscriminate consumer spending. Lowered taxes also encouraged private spending on credit, while consumer debt climbed and already too-low private savings for productive investment decreased.

By the 1980s it thus seemed probable that with the political sensitivity of the great pileup of state services and payments, democratic America was drifting into one of its periodic logjams of accumulated interests that could not be broken except in a national crisis like World Wars I and II and the crash of 1929. It remains to be seen whether the giant debt, foreign trade imbalances, and heavy dependence on overseas investors and oil will create a major crisis forcing Americans to face the baleful consequences of having sung the song of state benefits but not wanting to pay the piper.

In the 1980s, the sense of spreading dysfunction in American government as well as the stream of reform proposals helped widen America's ceaseless probing into the national condition. This new round of old debates included a revival of philosophic inquiry about democracy from writers like Sheldon Wolin, Walter Berns, and Michael Walzer, as well as important books about government dysfunction from such leading experts as Robert Dahl, Alice Rivlin, Charles Lindbloom, and Hugh Heclo and studies of specific policies from a large coterie of highly regarded students.[111] For all of the obvious connections of such inquiry with the long tradition of America-watching, there were new concerns in this round of discourse. None was more evident than in talk of "the state." One scholar summarized a revived interest in political history as "bringing the state back in."[112] In the academy this was a reaction against

111. Sheldon Wolin, *Politics and Vision* (Boston, 1960); Walter Berns, *In Defense of Liberal Democracy* (Chicago, 1984); Michael Walzer, *Radical Principles: Reflections of an Un-Reconstructed Democrat* (New York, 1980). For Dahl, Lindbloom, and Heclo, see below. Otis Graham directed me to many recent studies dealing with the revived interest in the state. For general theories, see Martin Conroy, *The State and Political Theory* (Princeton, 1984).

112. Peter B. Evans *et al.*, eds. *Bringing the State Back In* (Cambridge, Mass., 1985); "The State," *Daedalus* (Fall, 1979); Stephen Krasner, "Approaches to the State: Alternative Conceptions and Historical Dynamics," *Comparative Politics*, VI (1984), 223–46; J. P. Nettl, "The State as a Conceptual Variable," *World Politics*, XX (1967).

a generation of social history in which, if politics and government were considered at all, they were virtually epiphenomenal. But "bringing the state back in" might also imply that the state had not counted for much throughout most of American history and that, understandably, it had been neglected by scholars. That assumption was to take appearances for reality. It ignored, for example, the state's long covert role, especially in sponsorship of enterprise. By also neglecting the thick record of slow pileup of regulatory activity beyond the headline issues like antitrust laws and by failing to observe the waxing and waning of intervention among levels of government, it could seem that the state had been "out." In fact, it has always been "in," with its functions and powers building up across generations, parties, all presidencies and Congresses, and despite chronic state-shaming.

The inquiry of the last decade or so about the state has differed markedly from the progressive intellectuals' search for a state before 1914. The major emphasis recently has been to acknowledge the permanence of large and active government in American life. Yet, at the same time that the state had become a mighty presence, the manner of its growth (what has been called here "pileup"), the ways its pieces are cobbled together, financed, staffed, administered, subject to review and revision, and confusedly presented to the electorate by politicians and interest groups, made it difficult for citizens to make sense of what had happened to America.[113]

"Pileup" meant unwieldy size, high costs, and, most of all, a nearly endless series of dysfunction in most of America's 100,000 governments. Debates in the 1980s, however, continued to confuse the issues of size, cost efficiency, and ideology. If effectiveness per dollar spent were emphasized against decrying of bigness per se, not enough was known about how, activity by activity, function by function, increases in size affected efficiency and effectiveness. In actually disbursing funds, giant federal activities like issuing social security checks, farm benefit payments, and income-tax refunds produced few citizen complaints. On the other hand, bidding and contracting, especially in the Brobdinagian Pentagon or health-care reimbursement, pululated cyclically with horror stories or scandals. But even if another controversial activity, welfare administration, were to be done better, the scope and organization of aid would still lead to concerns that in millions of lives much of every week would be spent in different queues, sitting on agency benches, holding numbered tickets to be called to fill out a form or to be seen by the

113. A well-argued class analysis of the difficulties is in John F. Manley, "Neo-Pluralism: A Class Analysis of Pluralism I and Pluralism II," *American Political Science Review*, LXXVII (1983), 368–89.

job counselor, case worker, or doctor in the Medicaid clinic. Most Americans had only a glimpse of this welfare round-of-life, but it did involve questions about bureaucratic overload for millions of poorer citizens heavily dependent on state support.

Many of those who were most judgmental about welfare thickened the very large and common error of ignoring how much the dysfunctions of government accompanied the growing record of degenerating management in American society; how corporations, banks, savings and loan institutions, universities, professional societies, merchandising empires, and so on, similarly suffered from grandiosity, jargonish and abstract goals, inexpert and slovenly administration, bureaucratic bloat, poor market analysis and budgeting, too little reinvestment and too much pay-out to stockholders and executives, pointless "printout," prestige and favor and glamour seeking, the easy life at the club or lake, and accepting inhouse the delusions and fantasies about the reasonableness of it all depicted for outsiders by departments of public relations.[114] No answers for the major problems of the permanently big state would be adequate that avoided the habits and demands of America's big society.

Robert Higgs's recent libertarian analysis and prescriptions about big government are far from mainline, but his title, *Crisis and Leviathan* (1987), sums up the gathered sense of difficulty of both liberals and conservatives about running today's state. Higgs mistakenly assumes that America before 1890 regarded itself as adequately self-sufficient to eschew state investment or public action against private excess. Today, our needy and injury-sensitive democracy, even without major crisis, will no longer tolerate, for the sake of the individual liberty so esteemed by Higgs, government passivity in the face of immoderate unemployment, competition from foreign textiles, shoes, and steel, bank failures, mortgage foreclosures, water pollution, or "toughing it out" after natural disasters like drought and flood.

However forlorn Higgs's libertarian responses to Leviathan may be, his wide and irreverent inquiry reminds us of how wide the range of state watching and state talk has become. Nothing about the state now escapes scrutiny by academics, legislatures, commissions, and columnists. There is a plethora of conflicting opinion that at least *seems* qualified. It confronts us with a cascade of indictments, findings, and policy proposals about Leviathan in travail that dwarfs the earlier efforts at state defining among the 1914 progressive intellectuals and policy-makers.[115]

114. The economic aspects of productivity and managerial failings are summarized in William Bowen, "How to Regain Our Competitive Edge," *Fortune*, March 9, 1981, pp. 74–90.

115. There is a good cross section of opinions in David Lowery and William D. Berry,

But amid the flood of debate about the state, what *was* to be done? Besides so many answers, what were the best questions? Size? Competence? Personnel or procedures? Doable or impossible tasks? "Who, whom" questions about power—who had it to use against whom—had produced an enormous and contentious literature about state malaise. The facts above government operations were themselves in dispute and did little to clarify what American priorities or obligations ought to be in dealing with government dysfunction. If one type of analysis suggests that the government agencies, like the dozens in farm policy, do largely what their constituency wants,[116] another line of inquiry reveals that in the history of labor relations or international economic policy government officials have pretty much run their own show.[117] "Who governs" preoccupies one group of political scientists[118] while the question "*Whoever* governs, what will the big state give to whom?" stimulates quite another emphasis about contemporary conditions.[119] In recent academic study of the major branches of federal power, one line of scholarship stresses how historical failures to provide the presidency a permanent corps of top-level civil servants to formulate and manage policy has led to short-term, disjointed, uneven service by a "government of strangers," the three thousand or so senior administrators whom the president can now appoint and dismiss. Political convenience and flexibility with such staffing are purchased at the cost of forsaking long-term governmental experience and tempered expertness in public policy circles.[120]

Another line of study of the presidency, however, indicates how much would-be strong presidents, even with good staff, are now denied a seeming presidential moment by the plethora of pluralistic checks and balances.[121] Even the strongest of presidents will be challenged by the permanent civil-service bureaucracy, the coordinate branches of Congress

---

"Growth of Government in the U.S.: An Empirical Assessment of Competing Explanations," *American Journal of Political Science,* XXVII (1983), 665–94.

116. Charles L. Schultze, *The Distribution of Farm Subsidies: Who Gets the Benefits* (Washington, D.C., 1971).

117. Howell Harris, "The Snares of Liberalism," in *Shop Floor Bargaining and the State,* ed. Steven Tolliday and Jonathan Zeitlin (Cambridge, Mass., 1985). Stephen Krassner, *Defending the National Interest: Raw Material Investments and U.S. Foreign Policy* (Princeton, 1978).

118. Robert Dahl, *Who Governs* (New Haven, 1961).

119. Benjamin I. Page, *Who Gets What from Government* (Berkeley, 1983); Joseph Pechman and Benjamin Okner, *Who Bears the Tax Burden* (Washington, D.C., 1974).

120. Heclo, *A Government of Strangers.*

121. The plaint is made clear by a chastened pluralist Charles E. Lindbloom, "Another State of Mind," *American Political Science Review,* LXXVI (1982).

and the courts and their large staffs, long-term appointees like the Federal Reserve Board, let alone the skillful, well-financed lobbyists for industry, education, and the senior citizens. Each of these has more influence with the Congress and bureaucracy than with the popularly elected chief executive.[122]

Studies of Congress, the Pentagon, the executive departments, and the courts reveal similar stories of growth in functions attendant with complicated operations, cross-purposes, tolerance of ineptitude, flashy programs, or hidden mess, decline of hard work, sloppy inhouse supervision, and inhouse vengeance against whistle-blowers. With Congress, repeated efforts to streamline, improve staff, and reform procedures, especially in key functions like budgeting and appropriation, have produced larger staffs but slim results.[123] Report after report about the justice system tells of overloaded courts, overlong trials, eccentric sentencing, overcrowded prisons, unevenly qualified or overworked or understaffed judges, excessive plea-bargaining. All of this accents unfairness, unevenness, decreasing effectiveness, and lessening confidence in American justice.[124]

Other "systems" generated similar tales. Washington may collect multiple billions in income taxes, but its costly computer system to catch tax-cheaters identified so many questionable returns that the chances of being audited by the limited corps of examiners were smaller than before the system was redesigned. Congress passes a massive simplification of the tax rates in 1986, but the public is dismayed by the complex forms needed to clarify withholding and substantiate deductions. The overtouted reorganization of the postal service provides erratic service with declining deliveries and pickups and bizarre delays in arrivals of even "special deliveries." All this occurs despite recurrent reorganization, almost annual increases in the cost of postage, starting salaries of $24,000 for clerks, and massive and expensive mechanization. After spending more than $1 billion on automation for greater efficiency, a 1990 study found it no greater.[125] The government cannot create, run, or regulate an adequate rail or bus system for passengers. Its Atomic Energy Commission and its successor, the Nuclear Regulatory Commission, try to move the nation, including the hallowed TVA, to nuclear

122. Hugh Heclo and Lester Salomon, eds., *The Illusion of Presidential Government* (Boulder, Colo., 1981).

123. Samples of the disarray are presented in Joseph Pechman, ed., *Setting National Priorities: Agenda for the 1980s* (Washington, D.C., 1980), especially the essay by James Sundquist on competence.

124. James Q. Wilson, *Thinking About Crime* (Rev. ed.; New York, 1983).

125. "Report says Postal Service slow to boost productivity," *News and Observer* (Raleigh, N.C.), May 10, 1990.

power at immense, spiraling costs and dangers proportionate to the complexity of safety controls that unevenly competent personnel must monitor. Washington dangerously mismanages its own atomic facilities at the Hanford, Washington, complex, incurs over 1,000 violations at the TVA atomic plants in just five years, and goes so deeply into debt in financing TVA expansion that some TVA electric rates rise 50 percent in three years and 7,500, or 22 percent, of employees have to be fired.[126] Federal budget procedures and welfare systems are regularly denounced by both parties as scandals. Massive public housing to replace slums turns the government into the nation's largest slumlord—and impotent, to boot, before the degeneration, vandalism, and crime in many of the older "projects." Some of these in cities like St. Louis, Chicago, and Newark even have to be abandoned or blown up. Starting in the 1970s, to counter the inadequate funds in the social security unemployment trust accounts, the administering states, lacking higher taxes to replenish the funds, tightened eligibility rules. Simultaneously, there was an increase in the numbers of unemployed who had not worked enough or earned enough to qualify for any benefits. In the 1970s, the jobless on relief had already hit a low of 41 percent, but by 1988, under the new rules, only 32 percent of jobless could qualify. This also reduced the billions of dollars paid in unemployment benefits that could figure in attempts to stimulate demand during recessions.[127] For almost twenty years, the nation's Medicare and Medicaid system of reimbursement to "providers" at their stated costs stimulated hospitals and doctors to overorder diagnostic tests, pile on "patient days," and unnecessarily replicate in many localities expensive but glamorous diagnostic devices such as magnetic resonance scanners, confident that "the government will pay." Reimbursement at stated costs did follow. The soaring price for care surpassed inflation rates and eventually passed to taxpayers and also to premium payers in private insurance rates. The latter reflected the mounting costs of providing the doctors with the latest diagnostic devices and with the freedom to order whatever procedures they wished. This freedom led to the hospitals increasing their allowances for bad debts as their patients' insurance claims began to be rejected for unwarranted or unauthorized services and to cover huge, mismanaged "accounts receivable." In seeking to improve public service, the national administration perennially makes forays into private firms or universities in the provinces for needed talent, but Washington can hold them for only a few years be-

126. *Newsweek*, January 18, 1982.
127. "Jobless Insurance System Aids Reduced Number of Workers," New York *Times*, July 26, 1988. On other problems of the system and its general history, see "Fixing Social Security," *Newsweek*, May 7, 1990.

fore they exit through the "revolving door" to return to the seeming sanity and higher salaries in the law, media, or consulting firms. Naturally, these want to use the savvy and access that the former bureaucrats have acquired during their stint for the state.[128] The national government not only pays farmers, largely the wealthiest, the guaranteed tens of billions of dollars annually but commits itself to storing, at enormous public costs, the excessive production that the guarantees stimulate.[129] Under Jimmy Carter, Washington began to free savings and loan associations to earn more, compete more with stockbrokers' money management accounts, and offer more services than their classic, but low-profit, home mortgage loans. But declining bank inspection and new appetites in the liberated bankers led to leaping interest rates to attract deposits. The latter were used to finance billions of dollars of risky or illegal loans or for the personal benefit of the bank officers and their friends. The assurances were that depositors faced no risk because of deposit insurance. Federal power thus waned mightily in the 1970s on behalf of greater freedom in the banking world, but less than a decade later government was warned to prepare to wax with hundreds of billions of dollars in appropriations to bail out the now overextended private system. Such lists of failures in the general litany about how America is misgoverned are endless, familiar, and drearily ritualistic for all their truth.

The size, complexity, and messes of big society with its mammoth private institutions invite big government intervention either as friend, *e.g.,* to guarantee private loans, or as countervailing power, *e.g.,* to lower long-term interest rates. As friend or foe, the need for legislation or court action is often so large that it entails immense complications for the state in trying to put things right. What intervention may involve is suggested by the story of the federal prosecution of IBM under the antitrust laws. A complex indictment of the immense operations of this computer empire in 1969 led to thirteen years of litigation. More than 66 million pages of documentation, in addition to the huge size of the trial record, had accumulated. The trial costs for Washington ran past $13 million. About three hundred attorneys came and went on both sides.[130] This single government action in the courts was stunningly complex, but it may be the only size action possible for the state in dealing with en-

128. The National Academy of Public Administration presents its advice on better management (largely for executive functions) in an appendix to Heclo and Salomon, eds., *The Illusion of Presidential Government.*

129. Robert J. Samuelson, "The Farm Mess Forever," *Newsweek,* November 18, 1985.

130. "End of Action on I.B.M. Follows Erosion of Its Dominant Position," New York *Times,* January 9, 1982. Follow-up articles appear January 10, 11. See also the "absurdities of the IBM case" in Washington *Post,* April 18, 1982.

terprises on the IBM scale. Yet, the effort was fruitless. By 1982, there was no satisfactory end in sight and the government had to drop the case. If the judge died, among other possibilities, what successor could master the trial record? More weightily, after thirteen years, market conditions had so lessened IBM's eminence that a guilty verdict based on the 1969 evidence would have been out of date. The tale of a more successful immense antitrust action, against AT&T and the Bell system, suggests that competition, if indeed restored by government action, may still have baleful effects on consumer costs and the simplicity of service.

Although invited to endless tasks by the aroused expectations in an immense economy, government policy is heavily circumscribed by structural changes in American life. These include a larger and older population, a shift from heavy goods manufacturing to services, the changing composition and rootedness of a society of "ethnics" that seems increasingly less a community than an enclave of cultures, 40 percent of black and 25 percent of all youth not only unemployed but disqualified for most jobs by dropping out of school, most women entering the work force, the discontent with the relentlessly routinized work needed to make big society work, signs of the decreasing effectiveness of decent socialization of children by parents. All such aspects of national life are replete with needs that will invite new programs like government-funded child care. But the even deeper discontents of those groups now demanding psychological satisfactions like fairness or fulfillment or respect (see below) suggest objectives that no president and Congress can hope to affect more than marginally. And with deficits immense, tax increases horrifying, program costs soaring, and the sense of staunchable wounds insistent, should limited funds go to help keeping alive doomed Alzheimers or AIDS victims or to improving the infant and child mortality rate?[131]

Washington power is even more limited by the global changes that affect many domestic interests, crowd our consciences, and tempt us to great programs beyond our frontiers. Turmoil in the former Soviet Union, famine in sub-Saharan Africa, explosive population growth in the third world, the deforestation of the Amazon, Niger, the Congo, and Irrawaddy, the thickening clouds of pollution over Mexico City, Tokyo, Seoul, and Bombay, the leaping increases in heterosexual AIDS cases in Africa, the rising textile industries in Taiwan and Thailand, automobiles from Korea as well as Japan, European allies who will, issue by issue, go their own way, the uniting of Germany, and the freeing of Soviet satellites—all these and more in the global village are not our deci-

---

131. Richard D. Lamm, "We Can't Fund All Our Dreams," *News and Observer* (Raleigh, N.C.), May 28, 1989.

sions and set limits on what American government can do, however great its sense of mission and its willingness to spend billions to better the world as we see fit. Regardless of what party, president, or Congress wants, a single world economy deeply affects what the American economy can profitably produce, the prices we can charge, the profits and deficits business or government can anticipate, the investments we can make, and thus the policies the state can pursue in all these respects.

But other than the invitation to mess, frustration, and lies in attempting the impossible or the grandiose at home or abroad, do "structural" situations preclude governing better within limits that are honestly admitted? Responses to the poor national record of our 100,000 governments is amply clear: allegations of serious limits or faults are dismissed by politicians such as George Bush as "knocking America" or "selling America short"; others resort to ritualistic decrying about decline but will not fight for more than gestures of reform; still others like Senator Warren Rudman leave public life in frustration over stalemate or sellout. Meanwhile the state grinds on with excessive, alienating unevenness and delivering decreasing value for money.

For looming temptations for new state action after Reagan, like child care, universal health insurance, or restoring American "competitiveness," fifty years of experience with out-in-the-open state intervention suggest at least a few guidelines for assessing prospects. Expert opinions about American needs will be divided, and even top-notch commissions of inquiry about the facts and policy alternatives will not escape bias. Large-scale, blanket programs, especially those called "wars," are likely to be counterproductive. Plans for massive urban renewal, for example, bring too little renewal and too much destruction of what communal ties old and run-down areas were able to retain. Sweeping nationwide designs, particularly in social services, will often conflict badly with regional, ethnic, and racial differences. The program designed for fragmented black families in Watts may make less sense in the Hispanic towns of Texas, where family ties may be stronger. Small, much-hailed "pilot programs" can proliferate to become formulaic or mere gestures. All programs beget bureaucracies and constituencies with vested interests in the existing program and in its "looking good," its ample funding, and its full complement of jobs. Policy that invokes "pluralism" or "multiculturalism" to justify entitlements for minorities also plays to and pays off interest groups. Rewards go less to the best deserving than to the best connected. Victories in interest-group pluralism act to restrict funds for other groups that may be equally deserving but are less influential than the American Farm Bureau Federation, the American Medical Association, the American Association of Retired Persons, or the National Education Association. All interest groups contending for public money emphasize large immediate gains, underestimate longer-range and cumulative costs, and ignore negative consequences of even well-intentioned and well-launched projects. Overstimulated needs, program costs deliberately understated to seem affordable, and bureaucratic promises of great achievements help lead to "the quiet side of public spending."[132] Off-budget and supplementary appropriations thus obtain what publicized hearings and realistic financing dare not ask for or reveal.

The record of such dangers and tricks of the big state in league with needy society is known to all veteran legislators and bureaucrats. By the different standards of a Hugh Heclo or Charles Lindbloom or Theodore Lowi, the hyperplural system with its countless power centers veers toward discredit and injustice.[133] Ominous for change, however, is that it *pays* both petitioners and their public servants. Those not yet rewarded live in hope of connecting. For many already established in the great queue, the state always seems to appropriate too little and unfairly. In any case, government no longer has to rule, as Machiavelli contended, by fear and force but by paying, and massively.

The Perils of Pluralism

In the 1960s the play of expectations and entitlements gained new force. Many ethnic, religious, and racial minorities that had felt excluded from national respect sought the state for various types of targeted aid. The phrase used at first to honor these new departures for government power was "respect for pluralism." If the entry of a word into popular parlance is a test of its cultural potency, *pluralism* became such a word, encompassing as it does the vast, intricate dealings of racial, ethnic, religious, and gender interest groups in American life and politics.

Historically, until the 1950s, the word *pluralism* had been a highbrow term. Originating in the Middle Ages to describe plural officeholding, in modern America it passed from the philosophies of William James and George Santayana into political-legal parlance during World War I.[134] Harold Laski, who had studied with James, seems to have been the

132. Herman B. Leonard, *Checks Unbalanced: The Quiet Side of Public Spending* (New York, 1986).

133. Theodore J. Lowi, *The End of Liberalism* (New York 1969). Ironically, recent reforms add to the complexity and slowness of government action. The expanding role of the Congressional Budget Office requires more time, information, and weighing of expert views in considering major legislation. Campaign expenditure restrictions dilute the threats party leaders can use to enforce discipline in moving bills through Congress. The less pork there is for distribution, the freer Congressmen and senators are to go their own ways.

134. There is no adequate general history of these important changes in American

first to use it for political purposes in developing his critique of Hobbesian sovereignty. Soon the word also became a term used to analyze American diversity. "Cultural pluralism" was first defined in the writings of another of James's admirers, the philosopher Horace Kallen.[135] In both political and cultural analysis, *pluralism* was to have descriptive and prescriptive meaning. Laski depicted the increasing, conflicting multiplicity of groups that set limits on American government's pretensions to having the final word. Without at first using the word *pluralism*, Kallen and his contemporary Randolph Bourne emphasized the growing diversity of American minorities and the many cultural and religious loyalties these groups encouraged.[136]

Despite their different interests, the three writers were similar in also advocating pluralism as a national ideal. Laski urged the government to respect the power of groups such as labor unions, and consumer societies to manage their own affairs free of state restrictions. At about the same time, 1916, the young socialist Randolph Bourne joined Kallen, albeit with different perspectives, to argue against adherence to a single community ideal calling itself "Americanism." Instead, they urged that a morally adequate ideal of community should ungrudgingly tolerate the host of America's intense and diverse national and religious loyalties. Bourne called his ideal "trans-national America" because he sought a more inclusive loyalty that would reach across the many nationalities that had come to make up American society. The new loyalty, however, retained a core of such historic ideals as freedom for belief and equal opportunity, the rule of law, and majority rule.

This early twentieth-century stir about law and power, ideals and loyalties, had much to do with the very tender questions raised by the post-1880 programs to Americanize immigrants and the politics of preparedness and war mobilization after 1915. At the same time, as John Higham has contended, the idea of a less monistic American life helped arouse younger intellectuals, like the Spanish-American George Santayana and the Jewish journalist Abraham Cahan, against the WASP elite that had domi-

---

thought. The best short prologue to the philosophic issues remains Morton G. White, *Social Thought in America: The Revolt Against Formalism* (New York, 1949). Compare with these full-length studies of pluralism in flower: Henry Kariel, *The Decline of American Pluralism* (Stanford, 1961); Darryl Baskin, "American Pluralism: Theory, Practice, and Ideology," *Journal of Politics*, XXXII (1970).

135. Harold J. Laski, *Studies in the Problem of Sovereignty* (New Haven, 1917); Herbert A. Deane, *The Political Ideas of Harold J. Laski* (Hamden, Conn., 1972); Horace Kallen, "Democracy Versus the Melting Pot," *The Nation*, C (1915), 190–94, 217–20.

136. Randolph Bourne, "Trans-national America," *Atlantic Monthly*, CXVIII (1916), reprinted in Bourne, *War and the Intellectuals*.

nated cultural life before 1900.[137] If the cultural pluralists opposed a single standard of "Americanism," in 1919 Theodore Roosevelt bluntly responded on behalf of the latter. In one of his last letters, he declared that Americanism meant that there was to be "room in America for but one flag, the American flag . . . and room for but one language here and that is the English language, for we intend to see that the crucible turns our people out as Americans, of American nationality, and not as dwellers in a polyglot boardinghouse."[138]

Such implicit absolutism about American ideals had long coexisted with the First Amendment pledges to freedom of belief and speech. Of course, even before the twentieth century there had been repeated tension between dominant social ideals and the supposedly guaranteed liberties for minorities such as Roman Catholics, Mormons, the Chinese, and abolitionists. But it was not until after the giant wave of so-called new immigrants from southern and eastern Europe after 1880 and then during the struggles about patriotism during World War I that the tensions between the cultural standard called Americanism and constitutional and cultural liberty became a large issue in American debate and law. Before 1914, there had been very little America civil-liberties law dealing with the insistent monism about the ideals that qualified one for first-class citizenship. The going WASP culture was the powerful norm posited for everyone from blacks to Native Americans to Slavic immigrants. Whatever its price, this culture seemed unchallengeable, and immigrants seemed to conform to its demands about language, the flag, dress, hygiene, and other such matters. The Wilsonian prosecutions of dissenters against the war, some of them foreign-born radicals, intensified the public debate about dissent against the war and community standards of loyalty.[139] That struggle has never ceased, as recent controversies about service in the Vietnam War, burning the flag, and that derivative from pluralism, called multiculturalism, have demonstrated.

About the state, the law, and loyalties, much of the serious American discourse has its source in the opinions of Justice Oliver Wendell Holmes. Starting in 1919, Holmes's dissents in civil liberties cases before the Supreme Court revealed some of the dilemmas in confronting pluralist views of American society, especially in assessing the legitimacy or wisdom of law that tried to restrict the expression of unpopular antiwar,

137. John Higham, *Send These to Me* (Baltimore, 1984), 87–92.

138. Theodore Roosevelt to the American Protective Association, 1919, in *The Letters of Theodore Roosevelt,* ed. Elting E. Morison (8 vols.; Cambridge, Mass., 1954), VIII, 1,422.

139. Harry N. Scheiber, *The Wilson Administration and Civil Liberties, 1917–21* (Ithaca, N.Y., 1960).

anticapitalist opinions.[140] Holmes's own views were based on his brand of relativism about ideals.[141] As an evolutionist, he believed that there was no scientific or philosophic basis for positing permanence for any "value" or for saying that values themselves could be true rather than useful. The American cause in World War I, or any other cultural ideal parading as the truth, did not intrinsically merit supreme loyalty and service over other loyalties to pacifism or bolshevism or imperial Germany. If no ideal or belief could thus pass muster as truth, how could the democratic state ever legitimately enforce its "favorite truth"? However stirring, patriotic ideals expressed for Holmes only transitory preferences. Yet such laws as the Espionage and Sedition Acts of 1917 held citizens accountable for uttered beliefs. Holmes's wrestling with ensuing questions about loyalty shows an unresolved struggle to find public status for his profound skepticism. Although an ideal or loyalty could be, at best, temporarily useful, realism about democratic society suggests that, like any other, it sustains itself and gives itself identity through unsurrenderable ideals. For that "fighting faith" it may even imprison or kill.[142] During World War I the state's claims for the rightness of the cause of democracy were pressed against dissenting radicals like Schenck, Abrams, and Debs, who questioned whether "Mr. Wilson's war" was indeed a struggle to make the world safe for democracy. After siding with the majority in 1919 that Schenck and Debs had violated the Sedition law, Holmes in subsequent dissents reiterated that prosecution for expressing unpopular opinions could be understood not because America had truth and right on its side but because the state had what he called the "ultimata ratio," the power to do as it wished on behalf of what it took to be true.[143] "Took to be true" because, like any individual, society and state had to have some basis for judgments. If they believed strongly in their ideals, as Holmes confessed, they "can't help" positing them as truth. But that did not *make* these ideals true or entitle government to proscribe other views.

140. Max Lerner, ed., *The Mind and Faith of Justice Holmes* (Boston, 1943), contains the famous dissents and other opinions, with the editor's comments.

141. There is a good reprise of Holmes's relativism in White, *Social Thought in America*. For the full career, see David H. Burton, *Oliver Wendell Holmes, Jr.* (Boston, 1980).

142. Arguments about Holmes's ideas are collected in David H. Burton, ed., *Oliver Wendell Holmes: What Manner of Liberal?* (Huntington, N.Y., 1979).

143. Holmes's concurrences in the 9–0 Supreme Court decision against Schenck and in the Debs case in 1919 can be found in Lerner, *Mind and Faith of Justice Holmes*. His concurrence in the conviction of Frohwerk, also in 1919, is in *Frohwerk v. United States*, 249 U.S. 204 (1918). Later that year he moved into the dissenting role for which he is better remembered. But the first three cases are important for majoritarian themes that did not disappear from Holmes's later dissents.

Holmes never worked out systematically the vexatious questions that he and the court repeatedly faced in the aftermath of the wartime Espionage and Sedition Acts and the "Red scare" of 1919 and 1920. To the extent that his memorable phrases still form the main premises of civil libertarians, the ambiguities in his attempts to draw lines between free expression and state-enforced orthodoxy endure.[144] His efforts to increase American tolerance, or as we might now say, "respect for pluralism," were not helped by his inability to resist his literary flourishes in phrases like "best test for truth," "free marketplace for ideas," "clear and present danger." In dealing with dissenters, a phrase like "the best test for truth" is confusing. If ideals cannot be true, how can one test for truth or authoritatively invoke any public ideal to which there was, allegedly, a "clear and present danger"? Abrams and the other wartime dissenters went to jail because the American government acted as though their pamphlets or speeches, as ideas, did imperil waging war on behalf of American truth.[145] In effect, the majority of the court refused to view the world as the ever-evolving cosmos without any moral certainties that Holmes stoically accepted. Even if, as he wrote, "time has upset many fighting faiths," for any moment, at least, the court held that the current American faith was invocable against dissenting minorities.

With the end of the war these first forays into pluralism about loyalty and dissent diminished. For the next generation or so, pluralism as a word and as a doctrine remained largely within the academy. Horace Kallen, joined by John Dewey, continued to explore the themes, and younger minds like Robert MacIver further developed arguments against absolute sovereignty and for cultural diversity.[146] When it came to public policy about immigrants and blacks, most liberals were assimilationists, not pluralists. Against historic prejudices they urged the admission of minorities to the full benefits of equal opportunity. They did not question the cultural hegemony of Anglo-American customs, law, and language. Their assimiliationism was a more generous Americanism, but it remained monistic nonetheless. When the sociologist

144. Post-Holmesian developments in civil liberties are traced in Milton R. Konvitz, *Expanding Liberties* (New York, 1966). See also Archibald Cox, *Freedom of Expression* (Cambridge, Mass., 1981).

145. Richard Polenberg, *Fighting Faith: The Abrams Case, the Supreme Court, and Free Speech* (New York, 1987).

146. Horace Kallen, *Culture and Democracy in the United States* (New York 1924); John Dewey, *The Public and Its Problems* (New York, 1927). There are postwar summaries of pluralist ideas of authority and their critics in Francis W. Coker, *Recent Political Thought* (New York, 1934), Robert MacIver, *Community* (London, 1920), and *The Modern State* (London, 1926).

Robert E. Park launched his important studies of American racism in the 1920s, he was committed not to maintaining an African cultural heritage within American freedom but to extending a common identity and uniform justice for all races in America.[147] As yet, other writers had done little to explore the distinctive historical-cultural differences among American groups and how they might "pluralistically" coexist.[148] For most liberal scholars before the 1950s, including the illustrious Gunnar Myrdal, there seemed to be nothing culturally distinctive in black life that merited encouragement. Blacks were, simply, Americans with darker skins who had been denied their rights. As for more recognition of the cultural loyalties of recent immigrants, if they did not wish to adopt traditional Americanism by following advice like Theodore Roosevelt's and forsake the old-country ways, they were increasingly urged to "contribute" to that new cultural monism, an amalgam of all customs and beliefs in the much-lauded melting pot of democracy.

Among the immigrants themselves after 1920, or at least for their spokesmen, the early calls of Kallen and Bourne for openly maintaining old identities within American freedom seemed to fall on deaf ears. In dealing with the America outside their enclaves, the first and second generations of the post-1880 immigrants bet that Roosevelt had read their prospects correctly.[149] The road to success in America required seeming as American as possible, in language, habits, religion, patriotic loyalty, and even, if "making it" so required, Americanizing the old-country family name or converting to some branch of American Protestantism.

We lack substantial histories of how all these painful drives to a place under the American sun worked themselves out after 1920. An accumulating analysis building on the pathbreaking work of scholars like John Higham, Nathan Glazer, and Milton Gordon has tantalized us about how complex and rich the tale of diversity is and how basic it also is to understanding recent, if not all of, American history.[150] These stud-

147. The essays before 1930 are in Robert Ezra Park, *Collected Papers* (New York, 1974).

148. Higham, *Send These to Me*, 214–20.

149. The view from the 1940s that few groups had been resisting assimilation is strongly maintained in the second volume of the influential series under W. Lloyd Warner, *Yankee City: The Status System of a Modern Community* (New Haven, 1942). Ten years later, Will Herberg found in the reformulated doctrines of the three principal American religious groups small signs of resistance to assimilation. Herberg, *Protestant-Catholic-Jew* (Garden City, N.Y., 1955).

150. A notable attempt to emphasize the importance of pluralism across American history is in Daniel J. Boorstin, *The Americans* (3 vols.; New York, 1958, 1965, 1973). For early America, see Gary B. Nash, *Red, White, and Black: The Peoples of Early America* (Englewood Cliffs, N.J., 1982). For the same period but about whites' contests with whites, see Bernard Bailyn, *Voyagers to the West* (New York, 1986). The large, long-term

ies also make clear that the first pleas for cultural pluralism by Bourne and Kallen had completely neglected problems of race and had underestimated the power struggle immigrants would have to undertake against the dominant culture. Even more, no one emphasized the historic enmities among cultural and racial minorities or foresaw the bitter fights for honor and reward once the state offered them. The struggles after 1920 within the localities and states by various "ethnics" for political posts and social acceptance as good Americans presaged a culture far more barbed and power-conscious about place and pay-off than the first pluralists anticipated. The general experience of immigrants with WASP America suggested that insisting on a distinctive identity, as Kallen had urged on American Jews, would bring the lowest jobs, barriers in housing, schools, clubs, and professionals, often through open and enforced quotas, and social disdain and mockery. The determination to bypass such prejudice and win shares from the American pot of gold strengthened the drive at least to seem assimilated and not to parade the immigrant's previous culture. But among their own, inside the families and neighborhoods, the old ways, languages, and especially religious faiths resisted giving way to Americanization or melting into something else, even if ever changing, ever new. The old ways figured in intense ethnic rivalries and intergenerational struggles to hold to the heritage while trying to play simultaneously the American game of seeming no different from anyone else.[151] The aim was to be acceptable when crossing onto WASP terrain in schools and employment. The battles varied depending on the ethnic group and its ideals, its size, its location in America, and the time the group had been here. Catholic immigrants, for example, not only sharply divided along national lines of Irish, Italian, Slovak, and German in parish affairs but created virtually alternative Americas of churches, stores, parochial schools and colleges, fraternal societies, festivals, and rules about dating and marriage.[152] These Catholic Americans derived special energy from a powerful church with a worldwide hierarchy, impressive resources, and good reasons to keep its followers mindful of a Catholic way of life against the temptations of the domi-

tale of immigration and the enduring influence of ethnic groups has been the lifework of Oscar Handlin ever since he published *The Uprooted* (1951). For Milton Gordon, see *Assimilation in American Life: The Role of Race, Religion, and National Origins* (New York, 1964).

151. Higham, *Send These to Me*, 214–15; George M. Marsden, *Religion and American Culture* (Orlando, 1990), 187–93; Ronald H. Bayor, *Neighbors in Conflict: The Irish, Germans, Jews, and Italians of New York City, 1929–1941* (Urbana, Ill., 1988).

152. Robert A. Orsi, *Madonna of 115th Street: Faith and Community in Italian Harlem, 1880–1950* (New Haven, 1955).

nant Protestant America. In his private life Al Smith was an observant Catholic, but on the public scene, Catholicism was presented "only" as his religion, a faith like the others that all good Americans maintained.[153] When a LaGuardia or Cermak or a Lehman won elections in their locales before World War II, they came before the public as "just as American" as their WASP predecessors. Virtually nothing was said about their Italian, Slovak, or Jewish background or involvements with those minorities. Still, they obtained many votes from among "their own kind" precisely because they were somehow recognizable as "one of our own."[154]

Given the priority on seeming publicly as American as possible, it followed that most of the struggles for acceptance by immigrants before 1940 did not call for programs for government enhancement of minority identity. Instead, the first and second generation of ethnics took on WASP America by becoming "acceptable" and claiming for themselves that great established American ideal, equal opportunity. The premise was that all citizens deserved the chance to show their worth without their "background" disqualifying them in advance for jobs, schooling, and housing. And if the background was not emphasized before WASP potentates by using foreign languages, dress, and foods, so much the better.

Although most of the histories of cities and states after 1920 about these struggles still need to be written, we are left with the strong impression that special government recognition for minorities involved largely ceremonial matters like allowing government employees time off for celebrating Mardi Gras or St. Patrick's Day. But within the local political parties, the ethnics were learning the ropes and winning places. Among the same minorities, however, problems about sustaining identities were weightier than having a WASP mayor march in a Hibernian parade. Sore points for ethnic and religious minorities before 1945 included questions like the place of Catholic and Jewish schools in the community system, the obligatory flag salute or reading from Protestant bibles in schools, quotas in employment and college admissions, absences from school or jobs for religious observances, provisions for translation in courtrooms and other public offices for non-English-speaking citizens, and the fairness of jury selection, electoral districting, nominating candidates, and voting requirements.[155]

153. Oscar Handlin, *Al Smith and His America* (Boston, 1958), 182–84.
154. Arthur Mann, *LaGuardia Comes to Power* (Philadelphia, 1965).
155. John W. Allswang, *A House for All Peoples: Ethnic Politics in Chicago, 1890–1940* (Lexington, Ky., 1971); Joseph C. Roucek and Bernard Eisenberg, *American Ethnic Politics* (Westport, Conn., 1982); Michael Novak, *The Rise of the Unmeltable Ethnics* (New York, 1972).

While these local struggles went on, nationally, the New Deal relief legislation did not single out any racial, ethnic, or religious group for special qualification or disqualification. Indeed, one of the sore points in New Deal programs was that local officials in the South tried to disqualify blacks from federal farm relief funds, although the intention of the law was to treat all needy farmers equally.[156] The one large matter after 1920 in which public policy was openly one-sided was the immigration quota system of 1924 that clearly favored northern Europeans for entry. But the complaint was that the system did not treat all groups equally, with a blind eye to national origins. The quotas or exclusions violated the equal opportunity to come to America and to try the great game.[157] Supreme Court decisions after the 1930s against the white primary and required public oaths and ceremonies like the flag salute were to the same effect.[158] If Jehovah's Witnesses or any blacks profited from such federal intervention, they did so as a by-product of attempts to enlarge general freedom of conscience and a race-free politics, not the court's desire to single out or reward a special group. In national politics, electoral appeals to minorities or the staffing of political parties and the White House with specialists in their needs and wishes did not take hold until well after World War II. Presidents might bring a few Jews and Catholics into their cabinets or the judiciary despite growls from the old stock, but not until the 1960s did presidential candidates court minorities through photographs of themselves eating pizza or donning yarmulkes. The accepted style for presidential candidates was to speak to all citizens simply as "my fellow Americans" and to deprecate or keep silent about other loyalties. As late as 1952, when Samuel Lubell published *The Future of American Politics,* which stressed the patterns of recent voting by minorities, it came as a surprise how much national balloting in the previous generation seemed to have been colored by what German, Irish, Slavic, Italian, and Jewish Americans thought about foreign policy and related matters like immigration.

The merging of minority drives for respect and reward with ideals of cultural pluralism began during World War II. That was an appropriate moment not only for rediscovery of Americanism but also, somewhat contradictorally, for minorities to come into their own and from under

---

156. Nancy Weiss, *Farewell to the Party of Lincoln* (Princeton, 1983). On the more general subject of blacks during the New Deal, see Paul Mertz, *New Deal Policies and Southern Rural Poverty* (Baton Rouge, 1978); and see Paul Conkin, *Tomorrow a New World* (Ithaca, N.Y., 1959), 200–203, on the TVA towns for whites only.

157. John Higham, *Strangers in the Land* (New Brunswick, N.J., 1955).

158. Commager, ed., *Documents of American History,* 613–22, on the flag salute, 676–78 on the white primary.

the shadow of being "aliens," "un-American" or "hyphenated." Being 100 percent American now began to invite asserting the old identities publicly, symbolized by such prosaic changes as introducing pizza into daily American fare and quickly making it as American as apple pie. The lumpy blend of traditional incompatibles, Americanism and ethnicity, also began to influence intellectuals for whom ideas of cultural pluralism had slowly been gaining appeal since 1920.[159] As the Americanized grandchildren of immigrants began to gain jobs and promotions despite previous or lingering prejudice,[160] it became easier to acknowledge a Jewish or Catholic background. There was less need to ape the Brahmins or WASPs and fly false colors of an assumed WASP identity.

In the general population, there was another incentive to abandon a demeaning assimilation. In the face of the totalitarian attacks on races and creeds other than those approved by the state, America in World War II began to appreciate the murderous potential of prejudice. The nation began to proclaim proudly its diversity and dedication to equal justice for all minorities. Official celebrations of cultural diversity, what some have called soft pluralism, became irresistible against fascist hatred for decadent democracies of impure breeds and racial mongrelization. Affirming their patriotism also by joining the armed forces was another way for German-and Italian-Americans and the Nisei Japanese-Americans to dissociate themselves from the fascist ancestral lands overseas. Still, the older hunger for cultural monism and racist standards lingered in such acts as sending Japanese-Americans *en masse* to detention camps and in keeping the armed forces heavily segregated.

The assertions of diversity and pride in heritage were still heavily ceremonial and celebratory and did not involve government funding to promote or reward minorities or their mores as such. By 1945 it followed that minority groups began to run on two tracks. They were still drawn by the advantages of assimilation, but they were also now encouraged openly to cherish their old identities in public ceremonies, festivals, and publications such as, for notable example, the new American-Jewish magazine *Commentary*. During the war, the proud observance of "I Am an American" Day had emphasized the diverse composition of "American." At public meetings and ethnic holidays by the 1950s, Irish, Italian, or Israeli flags were flown alongside the Stars and Stripes. Soviet hegemony over Eastern Europe and the founding of Israel in 1948 encouraged minorities to press openly for foreign policies favorable to cap-

159. Higham, *Send These to Me*, 214–20.
160. Diana Trilling, "Lionel Trilling: A Jew at Columbia," *Commentary*, LXVII (1979).

tive or new nations. Secretary of State Dulles' promise to seek liberation, not merely containment, for nations behind the Iron Curtain was calculated in part to have electoral appeal for Americans with ancestors east of the Oder-Neisse line.

Although legitimating pluralism in such varied ways had important cultural roots and seismic effects, the demographic growth and time in America of the post-immigrant minorities created greater self-confidence and know-how. Also, large numbers of recent citizens had organizations and votes that carried weight in a democratic polity. Whatever the reasons for the flowering of pluralism, it brought to the fore the long-lingering questions of how encouraged minority concerns could harmonize with each other as well as fit, as originally intended, within a lauded common American patriotism. Broadening pluralism also had to encourage resistances both to Americanization and to the melting pot. It was also clear that any substantial, distinctive cultural identity ultimately must rest on some unsurrenderable ideal: a language, a faith, dietary laws. If everything from the past was surrenderable or dilutable, what was the sense of championing cultural pluralism against the claims of both Americanization and the melting pot? For Jews who observed the Mosiac law, "American" or "Yankee" ways, pure or mixed with Jewish observances, could imply contamination or even defilement. Devout Catholics had to be leery about the strong Protestant coloration and free churches of American life. Similarly, many immigrant parents had to be reluctant to anticipate their children's challenging the patriarchal family and its common life through language, church, and those old-country ways. Yet, paradoxically and painfully, only Americanization continued to suggest success for those same parents.

The more pluralist doctrine caught on, the more the cultural consequences of its political and social victories became problematic. It was one thing for Randolph Bourne to ask American society to recognize and respect diverse ideals and to find room for them alongside his socialist egalitarianism, free speech, broadened majority rule, and so on. But it was another game to call upon government, for example, to use the schools and other modes of public spending to enliven plural loyalties because Jews or Hispanics or blacks or Asians or Native Americans might not wish to become 100 percent WASP or, rather, might wish to keep what they wanted from their ancestral cultures while they also "did the American thing," like becoming consumers, baseball fans, or movie goers.

Whatever choices were made, there lingered an ambiguity at the heart of a hearty pluralism like Kallen's: an *individual* Jew's free choice to assimilate could conflict with claims of his minority *group* that a 100 percent American identity was a chimera and that satisfactory and honest identity would only come by staying with one's "own kind" and by not shamefully denying the past by "trying to pass," even in the name of an American right to choose.[161] This theme was prophetic of claims made three generations later during debates about multiculturalism. Strong loyalty to a separate heritage could shrink or oppose much that a pluralistic America would still need in shared custom and belief. Sociologically, it seems impossible for any society to work well without strong common beliefs. Morally, an attack against the prejudice and cultural privilege of the past should not jettison such old ideals as the rule of law, equal protection of the laws, equal opportunity, and votes for all adults. Neither Bourne nor Kallen had questioned those older American ideals, for they had envisioned minority loyalties as fruitful adjuncts to the best of the existing American ideals. As pluralism strengthened its appeal after 1950, practical issues about both the old and the new ethnic identities had to be confronted. Specifically, what was to be rejected or abandoned, what resisted or retained, what mixed or diluted? And how could any search for identity in a liberal democracy be other than individual? If pluralism began as a defense of group ideals, could it avoid ending as an enlarged individualism, with everyone making up his own America? If white culture or the WASP world turned out to be less alluring than assimilationists assumed, could Hasidism or the Black Muslims substitute for the dominant ethos? On what basis could coexistence and crossover be negotiated? For example, the sheer weight of the numbers who spoke only English seemed to guarantee that it would remain the common language of America. Its pervasiveness *had* to erode the hold of other languages, even if they were given tolerance or social leeway as words like *ciao, chutzpah,* or *chic* came into general parlance. If minority languages were gradually displaced by English, how much vitality would be left in the minority cultures? Pluralist strategy, when involving strong assertion about language and other cultural distinctions, found it difficult to avoid being too particular. And that particularity in the heritage of many minorities included deep Old World animosities toward other countries. Irish-English hatred, for a notable example, had not disappeared after a tide of Irish immigrants began to arrive in America after the 1840s. More than a century later, group sentiments and competitiveness about superiority, precedence, and preferment were to be stimulated by pluralist designs to keep the old-country cultures vibrant and honored. The historical and socio-

---

161. Higham, *Send These to Me,* 205–10; Norman Podhoretz, *Making It* (New York, 1967), on the problems of Jewish identity as they affected the founding and mission of *Commentary* in the 1940s.

logical pertinence of these American dilemmas remains to be appreciated, let alone gauged adequately for their political effects.[162]

The pursuit of countervailing minority power against the old American WASP culture was to bring costs along with its rewards. As competition enlarged among minorities for power and status, it sporadically invited counter-power-mongering, counter-ignorance, counter-prejudices, and counter-hatreds like those of Catholics against Protestants, Christians against Jews, Cypriots and Turks against Greeks, Sicilians against mainland Italians, and, most notably, white Americans against blacks. All such darker antagonisms came in the bright pluralist package known as "respect for heritage."

There was an early foretaste of difficulties in the later pluralist logic about support for diversity as the nation became aware of what the defeat of the Native American tribes had done to tribal life and as efforts were made in the courts and in legislation in the 1920s to improve tribal conditions. Were American Indians (as they were then called) conquered nations or cultures in residence on United States soil? Were they now citizens under American law only in some respects? Were they entitled to all American rights? Preserving tribal life could run almost at right angles to the ideal of full American rights for all who lived within the United States.[163] If, as one view of pluralistic Americanism implied, Native Americans should be as free as anyone to exercise the full range of American rights, including the right to buy and sell property and to live where one liked, that goal could subordinate the old tribal ties and claims over their members and lands to United States law and justice. If Native American culture was to be encouraged, which was to have priority: tribal custom under medicine men or public school teachers on the reservations; smoke and drum signals or telephones and radios; the words of the chiefs or majority rule (including women) at tribe meetings; individual, private

162. Ray A. Billington, *The Protestant Crusade* (Gloucester, Mass., 1963), and Higham, *Strangers in the Land*, give earlier parts of the story of anti-immigrant prejudice. A recent assessment of the effects of the reverse prejudice behind extreme claims of multiculturalism is in Arthur Schlesinger, Jr., *The Disuniting of America* (New York, 1992).

163. Earlier legal dilemmas about Native American rights are best revealed in the singular work on their behalf in the law and the courts undertaken by Felix S. Cohen. For a summary, see his "Indian Rights and the Federal Courts," *University of Minnesota Law Review* (1940). See also his *Handbook of Federal Indian Law* (Albuquerque, 1971). A general, more recent work on the federal government and the Indians is Francis P. Prucha, *The Great Father: The United States Government and the American Indians* (2 vols.; Lincoln, Nebr., 1984). For the mid-century dilemmas of a leading administrator of Indian affairs, see John Collier, *Indians of the Americas* (New York, 1947). Compare with Lawrence C. Kelly, *The Assault on Assimilation: John Collier and the Origins of Indian Policy Reform* (Albuquerque, 1983). Vine Deloria, *We Talk, You Listen: New Tribes, New Turf* (New York, 1970), represents some later versions of old dilemmas within the tribes.

homesteads or tribal property in common? The white "American way," if invoked by individual Indians to claim the rights of American citizens, could further weaken the already decimated tribal bonds.[164]

Another preview in the 1920s of later pluralist tensions was in the black nationalist movement.[165] Most blacks then were not won by the appeals of Marcus Garvey to nurture a distinctive black or African heritage, including plans for returning to Africa on Garvey's Black Star steamship line. Their goals were heavily integrationist. Most black leaders not only opposed the interloper Garvey but, as integrationists, needed to play down whatever he said about remaining distinctively black. They insisted that blacks were no different than other Americans except for the accident of skin color. To say that blackness made for unexpungeable differences could encourage not only black cultural separatism but also a strongly restrictive white racism with an emphasis on permanent racial differences reminiscent of Garvey's idea. One great difference, however, between blacks and ethnics in estimating the appeal of an older tradition was not only ineradicable color but that, after three centuries in America, a black culture from Africa was far less vibrant than the still fresh and practiced European traditions of whites. An African heritage that had to be *resuscitated* would be far thinner for blacks than the still lively old-country heritage was for recent immigrants from Europe. "Africanism" often seemed abstract, almost fabricated, compared with the enduring and large givenness of the religion, language, customs, foods, songs, and tales in the post-immigrant neighborhoods in America. There were other lessons for the future from Garveyism. As a description of a culture, *African* is as general as *European* or *Asian*: there are many Africas, and not all of them are black. And would a more fulsome American Africanism include tribal wars, slavery, and the subjugation of women? With the collapse of the Garvey movement, such questions remained dormant until the 1960s, when the power of the pluralist call to affirm a former culture forced established black leaders to share places, albeit dubiously, with black nationalists like Elijah Mohammed and Malcolm X.[166] In contrast, by the 1970s it would have been strange for Italian-Americans like Frank Sinatra or the popular indus-

---

164. A wide-ranging survey and analysis of the clash of cultures is in Harold E. Fey and D'Arcy McNickle, *Indians and Other Americans* (New York, 1970).

165. Judith Stein, *The World of Marcus Garvey: Race and Class in Modern Society* (Baton Rouge, 1986); Theodore Draper, *The Rediscovery of Black Nationalism* (New York, 1970).

166. E. U. Essien-Udom, *Black Nationalism* (Chicago, 1964), chap. 11, on black responses to the Black Muslim movement; Eugene Wolfenstein, *The Victims of Democracy: Malcolm X and the Black Revolution* (Berkeley, 1981).

trialist Lee Iacocca to find significant opposition to their newly extolling their Italian roots.

By 1945, growth in political power and negotiating skills had gradually brought place and respectability in many localities for ethnic minorities.[167] Blacks did not proportionately profit, but, although slowly, larger numbers were completing high school and college or moving into professional or higher paying jobs. From those ranks of the black bourgeoisie were to come many of the leaders of the civil rights movement.[168] As ethnic and religious barriers to equal rights for blacks in jobs, education, housing, and the professions began to decline and as minorities felt more honor and strength in political contest, difficulties like those of the Native Americans and the Garvey movement about the loss of heritage rose within minority enclaves. Ethnic leaders now began to question the paramountcy of everything "American" and to try to set themselves off not only from the old American stock but from other minorities.[169] Although the post-1945 pluralist creed also proclaimed brotherhood and comity among Americans of "richly different backgrounds," the less sentimental view has to stress how much the numbers and group awareness of the ethnics and the successes of ethnic and racial politics began to create that political minefield of sensitivities and interests about minority needs and recognition that came to be called multiculturalism.[170]

Endorsement of pluralist ideals enormously complicated the tasks of governing a nation of interest groups for which honor for minorities and economic entitlements became entwined. For all their spread after 1933, New Deal economic entitlements had involved measurable, finite, material needs. After all, there were so many farmers raising this or that crop with this or that dollar income and acreage who might merit price supports. But entitlement programs after 1965 aimed at enhancing feelings of precedence and prestige or at repairing psychological hurt and a sense of cultural deprivation were trying to accomplish goals that may be limitless. It was the vague boundaries of such sensitivities that were to make for enormous political complications. Civil rights programs, court decisions about the racial, gender, and ethnic (not merely economic) representation on juries, minority membership in police and fire forces and the military, exemption from certain duties during

167. Nathan Glazer and Danid P. Moynihan, *Beyond the Melting Pot: The Negroes, Puerto Ricans, Jews, Italians, and Irish of New York City* (Cambridge, Mass., 1963).

168. Harvard Sitkoff, *The Struggle for Black Equality, 1954–1980* (New York, 1981); Sar Levitan, William Johnston, and Robert Taggert, *Still a Dream: The Changing Status of Blacks Since 1960* (Cambridge, Mass., 1975).

169. Novak, *The Rise of the Unmeltable Ethnics;* Edgar Litt, *Beyond Pluralism: Ethnic Politics in America* (Glenview, Ill., 1970).

170. Nathan Glazer, *Ethnic Dilemmas, 1964–1982* (Cambridge, Mass., 1983).

military service for women as well as for observant Jews or Moslems, the cultural images and other content of curriculum, scores on intelligence, aptitude, and achievement tests, representation on the platform at civic and public school ceremonies, fears for the fate of fellow ethnics or religiosi behind the Iron Curtain or in countries like Israel or Communist China—all these and others created great difficulty in fulfilling the demand that the state fund and honor minority wishes in domestic as well as foreign policies. And the webs of these entitlements were to be spun not only from Washington but at every level of government that minorities could affect.

In the immediate prelude to the appearance of these new webs, it is striking that the most consequential federal interventions about minority rights up to 1965, the Brown decision against segregated schools (1954) and the civil rights legislation of 1964 and 1965, were still cast in the traditional mode of government enlarging opportunity. Most black and white leaders for civil rights then viewed the century of segregation and of violating blacks' voting rights as denying them as individuals the chance to show what they could achieve, given a fair shot. The message of Martin Luther King, Jr., was strongly to that effect: enforce for blacks the constitutional rights that had become law by 1870, and America would be in sight of the promised land.[171] What in fact followed the landmark actions of 1954, 1964, and 1965 transformed pluralist emphasis on guaranteeing opportunity into the notably different politics of affirmative action. Black disappointments with legal and political equality, the great goal before 1965, led to demands for racially targeted programs that would enable blacks to "catch up" in education, housing, jobs, government contracts. They then could move into positions where their new legal and political rights would bring more substantial results in income and better jobs. The Equal Employment Opportunity Commission, authorized in the 1964 legislation, soon filed suits for racial preference in hiring and promotion. Another signal for this new departure was given by Lyndon Johnson just after the momentous legislation of 1964 and 1965 in what became known as his famous parable of the footrace: "You do not take a person who for years has been hobbled by chains and liberate him, bring him up to the starting line of a race and then say, 'You are free to compete with all others,' and still justly believe that you have been completely fair."[172]

The political logic and very complicated strategies to make the race

171. Taylor Branch, *Parting the Waters: America in the King Years, 1954–1963* (New York, 1988).

172. Quoted in Daniel Seligman, "Affirmative Action is Here to Stay," *Fortune,* April 19, 1982.

fairer were clear. The case had been made obvious in the Reconstruction debacle a century earlier. With blacks being numerically only a small part of the American population in 1965, they could be at constant disadvantage electorally in Congress and in most state legislatures even if all qualified blacks did vote. The other America would have to decide, as a matter of equity and social comity, to help blacks make more of their lives than available through their formal legal and electoral equality. Without such help it seemed that American society would not move fast enough to bring blacks adequate reward. In logic, racially targeted state action seemed inescapable. In the 1960s, black leaders and their white allies began to press the government for special support for blacks as a race. At the federal and other levels, various programs of affirmative action soon followed. Many are still in place in the 1990s.

But a larger signal had been given. If blacks could obtain affirmative action, why could not women, gays, the disabled, and an ever-growing list of ethnic groups? The new politics of "hard pluralism," of laws underwriting minority aspirations and granting various tangible benefits, was alerting many minorities about honor and reward for their group and was sharpening their discontents about their inadequate status. We must recall how far the politics of expectations and entitlements, of going to the state for *economic* needs, had already proceeded in the thirty years since 1933 and how much sensitizing of and muscle-flexing among ethnics had already occurred in cities and states before 1965. Also relevant by then was the near-prospect of more than 50 percent of living Americans having had no ancestors in America before 1900. Many voters were thus potentially available to become sensitive to ethnic issues. By 1965, moreover, the third and fourth generations were already more secure in one important American part of their identity, *i.e.*, in the money and power many had already wrested from the system. Local politics had also taught their leaders savvy about the political game and how to press their needs. And the ballot, pressure groups, and the media, as well as the rhetoric of pluralism, were readily available to make their ethnic loyalties into potent political forces. For quite different purposes, therefore, and with rising anxieties and expectations about the distribution of cultural entitlements, a widening array of minority leaders sought the state for redress and reward.

The new departures in entitlements that occurred across all tiers of American government added laws openly aimed at increasing income, contracts, jobs, promotions, school admissions, and cultural enhancement such as the teaching of Swahili and Afro-American history in high schools and colleges. From the outset, such targeted support angered many citizens, by no means only WASPs, required to step aside if tra-

ditional hiring and promotion practices stood in the way of better results for a disadvantaged group. Anger, if not rage, about affirmative action was to become one of the most potent forces in American politics
after the 1970s. In the Nixon years, his strategists were already appealing to voters' feelings of cultural alienation from the Democrats in
order to solidify "the emerging Republican majority." With those cultural battle lines already drawn, post-Nixon politicians like Ronald Reagan were quick to denounce mandated quotas or goals as radical devi-
ations from the American mainstream ideal of legal equality to seek
opportunity. Those in the media who approved the new programs seemed
reluctant to recognize or report how divisive the new "equality of results" was, fearing to amplify antagonism by acknowledging it. But
the politicians knew soon enough where the votes were as cities like
Boston, Chicago, and Los Angeles were stirred by political wars and violence over ethnic and racial turf. The resentment, however, did not follow clear class or other group lines. Greek-Americans, for example, could
be angered as whites or males or Greeks against favors for blacks or
females or, in foreign policy, for Turkey, a NATO ally.

The logic for the special entitlements had been latent in the earliest
pluralist arguments. If state and society were to sustain the widest possible pluralism, government should intervene to create a more diverse
share of jobs and to enhance, with special schooling or cultural programs, recognition for groups that felt disadvantaged in ordinary social
competition. Prejudices and slights that the republic had blithely lived
with under WASP domination before about 1920 became publicly de-
nounceable in an America now heavily populated by minorities with
adroit leaders and allies. Stories that "everybody knows" and floods
of investigations and reports easily showed prejudice or insufficient sensitivity about blacks, women, gays, Koreans, Hispanics, single parents,
AIDS victims, the handicapped, *et al*. The expansive pluralist argument
was thus clear: the state should try to redress the balance. Merely prohibiting discriminatory treatment and requiring open advertising that
encouraged minorities to apply for jobs, with promises to interview them,
were not enough.

As the state went to work more extensively for minority betterment
it sometimes pitted once-allied minorities against each other. Jews and
liberals who had been old friends of blacks in fights before the 1960s for
justice were driven away by mandated affirmative action for blacks.
Whites like the South Boston Irish had long included extreme negro-
phobes. Some became violent against state-ordained busing and racial
mixing in Boston schools and neighborhoods. White flight to the suburbs was an attempt to escape from mixed schools and other contacts

with blacks and the feared deterioration of property values and public education.[173] Pluralist justice for specific groups thus seemed to come at the cost of generally decreasing what there was of community among Americans. Earlier in the century, the community implicit in the dominant Americanism had often meant white rule with black subordination, "Anglo" superiority with "Mex" acquiescence, or boss rule over ghetto immigrants. Pluralist ideology had originally envisioned cultural recognition producing stronger, not weaker communal ties among all Americans and certainly not in derogation of all common cultural ties such as extreme black nationalists, for example, seemed to voice. In the original pluralist ideal, respect would replace prejudice and increase "understanding." Instead, in their painful struggles for state support to enhance their sense of their rights and for respect against aggressive or insensitive outsiders, ethnic, racial, gender, and sexual interest groups vied abrasively against each other for state support. They often tried to appear more virtuous than their putative oppressor or rivals for rewards. They glossed over those powerful prejudices within their own circles against whites or males or heterosexuals that clouded their appeals for an America that was more tolerant and more given to good will and fair shares for all. Governments became increasingly alert to minority sensitivities in devising personnel politics, making appropriations, declaring new holidays or public places like those honoring Martin Luther King. Granting extra points to blacks taking civil service examinations or similar favors in appointments within bureaucracies fostered an even greater stake in the state for beneficiaries than existed in the 1930s. Then all groups drew nearer to government for jobs, welfare payments, paving contracts, and so on, but only as generally down-and-out citizens or "the needy." As more affirmative action programs were enacted by the 1980s they stimulated groups to learn how to milk the state to strengthen a growling separateness, and to promise "trouble" if favors were not granted. The union of economic and cultural entitlements invited extremist black stances like "mau-mau-ing" white officials with talk of violence or shutdowns if demands for jobs or community programs were not met.[174] In response, white militants organized and white parents denounced favoritism for blacks at school board and city council meetings. Many whites whose sympathies for blacks had been all-important in

173. Glazer, *Ethnic Dilemmas,* chap. 2, "Negroes and Jews: The New Challenge to Pluralism." For national white animosity, see Peter Benzen, *Whitetown, USA* (New York, 1970).

174. The technique of "mau-mau-ing," named after the ferocious Kenyan resistance to the British, is described in Philip S. Foner, ed., *The Black Panthers Speak* (Philadelphia, 1970), 45–47. See also Draper, *Black Nationalism,* chap. 7.

passing the civil rights legislation of 1964 and 1965 were driven off by zealous black leaders who sneered at "guilty white liberals" or "honkies" getting high on doing something for blacks. And some black leaders, amid the sporadic racism of their own followers, often took any white hostility to their entitlements as evidence of how irreversibly racist all of white America was. Unprejudiced liberal doubts about the *principle* of affirmative action were similarly suspect as white racism.[175]

By 1990, the barbedness of state-succored multiculturalism was apparent in countless daily news stories. One from New York City particularly illustrated the maze of obstacles confronting officials trying just to contain racial and ethnic unrest, let alone restore group harmony. Following a controversial mild verdict against a white youth implicated in a gang murder of a young black, Mayor David Dinkins delivered an unusually forceful speech against hatred and appealed for peace and comity as the American way. Strong approval for the TV talk by voices like the New York *Times* was diluted by negative responses elsewhere about the timing of the speech and by even darker inferences that well-known confrontational minority leaders drew from it. Because of the seeming imminent threat of violence on that day, Friday, the mayor spoke that evening, the Jewish sabbath. An Orthodox Jewish councilman announced that he was "shocked and hurt" by the mayor's insensitivity. But this same "insensitivity" pleased anti-Semitic black and Hispanic leaders who thought the mayor had previously been too deferential to Jewish voters. Because the mayor had also complained about a black boycott of a Korean-American store, other black leaders railed about a black mayor's failure to line up with other blacks against the Korean. They denounced Dinkins as a traitor to his race who "had too many yarmulkes on his head," a revealing reference to the recent habit of politicians' donning Jewish prayer caps when they courted Jewish support. Still others who approved the substance of Dinkins' appeal for harmony complained about his tardiness and his well-known caution about "speaking out."

As in so many other cases, this nasty squabble came to no resolution. Like an alarming fever it ran its course, but left another layer of hurt and rancor on the record of pluralism turning pathological. The principal leftover questions voiced by New Yorkers were how long such hatred could continue without war in the streets, and when, not if, what James Baldwin had once called "the fire next time" would ignite. That white and black demagogues were available to exploit *any* verdict in the New York trial of the white youth was no surprise. What was incalculable

---

175. Glazer, *Ethnic Dilemmas*, pt. 3.

were the size and marshallable militancy of the groups to which the demagogues appealed.[176]

The nostalgic words that entered talk in the 1980s about America's
loss of "social contract," *e.g.*, concord, comity, consensus, social solidarity, civil religion, "habits of the heart," mutuality, could imply an
American past without social struggle or group antagonisms. More ominously, however, any "decline of community" today suggests that if cultural conflicts cannot be negotiated without state intervention, government decisions in minority disputes will reflect only the success of angry
shouts and threats in the legislatures and courts. Social negotiation failing, bitter searches for advantages over other groups inevitably will
enlarge the role of the state in setting cultural priorities and settling squabbles. In the especially sensitive matter of political apportionment, there
developed an increasingly powerful feeling that the only fair district lines
were those promising the election of "one of our own" who "knows our
problems" instead of an "outsider." The byzantine complexities of
ethnic gerrymandering implied that there was no trustable platoon in
America beyond the borders of one's own racial or ethnic enclave. Out
there, in the rest of America, there was only a hostile jungle of the majority or other minorities. The logical response was that the oppressed
elect as many as possible blacks or Puerto Ricans or gays or women or
opponents of abortion.

In one sense, it is traditional American politics to elect someone who
would fight for your interests. What is new, or at least much larger, is the
implication that race or nationality or gender are better guides to nominating and voting than stands on issues like unemployment or improved
schooling. Community ties, unlike "conformity" in American history,
have never been very strong before the appetites set loose by American
competitive individualism. But what feeling there has been among us for
the larger platoon seems especially strained by rising suspicions in our
little platoons about the motives of "other groups" and what "they"
would do to "us" when and if blacks, Zionists, Hispanics, gays, Moonies,
the "moral majority," increase their influence with the state. Today,
the state has to consider that its rehabilitation and resettlement aid to
Vietnam refugees on the Gulf coast deeply offends native fishermen (white
and black) who resent the underwritten new competition from Asian
outsiders.[177] At one point, black extremists held that the government promotion of contraception and the failure to fund more research about
sickle-cell anemia were prompted by genocidal intentions against Amer-

176. "Around City Hall," *New Yorker*, May 28, 1990.
177. "Vietnamese Work Force Encroaches on Natives of Texas Shrimping Towns,"
Washington *Post*, December 26, 1984. See also, New York *Times*, April 7, 1985.

ican blacks.[178] Similar feelings of abuse, persecution, and homophobic genocide have been voiced by some gay group leaders because increases in research and treatment funds for AIDS have not seemed large enough, even though from 1984 to 1992 they went from $100 million to $7 billion in state and federal funds, a sum greater than that for research and treatment for any older and greater killer like cancer and heart disease. Bureaucrats were increasingly hard pressed by the swirl of sensitivities thay had to consider. In order to avoid any minority group rancor and possible crippling of the project, the U.S. Navy specified, when seeking designs for a new memorial in Washington, that any human figures in it not reveal *any* "ethnic type." Facelessness is another tendency of pluralist policy-making by a government that has been driven by the fierceness of ethnic contests to try to offend no one.[179] Was government in the midst of the fabulous fandango of an American culture that had fulfilled so much of the program of cultural pluralism thus to be driven to inanity like the navy project or was it to be engaged largely in a frightened parceling out of entitlements among deeply antagonistic interest groups held together only by expectations of continuing pay-off or pay-out? What would happen if, especially with deficits restricting budgets, the payments stopped, diminished, or were redeployed to groups or purposes that enraged the deprived or unrewarded? Watts and other rampages were viewed as portents of alienated rage.

Another quite different peril of pluralism involved civil rights for hate groups in American society. Is the pluralist state bound to treat the creeds of the Klan or American Nazis or, for that matter, ethnic prejudices against other groups merely as "opinions"? Should the law stop the public expression of hatred, as when the American Nazis parade in Skokie, Illinois, to insult the many descendents of holocaust victims who live there? Does Holmesian freedom for "the ideas we hate" square with another pluralist emphasis on the value of tolerance or brotherhood among groups?[180] Already in the 1940s, pluralism taken as an absolute affected American liberal anti-Catholics like the journalist Paul Blanshard. He found it very difficult to make room in America for a Roman Catholic Church that, as he saw it, was not pluralist within its own confines and that supposedly would cancel American pluralism if it could extend its influence and power.[181] Fifty years later, a similar logic had led to what

178. Robert G. Weisbord, *Genocide? Birth Control and the Black American* (Westport, Conn., 1975).

179. Washington *Post,* December 31, 1986.

180. Robert P. Wolff, Barrington Moore, Jr., and Herbert Marcuse, *A Critique of Pure Tolerance* (Boston, 1965), 81–117.

181. Paul Blanshard, *American Freedom and Catholic Power* (Boston, 1949).

was called political correctness. In extreme form and in the name of respect for multiculturalism, several universities and localities banned expressions of hate or disdain for blacks, women, and homosexuals. Hateful ideas were thus to be eliminated from public discourse because some authority decided that they were offensive as well as intrinsically wrong morally.

Fortunately, millions of minority members resisted extremism even on behalf of their sensitivities and even while vigorously maintaining their group loyalties. Extremism was also blunted by an America with jobs and education increasingly open to all and without denigrating minority loyalties. But how many self-conscious American minorities while remaining law-abiding and opposed to antihate laws were not privately acquiring the all-important pluralist temperament of tolerance, forbearance, and avoidance of abrasive absolutes? The depth of psychological commitment to a pluralist America and to policies of tolerance and "dialogue" among all groups is unclear even if most citizens acquiesce in law and order and do not riot in Los Angeles or assault blacks in Boston or Koreans or Hasidic Jews in Brooklyn. Indeed, the pluralist rhetoric about "dialogue" had become so pervasive on another part of the surface of public life that it seemed almost a psychological denial of much of the harsh feelings about other groups that minorities such as some American Arabs and Zionists brought to their struggles for more influence over Middle East policies. Even a Klan leader in the 1980s seemed affected by ideas of all Americans belonging together when he allegedly said, "All white people should vote for a white candidate regardless of race."

Whatever the moral appeal of pluralism and of its realism about the weight of minorities in American history, the all-important psychological capacity of citizens to live without irritable searching for finality about their favorite beliefs and ideals remains very difficult to achieve. It is very rare, and not only in America, to accept the tentativeness or skepticism about one's own fighting faith or cultural "can't help" that play so attractively in the cultural pluralism of Holmes or John Dewey. Even for pluralists, a restraint about judgment or interfering against "other creeds" is severely taxed by parents whose religious ideals dictate no medical care, transfusions, or injections for their sick children, or in answering those who claim that even a *peaceful* Nazi demonstration in Skokie will be too insulting and provocative, or by minorities demanding bilingualism in public education or tax vouchers for alternative education for groups offended by the moral neutrality or secularism of public schools without prayer.

In the logic of cultural relativism, however, what gives pluralist "respect for individual heritage," surely a vague judgment, invokable priority over racist ideas? When it comes to state action, are not hate or respect only matters of opinion? In the Holmes construction, do not the moral ideals of a Jesus of Nazareth and an Adolph Hitler stand equal, before the state, in free-market contest? And is the pluralist freedom that would refuse the state the right to endorse either view itself ultimately relative, only another transitory fighting faith, however dearly bought and costly to follow? Or is pluralist doctrine about maintaining freedom amid diversity uncompromising and eternal and thus, paradoxically, itself invokable as a truth—an absolute—against any "clear and present danger" to diversity? These remain largely unanswered questions in pluralist theory.[182]

Hansen's Law for the student of immigrant history stated that what the second generation (1920 to 1940) strove to forget during the struggles to be accepted as American, the third generation attempted to reinvigorate.[183] There are signs, however, to the contrary of the barbed ethnicity so featured here. The fourth generation after immigration, not yet mature in Hansen's time (the 1930s), now drifts away from or irreparably waters down what the third generation revived.[184] This change within ethnic enclaves may be occurring even though ethnic leaders still patrol the ramparts, declaiming against affronts or loss of cultural respect. Ethnicity, less so racial feeling, may be lessening because the victories of pluralist ideals and the immense fact of American diversity lowered the threat of the old aggressive Americanism. Similarly, the lure of economic success required minorities to learn to get along with other groups and to be less shrill about their self-esteem. Religious sectarianism also declines because, as Will Herberg observed, assimilation and the need for dialogue about "shared values" and "brotherhood" honed down the sharper tenets of traditional religious orthodoxies like the divinity of Jesus Christ or the chosenness of the Jewish people.[185]

Among the many crosscurrents in pluralist contests, hostile as well as nostalgic identities probably have their hardest going against the tendencies of a continental consumer society. If the assertion of powerful ethnic feelings once had advantages beyond giving the individual his choice of identity, it was as a counterweight to old democratic tendencies to cul-

182. A controversial exploration of invoking pluralism against antipluralists, *i.e.*, the Communist Party, was developed by Sidney Hook in *Heresy, Yes—Conspiracy No!* (New York, 1953).

183. Marcus Lee Hansen, "The Third Generation in America," *Commentary*, XIV (1952).

184. Higham, *Send These to Me*, chap. 10.

185. Herberg, *Protestant-Catholic-Jew*.

tural conformity. That much-marked American impulse is now accented by an industrial culture with mass production and ceaseless advertising bringing citizens to greater uniformities of belief, taste, and style. Yet as American affluence increased after World War II, so did ethnic assertiveness. How can pluralist commitments to enhance cultural diversity be reconciled with the strong structural countertendencies of industrial society to homogeneity? At the same time, how is pluralist thought to contend with those remaining streaks of fanaticism about saving group ideals that the sense of engulfment by a homogeneous, secular materialism seems to accent among religious minorities such as the Hasidic Jews or the minority called "moral majority" of beleaguered Christians? American materialism, although so deplored, has diverted some potential zealots to channel energies into earning money, keeping up with the Joneses, and pleasing all types of customers rather than waging ethnic or creedal battles. Maintaining a special, insistent, and visible minority identity and observing a sabbath on a Friday or Saturday may drive away customers who want to shop in stores staffed by "folks like us" or on just those weekend days. A special identity marked by wearing dashikis or long sidelocks or refusing to eat in the company cafeteria because it served pork may also clash with the work style, holidays, or food choices of the majority of other workers. The bland bureaucratic style of getting along that the great-grandchildren of immigrants encounter as they enter large American firms or government service further undercuts honoring the old culture that the third generation rediscovered. Ethnic defensiveness is either not necessary with a boss who may be another ethnic or it stirs too much anxiety about "being special" and losing out for promotion. That more petulant pluralism called multiculturalism may now be "in," but it still may not pay well to insist on the exclusivity and superiority of your group's unsurrenderable ideal. The Old Amish, determined to remain true to their ideals of Christian simplicity and resistance to temptations and frivolities, have to forego government price supports for their produce as well as microwave ovens, dishwashers, and tractors and trucks for the farm. Orthodox Jewish parents may want to eat only kosher food, but their children at play or in school with gentile children may sneak in the forbidden Big Mac or pepperoni pizza. Overassertive ethnicity about the fate of brother Palestinians or extreme racist ideas may not only keep a true believer at an economic disadvantage but may send him to jail for violence at a rally or even to an early grave as a casualty in a violent demonstration against the Los Angeles justice system. On the other hand, failure to admit more blacks to a larger share of American money and comforts can alienate some black leaders. They sense insincerity in the now professedly multicultural America's reluctance, for example, to fund the study of African cultures in the schools or in its failure to select every black candidate who is nominated or runs for office.

If one thus searches along the full and still-poorly-charted spectrum of pluralist plethora and contest in America, one finds not only the hoped-for approval and growth of minority voices and greater options for belief and policy but a culture far more openly in disarray about its differences than foreseen by Kallen or Bourne. It is a culture beset by tensions, envy, anxieties, frustrations, and bitterness at the costs of affirming and financing pluralist ideals. What began as a noble cultural ideal ends all too often in political mire.

While minority expectations for state support became more numerous and stronger, money is always short. If Congress or the courts declare cuts and limits in entitlements, who among the hypersensitive minority groups would be the first to feel them and the humiliation? Many blacks, Hispanics, and others now believe their groups forever "entitled" to what they have been able to obtain from government. Some of their leaders like Jesse Jackson construe entitlement cuts as willfully prejudiced rather than politically less attentive to black claims. Since cuts in entitlements, like their initiation, derive from the rough trading of group politics, fairness all around, let alone *feelings* of fairness, is chimerical to anticipate. If, over fifty years, expectations about what government could do grew too high and entitlements became sacrosanct, with any consensus about a common Americanism now thinner or far more brittle, little that is fair can be made to seem fair against intransigent minorities. Fear and anger about their status and rewards may be compounded by militants or politicians or affirmative action bureaucrats with heavy interests in keeping minority awareness and income high and rivalries about entitlements fecund.

Although both major parties have developed diverse constituencies awaiting entitlements, the present-day Democratic party especially suffered from enlarging its alliances with minority groups. Increasingly since the 1930s Democrats have championed themselves as defenders of minorities, but by the 1980s they were charged with being captured by "special interests," including not only labor unions but blacks, abortionists, feminists, and gays. The party rules after 1968 mandated choosing convention delegates by guaranteeing quotas of seats to women and various minorities. The sensitivity to local minorities needed, district by district, state by state, to gain delegate votes for the Democratic presidential nomination had the ironic effect of driving the *national* majority, especially white males, toward Republicans or conservative Democratic candidates or away from the voting booth. Such realignments played the theme of the Democrats as the partisans of extremists, outside the "mainstream," or as another phrase, anti-gay in intent, put it, as "San Francisco Democrats."

By the 1990s, however fierce the American minority contest still seems, we return to those other signs that the multicultural society of aggressive minorities may fade, its pugnacious diversity turning out to be transitory. At their best, the temptations of mainstream America have become more weighty in offering not only greater income but also cultural enhancement through more accessible higher education and countless local orchestras, ballet and drama companies. For those resisting such blandishments, the costs of remaining "special" or in exile at home can come very high, as most of the communes of the 1960s discovered.[186] Despised capitalist society provides antibiotics and special-care units for sick children and agricultural research that increases the yield of the commune soybean fields and catfish ponds. Today, the same government that may be urged in the name of multiculturalism to accept bilingualism also underwrites an extraordinary economy with job opportunities that have little room for anything other than a common tongue of English in daily business life. For more recent minorities, however, especially those millions arriving in the Southwest from Mexico and other Western Hemisphere nations, the success of predecessors in establishing local bilingualism and a general pluralist permissiveness about maintaining cultural identity, intermarriage, multilingual ballots, and places for minority members on the ballot suggest that newer minority relations with the extant culture are quite other than the situation that confronted the immigrants who came before 1914.[187] The earlier immigrants faced an Americanism adamant about English, schooling only in WASP values, and cultural esteem for the self-sufficient individual. The immigrant was expected to foreswear labor unions, save for rainy days of unemployment and old age, wear clean white shirts and ties if salaried, and pay cash on the barrel for all purchases. This almost vanished America created immense pressure to conform to such ideals and mores. Today's America for arriving immigrants includes far more "laid-back" styles in work and leisure, welfare state services, encouragement of folk traditions, languages, and cuisine, and democracy's now deep-set politics of enlarging economic and cultural entitlements.[188] These changes promise a foaming political brew, especially from Texas to California but also in scattered other states like New York and Illinois in which many Mexicans or other Hispanics are settling and will be voters. But how long even

186. "The Graying of Aquarius," *Newsweek*, March 30, 1987.
187. Glazer, *Ethnic Dilemmas*, 331–36; Higham, *Send These To Me*, 65–70.
188. David M. Reimers, *Still the Golden Door* (New York, 1985).

encouraged and profitable separateness will endure is not clear. However strong their customs may be while immigrants are still new arrivals, poor, and living in separate geographic and cultural enclaves, eventually most minorities in American history have made peace, however troubled, with the nation's opportunities, cash, and comforts.

Stymied by Success

Rhetorical attacks on the welfare state for the poor obscured the deeper, more difficult issues of the future of the entitlement state for all citizens. Conservative criticism stressed freedom from government, the old American liberty to do with one's own as one liked. It opposed having the lodge, club, job, business, or farm regulated by government or a nest egg destroyed by taxes, inflation, or costs for debt service to provide favors for others. The deeper view is historical. The nation had "jest grewed" to a size and complexity that made for unprecedented and unignorable impingement of needs and interests on each other, regardless of attitudes toward the role of government. If Chrysler Motors fails, the effects roll from coast to coast in jobs lost, home mortgages foreclosed, Chrysler suppliers and dealers shut down, banks with loans to Chrysler out-of-luck—the list goes on. Recall, as examined earlier, that long before the era of big business and the great state, the continental play of freedom and of Jeffersonian ideals of competition were already creating needs for state funding of turnpikes and canals, for example, to enhance opportunity. Recall, too, that painful results from free enterprise in land booms or in issuing dubious paper money also drove citizens to seek ever-more-obliging democratic politicians for relief. The resulting, long-woven interest net, not the recent safety net of the welfare state, is the historic and deeper problem for American legislation and justice. Especially with its new strands of entitlements for ethnic and racial groups, the unravelable interest net makes state retrenchment too costly for mainstream citizens with their own substantial entitlements and very perilous for their legislators to attempt. The size and thickness of the web of the state, so carelessly woven for more than a century, made the deeper labor of bringing it under control formidable. Effectiveness, efficiency, doing a good job for citizens on important tasks that private abilities could not demonstrably accomplish—those were the real tasks that lay inside the nation's Augean stables. Increasingly, they needed cleaning, but the Augean image, of course, suggests that the task might be fruitless. Where the entitlement state recently waned in one program, like legal-aid funding, it waxed in another, like more liberal student loans or AIDS research or expanded Head Start. There was little sign of Herculean leaders or, even more, of major political parties that would nominate such leaders. The purported gridlock or "deadlock of democracy," *i.e.*, the inability of the traditional two-party system to move on large, pressing national matters, pertained not only to president, Congress and the party system, which had long been featured as causing the jam,[189] but to the mutually frustrating interest groups, among them the forty thousand Washington-registered lobbying associations, that tried to bend the political system to advance their entitlements. The problem was, after all, not in government itself, much as Reagan or Gingrich tried to locate it there, but in what the interest groups in free society, including those who were to vote for a Republican Congress in 1994, had come to expect of the state. What matters is not that we have such groups. They are intrinsic to our open and competitive society. What is needed is the politics beyond the lowest common denominator that satisfies only the latest coalition of groups and leaves broader concerns of public policy untended or touched only by gestures.

Once presidents, Congresses, and both parties after the 1930s gradually made it seem that the state was in the business of repairing all tears and frays in the social fabric, it was difficult for any group to be content with the traditional arguments that Americans were largely on their own with only "bad luck," "weakness of character," or "poor judgment" as explanations for personal disaster. Instead, the enlarging scope of government and victories in enlisting its aid over three generations nourished a belief that there is no social opportunity or individual misfortune that cannot be tended by state intervention.[190] Like modern capitalism feeding fantasies about miracles of riches, comfort, and happiness through productivity, the ardor of the search for salvation by state action makes one wonder whether any foreseeable government for Americans could respond adequately to the desires stimulated by what the state already does or promises. Phrases like a New Deal, Great Society, War on Poverty, and New American Paradigm arouse sweet visions of the good life under the service state and its politicians. Government inevitably fails to live up to excessive promises and to keep pace with the appetites and constituencies it has aroused. The welfare benefits office, U.S. employment commission or VA regional offices turn out to be poor substitutes for the Holy Grail of a great society and welfare state promising an end, at last, to such ills as poverty and discrimination. The cadences of King's "I have a dream" mark time for many causes other than civil rights. However, the spectacle of the state that cannot deliver turns evermore

189. Burns, *Deadlock of Democracy.*
190. My sketch of the dynamics of state growth takes off from Schumpeter's analysis of capitalist economic development in *Capitalism, Socialism, and Democracy.*

disappointing and erodes confidence and credibility in it. It alienates intellectuals who may have believed in it earlier but who, in anger at its
failures, lies and intrinsic imperfection, turn their gifts from serving or
praising the welfare state as liberals, to analysis and criticism of it as conservatives or "neo-liberals." Ironically, as Schumpeter suggested about
the fate of advanced capitalism in its turns toward statism, the only
answer for the sickness of the great state seems to be more intrusive government, if only to correct earlier errors and to guard against repeating
mistakes with yet another layer of bureaucracy toward a pain-free society.[191] If capitalist culture's frustrations and interventions lead almost
imperceptibly to overtouted state socialism (in the Schumpeter view),
does state stymie portend some similar pseudo-transcendence in politics?

Over the generations, as we have seen, the state has played a variety
of roles in serving changing national needs. In the Jefferson-Jackson
mode it was an umpire for fairness, pledged to act on behalf of the majority to keep economic contests and state benefits fair. Meanwhile, individuals were to take care of most of their needs by self-help. But a fair
chance at equal and expanding opportunities to enhance growth implicitly demanded the second model, sponsorship, with the state building internal improvements, dams, or space rockets to enlarge enterprise
so that more Americans could have a hopeful run toward the rainbow.

However widened the American game by 1840, it chronically failed
to satisfy all citizens that opportunities or results were adequately equal.
The very openness of the game invited private powers to try to dominate
their marketplace or community. State sponsorship open to all to seek
often did not seem evenhanded in the actual grants for railroads or in
guaranteeing silver purchases. Encouraged activities like the railroads
used their advantages in protested rates, poor service, or favors like re-
bates. The perception of dominated markets and of abusive private powers thus led to a third type of government activity, the regulatory state
on behalf of the "public interest." Overall, however, regulation eventually came to seem no less ambiguous than umpiring or sponsoring. Decisions in the name of the public interest are chronically open to charges
of favoritism, slack, corruption, or excessive zeal.

Umpiring, sponsorship, and regulation helped create the fourth role
for government, the client state. Over the decades, the client state gave
its ear to farmers wanting free homesteads, lumber interests intent on
their style of forest conservation, prohibition groups wanting alcohol
banned, and affirmative action forces seeking set-asides for black contractors.

191. Otis L. Graham, *Toward a Planned Society: From Roosevelt to Nixon* (New
York, 1976).

More lofty than the preceding styles was the fifth, the crusading state. That role is intrinsic in classic expressions of American purpose like the "pursuit of happiness," a "more perfect union," "promote the general welfare." This mode marks dramatic, breakthrough moments in our history, when slaves were freed or battles waged for a world made safe for democracy or for the Four Freedoms. The style often uses the rhetoric of a war—against poverty or racism, or to secure family values. The chronic danger is the temptation to grandiosity and self-delusion in generous wishes, like ending racism or ridding the world of "power politics" and the "old diplomacy." Great moments when the state seems to act for the highest moral interests are those that need most scrutiny for what Reinhold Niebuhr called "irony." Under the spell of doing God's work, citizens and leaders act with too little reflection about the selfish interests and unpleasant consequences that may come in the train of attempting the holy.

Cautionary notes are most pertinent for the latest and sixth model of how American government works, the broker state. This model evolved largely to describe post–New Deal America. Government tries to abandon old pretensions to playing the distant impartial umpire, to sponsoring only well-connected or party-loyal clients, or to pursuing a national vision. Instead, it claims to open itself impartially to the American winds of doctrine and interest. A *New Yorker* cartoon caption expressed it wittily: "Elect Fred O. Pittley, The Candidate of *All* the Special Interests." The broker state professes to free itself from exclusive ties to the interests of middle or rich Americans and asks all citizens, who wish to, to find a place at its hearings for competing supplicants and lobbyists. It announces that it now stands ready, with its massive resources, to enter quickly and openly the game as the quarrelsome factions conclude their bargains with each other under its brokering. Government no longer has confidence that free competition will produce what the nation needs without its intervention, so it actively tries to bring together interest groups, like buyers and sellers, to create "deals." In the words of the Italian socialist leader Bettino Craxi, "There are no more ideals. We simply manage interests."[192] In America as in Italy, the daily deal itself, rather than its rightness or broader implications for the economy or society, is the politician's objective. Getting through his day and revealing as little as possible about where the broker himself stands is the practice. Indeed, it is dubious that he "stands" anywhere, given his shifting loyalties. Perennially, the broker state makes itself available to the ebb and flow of interests of all sorts and seeks to reward each group

192. Quoted in "Don't Blame Fate, Blame the Italians," New York *Times*, March 9, 1993.

or coalition as liberally as it can. Arranging the pay-off with yet another entitlement and moving on to face the loudest squabble about the next big issue is routine. The impetus is unrestricted by any feeling for contradiction among the various deals the broker has created or entitlements he has enacted. Wheeling and dealing may be the best that the giant brokering democracy can do against the interest groups that are nurtured by its fabulous wealth and its egalitarian ideal of a chance and a hearing for all. Therein lie deeper rubs for effective legislation, budgetary costs, and public confidence.

Legislatures facing reelection and badgered by dozens of views about tax reform or nuclear waste disposal, including many with at least some cogency, can scarcely be expected to find the time, energy, knowledge, and reflection to peer into the depths or even the medium distance of the pressing issue of the next twenty-four hours. Sufficient only unto the day are the decisions a clamorous democracy receives from its brokers: a Vietnam War without tax increases, welfare support that encourages fathers to live apart from the family, tax cuts for everyone while defense expenditures massively increase, Gramm-Rudman-Hollings evasions that politically touchy deficits can be cut by bureaucrats rather than by politicians who must stand for reelection. Even defense needs, for all their high patriotic urgency, provide little escape for the broker state to longer-view, more resolute policies. Weapon and supply contracting involves a huge squabble of interest groups, each with close ties to local citizens, legislators, bureaucrats and White House friends. Hot issues like the location or closing of missile bases, the seaports for nuclear and nuclear-armed ships, and the hauling and disposing of nuclear waste bring negative entitlements into play, brokering among voices and voters asking *not* to be contaminated by waste disposal policies of that same federal power whose contracts for nuclear-weapons factories they had earlier sought.

When funds from the state for some programs began to falter in the 1980s, the game turned ugly and the fragility of the contracts between the broker and the customers for promised benefits became apparent. Those still waiting, unrewarded or underrewarded, for their hearings before the brokers *know* how rich America is and what it can afford *somehow,* if only the broker will work for the new supplicants. The broker-politician, however, tries to forgo exclusive ties to specific interests as well as to resist representing one broad principle, like the right to life or to choice, that could mark him a "single issue" man and too far from the fuller fray of brokering for all comers who may be contributors to campaign funds. Being on call and with an ear for everyone seems irresistible. There is so much government money to spend, such immense campaign costs, so many diverse supplicants aroused by impingement, expectations, and entitlements. And underlying it all is an astonishing history of national capacity to produce wealth and to suggest an extraordinary well-being for every citizen. Like the Wall Street investment specialists who move amorally among giant enterprises, putting together conglomerates, mergers, buy-outs and take-overs, not for productivity, jobs, or economic growth, but for commissions and "the game," the broker state offers its services at the low cost of campaign contributions and votes at election time. But all brokers in politics as well as business depend on the phones ringing. Across the republic is a huge cacophony of voices, each ready to get on the phone with the broker, with both parties eager for a deal, the official accepting every incoming call, not judging anyone in advance. It is Madisonian particularism with a vengeance, but it is saved from a dead end by the immense resources of this nation and the nimbleness of its brokers in creating the impression that this giant society *is* governed. In reality, the state merely gets through each day as best it can. And perhaps muddling through is the best we can do for ourselves, given our history and ideal of trying to do the best for everyone pursuing happiness.

All six of these modes of the state are abstractions from our history. In reality, the modes overlap, but inevitably all invoke the "public interest." Sometimes that priority becomes clear and is validated by a national consensus as, notably, in 1864 and 1865 when both North and South were taking different steps to end slavery. Usually, however, on smaller as well as greater matters, citizens invoking the public interest legitimately differ about what that public interest is. Even with the best will in the world in pursuing it, the public interest is intellectually difficult to discern in the welter of democratic America's views of policy. Jobs for lumbermen and protection of the forests and fauna are both legitimate goals. Defense costs show no clear paths to the public interest, since attention to health, education, and welfare as well as adequate national defense in an unstable revolutionary world are major, competing objectives. In the Reagan defense buildup we confronted conflicting experts with similar competence and credentials about what the public interest dictates in making choices among rockets, Stealth bombers, conventional forces, a six-hundred-ship navy, a "strategic defense initiative," and so on, let alone making post–Cold War cuts in any of these.[193] Taken up by the brokers, action on most of these proposals involves trade offs and not, as the partisan stand on one proposal or another maintains, implicitly clear definitions of what the public needs or wants. Worst of

193. Asa A. Clark *et al., The Defense Reform Debate* (Baltimore, 1984), pts. 6, 7.

all, the public interest can be a pernicious abstraction, the next-to-the-last refuge of scoundrels, such as invoking national security to hide illegal aid to Nicaraguan Contras, covering up White House felonies, or transporting Japanese-Americans wholesale to detention camps.

If we take just a few steps back from this baffling and intricate system in which it seems impossible to achieve agreement about the public interest, perhaps we can still appreciate how energetically democratic it is, how many voices it permits to be heard, how many needs it attempts to serve, how much it tries to abide, amid our rising strife among minorities, by a rule of live-and-let-live. There may be some solace for us from knowledgeable foreign observers over the last generation who have *admired* the different ways in which America copes with its domestic affairs, given the unprecedented proportions and pressures of its continental tasks.[194] They also sympathize with our dilemmas about dysfunction, for they know that safety and peace abroad, for allies as well as ourselves, depend on our abilities to "deliver" and to remain dependable in our commitments. Like us, they also worry that much of what American government does at home, it does poorly.

The saving and impressive aspect of the bemoaned mess, they remind us, is how rich and politically free the nation remains. If anything, the overseas critique is that for a nation of its size and power, America is *un*dergoverned, *i.e.*, not under effective control, just as the country seems to these friends to be ill-disciplined in private endeavor and personal and civic morality and undependable in international commitments. For the unfriendly critics abroad, on the right wing, the mess is the long-bewailed democratic barbarism; for the left around the globe, it is capitalist corruption. Among us, government at every level oversells and underdelivers and drives citizens of every class, from the welfare-office frequenter to the millionaire contractor, to distraction or to despair by increasingly Kafkaesque rules and regulations, insensitivity and waste.

But, again, in the political darkness of new tyrannies that deepened over most of the globe after 1945, America remained a beacon for common folk abroad, a nation impressive in liberty and abundance. For tens of millions overseas in starvation or standing in line to buy cabbage or potatoes, America's freedom was not seen as anarchy or as a capitalist sham. Its cornucopia supermarkets and discount stores were not suspect consumerism. Paradox though it may seem, America amid its disorders had even increased basic freedoms during fifty years of growing state ac-

---

194. Godfrey Hodgson, *America in Our Time: From World War II to Nixon—What Happened and Why* (Garden City, N.Y., 1976); Henry Fairlie, *The Spoiled Child of the Western World: The Miscarriage of the American Idea in Our Times* (Garden City, N.Y., 1976); Jean-Jacques Servan-Schreiber, *The American Challenge* (New York, 1968).

tivity since the New Deal intervention. Blacks can now vote and protest as they will. Open expression of religious and ethnic prejudice is increasingly frowned on. The once-deplored and held-back ethnics, the Italians, Poles, Chinese, Jews, have "arrived" in political positions, money, and influence. The freedom of the press and of public expression of "lifestyle," especially in sex, pornography, and nudity, are astonishing for those who can remember distant days when Playboy bunnies were daring and enticing. The divorce rate hovers near 50 percent but divorce no longer brings much shame or social ostracism. Loyalty and dissent issues became rarer and invocations of state security far more circumspect after the McCarthy nastiness. "Red raids" have not recurred. Racist immigration restrictions of 1924 and 1952 have been repealed, and recent immigrants are under far less pressure to conform to "American" mores. The police are far more constrained by Miranda rules and review boards. Sealed-off company towns and unchecked corps of Pinkerton and Burns hired detectives are scarcely heard of. Labor organization and collective bargaining are far more available, even if union membership seems less appealing. A Freedom of Information Act has further limited the effectiveness of appeals to national security to keep state secrets, and a succession of supposed dire threats to the republic like Senator Knowland, Martin Dies, Joseph McCarthy, Richard Nixon, David Duke, and the leaders of the "moral majority" are habitually cut down to size. Abroad, it is no wonder that America continues to have impressive allure for common folk who can think of leaving Vietnam or Pakistan or Russia for other lands and who still see in the United States freedom, opportunity, and youth, regardless of reports of scandal or sclerosis.

Fortunately, not fifty but several hundred years of capital underlie current American investment in the rule of law, popularly elected governments, freedom for faith, opinion, and association, and economic growth amid social diversity. But that huge capital and any confidence in America it still breeds are not inexhaustible. The twentieth century elsewhere shows dismayingly rapid turns of fortune for the overconfident among great and rich powers in Berlin, Vienna, or London. As Tocqueville warned at the beginning of the age of democracy, in its passions for freedom and equality America tends to betraying extremes of belief and action in pursuing both of its ideals. Uncriticized and uncorrected, its powerful excesses of spirit and Mammon, with Mammon and spirit now under state sponsorship, may waste even such enormous capital as we possess.

Nostalgia on left and right too easily suggests that yesterday had it much better. But the historian who looks into the American past for "true community" or unambiguous liberty or those unifying "habits of the heart" that citizens and leaders could take for granted is hard put to find much of these in even the most distant American times.[195] Instead, from the beginning, America was at once so busy, so fragmenting, so centripetal, so involved in its conflicts between man and God, fathers and sons, the hearth and society, purity and power. The New England puritan affirmed his covenant-communal ideal and tried to keep eyes on the sparrow and profit within bounds, yet he pursued his profits that helped undercut the covenant of the saints.[196] In time, liberty and enterprise in farming led to huge productivity by great plantations or bonanza farms, but they also recurrently produced gluts or employed slave labor.[197] The idea, therefore, that a year like 1660, 1865, or 1914 represents a dissolution of community, a momentous "fall," or an end of innocence is difficult to sustain. In our past, Christian, humanitarian, or republican ideals were trumpeted, but always with fear that they were losing their hold on citizens. All those would-be common faiths that depended on some kind of citizen self-restraint or "virtue" coexisted with concealed, or even openly justified, strong, and contrary individual energies. Selfishness and self-interest constantly undermined republican virtue as well as Christian love or the Golden Rule. Opportunity often blighted as many lives as it embellished so that, as Richard Hofstadter tellingly put it, a crass American individualism has often been at odds with a rich and confident American individuality.[198] So every American generation since 1660 has produced its Jeremiads and theories of "declension" about Americans desecrating their ideals in pursuing diamonds as big as the Ritz.

Our national balance sheet now reveals, amid enormous wealth and power, the increasingly fearsome costs of the piled-up state. That state encourages a corrosive multiculturalism far other than the diversity that the first cultural pluralists had in mind. It does not do many of its tasks even adequately, and after tempting and taunting citizens about pie in the sky, it frustrates and fails them perhaps as much as it repairs and liberates them. When the books are closed, what services the state delivers cost too much. Well may we may pray that there is still time. It took only four years, from 1914 to 1918, for the political collapse of Eu-

195. Robert N. Bellah *et al.*, *Habits of the Heart: Individualism and Commitment in American Life* (Berkeley, 1985).

196. Bernard Bailyn, *The New England Merchants in the Seventeenth Century* (Cambridge, Mass., 1955).

197. Edmund S. Morgan, *American Slavery, American Freedom* (New York, 1985), on the origins of our deepest paradox.

198. Richard Hofstadter, *The Progressive Historians: Turner, Beard, Parrington* (New York, 1968), 145–46.

rope with its old democratic as well as autocratic empires, only three from the American prosperity of 1929 to the near-immobilism of 1932, and only seven months from a Russia delivered from a czar to democracy to the Leninist coup. Happily, the vicissitudes of history also show that generations of Soviet hegemony over Eastern Europe and over its own peoples could collapse in less than twelve months. But diasastrously or happily, the lesson remains how low and quickly the mighty can fall.

Left to their freedom and to overflattering by underdemanding leaders, Americans will continue to be guided by their private pleasures and pains. No balancing by a "hidden hand" beyond government will bring them to harmony, let alone to habits of the heart that enrich all lives. We cannot foresee that 250 million citizens will see the light against the interest net, repent, and send back their Treasury checks. We do not need to wait, however, for that lauded change of heart to well up across the broad fields of the republic. We do need shrewd and courageous presidents who can get around the sloth and self-absorption of the common life. But national politics has become so faction ridden, so lacking in comity, and so leery of outspoken leaders that the circumstances favorable to the nomination, election, and legislative success of such presidents remain very dubious. It is difficult to believe that the "right man" as president can be visible until he is in the White House and finds himself willing to take risks against what the daily polls and cautioning pols say. Having the right man in place, in any case, has always been largely a matter of chance. Power as commander-in-chief and blood and death during a terrible war formed *our* Abraham Lincoln and made him the Lincoln who belongs to the ages rather than the affluent railroad lawyer and crafty politician. The record for the forceful, insightful leader making it to the presidency and then triumphing is not very impressive or encouraging. Theodore Roosevelt (with his significant limitations of big talk while wielding a small stick) came to the White House by an assassin's bullet. In 1912, only a split in the Republican Party gave Wilson (with all his limitations as well as strengths) his chance. The Herbert Hoover who seemed so well qualified for the presidency in 1928 found his gifts inadequate for what events flung at him in his White House years. And his opponent in 1932, who *was* to come to greatness, campaigned principally against Hoover's big spending and growing bureaucracy. Even if at work in the White House, gifts of moral passion and persuasion like Wilson's can come to dubious results, even tragic endings. A compelling need like Lyndon Johnson's to be among the great ones by doing the Lord's work against poverty or racism may count, but so do the ability to eschew slogans, study hard, and speak sense, not preach pretentious "wars" and "crusades" to the American people. And "count" also do the political skills to dramatize the genuine issues, to persevere with them, and to deliver on them. Only such leaders can persuade the American voters to rise to higher horizons. To create a presidential moment, however, these leaders need the help of a dozen or so top-rate, Washington-wise, incorruptible colleagues at the White House rather than the latest crop of *naifs* from the Ivy League or Atlanta or California or Little Rock provinces. Twelve good men and true could start to make major changes toward a more modest and productive politics while teaching and cajoling the nation to travel with them, even if the polls are not initially encouraging and the constituency-conscious Congress quivers.

But Americans can only anticipate from their society what it is capable of producing most of the time. Will our knock-about democratic politics attract and advance the talent we need? Left to drift under flattering politicians, this massive democracy has long been led to prefer what is easy. Left ignorant, it goes too quickly for merely ritualistic exorcism of evils or invocations of "sacrifice." It settles for gestures like repeatedly ineffective but much-touted antideficit programs or tinkering with health-care delivery. The media commentators do not help. They tend to bring us only today's perspective, the hot issue that may increase the ratings but may be gone by the next evening. The C-Span culture of news around the clock negates any sense of history or room for reflection. There is no time or memory that might suggest, for example, that freedom has endured worse threats than Joseph McCarthy or David Duke. Alternately, when columnists strive for perspective, they speak the reassuring or stylishly gloomy slogan, not the really demanding concept. Let even half-fresh ideas for the 1980s like "national industrial policy" or "competitiveness" or "productivity" appear and they are at once taken up by the networks, debated superficially on *Meet the Press* or *Face the Nation,* turned into grandiose platform planks, and deprived of all meaning except safe, glamorous banality. What value there was in the original version, when tried out on the hustings, is taken to prove the original version "too complicated," *i.e.,* politically too hot to handle or beyond the candidate's grasp. Different versions of the idea of a "new competitiveness" might have serious content among some brains trust or other at Harvard or Stanford, but when the idea is released across the republic, it creates only a few swells or eddies against the politician's faddish versions and strengthens everyone's deeper preference not to rock *my* boat. We are asked, instead, to accept what sounds good and costs little—in our word, gestures. But the politics of democracy, not God on high, has created this. This order of things was not written in heaven, destined to endure without giving way to chronic civil violence or cocky leaders promising to restore order against the Washington crowd.

The would-be strong president may not be able to make our faction-ridden system move beyond more brokers' deals. He may well need a crisis like 1861, 1913, or 1932 to permit unusual ability to come into play. But at times a strong leader can create presidential moments, as Lyndon Johnson did in 1964, for better and for worse. Johnson announced to his elated lieutenants right after his great victory over Goldwater that he was determined to bring America toward his Great Society for racial justice and social well-being. Yet even Johnson, one of the supreme players of our political system and one of the most damaging simplifiers of government capabilities, also warned his energetic advisers that they had only about eighteen months to *make* his moment, to press for the Great Society agenda. And he was right, for in just about that time he was into the Vietnam swamp that eventually ruined his pretensions of bringing off the victory that had eluded the French, who had known the country for eighty years and far better than we. If Ronald Reagan wanted to use his moment in the election of 1980 to bring off a Reagan revolution, that plan was aborted in shorter time than Johnson's, when it was apparent in the fall of 1981 that the Reagan tax-cuts would not be supplemented by a White House fight to contain the entitlements of mainstream Americans.

Making the case by cajoling or crushing the politicians, along with reaching over the legislators' heads to their constituents, remains the presidential task in the bumbling, buzzing confusion of the great democracy. The president is still the only official who can present a national agenda, keep it in the headlines, and drive Congress toward it while he persuades the public and his own bureaucrats to come along. As the leading national teacher, only the president is virtually guaranteed the prime-time and lead-story opportunities to make his case before the American people. That he will do so is, of course, always an act of faith. Are his will, skill, and calling for politics matches for his insights and stirring words? Where are the votes? Such questions are never more appropriate than today, when sympathetic students of presidential power warn how circumscribed even a strong leader is by the other powers in Madisonian Washington.

There is a larger and more difficult act of faith, however, beyond the strained hope for the strong president and the presidential moment. Politically, it comes from what is enduring in the heritage of Jefferson: that the American people, blessed with plenty, opportunity, and reward, and thus with unusual resistance to extremism, would respond well to the president who gives the facts, persists with the reasoned case and provides the assurance in specific proposals for fairness in both sacrifice and advantage. If there is still a rousable capacity for a common effort against difficulty in the American people, despite the ravages of recent multicultural politics and the thinning of public comity, it points to the continuing pertinence of Adlai Stevenson's plea, "Let's talk sense to the American people." Despite what many aver, taming the state and reweaving the interest net are not yet issues of basic freedom, blessed as America still is with that wealth and that open society that "fortuna" has brought only to the Atlantic portion of the globe. Rather, stuck with the state as we now are, the issues are that we truly be *governed,* that we get our money's worth from a trillion-dollar budget, that government knows what it is doing and politicians know what not to do or what they cannot do, that the big state makes good on its promises, and that it rouses expectations only for policies that have some substantial chance to succeed. For large and near prospects, there surely is an issue that the state itself not contribute, as its pretentiousness and cross-purposes in policy now do, to the disorder or skepticism about "ordinary" politics, without extremism and without demonic leaders, that elsewhere in this terrible century have shaken or destroyed political liberty.

POSTSCRIPT: PROGRAMS

What Is Not to Be Done

1. Go on as we have: politicizing newly discovered needs of citizens; piling up programs; making mere gestures at reform; arousing and aggravating cultural differences; relying on traditional checks and balances to block unwise programs; dwelling on dollar costs rather than effectiveness of programs; expediently shifting responsibilities and costs from one level of government to another (waxing and waning).

2. Pretend that any program can be kept from being nonpolitical.

3. Pretend that American democracy can deliver on anything and that failure to do so is "knocking America" or a right-wing conspiracy.

4. Assume that we can directly weaken the now regnant culture of expectations and entitlements.

5. Fail to tell citizens their genuine alternatives about government policies.

What Is to Be Done

1. Resist the culture of entitlements *politically,* not by fruitless and ritualistic exhortations against an entrenched national style of seeking the state for satisfying needs. Instead, primarily, resistance requires safeguarding legislators against immediate pressures.

2. Extend term in the U.S. House of Representatives to four years. Set term limits only for the U.S. Senate.

3. Fully finance all federal elections and, eventually, state and local contests.

4. Provide free or stipulated, negotiated, low-cost access to TV and radio for major parties and third parties meeting formal criteria for qualifying for time.

5. Set low, varying limits on congressional staffs depending on number of terms legislator has served and size of his or her constituency.

6. Use temporary, *ad hoc,* national commissions of experts to decide about issues such as military base closings or social security fund-

ing that are too sensitive to handle by direct legislation. The decisions will be binding unless countered by specified presidential and congressional overrides.

7. Forbid all lobbying involving any tangible *quid pro quo* to any government official or staff involving a vote, introduction of legislation, or assured good will toward any group. A promise to support at the polls only with votes shall not be banned.

8. Choose federal judges from ever-revised ratings of candidates prepared by U.S. Supreme Court justices, appointed groups of respected senior lawyers, and distinguished law school professors.

9. Make budgets selectively longer or shorter term for such subjects as military or educational policy. Separate budgets for capital and operating costs. Use zero-base and sunset criteria wherever possible.

10. Return all possible federally collected dollars to lower levels of government but with clear, auditable, and enforceable general criteria for expenditure and accountability and with assured penalties for ignoring the critieria.

11. Target all major income tax actions toward verifiable attempts to improve productivity and/or to increase jobs. Capital-gains relief can be used only if profits are provably reinvested in new or expanded capital enterprises.

12. Fund annually one thousand national "government service," four-year undergraduate scholarships usable at any bona fide four-year college or university. In exchange, the scholars will pledge themselves after graduation to five years of full-time work in any level of government starting at going salary levels. The curriculum for all winners must require a major in general humanities, *e.g.,* history, literature, and philosophy, and a minor in any specialty likely to be useful in civil service, *e.g.,* economics, transportation, agriculture.

What Is Likely to Be Done

Short of a national crisis such as in 1860–1861, 1933, or 1941, precious little.

Bibliography

PRIMARY SOURCES

Acts and Laws of the State of Connecticut in America. Hartford, 1786.

Adams, Brooks. *The Degradation of the Democratic Dogma.* New York, 1920.

Adams, Charles Francis, Jr. *Chapters of Erie and Other Essays.* New York, 1967.

———, ed. *The Works of John Adams.* 10 vols. Boston, 1850–56.

Adams, Henry. *The Education of Henry Adams.* Boston, 1918.

———. *Democracy, an American Novel.* New York, 1880.

Adams, John. *The Selected Writings of John and John Quincy Adams.* Edited by Adrienne Koch and William Peden. New York, 1946.

———. *The Spur of Fame: Dialogues of John Adams and Benjamin Rush, 1805–1813.* Edited by John A. Schutz and Douglas Adair. San Marino, Calif., 1966.

Annals of the Congress of the United States. 1st Cong., 1st Sess. Vol. I. Washington, D.C., 1834.

Bourne, Randolph. *War and the Intellectuals: Collected Essays, 1915–1919.* Edited by Carl Resek. New York, 1964.

Brandeis, Louis D. *Other People's Money and How the Bankers Use It.* Edited by Richard M. Abrams. New York, 1967.

Buchanan, James. *The James Buchanan Papers.* Edited by Lucy Fisher West. Microfilm. Philadelphia, 1974.

Burckhardt, Jakob. *Force and Freedom.* New York, 1943.

Burke, Edmund. *Reflections on the French Revolution.* New York, 1935.

———. *The Works of the Right Honorable Edmund Burke.* 6 vols. London, 1854.

Calhoun, John C. *A Disquisition on Government and a Discourse on the Constitution and Government of the United States.* New York, 1968.

Cappon, Lester J., ed. *The Adams-Jefferson Letters.* 2 vols. Chapel Hill, 1959.

The Colonial Records of the State of Georgia. Edited by Allen Candler. Atlanta, 1904–16.

Conner, R. D. W., ed. *A Pocket Manual of North Carolina for the Use of Members of the General Assembly, Session 1911.* Raleigh, 1911.

Croly, Herbert. *The Promise of American Life*. New York, 1909.

Crocker-Langley. *San Francisco Directory*. San Francisco, 1910.

Dewey, John. *Individualism Old and New*. New York, 1929.

———. *Influence of Darwin on Philosophy*. New York, 1910.

———. *Liberalism and Social Action*. New York, 1935.

———. *The Public and Its Problems*. New York, 1927.

———. "The Social Possibilities of War." In *Characters and Events: Popular Essays in Social and Political Philosophy by John Dewey*, edited by Joseph Ratner. New York, 1929.

Elliott, Jonathan, ed. *The Debates in the Several State Conventions on the Adoption of the Federal Constitution*. 5 vols. Philadelphia, 1836–59.

Emerson, Ralph Waldo. "The Fugitive Slave Law." In Emerson, *Miscellanies*. Boston, 1878.

Farrand, Max, ed. *The Records of the Federal Convention of 1787*. 4 vols. Rev. ed. New Haven, 1937.

Follett, Mary P. *The New State*. New York, 1918.

Goodwin, Isaac. *Town Officer: Or Laws of Massachusetts*. N.d.; rpr. Worcester, Mass., 1825.

Hamilton, Alexander. *The Papers of Alexander Hamilton*. Edited by Harold C. Syrett and Jacob M. Cooke. 27 vols. New York, 1961–81.

Hamilton, Alexander, James Madison, and John Jay. *The Federalist*. New York, 1888.

Historical Commission of South Carolina. *The Colonial Records of the State of South Carolina*. Columbia, S.C., 1951–.

Historical Statistics of the United States. 2 vols. Washington, D.C., 1975.

Hobhouse, L. T. *The Metaphysical Theory of the State*. London, 1918.

Holmes, Oliver Wendell, Jr. *The Common Law*. Boston, 1881.

Hobbes, Thomas. *Leviathan*. Oxford, Eng., 1946.

Hoover, Herbert. *Addresses upon the American Road, 1948–1950*. Stanford, 1951.

———. *American Ideals Versus the New Deal*. New York, 1936.

———. *American Individualism*. Garden City, N.Y., 1922.

———. *Memoirs*. 3 vols. New York, 1951–52.

Howe, Mark Dewolf, ed. *Holmes-Laski Letters*. 2 vols. Cambridge, Mass., 1953.

James, William. *A Pluralistic Universe*. New York, 1909.

Jefferson, Thomas. *The Complete Jefferson*. Edited by Saul Padover. Freeport, N.Y., 1943.

———. *The Life and Selected Writings of Thomas Jefferson*. Edited by Adrienne Koch and William Peden. New York, 1944.

———. *The Papers of Thomas Jefferson*. Edited by Julian P. Boyd. 25 vols. to date. Princeton, 1950–.

———. *The Writings of Thomas Jefferson*. Edited by Paul L. Ford. 12 vols. New York, 1892–99.

Keynes, John Maynard. *Essays in Biography*. New York, 1933.

———. *Essays in Persuasion*. New York, 1932.

Langley. *San Francisco Directory*. San Francisco, 1880.

Laws of the State of Delaware. 2 vols. New Castle, Del., 1797.

The Legislative Manual and Political Register of the State of North Carolina for the Year 1874. Raleigh, 1874.

Lilienthal, David. *Big Business: A New Era.* New York, 1953.

———. *TVA: Democracy on the March.* New York, 1944.

Lincoln, Abraham. *Collected Works of Abraham Lincoln.* Edited by Roy P. Basler. 8 vols. New Brunswick N.J., 1953.

Lippmann, Walter. *Drift and Mastery.* New York, 1914.

———. *Public Opinion.* New York, 1922.

Madison, James. *The Papers of James Madison.* Edited by William T. Hutchinson *et al.* 16 vols. Chicago, 1962–.

Malone, Dumas, ed. *Correspondence Between Thomas Jefferson and Samuel DuPont de Nemours, 1798–1817.* Boston, 1930.

Maryland Historical Society. *Archives of Maryland.* Annapolis, Md., 1883–1919.

McKenney. *Oakland City Directory.* Oakland, 1883.

Mill, John Stuart. *Prefaces to Liberty: Selected Writings of John Stuart Mill.* Edited by Bernard Wishy. Boston, 1959.

Montesquieu, C. D. S., Baron de. *The Spirit of the Laws.* New York, 1949.

Perkins, Frances. *The Roosevelt I Knew.* New York, 1946.

Persons, Stowe, ed. *Social Darwinism: Selected Essays of William Graham Sumner.* Englewood Cliffs, N.J., 1963.

Polk-Husted Directory Co. *Oakland City Directory.* Oakland, 1913.

Raleigh City Directory, 1880. Raleigh, 1880.

Raleigh City Directory, 1910. Raleigh, 1910.

Recent Economic Changes in the United States. 2 vols. New York, 1929.

Roosevelt, Franklin D. *Complete Presidential Press Conferences.* Vol. XXII of 25 vols. New York, 1942.

Roosevelt, Theodore. *The Letters of Theodore Roosevelt.* Edited by Elting E. Morison. Vol. VIII of 8 vols. Cambridge, Mass., 1951–54.

Rush, Benjamin. *The Selected Writings of Benjamin Rush.* Edited by Dagobert D. Runes. New York, 1947.

Schumpeter, Joseph A. *Capitalism, Socialism, and Democracy.* New York, 1942.

Spinoza, Benedictus de. *Political Theological Treatise and Political Treatise.* London, 1883.

Steffens, Lincoln. *The Shame of the Cities.* 1904; rpr. New York, 1957.

Stiles, Ezra. *The United States Elevated to Glory and Honor.* New Haven, 1783.

Thorpe, F. N., ed. *The Federal and State Constitutions, Colonial Charters, and Other Organic Laws . . . Forming the United States of America.* 7 vols. Washington, D.C., 1909.

Tocqueville, Alexis de. *Democracy in America.* 2 vols. New York, 1946.

———. *The Old Regime and the French Revolution.* Garden City, N.Y., 1955.

———. *Recollections.* New York, 1949.

Truman, Harry S. *Memoirs.* 2 vols. Garden City, N.Y., 1955–56.

U.S. Department of Commerce, Bureau of the Census. *Historical Statistics of the United States: Colonial Times to 1970.* Vol. II of 2 vols. Washington, D.C., 1975.

Veblen, Thorstein. *The Theory of Business Enterprise.* New York, 1904.

Washington, George. *The Writings of George Washington.* Edited by John C. Fitzpatrick. 39 vols. Washington, D.C., 1931–44.

Webster, Pelatiah. *Essay on Free Trade and Commerce.* Philadelphia, 1779.

Weyl, Walter. *The New Democracy.* New York, 1912.

Wells, H. G. *The Great State.* New York, 1912.

Wilson, Woodrow. *Congressional Government: A Study in American Politics.* 1885; rpr. Baltimore, 1981.

———. *The New Freedom.* New York, 1914.

———. *The Study of Public Administration.* 1887; rpr. Washington, D.C., 1955.

SECONDARY WORKS

BOOKS

Abbott, Grace. *From Relief to Social Security.* New York, 1966.

Abernethy, Thomas P. *Western Lands and the American Revolution.* New York, 1937.

Abrams, Richard M. *Conservatism in a Progressive Era: Massachusetts Politics, 1900–1912.* Cambridge, Mass., 1964.

Adams, James Truslow. *Provincial Society, 1690–1763.* New York, 1929.

Adams, Sherman. *Firsthand Report: The Story of the Eisenhower Administration.* New York, 1961.

Ahlstrom, Sidney A. *Religious History of the American People.* New Haven, 1972.

Alexander, Charles C. *Holding the Line: The Eisenhower Era, 1951–1961.* Bloomington, Ind., 1975.

Alexander, De Alva S. *History and Procedures of the House of Representatives.* Boston, 1916.

Allswang, John M. *A House for All Peoples: Ethnic Politics in Chicago, 1890–1940.* Lexington, Ky., 1971.

———. *Bosses, Machines, and Urban Voters.* Port Washington. N.Y., 1977.

Ambrose, Stephen E. *Eisenhower.* 2 vols. New York, 1983.

Anderson, Donald E. *William Howard Taft.* Ithaca, N.Y., 1973.

Andreano, Ralph L., ed. *The Economic Impact of the American Civil War.* Cambridge, Mass., 1962.

Andrews, Charles M. *The Colonial Period of American History.* 4 vols. New Haven, 1934–37.

Andrews, J. Cutler. *The North Reports the Civil War.* Pittsburgh, 1955.

Appleby, Paul. *Big Democracy.* New York, 1945.

Arnold, Thurman. *The Folklore of Capitalism.* New Haven, 1938.

Ausubel, Herman. *Historians and Their Craft.* New York, 1950.

Bailey, Kenneth P. *The Ohio Company of Virginia and the Westward Movement, 1747–1792.* Glendale, Calif., 1939.

Bailey, Stephen. *Congress Makes a Law.* New York, 1957.

Bailyn, Bernard. *Education in the Forming of American Society.* Chapel Hill, 1960.

————. *Ideological Origins of the American Revolution.* Cambridge, Mass., 1967.

————. *The New England Merchants in the Seventeenth Century.* Cambridge, Mass., 1955.

————. *Origins of American Politics.* New York, 1968.

————. *Voyagers to the West.* New York, 1986.

Baldwin, S. E. "Early History of the Ballot in Connecticut." In *Papers of the American Historical Association.* Vol. IV. New York, 1890.

Banning, Lance. *The Jeffersonian Persuasion.* Ithaca, N.Y., 1978.

Barrett, Jay Amos. *Evolution of the Ordinance of 1787.* New York, 1891.

Barrow, Thomas C. *Trade and Empire.* Cambridge, Mass., 1967.

Barth, Alan. *The Loyalty of Free Men.* New York, 1951.

Baruch, Bernard. *American Industry in the War.* New York, 1941.

Bayor, Ronald H. *Neighbors in Conflict: The Irish, Germans, Jews, and Italians of New York City, 1929–1941.* Urbana, Ill., 1988.

Beale, Howard K. *The Critical Year.* New York, 1930.

Beard, Charles A. *The Economic Origins of Jeffersonian Democracy.* New York, 1915.

————. *Toward Civilization.* New York, 1930.

Beard, Charles, and Mary Beard. *The Rise of American Civilization.* New York, 1927.

Becker, Carl. *The Declaration of Independence.* New York, 1922.

Bellah, Robert N., *et al. Habits of the Heart: Individualism and Commitment in American Life.* Berkeley, 1985.

Belz, Herman. *Reconstructing the Union.* Ithaca, N.Y., 1969.

Bemis, Samuel F. *John Quincy Adams and the Union.* New York, 1956.

Benedict, Michael L. *A Compromise of Principle: Congressional Republicans and Reconstruction, 1863–1869.* New York, 1974.

Bennett, David H. *Demagogues in the Depression.* New Brunswick, N.J., 1969.

Benson, Lee. *The Concept of Jacksonian Democracy.* Princeton, 1961.

Bentley, George R. *A History of the Freedmen's Bureau.* New York, 1970.

Benzen, Peter. *Whitetown, USA.* New York, 1970.

Bercovitch, Sacvan. *The American Jeremiad.* Madison, Wis., 1978.

————. *The Puritan Origins of the American Self.* New Haven, 1975.

Berle, Adolph A. *The 20th Century Capitalist Revolution.* New York, 1954.

Berle, Adolph A., and Gardiner C. Means. *The Modern Corporation and Private Property.* New York, 1932.

Berlin, Ira. *Slaves Without Masters.* New York, 1975.

Berns, Walter. *In Defense of Liberal Democracy.* Chicago, 1984.

Bernstein, Barton J., ed. *Towards a New Past: Dissenting Essays in American History.* New York, 1968.

Berthoff, Rowland. *An Unsettled People.* New York, 1971.

Billington, Ray A. *The Protestant Crusade.* Gloucester, Mass., 1963.

————. *Westward Expansion.* 5th ed. New York, 1982.

Blanshard, Paul. *American Freedom and Catholic Power.* Boston, 1949.

Blum, John M. *Woodrow Wilson and the Politics of Morality.* Boston, 1956.

Bonomi, Patricia U. *A Factious People.* New York, 1971.

Boorstin, Daniel. *The Americans: The Colonial Experience.* New York, 1958. Vol. III of Boorstin, *The Americans.* 3 vols.

———. *The Genius of American Politics.* Chicago, 1953.

Braeman, John, *et al.,* eds. *The New Deal: The State and Local Levels.* 2 vols. Columbus, Ohio, 1975.

Branch, Edward D. *The Sentimental Years.* New York, 1934.

Branch, Taylor. *Parting the Waters: America in the King Years, 1954–1963.* New York, 1988.

Breen, Timothy H. *The Character of the Good Ruler.* New Haven, 1970.

Bremner, Robert H. *Children and Youth in America.* 2 vols. Cambridge, Mass., 1970–74.

Bridenbaugh, Carl. *Mitre and Sceptre.* New York, 1962.

———. *Vexed and Troubled Englishmen, 1590–1642.* New York, 1968.

Brock, William R. *An American Crisis: Congress and Reconstruction, 1865–1867.* New York, 1963.

Brodie, Fawn M. *Thaddeus Stevens, Scourge of the South.* New York, 1959.

Broek, Jacobus ten. *Equal Under Law.* New York, 1965.

Brown, Keith C., ed. *Hobbes Studies.* Cambridge, Mass., 1964.

Brown, Richard D. *Modernization: The Transformation of American Life, 1600–1865.* New York, 1976.

Brown, Robert E. *Middle Class Democracy and the Revolution in Massachusetts, 1691–1780.* Ithaca, N.Y., 1955.

Bruce, Philip A. *Institutional History of Virginia in the Seventeenth Century.* 2 vols. New York, 1910.

Bruchey, Stuart. *The Roots of American Economic Growth, 1607–1861.* New York, 1968.

Buel, Richard, Jr. *Securing the Revolution: Ideology in American Politics, 1789–1815.* Ithaca, N.Y., 1972.

Bumsted, J. M., and J. E. Van de Wetering. *What Must I Do To Be Saved?* Hinsdale, Ill., 1976.

Burner, David. *Herbert Hoover: The Public Life.* New York, 1978.

———. *The Politics of Provincialism: The Democratic Party in Transition, 1918–1932.* Cambridge, Mass., 1967.

Burns, James MacGregor. *Congress on Trial.* New York, 1949.

———. *Deadlock of Democracy.* Englewood Cliffs, N.J., 1963.

Burton, David H. *Oliver Wendell Holmes, Jr.* Boston, 1980.

———, ed. *Oliver Wendell Holmes: What Manner of Liberal?* Huntington, N.Y., 1979.

Butterfield, Herbert. *The Englishman and His History.* Cambridge, Eng., 1944.

———. *The Whig Interpretation of History.* London, 1931.

Campbell, Stanley W. *The Slave Catchers: Enforcement of the Fugitive Slave Law, 1850–1860.* Chapel Hill, 1970.

Caro, Robert. *The Power Broker: Robert Moses and the Fall of New York.* New York, 1974.

Carpenter, Jesse T. *The South as a Conscious Minority, 1789–1861.* New York, 1930.

Carter, Dan T. *When the War Was Over: The Failure of Self-Reconstruction in the South, 1865–1867.* Baton Rouge, 1985.

Chalmers, David M. *The Social and Political Ideas of the Muckrakers.* New York, 1964.

Chambers, Clarke A. *Seedtime of Reform: Social Service and Social Action, 1918–1933.* Minneapolis, 1963.

Chandler, Alfred D., Jr. *Strategy and Structure: Chapters in the History of Industrial Enterprise.* Cambridge, Mass., 1962.

———. *The Visible Hand: The Managerial Revolution in American Business.* Cambridge, Mass., 1977.

Channing, Steven A. *Crisis of Fear: Secession in South Carolina.* New York, 1970.

Chase, Stuart. *The Tragedy of Waste.* New York, 1925.

Chatters, Carl H., and Marjorie Leonard Hoover. *An Inventory of Governmental Activities in the United States.* Chicago, 1947.

Chinard, Gilbert. *Thomas Jefferson, the Apostle of Americanism.* Boston, 1929.

Clark, Asa A., *et al. The Defense Reform Debate.* Baltimore, 1984.

Clark, Peter, and Paul Slack, eds. *Crisis and Order in English Towns, 1500–1700: Essays in Urban History.* Toronto, 1972.

Clarkson, Grosvenor B. *Industrial America in the World War: The Strategy Behind the Line, 1917–1918.* Boston, 1923.

Clough, Shepherd B. *A History of the Flemish Movement in Belgium.* New York, 1930.

Cochran Thomas C., and William Miller. *The Age of Enterprise: A Social History of Industrial America.* New York, 1961.

Coffin, Victor. *The Province of Quebec and the Early American Revolution.* Madison, Wis., 1896.

Cohen, Felix S. *Handbook of Federal Indian Law.* Albuquerque, 1971.

Coker, Francis W. *Recent Political Thought.* New York, 1934.

Colbourn, H. Trevor. *The Lamp of Experience: Whig History and the Intellectual Origins of the American Revolution.* Chapel Hill, 1965.

Cole, Arthur C. *The Irrepressible Conflict, 1850–1865.* New York, 1938.

Collier, John. *Indians of the Americas.* New York, 1947.

Collins, Robert M. *The Business Response to Keynes, 1929–1964.* New York, 1981.

Commager, Henry Steele, ed. *Documents of American History.* New York, 1949.

———. *Majority Rule and Minority Rights.* New York, 1943.

Conkin, Paul. *Tomorrow a New World.* Ithaca, N.Y., 1959.

Connelly, Thomas L., and Barbara L. Bellows. *God and General Longstreet: The Lost Cause and the Southern Mind.* Baton Rouge, 1982.

Conroy, Martin. *The State and Political Theory.* Princeton, 1984.

Cook, Adrian. *The Armies of the Streets.* Lexington, Ky., 1974.

Cooper, John M. *The Vanity of Power: American Isolation and the First World War, 1914–1917.* Westport, Conn., 1969.

Coulter, E. Merton. *The Confederate States of America, 1861–1865.* Baton Rouge, 1950.

————. *The South During Reconstruction, 1865–1877.* Baton Rouge, 1947.

Cowley, Malcolm. *Books That Changed Our Minds.* New York, 1939.

Cox, Archibald. *Freedom of Expression.* Cambridge, Mass., 1981.

Cox, Lawanda. *Lincoln and Black Freedom: A Study in Presidential Leadership.* Columbia, S.C., 1981.

Cox, Lawanda, and John H. Cox. *Politics, Principle, and Prejudice, 1865–1866.* New York, 1963.

Craven, Avery O. *The Coming of the Civil War.* New York, 1942.

————. *Edmund Ruffin, Southerner.* New York, 1932.

Craven, Wesley F. *The Legend of the Founding Fathers.* New York, 1956.

————. *The Southern Colonies in the Seventeenth Century, 1606–1689.* Baton Rouge, 1949.

Cremin, Lawrence A. *The American Common School.* New York, 1951.

————. *American Education: The Colonial Experience, 1607–1783.* New York, 1970.

————. *American Education: The National Experience, 1783–1876.* New York, 1980.

————. *The Transformation of the School.* New York, 1961.

Cress, Lawrence D. *Citizens in Arms.* Chapel Hill, 1982.

Croly, Herbert. *Marcus Alonzo Hanna.* New York, 1912.

Crossman, R. H. S. *New Fabian Essays.* New York, 1952.

Cuff, Robert D. *The War Industries Board: Business-Government Relations During World War I.* Baltimore, 1973.

Curti, Merle. *Probing Our Past.* N.d.; rpr. Gloucester, Mass., 1962.

Curtis, Bruce. *William Graham Sumner.* Boston, 1981.

Curtis, James C. *Andrew Jackson and the Search for Vindication.* Boston, 1976.

Curtis, Michael K. *No State Shall Abridge.* Durham, N.C., 1986.

Dahl, Robert. *Who Governs.* New Haven, 1961.

Dangerfield, George. *The Awakening of American Nationalism, 1815–1828.* New York, 1965.

————. *The Era of Good Feelings.* New York, 1952.

Davis, David B. *Ante-Bellum American Culture.* Lexington, Mass., 1979.

————. *The Problem of Slavery in the Age of Revolution, 1770–1823.* Ithaca, N.Y., 1975.

Deane, Herbert A. *The Political Ideas of Harold J. Laski.* Hamden, Conn., 1972.

Dearing, Charles L. *American Highway Policy.* Washington, D.C., 1941.

Dearing, Mary R. *Veterans in Politics: The Story of the GAR.* Baton Rouge, 1952.

Deloria, Vine. *We Talk, You Listen: New Tribes, New Turf.* New York, 1970.

Demant, V. A. *Religion and the Decline of Capitalism.* New York, 1952.

Deutsch, Karl. *Nationalism and Social Communication.* Cambridge, Mass., 1966.

Diamond, William. *The Economic Thought of Woodrow Wilson.* Baltimore, 1943.

Dickson, R. J. *Ulster Emigration to Colonial America, 1718–1775.* London, 1966.

Diggins, John P. *The Bard of Savagery: Thorstein Veblen and Modern Social Theory.* New York, 1978.

———. *Mussolini and Fascism: The View from America.* Princeton, 1972.

———. *The Proud Decade.* New York, 1988.

Dinnerstein, Leonard, and David Reimers. *Ethnic Americans: A History of Immigration and Assimilation.* New York, 1975.

Dodd, Edwin M. *American Business Corporations Until 1860.* Cambridge, Mass., 1954.

Donald, David H. *Charles Sumner and the Rights of Man.* New York, 1970.

———. *Lincoln Reconsidered.* New York, 1956.

———. *The Politics of Reconstruction, 1863–1867.* Baton Rouge, 1965.

———, ed. *Why the North Won the Civil War.* Baton Rouge, 1960.

Donoughue, Bernard. *British Politics and the American Revolution: The Path to War, 1773–1775.* New York, 1964.

Dorfman, Joseph. *The Economic Mind in American Civilization.* 3 vols. New York, 1946.

Douglas, Lewis W. *The Liberal Tradition.* New York, 1935.

Douglas, Paul H. *American Apprenticeship and Industrial Organization.* New York, 1921.

Douglass, Elisha P. *Rebels and Democrats.* Chapel Hill, 1955.

Draper, Theodore. *The Rediscovery of Black Nationalism.* New York, 1970.

———. *The Roots of American Communism.* New York, 1957.

Du Bois, W. E. B. *Black Reconstruction.* New York, 1963.

Durden, Robert F. *The Gray and the Black: The Confederate Debate on Emancipation.* Baton Rouge, 1972.

Dykhuizen, George. *The Life and Mind of John Dewey.* Carbondale, Ill., 1973.

Dykstra, Robert R. *The Cattle Towns.* New York, 1968.

East, Robert A. *Business Enterprise in the American Revolutionary Era.* New York, 1938.

Echeverria, Durand. *Mirage in the West: A History of the French Image of American Society to 1815.* Princeton, 1957.

Eckenrode, Hamilton J. *The Revolution in Virginia.* Boston, 1916.

———. *The Separation of State and Church in Virginia.* Richmond, Va., 1910.

Eldersveld, Samuel J., et al. *The Citizen and Administrator in a Developing Democracy.* Glenview, Ill., 1968.

Ellis, John Tracy. *Catholics in Colonial America.* Baltimore, 1965.

Elson, Ruth. *Guardians of Tradition: American Schoolbooks of the Nineteenth Century.* Lincoln, Nebr., 1964.

Erickson, Charlotte. *American Industry and the European Immigrant, 1860–1885.* Cambridge, Mass., 1957.

Erikson, Kai. *Wayward Puritans.* New York, 1966.

Ernst, Joseph A. *Money and Politics in America, 1755–1775.* Chapel Hill, 1973.

Essien-Udom, E. U. *Black Nationalism.* Chicago, 1964.

Evans, G. H., Jr. *Business Incorporations in the United States, 1800–1943.* New York, 1948.

Evans, Peter B., et al., eds. *Bringing the State Back In.* Cambridge, Mass., 1985.

Fabricant, Solomon. *The Trend of Government Activity in the United States Since 1900*. New York, 1952.

Fairlie, Henry. *The Spoiled Child of the Western World: The Miscarriage of the American Idea in Our Times*. Garden City, N.Y., 1976.

Fairman, Charles. *American Constitutional Decisions*. New York, 1948.

——. *Reconstruction and Reunion*. New York, 1971.

Farrand, Max. *The Framing of the Constitution of the United States*. New Haven, 1913.

Faust, A. B. *The German Element in the United States*. 2 vols. Boston, 1909.

Faust, Drew G. *A Sacred Circle: Dilemma of the Intellectual in the Old South, 1840–1860*. Baltimore, 1977.

Fehrenbacher, Don E. *Prelude to Greatness: Lincoln in the 1850s*. Stanford, 1962.

Fey, Harold E., and D'Arcy McNickle. *Indians and Other Americans*. New York, 1970.

Fine, Sidney A. *Laissez Faire and the General-Welfare State*. Ann Arbor, 1956.

Fischer, David Hackett. *The Revolution of American Conservatism*. New York, 1965.

Fisher, Sidney G. *The Making of Pennsylvania*. Philadelphia, 1932.

Fite, Emerson D. *Social and Industrial Conditions in the North During the Civil War*. New York, 1930.

Fite, Gilbert C. *George N. Peek and the Fight for Farm Parity*. Norman, Okla., 1954.

Foner, Eric. *Free Soil, Free Labor, Free Men: The Ideology of the Republican Party Before the Civil War*. New York, 1970.

——. *Politics and Ideology in the Age of the Civil War*. New York, 1980.

——. *Reconstruction: America's Unfinished Revolution, 1863–1877*. New York, 1988.

——. *Tom Paine and Revolutionary America*. New York, 1976.

Foner, Philip S., ed. *The Black Panthers Speak*. Philadelphia, 1970.

Forcey, Charles. *The Crossroads of Liberalism*. New York, 1961.

Ford, Henry J. *The Scotch-Irish in America*. Princeton, 1915.

Forgie, George. *Patricide in the House Divided*. New York, 1979.

Foster, William T., and Waddill Catchings. *The Road to Plenty*. Boston, 1928.

Franklin, Julian H. *John Locke and the Theory of Sovereignty*. Cambridge, Eng., 1978.

——. *Jean Bodin and the Sixteenth-Century Revolution in the Methodology of Law and History*. New York, 1963.

Frederickson, George M. *The Black Image in the White Mind*. New York, 1971.

——. *The Inner Civil War*. New York, 1965.

Freehling, William W. *Prelude to Civil War: The Nullification Controversy in South Carolina, 1816–1836*. New York, 1966.

Freeman, Douglas Southall. *George Washington*. 6 vols. New York, 1952.

Freidel, Frank. *Franklin D. Roosevelt: Launching the New Deal*. Boston, 1973.

Friedman, Milton. *Capitalism and Freedom*. Chicago, 1962.

Friedman, Milton, and Anna J. Schwartz. *A Monetary History of the United States, 1867–1960*. Princeton, 1963.

Galambos, Louis. *Competition and Cooperation: The Emergence of a National Trade Association.* Baltimore, 1966.

Galbraith, John Kenneth. *The Great Crash, 1929.* 3rd ed. Boston, 1972.

Galenson, David W. *White Servitude in Colonial America.* New York, 1981.

Galloway, George B. *History of the United States House of Representatives.* New York, 1961.

Garraty, John. *The New Commonwealth, 1877–1898.* New York, 1968.

Garraty, John, and Peter Gay, eds. *The Columbia History of the World.* New York, 1972.

Gelfand, Mark. *A Nation of Cities.* New York, 1975.

Gerteis, Louis. *From Contraband to Freedom: Federal Policy Toward Southern Blacks.* Westport, Conn., 1973.

Gilbert, James. *Designing the Industrial State: The Intellectual Pursuit of Collectivism in America, 1880–1940.* Chicago, 1972.

Gillette, William. *Retreat from Reconstruction, 1869–1879.* Baton Rouge, 1980.

———. *The Right to Vote: Politics and the Passage of the Fifteenth Amendment.* Baltimore, 1965.

Gipson, Lawrence H. *The Coming of the Revolution, 1763–1775.* New York, 1954.

Glazer, Nathan. *Ethnic Dilemmas, 1964–1982.* Cambridge, Mass., 1983.

Glazer, Nathan, and Daniel P. Moynihan. *Beyond the Melting Pot: The Negroes, Puerto Ricans, Jews, Italians, and Irish of New York City.* Cambridge, Mass., 1963.

Going, C. B. *David Wilmot, Free-Soiler.* New York, 1924.

Goldwater, Barry. *The Conscience of a Conservative.* Shepherdsville, Ky., 1960.

Gollin, Gillian. *Moravians in Two Words.* New York, 1967.

Goode, Patrick G. *A Statement of the Expenditures of Government, Exhibiting the Prodigality and Extravagance of the Current Administration.* Washington, D.C., 1840.

Goodrich, Carter. *Government Promotion of American Canals and Railroads, 1800–1890.* New York, 1960.

Goodwin, George, Jr. *The Little Legislatures.* Amherst, Mass., 1970.

Gordon, Milton. *Assimilation in American Life: The Role of Race, Religion, and National Origins.* New York, 1964.

Gould, Lewis L., ed. *The Progressive Era.* Syracuse, 1974.

Govan, Thomas P. *Nicholas Biddle: Nationalist and Public Banker.* Chicago, 1959.

Graham, Ian C. *Colonists from Scotland: Emigration to North America, 1707–1783.* Ithaca, N.Y., 1956.

Graham, Otis L. *An Encore for Reform.* New York, 1967.

———. *The New Deal: The Critical Issues.* Boston, 1971.

———. *Toward a Planned Society: From Roosevelt to Nixon.* New York, 1976.

Green, Fletcher M. *Constitutional Development in the South Atlantic States, 1776–1860.* Chapel Hill, 1930.

Greene, Evarts B. *Religion and the State.* Ithaca, N.Y., 1959.

Greene, Jack P. *The Quest for Power.* Chapel Hill, 1963.

Greven, Phillip. *Four Generations: Population, Land, and Family in Colonial Andover, Massachusetts.* Ithaca, N.Y., 1970.

Grey, Susan. "Family, Land, and Credit: Yankee Communities on the Michigan Frontier." Ph.D. dissertation. University of Chicago, 1985.

Griffin, Clifford. *Their Brothers' Keepers: Moral Stewardship in the United States.* New Brunswick, N.J., 1960.

Griswold, A. Whitney. *Farming and Democracy.* New York, 1948.

Grob, Gerald. *Mental Institutions in America.* New York, 1973.

Gutman, Herbert G. *The Black Family in Slavery and Freedom, 1750–1925.* New York, 1976.

Haber, Samuel. *Efficiency and Uplift: Scientific Management in the Progressive Era.* Chicago, 1964.

Hacker, Louis M. *The Course of American Economic Growth and Development.* New York, 1970.

———. *The Triumph of American Capitalism.* New York, 1940.

Hackney, Sheldon. *Populism to Progressivism in Alabama.* Princeton, 1969.

Hadley, Charles D. *Transformations of the American Party System: Political Coalitions from the New Deal to the 1970s.* New York, 1975.

Hamby, Alonzo L. *Beyond the New Deal: Harry S. Truman and American Liberalism.* New York, 1973.

Hammond, Bray. *Banks and Politics in America: From the Revolution to the Civil War.* Princeton, 1967.

Handlin, Oscar. *Al Smith and His America.* Boston, 1958.

———. *The Uprooted.* Boston, 1951.

Handlin, Oscar, and Mary Handlin. *Commonwealth.* New York, 1947.

Hansen, Alvin. *Full Recovery or Stagnation.* New York, 1938.

Hansen, Marcus Lee. *The Immigrant in American History.* Cambridge, Mass., 1940.

Haraszti, Zoltan. *John Adams and the Prophets of Progress.* Cambridge, Mass., 1952.

Harlan, Louis R. *Booker T. Washington: The Making of a Black Leader, 1856–1901.* New York, 1972.

Harmon, Frances B. *The Social Philosophy of the St. Louis Hegelians.* New York, 1943.

Harris, Seymour, ed. *The New Economics.* New York, 1947.

Hartz, Louis. *Economic Policy and Democratic Thought.* Cambridge, Mass., 1948.

Haskins, George L. *Law and Authority in Early Massachusetts.* New Haven, 1960.

Hawley, Ellis W. *The Great War and the Search for a Modern Order.* New York, 1979.

Hay, Denys. *Europe in the Fourteenth and Fifteenth Centuries.* New York, 1966.

Hays, Samuel P. *Conservation and the Gospel of Efficiency: The Progressive Conservation Movement, 1890–1920.* Cambridge, Mass., 1959.

———. *The Response to Industrialism, 1855–1914.* Chicago, 1957.

Heald, Morrell. *The Social Responsibilities of Business, Company, and Community, 1900–1960.* Cleveland, 1970.

Heath, Milton S. *Constructive Liberalism: The Role of the State in Economic Development in Georgia to the 1860s.* Cambridge, Mass., 1954.

Hecksher, Eli. *Mercantilism.* London, 1935.

Heclo, Hugh. *A Government of Strangers: Executive Politics in Washington.* Washington, D.C., 1977.

Heclo, Hugh, and Lester Salomon, eds. *The Illusion of Presidential Government.* Boulder, Colo., 1981.

Heilbroner, Robert L., and Aaron Singer. *The Economic Transformation of America.* New York, 1977.

Henretta, James. *The Evolution of American Society, 1700–1815.* Lexington, Mass., 1973.

———. *Salutary Neglect: Colonial Administration Under the Duke of Newcastle.* Princeton, 1972.

Herberg, Will. *Protestant-Catholic-Jew.* Garden City, N.Y., 1955.

Herresshof, David. *American Disciples of Marx: From the Age of Jackson to the Progressive Era.* Detroit, 1967.

Herring, E. Pendleton. *Presidential Leadership.* New York, 1940.

Hesseltine, William B. *Lincoln and the War Governors.* New York, 1948.

Hibbard, Benjamin. *A History of the Public Land Policies.* New York, 1924.

Hidy, Ralph, and Muriel Hidy. *Pioneering in Big Business, 1882–1911: History of Standard Oil (New Jersey).* New York, 1955.

Higginbotham, Don. *The War of American Independence.* New York, 1971.

Higgs, Robert W. *Competition and Coercion: Blacks in the American Economy, 1865–1914.* New York, 1977.

———. *Crisis and Leviathan.* New York, 1987.

Higham, John. *Send These to Me.* Baltimore, 1984.

———. *Strangers in the Land.* New Brunswick, N.J., 1955.

Himmelfarb, Gertrude. *Lord Acton.* Chicago, 1957.

Hirschman, Albert O. *The Passions and the Interests.* Princeton, 1977.

Hirshson, Stanley P. *Farewell to the Bloody Shirt: Northern Republicans and the Southern Negro, 1877–1913.* Gloucester, Mass., 1968.

Hodgson, Godfrey. *America in Our Time: From World War II to Nixon—What Happened and Why.* Garden City, N.Y., 1976.

Hoff-Wilson, Joan. *Herbert Hoover: Forgotten Progressive.* Boston, 1975.

Hofstadter, Richard. *America at 1750.* New York, 1971.

———. *The American Political Tradition and the Men Who Made It.* New York, 1948.

————. *Anti-Intellectualism in American Life.* New York, 1963.

————. *The Idea of a Party System.* Berkeley, 1969.

————. *The Paranoid Style in American Politics, and Other Essays.* New York, 1965.

————. *The Progressive Historians: Turner, Beard, Parrington.* New York, 1968.

————. *Social Darwinism in American Thought.* Philadelphia, 1944.

Hofstadter, Richard, and Walter P. Metzger. *The Development of Academic Freedom in the United States.* 2 vols. New York, 1955.

Holt, Laurence James. *Congressional Insurgents and the Party System, 1909–1916.* Cambridge, Mass., 1967.

Honeywell, Roy J. *The Educational Work of Thomas Jefferson.* Cambridge, Mass., 1931.

Hont, Istvan, and Michael Ignatieff, eds. *Wealth and Virtue: The Shaping of Political Economy in the Scottish Enlightenment.* Cambridge, Eng., 1984.

Hoogenboom, Ari. *Outlawing the Spoils: A History of the Civil Service Reform Movement, 1865–1883.* Urbana, Ill., 1961.

Hook, Sidney. *Heresy, Yes—Conspiracy, No!* New York, 1953.

Howe, Irving. *World of Our Fathers.* Boston, 1957.

Howe, Irving, and Lewis Coser. *The American Communist Party: A Critical History.* New York, 1962.

Howe, John, Jr. *The Changing Political Thought of John Adams.* Princeton, 1966.

Howe, Mark DeWolf. *Oliver Wendell Holmes: The Proving Years, 1870–1882.* Cambridge, Mass., 1963.

Hughes, Emmet John. *The Ordeal of Power.* New York, 1963.

Huggins, Nathan T. *Slave and Citizen.* Boston, 1980.

Hurst, James Willard. *Law and the Conditions of Freedom in the Nineteenth Century United States.* Madison, Wis., 1956.

Huthmacher, J. Joseph. *Senator Robert F. Wagner and the Rise of Urban Liberalism.* New York, 1968.

Hyman, Harold M. *A More Perfect Union.* New York, 1973.

Isaac, Rhys. *The Transformation of Virginia, 1740–1790.* Chapel Hill, 1982.

Jackson, Sidney. *America's Struggle for Free Schools.* Washington, D.C., 1941.

Jaffa, Harry V. *Crisis of the House Divided: An Interpretation of the Issues in the Lincoln-Douglas Debates.* Seattle, 1959.

Jaher, Frederic C. *Doubters and Dissenters: Cataclysmic Thought in America, 1885–1918.* Glencoe, Ill., 1964.

Jameson, John F. *The American Revolution Considered as a Social Movement.* Princeton, 1926.

Jensen, Merrill. *The Articles of Confederation.* Madison, Wis., 1940.

Jordan, Philip D. *The National Road.* Indianapolis, 1948.

Jordan, Winthrop. *White over Black.* Chapel Hill, 1963.

Josephson, Matthew. *The Politicos.* New York, 1938.

Jouvenal, Bertrand de. *Sovereignty.* Chicago, 1957.

Kallen, Horace. *Culture and Democracy in the United States.* New York, 1924.

Kammen, Michael. *Empire and Interest.* New York, 1971.

————. *A Rope of Sand: The Colonial Agents, British Politics, and the American Revolution*. Ithaca, N.Y., 1968.

Kaplan, Lawrence S. *Jefferson and France*. New Haven, 1967.

Kariel, Henry. *The Decline of American Pluralism*. Stanford, 1961.

Karl, Barry D. *Charles E. Merriam and the Study of Politics*. Chicago, 1974.

Katz, Michael. *The Irony of Early American School Reform*. Cambridge, Mass., 1968.

Keezer, D. M., and Stacy May. *The Public Control of Business*. New York, 1930.

Keir, D. L. *The Constitutional History of Modern Britain, 1485–1951*. London, 1955.

Keller, Morton. *Affairs of State*. Cambridge, Mass., 1977.

Kelly, A. H., and W. A. Harbison. *The American Constitution: Its Origins and Development*. New York, 1948.

Kelly, Lawrence C. *The Assault on Assimilation: John Collier and the Origins of Indian Policy Reform*. Albuquerque, 1983.

Kendall, Willmoore. *The Conservative Affirmation*. Chicago, 1963.

————. *John Locke and the Doctrine of Majority Rule*. Urbana, Ill., 1941.

Kendall, Willmoore, and George W. Carey. *The Basic Symbols of the American Political Tradition*. Baton Rouge, 1970.

Kennedy, David M. *Over Here: The First World War and American Society*. New York, 1980.

————, ed. *Progressivism: The Critical Issues*. Boston, 1971.

Kenyon, John P. *Stuart England*. New York, 1978.

Kerney, James S. *The Political Education of Woodrow Wilson*. New York, 1926.

Kettner, James. *The Development of American Citizenship, 1608–1870*. Chapel Hill, 1978.

Kindleberger, Charles P. *The World in Depression, 1929–1939*. Berkeley, 1973.

Kipnis, Ira M. *The American Socialist Movement, 1897–1912*. New York, 1952.

Kirkendall, Richard J. *Social Scientists and Farm Politics in the Age of Roosevelt*. Columbia, Mo., 1966.

Kirkland, Edward C. *A History of American Economic Life*. New York, 1954.

————. *Industry Comes of Age: Business, Labor, and Public Policy, 1860–1897*. New York, 1961.

————. *Men, Cities, and Transportation: A Study in New England History, 1820–1900*. Cambridge Mass., 1948.

————. *The Peacemakers of 1864*. New York, 1927.

Klement, Frank L. *The Copperheads of the Middle West*. Chicago, 1960.

Knollenberg, Bernhard. *Origin of the American Revolution, 1759–1766*. New York, 1960.

Knox, Ronald. *Enthusiasm*. New York, 1950.

Koch, Gustav A. *Republican Religion*. Gloucester, Mass., 1933.

Koebner, Richard. *Empire*. Cambridge, Eng., 1961.

Kohn, Richard H. *Eagle and Sword: The Federalists and the Creation of the Military Establishment in America, 1783–1802*. New York, 1975.

Kolko, Gabriel. *The Limits of Power: The World and United States Foreign Policy, 1945–1954*. New York, 1972.

————. *Railroads and Regulation*. Princeton, 1965.

————. *The Triumph of Conservatism*. New York, 1963.

Konvitz, Milton R. *Expanding Liberties*. New York, 1966.

Kousser, J. Morgan. *The Shaping of Southern Politics: Suffrage Restriction and the Establishment of the One-Party South, 1880–1910*. New Haven, 1974.

Kramnick, Isaac F. *Bolingbroke and His Circle: The Politics of Nostalgia in the Age of Walpole*. Cambridge, Mass., 1968.

Krassner, Stephen. *Defending the National Interest: Raw Material Investments and U.S. Foreign Policy*. Princeton, 1978.

Kutler, Stanley I. *Judicial Power and Reconstruction Politics*. Chicago, 1968.

Labaree, Leonard W. *Conservatism in Early American History*. New York, 1948.

————. *Royal Government in America*. New Haven, 1930.

————, ed. *Royal Instructions to British Colonial Governors, 1670–1776*. 2 vols. New York, 1935.

Laidler, Harry W. *Concentration of Control in American Industry*. New York, 1931.

Lamoreaux, Naomi R. *The Great Merger Movement in American Business*. New York, 1985.

Lampard, Eric E. *The Rise of the Dairy Industry in Wisconsin: A Study in Agricultural Change, 1860–1920*. Madison, Wis., 1963.

Landes, David S. *The Unbound Prometheus*. New York, 1969.

Lang, James. *Conquest and Commerce: Spain and England in the Americas*. New York, 1975.

Larson, Arthur. *Eisenhower: The President Nobody Knew*. New York, 1968.

Larson, Henrietta M. *Jay Cooke, Private Banker*. Cambridge, Mass., 1936.

Lasch, Christopher. *The New Radicalism in America, 1889–1963*. New York, 1965.

Laski, Harold J. *Studies in the Problem of Sovereignty*. New Haven, 1917.

Lenski, Gerhard E. *The Religious Factor*. Garden City, N.Y., 1961.

Leonard, Herman B. *Checks Unbalanced: The Quiet Side of Public Spending*. New York, 1986.

Lerner, Max, ed. *The Mind and Faith of Justice Holmes*. Boston, 1943.

Leuchtenburg, William E. *Franklin D. Roosevelt and the New Deal, 1932–1940*. New York, 1963.

————. *In the Shadow of FDR*. Ithaca, N.Y., 1983.

————. *The Perils of Prosperity*. Chicago, 1958.

Levitan Sar, William Johnston, and Robert Taggert. *Still a Dream: The Changing Status of Blacks Since 1960*. Cambridge, Mass., 1975.

Levy, Leonard W. *Jefferson and Civil Liberties: The Darker Side*. Cambridge, Mass., 1963.

————. *Legacy of Suppression*. Cambridge, Mass., 1960.

Lewis, W. David. *From Newgate to Dannemora*. Ithaca, N.Y., 1965.

Leyburn, James G. *The Scotch-Irish: A Social History.* Chapel Hill, 1962.

Link, Arthur S. *Wilson: The New Freedom.* Princeton, 1956.

———. *Wilson: The Road to the White House.* Princeton, 1947.

———. *Woodrow Wilson and the Progressive Era, 1910–1917.* New York, 1963.

Litt, Edgar. *Beyond Pluralism: Ethnic Politics in America.* Glenview, Ill., 1970.

Litwack, Leon F. *Been in the Storm So Long: The Aftermath of Slavery.* New York, 1979.

———. *North of Slavery: The Negro in the Free States, 1790–1860.* Chicago, 1961.

Logan, Rayford W. *The Negro in American Life and Thought: The Nadir, 1877–1901.* New York, 1954.

Lowi, Theodore J. *The End of Liberalism.* New York, 1969.

Lubell, Samuel. *The Future of American Politics.* New York, 1952.

Lubove, Roy. *The Struggle for Social Security, 1900–1935.* Cambridge, Mass., 1968.

Lyman, Stanford M. *Chinese Americans.* New York, 1974.

Lynd, Robert S. *Middletown.* New York, 1929.

MacIver, Robert. *Community.* London, 1920.

———. *The Modern State.* London, 1926.

MacKesy, Piers. *The War for America, 1775–1783.* Cambridge, Mass., 1964.

MacNeil, Neil. *The Forge of Democracy.* New York, 1963.

Macy, Jesse. *The Anti-Slavery Crusade.* New Haven, 1919.

Maddox, Robert J. *The New Left and the Origins of the Cold War.* Princeton, 1973.

Maier, Pauline. *From Resistance to Revolution: Colonial Radicals and the Development of American Opposition to Great Britain, 1765–1777.* New York, 1972.

———. *The Old Revolutionaries: Political Lives in the Age of Samuel Adams.* New York, 1980.

Main, Jackson T. *The Anti-Federalists.* Chapel Hill, 1961.

———. *Social Structure of Revolutionary America.* Princeton, 1965.

———. *The Sovereign States, 1775–1783.* New York, 1973.

———. *The Upper House in Revolutionary America, 1763–1788.* Madison, Wis., 1967.

Maitland, Frederick W. *A Sketch of English Legal History.* New York, 1915.

Malone, Dumas. *Jefferson and the Rights of Man.* Boston, 1951.

———. *Jefferson the President: First Term, 1801–1805.* Boston, 1970.

———. *Jefferson the President: Second Term, 1805–1809.* Boston, 1970.

———. *Jefferson, the Sage of Monticello.* Boston, 1981.

———. *Jefferson the Virginian.* Boston, 1948.

Mandelbaum, Seymour J. *Boss Tweed's New York.* New York, 1965.

Mann, Arthur. *LaGuardia Comes to Power.* Philadelphia, 1965.

Markowitz, Norman D. *The Rise and Fall of the People's Century: Henry A. Wallace and American Liberalism, 1941–1948.* New York, 1973.

Martin, Waldo E. *The Mind of Frederick Douglass.* Chapel Hill, 1984.

Marty, Martin E. *Righteous Empire: The Protestant Experience in America.* New York, 1970.

Marsden, George. *Religion and American Culture.* Orlando, 1990.

Mason, Philip P. *A History of American Roads.* Chicago, 1967.

Mathieson, W. C. *British Slavery and Its Abolition, 1823–1838.* New York, 1936.

May, Henry F. *The Enlightenment in America.* New York, 1976.

———. *Protestant Churches and Industrial America.* New York, 1949.

McClellan, David. *Marxism After Marx.* Boston, 1979.

McCormick, Richard P. *The History of Voting in New Jersey.* New Brunswick, N.J., 1953.

———. *The Second American Party System.* Chapel Hill, 1966.

McCoy, Donald R. *Calvin Coolidge.* New York, 1967.

McFaul, John. *The Politics of Jacksonian Finance.* Ithaca, N.Y., 1972.

McFeely, William S. *Yankee Stepfather: General O. O. Howard and the Freedmen.* New Haven, 1968.

McLaughlin, William G. *New England Dissent.* 2 vols. Cambridge, Mass., 1971.

McPherson, James M. *The Struggle for Equality.* Princeton, 1964.

McWilliams, John. *Political Justice in a Republic.* Berkeley, 1972.

Meinecke, Friedrich. *Machiavellism: The Doctrine of Raison d'Etat and Its Place in Modern History.* New York, 1965.

Meier, August. *Negro Thought in America, 1880–1915.* Ann Arbor, 1963.

Meiklejohn, Alexander. *Free Speech in Its Relation to Self-Government.* New York, 1948.

Merrens, Harry T. *Colonial North Carolina.* Chapel Hill, 1964.

Merrill, Horace S. *Bourbon Democracy of the Middle West, 1865–1896.* Baton Rouge, 1953.

Mertz, Paul. *New Deal Policy and Southern Rural Poverty.* Baton Rouge, 1978.

Meyers, Marvin. *The Jacksonian Persuasion.* Stanford, 1957.

Middlekauff, Robert. *The Glorious Cause: The American Revolution, 1763–1789.* New York, 1982.

———. *The Mathers.* New York, 1971.

Miller, John C. *Alexander Hamilton: Portrait in Paradox.* New York, 1959.

———. *The Federalist Era, 1789–1801.* New York, 1960.

———. *Sam Adams.* Boston, 1936.

Miller, Perry. *The New England Mind: From Colony to Province.* Cambridge, Mass., 1953.

———. *Orthodoxy in Massachusetts.* Cambridge, Mass., 1934.

———. *Roger Williams.* Indianapolis, 1953.

Miller, William, ed. *Men in Business.* New York, 1962.

Miller, Zane. *The Urbanization of Modern America.* New York, 1973.

Millett, Allan R., and Peter Maslowski. *From the Common Defense: A Military History of the United States of America.* New York, 1984.

Mitchell, Broadus. *Depression Decade: From New Era Through New Deal, 1929–1941.* New York, 1947.

Moley, Raymond. *After Seven Years.* New York, 1939.

Montross, Lynn. *The Reluctant Rebels.* New York, 1950.

Moore, Albert B. *Conscription and Conflict in the Confederacy.* New York, 1924.

Moore, Edmund A. *A Catholic Runs for President.* Gloucester, Mass., 1968.

Moore, Edward C. *American Pragmatism: Peirce, James, and Dewey.* New York, 1961.

Morgan, Edmund S. *American Slavery, American Freedom.* New York 1985.

———. *The Birth of the Republic, 1763–1789.* Chicago, 1956.

———. *Inventing the People.* New York, 1988.

———. *The Puritan Dilemma: The Story of John Winthrop.* Boston, 1958.

———. *Roger Williams.* New York, 1967.

Morgan, Edmund S., and Helen M. Morgan. *The Stamp Act Crisis.* Chapel Hill, 1953.

Morris, Richard B. *The American Revolution Reconsidered.* New York, 1967.

———. *Government and Labor in Early America.* New York, 1946.

———. *Studies in the History of American Law.* New York, 1930.

Morris, Thomas D. *Free Men All: The Personal Liberty Laws of the North, 1780–1861.* Baltimore, 1974.

Moynihan, Daniel P. *Maximum Feasible Misunderstanding.* New York, 1969.

Mueller, Hans Eberhard. *Bureaucracy, Education, and Monopoly: Civil Service Reform in Prussia and England.* Berkeley, 1984.

Munro, W. B. *The Initiative, Referendum, and Recall.* New York, 1912.

Murdoch, Eugene C. *One Million Men: The Civil War Draft in the North.* Madison, Wis., 1971.

Murray, Charles. *Losing Ground: American Social Policy, 1950–1980.* New York, 1984.

Murray, John Courtney. *We Hold These Truths.* New York, 1960.

Myrdal, Gunnar. *An American Dilemma.* New York, 1944.

Nagel, Paul C. *One Nation Indivisible: The Union in American Thought, 1776–1861.* New York, 1964.

Namier, Louis B. *England in the Age of the American Revolution.* Rev. ed. London, 1961.

Nash, Gary B. *Red, White, and Black: The Peoples of Early America.* Englewood Cliffs, N.J., 1982.

Nash, Bradley D., and Cornelius Lynde. *A Hook in Leviathan: A Critical Interpretation of the Hoover Commission Report.* New York, 1950.

Nash, George H. *The Conservative Intellectual Movement in America Since 1945.* New York, 1976.

Nef, John U. *War and Human Progress.* Cambridge, Mass., 1952.

Nettels, Curtis P. *The Emergence of a National Economy, 1775–1815.* New York, 1962.

———. *The Money Supply of the American Colonies Before 1720.* Madison, Wis., 1934.

Nevins, Allan. *The American States During and After the Revolution*. New York, 1924.

———. *Ordeal of the Union*. 2 vols. New York, 1947.

———. *Study in Power: John D. Rockefeller, Industrialist and Philanthropist*. 2 vols. New York, 1953.

———. *The War for the Union*. 4 vols. New York 1959–71.

Nevins, Allan, and Frank E. Hill. *Ford: Expansion and Challenge, 1915–1933*. New York, 1957.

Nichols, Roy F. *The Disruption of American Democracy*. New York, 1948.

Noble, David W. *The Paradox of Progressive Thought*. Minneapolis, 1958.

Nock, Albert J. *Jefferson*. New York, 1926.

Novak, Michael. *The Rise of the Unmeltable Ethnics*. New York, 1972.

Olson, Alison G., and Richard Maxwell Brown, eds. *Anglo-American Political Relations, 1675–1775*. New Brunswick, N.J., 1970.

Orsi, Robert A. *Madonna of 115th Street: Faith and Community in Italian Harlem, 1880–1950*. New Haven, 1955.

Osgood, Herbert L. *The American Colonies in the Eighteenth Century*. 4 vols. New York, 1924.

———. *The American Colonies in the Seventeenth Century*. 3 vols. New York, 1904.

Ostrogorski, M. *Democracy and the Organization of Political Parties*. 2 vols. New York, 1902.

Owsley, Frank L. *States Rights in the Confederacy*. Chicago, 1925.

Page, Benjamin I. *Who Gets What from Government*. Berkeley, 1983.

Palmer, Robert R. *The Age of the Democratic Revolution*. Vol. I of 2 vols. Princeton, 1959.

Park, Robert Ezra. *Collected Papers*. New York, 1974.

Patten, Simon. *Essays in Economic Theory*. Edited by R. G. Tugwell. New York, 1924.

Patterson, James T. *Congressional Conservatism and the New Deal*. Lexington, Ky., 1967.

———. *Mr. Republican*. Boston, 1972.

———. *The New Deal and the States*. Princeton, 1969.

Pechman, Joseph, ed. *Setting National Priorities: Agenda for the 1980s*. Washington, D.C., 1980.

Pechman, Joseph, and Benjamin Okner. *Who Bears the Tax Burden*. Washington, D.C., 1974.

Peckham, Howard. *The Colonial Wars, 1689–1762*. Chicago, 1964.

Perman, Michael. *Reunion Without Compromise*. Cambridge, Mass., 1973.

Peristiany, J. G., ed. *Contributions to Mediterranean Sociology*. Paris, 1968.

Pessen, Edward. *Riches, Class, and Power Before the Civil War*. Lexington, Mass., 1973.

Peterson, Merrill. *The Jefferson Image in the American Mind*. New York, 1960.

Pierson, George W. *Tocqueville and Beaumont in America*. Gloucester, Mass., 1969.

Pocock, J. G. A. *The Machiavellian Moment*. Princeton, 1975.

———. *Virtue, Commerce, and History.* Cambridge, Eng., 1985.

Podhoretz, Norman. *Making It.* New York, 1967.

Pole, Jack R. *Political Representation in England and the Origins of the American Republic.* New York, 1966.

Polenberg, Richard. *Fighting Faith: The Abrams Case, the Supreme Court, and Free Speech.* New York, 1987.

———. *War and Society: The United States, 1941–1945.* Philadelphia, 1972.

Potter, David M. *The Impending Crisis, 1848–1861.* New York, 1976.

———. *Lincoln and His Party in the Secession Crisis.* New Haven, 1942.

———. *The South and the Sectional Conflict.* Baton Rouge, 1968.

Powell, Sumner C. *Puritan Village.* Middletown, Conn., 1963.

Pressly, Thomas J. *Americans Interpret Their Civil War.* Princeton, 1954.

Pribram, Karl. *A History of Economic Reasoning.* Baltimore, 1983.

Primm, James N. *Economic Policy in the Development of a Western State: Missouri, 1820–1860.* Cambridge, Mass., 1954.

Prothro, James W. *The Dollar Decade: Business Ideas in the 1920s.* Baton Rouge, 1954.

Prucha, Francis P. *The Great Father: The United States Government and the American Indians.* 2 vols. Lincoln, Nebr., 1984.

Quandt, Jean. *From the Small Town to the Great Community: The Social Thought of Progressive Intellectuals.* New Brunswick, N.J., 1970.

Quinn, David B. *England and the Discovery of America.* New York, 1973.

Raab, Felix. *The English Face of Machiavelli: A Changing Interpretation, 1500–1700.* Toronto, 1964.

Radosh, Ronald. *Prophets on the Right: Profiles of Conservative Critics of American Globalism.* New York, 1975.

Rae, John B. *The Road and the Car in American Life.* Cambridge, Mass., 1971.

Rainwater, Lee, and William L. Yancey. *The Moynihan Report and the Politics of Controversy.* Cambridge, Mass., 1967.

Randall, James G. *Constitutional Problems Under Lincoln.* New York, 1926.

———. *Lincoln, the Liberal Statesman.* New York, 1947.

Randall, James G., and David H. Donald. *The Civil War and Reconstruction.* Lexington, Mass., 1969.

Ransom, Roger, and Richard Sutch. *One Kind of Freedom: The Economic Consequences of Emancipation.* New York, 1977.

Rauch, Basil. *The History of the New Deal, 1933–1938.* New York, 1944.

Rawley, James A. *Race and Politics: "Bleeding Kansas" and the Coming of the Civil War.* Philadelphia, 1969.

Redlich, Fritz. *The Molding of American Banking.* New York, 1951.

Reeves, Thomas C. *Gentleman Boss: The Life of Chester Alan Arthur.* New York, 1975.

Reichard, Gary W. *The Reaffirmation of Republicanism: Eisenhower and the Eighty-third Congress.* Knoxville, Tenn., 1975.

Reimers, David M. *Still the Golden Door.* New York, 1985.

Remini, Robert V. *Andrew Jackson and the Bank War.* New York, 1967.

———. *The Election of Andrew Jackson.* Philadelphia, 1963.

Rice, Madeleine M. *American Catholic Opinion in the Slavery Controversy.* New York, 1944.

Richardson, James F. *The New York Police: Colonial Times to 1901.* New York, 1970.

Riegel, Robert. *The Story of the Western Railroads.* New York, 1926.

Rivlin, Alice M. *Reviving the American Dream.* Washington, D.C., 1992.

Roark, James L. *Masters Without Slaves: Southern Planters in the Civil War and Reconstruction.* New York, 1977.

Robbins, Caroline. *The Eighteenth-Century Commonwealthman.* Cambridge, Mass., 1959.

Robbins, Roy. *Our Landed Heritage.* Princeton, 1942.

Rorabaugh, W. J. *The Craft Apprentice.* New York, 1986.

Rose, Willie Lee. *Rehearsal for Reconstruction.* Indianapolis, 1964.

Rosen, Eliot. *Hoover, Roosevelt, and the Brains Trust.* New York, 1977.

Rosenkrantz, Barbara. *Public Health and the State.* Cambridge, Mass., 1972.

Ross, Edward A. *The Old World in the New.* New York, 1914.

Rossiter, Clinton. *Seedtime of the Republic.* New York 1953.

Rothbard, Murray N. *Salutary Neglect: The American Colonies in the First Half of the 18th Century.* New Rochelle, N.Y., 1975.

Rothman, David J. *The Discovery of the Asylum: Social Order and Disorder in the New Republic.* Boston, 1971.

Roucek Joseph C., and Bernard Eisenberg. *American Ethnic Politics.* Westport, Conn., 1982.

Rutland, Robert A. *The Birth of the Bill of Rights, 1776–1791.* Chapel Hill, 1955.

———. *The Ordeal of the Constitution.* Norman, Okla., 1966.

Rutman, Darrett. *Winthrop's Boston.* Chapel Hill, 1965.

Saloutos, Theodore, and John D. Hicks. *Agricultural Discontent in the Middle West, 1900–1939.* Madison, Wis., 1951.

Sargent, F. P., *et al. Immigration: The Problem.* Philadelphia, 1904.

Satz, Ronald N. *American Indian Policy in the Jacksonian Era.* Lincoln, Nebr., 1974.

Savelle, Max. *Seeds of Liberty.* New York, 1948.

Schattschneider, E. E. *Politics, Pressures, and the Tariff.* New York, 1935.

Scheiber, Harry N. *The Wilson Administration and Civil Liberties, 1917–21.* Ithaca, N.Y., 1960.

Schlesinger, Arthur, Jr. *The Age of Jackson.* Boston, 1945.

———. *The Crisis of the Old Order, 1919–1933.* Boston, 1957.

———. *The Disuniting of America.* New York, 1992.

———. *Orestes A. Brownson.* Boston, 1939.

———. *The Politics of Upheaval.* Boston, 1960.

Schlesinger, Arthur M., Sr. *The Colonial Merchants and the American Revolution, 1763–1776.* New York, 1918.

———. *New Viewpoints in American History.* New York, 1922.

Schochet, Gordon J. *Patriarchalism in Political Thought.* New York, 1975.

Schultz, Charles L. *The Distribution of Farm Subsidies: Who Gets the Benefits.* Washington, D.C., 1971.

Schumpeter, Joseph. *History of Economic Analysis.* New York, 1954.

Schwartz, Harold. *Samuel Gridley Howe.* Cambridge, Mass., 1956.

Schwartz, Jordan A. *The Interregnum of Despair: Hoover, Congress, and the Depression.* Urbana, Ill., 1970.

Seidman, Joel. *American Labor from Defense to Reconversion.* Chicago, 1953.

Selznick, Philip. *TVA and the Grass Roots.* Berkeley, 1949.

Servan-Schreiber, Jean-Jacques. *The American Challenge.* New York, 1968.

Shannon, Fred A. *The Farmer's Last Frontier, 1860–1897.* New York, 1945.

Sharp, James R. *The Jacksonians Versus the Banks: Politics in the States After the Panic of 1837.* New York, 1970.

Sharpless, Isaac. *A Quaker Experiment in Government.* 2 vols. Philadelphia, 1902.

Shonfield, Andrew. *Modern Capitalism.* New York, 1978.

Shryock, Richard H. *Medicine in America.* Baltimore, 1966.

Shy, John. *A People Numerous and Armed.* New York, 1976.

Sitkoff, Harvard. *The Struggle for Black Equality, 1954–1980.* New York, 1981.

Simpson, Alan. *Puritanism in Old and New England.* Chicago, 1955.

Sirmans, Marion E. *Colonial South Carolina: A Political History, 1663–1763.* Chapel Hill, 1966.

Skaggs, Jimmy M. *The Cattle Trading Industry.* Lawrence, Kans., 1973.

Sklar, Martin J. *The Corporate Reconstruction of American Capitalism.* New York, 1988.

Smith, Abbot E. *Colonists in Bondage.* Chapel Hill, 1947.

Smith, Denis Mack. *The Making of Modern Italy.* New York, 1968.

Smith, J. Allen. *The Spirit of American Government.* New York, 1907.

Smith, James C., ed. *Seventeenth-Century America.* Chapel Hill, 1959.

Smith, James Morton. *Freedom's Fetters: The Alien and Sedition Laws and American Civil Liberties.* Ithaca, N.Y., 1956.

Sosin, Jack M. *The Revolutionary Frontier, 1763–1783.* New York, 1967.

———. *Whitehall and the Wilderness, 1763–1775.* Lincoln, Nebr., 1961.

Soule, George H. *A Planned Society.* New York, 1932.

———. *Prosperity Decade.* New York, 1947.

Sproat, John G. *The Best Man: Liberal Reformers in the Gilded Age.* New York, 1968.

Stampp, Kenneth M. *And the War Came: The North and the Secession Crisis, 1860–61.* Baton Rouge, 1950.

———. *The Era of Reconstruction, 1865–1877.* New York, 1965.

———. *The Peculiar Institution.* New York, 1956.

Steel, Ronald. *Walter Lippmann and the American Century.* New York, 1981.

Steele, Ian K. *The Politics of Colonial Policy: The Board of Trade in Colonial Administration, 1696–1720.* Oxford, Eng., 1968.

Stein, Herbert. *The Fiscal Revolution in America.* Chicago, 1969.

Stein, Judith. *The World of Marcus Garvey: Race and Class in Modern Society.* Baton Rouge, 1986.

Stockman, David A. *The Triumph of Politics.* New York, 1986.

Storing, Herbert J., and Murray Day. *What the Anti-Federalists Were For.* Chicago, 1981.

Stourzh, Gerald. *Alexander Hamilton and the Idea of Republican Government.* Stanford, 1970.

Strauss, Leo. *The Political Philosophy of Hobbes.* Oxford, Eng., 1936.

Swisher, Carl Brent. *Roger B. Taney.* New York, 1935.

Sydnor, Charles J. *Gentleman Freeholders.* Chapel Hill, 1952.

Syrett, Harold C. *Andrew Jackson.* Indianapolis, 1953.

———, ed. *The Gentleman and the Tiger: The Autobiography of George B. McClellan, Jr.* Philadelphia, 1956.

Tager, Jack. *Intellectual as Urban Reformer: Brand Whitlock and the Progressive Movement.* Cleveland, 1968.

Tanner, Joseph R., ed. *Constitutional Documents of the Reign of James I, A.D. 1603–1625.* Cambridge, Eng., 1930.

Taylor, George Rogers. *The Transportation Revolution, 1815–1860.* New York, 1951.

Temin, Peter. *The Jacksonian Economy.* New York, 1969.

Terrill, Tom E. *The Tariff, Politics, and American Foreign Policy, 1874–1901.* Westport, Conn., 1973.

Thayer, Theodore G. *Pennsylvania Politics and the Growth of Democracy, 1740–1776.* Harrisburg, Pa., 1953.

Thelen, David P. *Robert M. La Follette and the Insurgent Spirit.* Boston, 1976.

Thomas, Emory M. *The Confederacy as a Revolutionary Experience.* Englewood Cliffs, N.J., 1970.

Thomas, John L. *Alternative America: Henry George, Edward Bellamy, Henry Demarest Lloyd, and the Adversary Tradition.* Cambridge, Mass., 1983.

Thomas, Norman. *After the New Deal, What?* New York, 1936.

Thorelli, Hans B. *The Federal Antitrust Policy: Origination of an American Tradition.* Baltimore, 1955.

Tolliday, Steven, and Jonathan Zeitlin, eds. *Shop Floor Bargaining and the State.* Cambridge, Mass., 1985.

Trefousse, Hans. *The Radical Republicans.* New York, 1969.

Trelease, Allen W. *White Terror.* New York, 1971.

Trinterud, Leonard J. *The Forming of an American Tradition.* Philadelphia, 1949.

Troen, Selwyn K. *The Public and the Schools: Shaping the St. Louis School System, 1838–1920.* Columbia, Mo., 1975.

True, Alfred C. *A History of Agricultural Experimentation and Research in the United States, 1607–1925.* Washington, D.C., 1937.

Tugwell, R. G. *Industry's Coming of Age.* New York, 1927.

———, ed. *The Trend of Economics.* New York, 1924.

Tyack, David. *The One Best System: A History of American Urban Education.* Cambridge, Mass., 1974.

Tyler, Alice Felt. *Freedom's Ferment.* Minneapolis, 1944.

Ubbelohde, Carl. *The Vice-Admiralty Courts and the American Revolution.* Chapel Hill, 1960.

Urofsky, Melvin I. *Louis D. Brandeis and the Progressive Tradition.* Boston, 1981.

U.S. House of Representatives Committee on Post Office and Civil Service. *History of Civil Service Merit Systems of the United States and Selected Foreign Countries.* Washington, D.C., 1976.

U.S. Senate Committee on Government Operations. *Confidence and Concern: Citizens View American Government.* Washington, D.C., 1973.

Voegeli, V. Jacque. *Free but Not Equal.* Chicago, 1963.

Von Abele, Rudolph. *Alexander H. Stephens.* New York, 1946.

Vossler, Otto. *Jefferson and the American Revolutionary Ideal.* Washington, D.C., 1981.

Walzer, Michael. *Radical Principles: Reflections of an Un-Reconstructed Democrat.* New York, 1980.

Ward, John William. *Andrew Jackson, Symbol for an Age.* New York, 1955.

Warner, Sam Bass. *Streetcar Suburbs: The Process of Growth in Boston, 1870–1900.* Cambridge, Mass., 1962.

———. *The Urban Wilderness: A History of the American City.* New York, 1972.

Warner, W. Lloyd. *Yankee City: The Status System of a Modern Community.* New Haven, 1942.

Washburn, Wilcomb E. *The Government and the Rebel.* Chapel Hill, 1957.

Webb, Sidney, and Beatrice Webb. *English Local Government from the Revolution to the Municipal Corporations Act.* London, 1908.

Weber, Eugen. *Peasants into Frenchmen: The Modernization of Rural France, 1870–1914.* Stanford, 1976.

Weinstein, James. *The Corporate Ideal in the Liberal State, 1900–1918.* Boston, 1968.

Weisbord, Robert G. *Genocide? Birth Control and the Black American.* Westport, Conn., 1975.

Weiss, Nancy. *Farewell to the Party of Lincoln.* Princeton, 1983.

White, Leonard D. *The Republican Era, 1869–1901.* New York, 1958.

White, Morton. *The Origins of Dewey's Instrumentalism.* New York, 1943.

———. *Social Thought in America: The Revolt Against Formalism.* New York, 1949.

White, Theodore H. *The Making of the President, 1960.* New York, 1961.

Wickwire, F. B. *British Subministers and Colonial America, 1763–1783.* Princeton, 1966.

Weibe, Robert. *Businessmen and Reform: A Study of the Progressive Movement.* Cambridge, Mass., 1962.

———. *The Search for Order, 1877–1920.* New York, 1967.

Wiley, Bell I. *The Life of Johnny Reb.* Indianapolis, 1943.

Will, George F. *The Morning After.* New York, 1986.

Williams, T. Harry. *Lincoln and the Radicals.* Madison, Wis., 1941.

Williamson, Chilton. *American Suffrage: From Property to Democracy, 1760–1860.* Princeton, 1960.

Williamson, Harold F., *et al. The American Petroleum Industry.* 2 vols. Evanston, Ill., 1959–63.

Wills, Garry. *Inventing America: Jefferson's Declaration of Independence.* Garden City, N.Y., 1978.

Wilson, Edmund. *Patriotic Gore.* New York, 1962.

———. *The Shores of Light.* New York, 1952.

Wilson, James Q. *Thinking About Crime.* Rev. ed. New York, 1983.

Wiltse, Charles M. *John C. Calhoun, Sectionalist, 1840–1850.* Indianapolis, 1951.

Wish, Harvey. *George Fitzhugh, Propagandist of the Old South.* Baton Rouge, 1943.

Wolfenstein, Eugene. *The Victims of Democracy: Malcolm X and the Black Revolution.* Berkeley, 1981.

Wolff, Robert P., Barrington Moore, Jr., and Herbert Marcuse. *A Critique of Pure Tolerance.* Boston, 1965.

Wolin, Sheldon. *Politics and Vision.* Boston, 1960.

Wood, Forrest. *Black Scare.* Berkeley, 1968.

Wood, Gordon S. *The Creation of the American Republic, 1776–1787.* Chapel Hill, 1969.

Woodward, C. Vann. *Origins of the New South, 1877–1913.* Baton Rouge, 1951.

———. *Reunion and Reaction.* Boston, 1951.

———. *The Strange Career of Jim Crow.* Rev. ed. New York, 1974.

Wright, Benjamin. *Consensus and Continuity, 1776–1787.* Boston, 1958.

Wright, Louis B. *Cultural Life of the American Colonies, 1607–1763.* New York, 1957.

———. *The First Gentlemen of Virginia.* San Marino, Calif., 1940.

Yarmolinsky, Adam. *The Military Establishment: Its Impact on American Society.* New York, 1971.

Young, Eleanor. *Forgotten Patriot: Robert Morris.* New York, 1950.

Young, Kimball. *Isn't One Wife Enough?* Westport, Conn., 1954.

Young, Roland A. *Congressional Politics in the Second World War.* New York, 1956.

Zemsky, Robert. *Merchants, Farmers, and River Gods.* Boston, 1971.

Zuckerman, Michael. *Peaceable Kingdoms.* New York, 1970.

ARTICLES AND ESSAYS

Agresto, John T. "Liberty, Virtue, and Republicanism: 1776–1787." *Review of Politics,* XXXIX (1977).

Ashcroft, Richard, and M. M. Goldsmith. "Locke, Revolution Principles, and the Formation of Whig Ideology." *Historical Journal,* XXVI (1983).

Bailyn, Bernard. "Politics and Social Structure in Virginia." In *Seventeenth Century America,* edited by James C. Smith. Chapel Hill, 1959.

Baker, Gordon. "Thomas Jefferson on Academic Freedom." *American Association of University Professors Bulletin,* XXXIX (1953).

Baskin, Darryl. "American Pluralism: Theory, Practice, and Ideology." *Journal of Politics,* XXXII (1970).

Berthoff, Rowland, and J. M. Murrin. "Feudalism, Communism, and the Yeoman Freeholder." In *Essays on the American Revolution,* edited by Stephen G. Kurtz and James H. Hutson. Chapel Hill, 1973.

Boatwright, Mody C. "The Myth of Frontier Individualism." *Southwest Social Science Quarterly,* XXII (1941).

Brebner, J. B. "Laissez Faire and State Intervention in Nineteenth Century Britain." *Journal of Economic History, Supplement VIII* (1948).

Brownlow, Louis. "The New Role of the Public Administrator." *National Municipal Review,* XXIII (1934).

Buel, Richard, Jr. "Democracy and the American Revolution: A Frame of Reference." *William and Mary Quarterly,* XXI (1964).

Callender, Guy S. "The Early Transportation and Banking Enterprises of the States in Relation to the Growth of Corporations." *Quarterly Journal of Economics,* XVII (1902).

Coben, Stanley. "Northeastern Business and Radical Reconstruction: A Re-examination." *Mississippi Valley Historical Review,* XLVI (1959).

Cohen, Felix S. "Indian Rights and the Federal Courts." *University of Minnesota Law Review* (1940).

Corwin, Edwin S. "The Progress of Constitutional Theory from the Signing of the Declaration of Independence to the Meeting of the Philadelphia Convention." *American Historical Review,* XXX (1925).

———. Review of Beard's *An Economic Interpretation of the Constitution of the United States. History Teachers' Magazine,* V (1914).

Cuff, Robert D. "We Band of Brothers—Woodrow Wilson's War Managers." *Canadian Review of American Studies,* II (1974).

Davis, David B. "Some Themes of Counter-Subversion." *Mississippi Valley Historical Review,* XLVII (1960).

Divine, W. R. "The Second Hoover Commission Report." *Public Administration Review,* XV (1955).

Fox, Dixon Ryan. "The Protestant Counter-Reformation." *New York History,* XVI (1935).

Frantz, Laurent B. "Congressional Power to Enforce the Fourteenth Amendment Against Private Acts" *Yale Law Journal,* LXXIII (1964).

Fuller, J. F. C. "The Place of the American Civil War in the Evolution of War." *The Army Quarterly,* XXVI (1933).

Gaus, J. M., and L. D. White. "Public Administration in the United States in 1933." *American Political Science Review,* XXVIII (1934).

Greven, Philip J., Jr. "Historical Demography and Colonial America." *William and Mary Quarterly,* XXIV (1967).

Griffith, Robert. "Dwight D. Eisenhower and the Corporate Commonwealth." *American Historical Review,* LXXXVII (1982).

Hammond, Bray. "Free Banks and Corporations: The New York Free Banking Act of 1838." *Journal of Political Economy,* XLIV (1936).

Hansen, Marcus Lee. "The Third Generation in America." *Commentary,* XIV (1952).

Hawley, Ellis W. "The Discovery and Study of Corporate Liberalism." *Business History Review,* LII (1978).

Hays, Samuel P. "The Social Analysis of American Political History." *Political Science Quarterly,* LXXX (1965).

Herberg, Will. "American Marxist Political Theory." In *Socialism in American Life,* edited by Donald Egbert and Stow Persons. 2 vols. Princeton, 1952.

Hexter, Jack. "Power Struggle, Parliament, and Liberty in Early Stuart England." *Journal of Modern History,* L (1978).

Holt, Michael F. "The Democratic Party." In *History of U.S. Political Parties,* edited by Arthur Schlesinger, Jr. New York, 1973.

Isaacs, Harold. "The New Pluralists." *Commentary,* LIII (1972).

Jensen, Merrill. "Democracy and the American Revolution." *Huntington Library Quarterly,* XX (1957).

Johnson, A. B. "The Legislative History of Corporations in the State of New York: The Progress of Liberal Sentiments." *Hunt's Merchants' Magazine,* XXIII (1950).

Kaczorowski, Robert J. "Searching for the Intent of the Framers of the Fourteenth Amendment." *Connecticut Law Review,* V (1973).

Kallen, Horace. "Democracy Versus the Melting Pot." *The Nation,* C (1915).

Kenyon, Cecilia M. "Men of Little Faith: The Anti-Federalists on the Nature of Representative Government." *William and Mary Quarterly,* XII (1955).

Keynes, J. M., and Harold J. Laski. "Can America Spend Its Way Into Recovery?" *Redbook,* December, 1934.

Kranel, Richard. "Prince Henry of Prussia and the Regency of the United States." *American Historical Review,* XVII (1911).

Krasner, Stephen. "Approaches to the State: Alternative Conceptions and Historical Dynamics." *Comparative Politics,* VI (1984).

Leach, Richard H. "The Impact of Immigration upon New York, 1840–1860." *New York History,* XXXI (1950).

Lindbloom, Charles E. "Another State of Mind." *American Political Science Review,* LXXVI (1982).

Lockridge, Kenneth A. "The Population of Dedham, Massachusetts, 1636–1736." *Economic History Review,* XIX (1966).

Lowery, David, and William D. Berry. "Growth of Government in the U.S.: An Empirical Assessment of Competing Explanations." *American Journal of Political Science,* XXVII (1983).

Maier, Pauline. "The Charleston Mob and the Evolution of Popular Politics in Revolutionary South Carolina." *Perspectives in American History,* IV (1970).

Main, Jackson T. "Government by the People: The American Revolution and the Democratization of the Legislatures." *William and Mary Quarterly,* XXIII (1966).

Manley, John F. "Neo-Pluralism: A Class Analysis of Pluralism I and Pluralism II." *American Political Science Review,* LXXVII (1983).

McGiffert, Michael. "American Puritan Studies in the 1960s." *William and Mary Quarterly,* XXXVII (1970).

Metcalf, Evan B. "Secretary Hoover and the Emergence of Macroeconomic Management." *Business History Review,* XLIX (1975).

Miller, Perry. "From the Covenant to the Revival." In *Religion in American Life,* edited by James Ward Smith and Abelard Jamison. Princeton, 1961.

Morgan, Edmund. "The First American Boom." *William and Mary Quarterly,* XXVIII (1971).

Morris, Richard B. "Insurrection in Massachusetts." In *America in Crisis,* edited by Daniel Aaron. New York, 1952.

Nettl, J. P. "The State as a Conceptual Variable." *World Politics,* XX (1967).

Palmer, Robert R. "The Dubious Democrat: Thomas Jefferson in Bourbon France." *Political Science Quarterly,* LXXII (1957).

Paul, Rodman. "The Origin of the Chinese Issue in California." *Mississippi Valley Historical Review,* XXV (1938).

Paxson, Fredrich L. "The Highway Movement, 1916–1935." *American Historical Review,* LI (1946).

Pole, Jack R. "Historians and the Problem of Early American Democracy." *American Historical Review,* LXVII (1962).

Price, Jacob M. "Economic Growth of the Chesapeake and the European Market, 1697–1775." *Journal of Economic History,* XXIV (1964).

Schlesinger, Arthur, Jr. "The Ike Age Revisited." *Reviews in American History,* XI (1983).

Shalhope, Robert E. "Towards a Republican Synthesis: The Emergence of an Understanding of Republicanism in American Historiography." *William and Mary Quarterly,* XXIX (1972).

Shannon, Fred A. "The Homestead Act and the Labor Surplus." *American Historical Review,* XLI (1936).

Simkins, Francis B. "New Viewpoints of Southern Reconstruction." *Journal of Southern History,* V (1939).

Smith, Daniel S. "The Demographic History of Colonial New England." *Journal of Economic History,* XXXII (1972).

Soltow, Lee. "Economic Inequality in the United States in the Period from 1790 to 1860." *Journal of Economic History,* XXXI (1971).

Stampp, Kenneth M. "The Concept of a Perpetual Union." *Journal of American History,* LXV (1978).

Tolles, Frederick B. "The American Revolution Considered as a Social Movement: A Re-evaluation." *American Historical Review,* LX (1954).

Trilling, Diana. "Lionel Trilling: A Jew at Columbia." *Commentary,* LXVII (1979).

Ver Steeg, Clarence L. "The American Revolution Considered as an Economic Movement." *Huntington Library Quarterly,* XX (1957).

Weber, Max. "The New Despotism." In *The Western World in the Twentieth Century,* edited by Bernard Wishy. New York, 1961.

Weinstein, James. "Organized Business and the City Commission and Manager Movements." *Journal of Southern History,* XXVIII (1962).

Wishy, Bernard. "John Locke and the Spirit of '76." *Political Science Quarterly,* LXXIII (1958).

Wolfinger, Raymond E. "The Development and Persistence of Ethnic Voting." *American Political Science Review,* LIX (1965).

Wood, Gordon S. "A Note on Mobs in the American Revolution." *William and Mary Quarterly,* XXIII (1966).

Wright, Benjamin. "Political Institutions and the Frontier." In *Sources of Culture in the Middle West,* edited by Dixon Ryan Fox. New York, 1964.

INDEX